A LOCOMAN'S LOG, 1937-85

A LOCOMAN'S LOG, 1937-85

Steam and diesel footplate life

Bill Alcock

Silver Link Publishing Ltd

ACKNOWLEDGEMENTS

I would like to thank the following for their help with illustrations: ASLEF, John Bloor, R. S. Carpenter, John Crook, John Edgington, R. J. Essery, K. C. H. Fairey, Michael Mensing, North Yorks Moors Railway, Dick Potts, Derek Sharpe, and Roger Siviter.

First published in June 1996

British Library Cataloguing in Publication Data

A catalogue record for this book is available from the British Library.

ISBN 1 85794 083 0

Silver Link Publishing Ltd
Unit 5
Home Farm Close
Church Street
Wadenhoe
Peterborough PE8 5TE
Tel/fax (01832) 720440

Printed and bound in Great Britain

CONTENTS

1	An early start, 1937-40	7
2	Firing, 1940-41	20
3	Through the freight links, 1941-44	36
4	Passenger and top link freight work, 1944-50	55
5	The 'Bradford' and Carlisle links, 1950-54	67
6	Passed out for driving, 1954-56	80
7	Monument Lane, 1956-58	97
8	Back to school, 1959-63	113
9	New routes, 1963-65	133
10	Freight links, 1965-67	146
11	Fire, storm and transformation of links, 1968-71	157
12	Tyseley changeover, 1971-74	173
13	Union matters, and the North link, 1974-80	189
14	HSTs and shunting, 1981-85	208
	Index	224

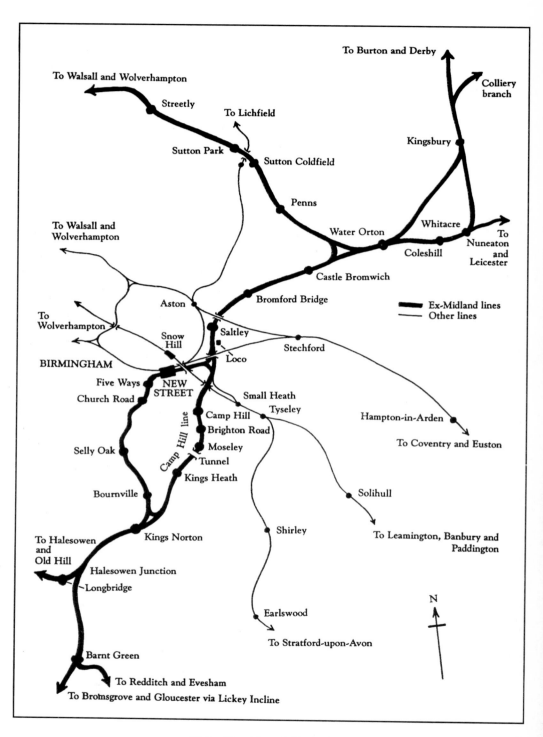

Midland lines through Birmingham

1
AN EARLY START
1937-40

I left school at the age of 14, in the summer of 1936. My parents' smallholding overlooked the old Midland railway line between Walsall and Birmingham, via Sutton Park, and as a small boy I used to look into the cutting at the end of our fields to watch the trains go by, especially on Saturdays in the summer when the 'Pines Express' would be diverted to this route on its run from Manchester to Bournemouth, to avoid Birmingham New Street station.

Later I would cycle to Lichfield Trent Valley station on the Euston to Crewe line to watch the LMS expresses go by, especially the 'Coronation', which would pass at around 11.30 am going north. I was so keen to be an engine driver.

At that time, to get a job on the railway you either had to have a relative working there, or someone had to recommend you. My father knew a boilersmith who worked at Bescot motive power depot (MPD), and he tried for over a year to get an interview for me. At last, in the summer of 1937, I was summoned to the shed offices.

Bescot was the parent depot for Ryecroft (which was also in Walsall), Aston, Monument Lane (Birmingham) and Bushbury in Wolverhampton. I had to take references from my local

vicar, Mr Talbot, and from Mr White, the Church Warden at our parish church where I sang in the choir; Mr White was also the shedmaster at Ryecroft. I also took school reports and a reference from the small brewery where I had been employed.

I had been primed on what questions I would be asked, in particular the rather daunting 'Are you prepared to move away from home?'. I knew that I must answer 'Yes' to this or I would not be considered as a footplateman.

I reported to the chief clerk, who looked at my references. He then asked me some mental arithmetic questions and took a sample of my handwriting. I was quite happy with mathematics as I had finished top of the school in it.

After about two hours of examination, I was ushered into the office of Mr Hughes, the Superintendent of the LMS Midlands area. He was a portly person with only one eye, having lost the other in the First World War.

Ex-LNWR 'Super D' 0-8-0 No 9091 stands beside the coaling plant at Bescot shed on 11 June 1949. *T. J. Edgington*

I had been told not to stare at him, but to look at him in a comfortable manner. He had my references and other papers in front of him, and said that he was satisfied with the questions the chief clerk had put to me; he asked me about the rail network of the Midlands, and questioned me on locomotives.

Then came the big question: 'Are you prepared to move away from home, my boy?'

I managed to squeak out a little 'Yes'.

'Right,' he said. 'You will be considered for a job at one of the locomotive depots.'

I thanked him and left, wondering which depot I would be sent to. I waited about three months and was beginning to think I had been forgotten when I received the important letter telling me that I was to report at 8.00 am on Monday 13 September 1937 at Ryecroft MPD, which was the nearest depot to my home, about 1½ miles away. It was also where Mr White, the Church Warden, was shedmaster. I gave a week's notice to the firm I worked for and prepared to start 48 years of railway work.

— o —

I arrived at Ryecroft Loco at 7.45 am and reported to the running shift foreman. The time clerk made out a clocking-in card and showed me how to insert it into the clock to record my time of arrival. When the office staff arrived at 9.00 am I was sent to the chief clerk and gave him my name, address, birth certificate, etc, then I was taken to the shedmaster's office.

Mr White recognised me and asked about my choir singing and where I lived, then said I would be working shifts, including nights, as a call-boy, calling drivers, firemen and guards for work. He then sent for the call-boy on duty and instructed him to take me to the stores to get a push-bike and oil lamp. I signed for them, and was instructed by the storeman to return them at the end of each shift.

The boy on duty was also instructed to take me with him to train me in calling up men and to show me where they lived. His name was Ken Jenvey, and his father was a driver at the depot. Our friendship was to last for 45 years.

While he was showing me the big address book of the men employed at the depot a shout came from the shift foreman's office for the call-boy. When we reported to the timekeeper gave Ken three tickets for a driver, fireman and guard, who were to report for duty that morning.

I found the railway cycle very heavy compared with my own, but Ken said, 'Don't ride your own cycle when on duty or you won't get any compensation if an accident occurs.'

We went to different parts of the town to call the men, then returned to the depot, where the time clerk was waiting with more tickets. This went on for most of the morning, and Ken explained that the depot had 'special men' who had to wait in all day waiting to be told what time they would be needed.

At the end of the shift I was told to report at 6.00 am next morning. There were five call-boys at Ryecroft and we worked shifts from 6.00 am to 2.00 pm, 2.00 pm to 10.00 pm, 10.00 pm to 6.00 am, and two others from 12.00 midnight to 8.00 am on a rota six days a week; every five weeks there was a Sunday shift, 6.00 am to 6.00 pm.

At about 12.15 am each morning the timekeeper would bring a book into the mess room containing about 150 names of drivers, firemen and guards who would be required to start work from 1.00 am to 8.00 am, and they needed to be called at least an hour before booking-on time. When you woke them you had to tell them the booking-on time and the train they would be working, for example book on at 2.15 am for the 3.30 am to Rugby. They had to acknowledge this, and if there was a query you had to return to the depot and sort it out with the time clerk or shift foreman, then return to the man concerned. All the men had to live within 2 miles of the depot so they could be called up or told of any alteration of their shift.

The three call-boys on duty sorted out which men were in their respective areas, and put them in time order in their notebooks. The 10.00 pm to 6.00 am boy covered the Butts area of Walsall, one of the midnight to 8.00 am boys covered the Ryecroft area, and the other one the Leamore area, a sprawling new council estate on the outskirts of the town.

Thus at the tender age of 15 we were responsible for getting the train crews to work on time. If anyone did not turn up or was late booking on, the call-boy responsible was 'on the carpet' in front of the shedmaster to explain why.

— o —

I had three weeks training on nights, one week on each area, learning the streets and the addresses of the train crews. After a few months there was no need to look up a man's address; you automatically knew where he resided.

We were supposed to give each man an hour's notice before his booking-on time, but some liked over an hour and some less. This was handy, because between about 4.30 and 5.30 am, five or six men booked on at the same time, living perhaps 2 miles apart, so it paid to know their requirements so that with a bit of juggling most could be satisfied.

The houses near the depot were old terraces or courts, with passages between leading to more rows of houses. This is where your bicycle's oil lamp came in handy, to stop you falling over anything lying about! Some men were heavy sleepers and occasionally you would need to throw small stones at the bedroom window or tap it with a clothes prop if there was one available. Very often the neighbours would wake up before the man concerned, and would open their windows to complain!

I commenced in the Leamore area, and on the first week I hardly returned to the depot from 1.00 until 6.00 am, but as I learned where men lived without referring to my address book I found I could return for a cup of tea and a sandwich at around 3.00 am, before the peak time of 4.00 to 6.00 am.

On one occasion I had to call a fireman at 3.20 am and was near his house at 3.00 am, but he didn't want more than the hour. As I did not have enough time to go back to the depot, I decided to wait the 20 minutes and

sat on his doorstep. However, I dozed off to sleep and awoke with a start when he opened the door and stumbled over me, having woken up and realised he was late, having not been called.

The following week, when I was on the day shift, I had to explain to the shedmaster why I had not called him. When I said what had happened, he said to me, 'Don't sit on doorsteps again - walk up and down to keep yourself awake.'

Some of the men were particular about the closing of gates, slamming of doors or knocking too hard. When you were in the mess room after returning to the depot, it was alarming when the door burst open and the cry 'Who called me this morning?' was heard. The boy concerned would be told what he had done wrong, and not to do it again.

The 6.00 am to 2.00 pm and the 2.00 pm to 10.00 pm shifts were concerned with calling up the 'special men', as the regular men were not called up after 7.30 am. The system on the old LNWR was that train crews in the 'special' link were given a different time over the 24 hours; starting from midnight on Monday morning, they had to remain at home to be called out at an hour's notice. When they finished their shift they were given a special paper denoting 12 hours rest, after which they would stand by for further duties for up to 10 hours.

Thus if a man started work at 1.00 am on Monday and finished his turn at 9.00 am, he would be available again at 9.00 pm on Monday night, but could be standing by till 7.00 am on Tuesday morning. If they were not called out within the 10 hours they would be paid a day's pay, and another special paper for 12 hours rest would be issued. However, rather than pay for 8 hours for nothing, the foreman would often bring them to work 15 minutes before the 10 hours were up, even if he had no work for them.

If this happened, it was emphasised to the call-boy to give them their full hour's notice, or they would claim a day's pay.

I was on duty on Christmas Day 1937, and it had been decreed by the Bescot Superintendent, Mr Hughes, that train crews who were not required for duty would be given a special paper time instead of paying them for a day's holiday. Mr White, the shedmaster, came to the depot after church service at around 12.30 pm, and inquired how many 'special' men had been called to work; he was told hardly any, but there were about 50 men standing by. He said, 'This is wrong! Send the call-boy to tell them they will not be required, so that they can enjoy their Christmas Day.'

I therefore had to go to 50 houses throughout Walsall and tell them the good news. Some wives said, 'Do you want him? He's gone to the club. Will you go there to tell him?'

When I arrived at the club, quite a few of the men were there, so I read the names from the list I had. They gave me threepences and sixpences, and some wives gave me mincepies or chocolates until my pockets were full.

On cold nights I called at local bakeries with the beat policemen; when hot misshapen pies or scones were rejected by the baker, we helped to dispose of them. In the summer we would meet at the local dairies where a nice cold cup of milk went down very well.

One morning, just before daylight broke, the oil in my cycle lamp ran out; it was not worth going back to the depot to refill it, so I decided to carry on. Unfortunately a policeman stopped me and asked what I was doing riding without a light. I explained about the oil running out, but he said he would have to report it and took my name and where I worked.

The next time I was on the 6.00 am to 2.00 pm shift I was on the carpet again, having a dressing down from the shedmaster. I mentioned this incident to the policemen I met at the bakeries; and when I told them his number, they remarked that he would report his own grandmother!

At about 4.30 am one morning I had a call to make at a house alongside Ryecroft Cemetery, and having a few minutes to wait I sat on the garden wall opposite the cemetery. I heard an unusual noise, and looking down the road saw something coming towards me glistening white in the moonlight. I immediately got on my cycle, thinking that it would

have to be fast to catch up with me, and with my heart beating fast I waited.

The apparition gradually got closer until I could see it was a man in an invalid chair with a white apron over his trousers; the noise was the cranking of the pedals! He used to sell newspapers, cigarettes and matches outside Walsall railway station in the early hours before the normal opening hours of the local shops. He certainly frightened me, and had I rushed away I would have sworn I had seen a ghost!

The Walsall police force was run by the Borough of Walsall, but on the outskirts of our calling-up area was the village of Rushall, which was policed by the County of Staffordshire, so policemen stationed at the police house would very often be from other parts of the county. At about 3.00 am one morning I was waiting to call someone in the village when a policeman approached me and inquired what I was doing hanging around at that time of night. I explained that I was a railway call-boy, and he asked me how old I was.

He did not believe that a 15-year-old should be out at that time of night working, and took me to his police house, despite my saying that I would be late with my calling-up. We had a cup of tea while he phoned his headquarters in Staffordshire regarding young persons being out on the streets at night. They in turn inquired at the railway headquarters and our depot, and I told them to tell Ryecroft MPD that driver Frank Smith would be late for work, as I had not yet been able to call him, and there would be others late if I was delayed much longer.

After a while police headquarters rang back to tell the officer that it was allowed. He told me to carry on, explaining that he was only looking after my welfare, and gave me a letter for my foreman to explain the delay. About a dozen men were late for work that morning! I subsequently became quite friendly with this policeman, and if I was waiting in the area and saw a light on in his office, I would call and have a cup of tea with him.

Little did we know that the law was about to be changed, and the following summer it became illegal for anyone under the age of 18 to be employed outside at night. The five call-boys then had to be employed at the depot cleaning engines, both inside the fire-box, removing clinker that was stuck to the boiler tubes and tube-plate and changing burnt fire-bars, and outside on the boiler and tender.

This is where I had my first official contact with locomotives, although I had ridden on them unofficially when I had spare time. After calling up on the afternoon shift I used to go along with Tom Mayo, the steam-raiser, who showed me how to shovel coal properly into the fireboxes, and how to work the injectors to put water into the boiler.

One Saturday afternoon the steam-raiser on duty must have had something to cele-brate, because when the pubs opened at 6.00 pm he disappeared for 15 or 20 minutes, then returned to his locomotives, then disap-peared again, telling me to look after his charges. At about 8.00 pm he returned, speaking thickly; he sat on the low wall out-side the sheds and started to sing. I told him I would look after his work - it was a good job Saturday was a quiet day.

When I went to clock off duty at 10.00 pm the running shift foreman called me to his office and asked me where the steam-raiser was. I said that he was on the wall at the front of the shed. He said, 'I know what has gone on and I'll speak to him later.'

We got to know the shed drivers and fire-men; on arrival at the depot, these men would clean out the fireboxes, coal and water the locomotives and marshal them in the shed. Occasionally an engine would have to be turned on the turntable and we would help them by pulling points, putting the vac-uum pipe on to the turntable motor and shovelling coal into the fireboxes. Eventually, when they trusted us, they would allow us to drive the smaller engines when the foreman was out of sight.

Ryecroft was a mainly passenger depot, employing about 300 men: drivers, firemen, fitters, labourers, office staff, cleaners and call-boys. (The passenger guards booked on at Walsall station.)

The locomotive fleet consisted of about 25 modern Fowler Class '3' 2-6-4 tank engines, used for the busy commuter services; five old LNWR Class '1' 0-6-0 tanks, which worked the push-and-pull to Dudley and Wolverhampton; and two ex-Midland Railway Class '2' 4-4-0 tender locomotives for Derby workings. The freight engines com-prised six ex-LNWR Class '8' 'Super D' 0-8-0 tender engines; three ex-LNWR 0-6-0 coal tender engines; two 0-6-0 Midland tenders; and two mixed traffic Stanier 'Black Five' 4-6-0s, Nos 5417 and 5418. The latter were used mainly for the night express freight train to London; the Ryecroft train crews would book off at Camden depot and lodge there before returning the next night. During the busy summer Saturdays and Sundays, along with the 'Super Ds' and the Midland tender engines they were used on passenger trains to Blackpool, Southport, Rhyl and Llandudno.

I can recall one August Bank Holiday Saturday, when the 'special' side of the engine board was showing about 20 excur-sions to seaside resorts. Locomotives were borrowed from Bescot, and two 'Jubilees' were borrowed from Bushbury. One fireman com-plained that he had been allocated a 'Super D' with a 'single man's tender' (ie the shovel-ling plate was flat instead of being raised about a foot, which was called a 'married ten-der' and was easier on the back). The train crews on these Saturday and Sunday Specials lodged at the resort and had a minimum of 9 hours off duty before working back home.

Two 'Super D' 0-8-0s at Ryecroft, still giving sterling service in 1957. *K. C. H. Fairey*

One day while I was cleaning on the 6.00 am to 2.00 pm shift I was told that a strange locomotive had arrived at the depot. On investigating I found that it was a converted ex-LNWR 'Claughton' painted in a bright maroon colour. Apparently one of our Stanier 'Black Fives' had failed on the return from Camden and the Ryecroft men had worked the 'Claughton' back to Walsall. A group of us cleaners spent some time scrambling all over and under it trying to identify the different working parts.

The Fowler 2-6-4 tank engines were worked by two crews a day, morning and afternoon, and they had the same engine allocated to them. They used to polish the boiler fronts, all the brass and copper valves and boiler water gauge glasses, and the insides of the cabs used to gleam. Some drivers and firemen would come to the depot in their own time on Sundays when their engine was standing cold and change the oil trimmings, which fed oil to the working parts.

I remember one driver, Sid Boughton, complaining that he had got the wrong locomotive! It appears that Nos 54 and 69 had been sent to Derby Works at the same time for general overhauls, and Sid was certain that the wrong numbers had been put on them before their return to Ryecroft. As I found out in later years, individual locomotives, although built to the same specifications, behaved differently, and Sid could tell those two apart.

The depot was supervised by the shedmaster, three running shift foremen and their timekeepers, a foreman fitter with three leading fitters, and a foreman cleaner; the office staff comprised a chief clerk and six or seven clerks who dealt with wages, mileages of locomotives for their periodical examinations, ordering spare parts and making up timetables of special trains.

After a few months of cleaning, a vacancy occurred for a telephone attendant in the running shift foreman's office, which meant working three shifts under the timekeeper and foreman. I applied and was successful.

I had to learn the railway telegraph code, where one word represented a whole regular-ly used sentence, taking and decoding messages for the person concerned, and sending out messages to the control office in Birmingham and to other depots. I also made the tea and was the general office dogsbody; when there were quiet periods in the evenings this involved fetching cigarettes and tobacco for the foreman and timekeeper, or going to the foreman's house with messages.

One foreman, Joe Pettifer, had a nice-looking daughter, and I did not need any second telling to go there. Another was Fred Wheeler, a big man who weighed about 18 stones and smoked a pipe as big as a bucket; he would send me for an ounce of St Bruno tobacco and an ounce of black twist. He would then spread a newspaper on his desk, cut the twist in thin slices, rub it fine, then rub the St Bruno, mixing it well with the twist. He would then put the mixture in his pouch, saving a pipeful, which, when alight, would nearly smoke us out of the small office. He also liked fish and chips, and two or three times on the afternoon shifts, if he didn't fancy his sandwiches, he would send me out for some and tell me to get a packet of chips for myself out of the money.

The messages I received concerned the running of trains and anything to do with train crews and their locomotives, such as a lack of water where locomotives were booked to replenish their tanks or tenders, or temporary speed restrictions through track repairs. These messages had to be given to the foreman, who placed them in the notice-case; on booking on, all drivers and firemen were allowed 10 minutes to study any alterations on their route. I also received messages for conductor-drivers, where a driver from outside the depot did not know the route, and from train crews liable to make overtime, asking for a relief crew to take over.

One afternoon I received a message from driver Jack Garn, who was working a freight train from Northampton, asking for relief. I passed the message to foreman Fred Wheeler, but as the train was near Rugby, he passed it to Control. (The Board of Trade regulations at that time stated that train crews must not work more than 11 hours in charge of a loco-

An unidentified ex-Midland '4F' 0-6-0 at Ryecroft Junction. Note the hut on the left, where footplate staff could phone the signalman when ready to leave Ryecroft depot. *Derek Sharpe*

motive or train.) I received another message from Jack about 1½ hours later, and the foreman again told Control; he was in no position to relieve him as he was out of his area.

At last Jack put his train off at Bescot sidings, and brought his engine to our depot. When he came to book off duty he was showing over 12 hours in charge of a locomotive, so Fred Wheeler called him into his office and asked him to change his time sheet to show under 11 hours in charge, promising to repay the overtime lost at another time. Jack was very annoyed at having to do this overtime after he had requested relief a couple of times, and refused Fred's request. Fred then had to make out a Board of Trade report stating why this overtime had occurred. Sadly these regulations were allowed to lapse during the war years, and I was on duty many times over 11 hours in charge, and on one occasion had over 27 hours on duty.

On 3 September 1939 war was declared, and passenger trains were reduced. Because Ryecroft was a passenger loco depot and Bescot was freight, there was a surplus of train crews at the former. Some men were transferred to Bescot to work the extra wartime freight trains, some applied for vacancies throughout the country, and others came back into the depot cleaning, taking my telephone attendant's position as they were senior in service to me. Junior men were made redundant, including me, and half

a dozen of us were transferred to Bushbury MPD, cleaning engines. Fortunately, it was only 10 miles away so I could cycle.

Bushbury was an express passenger locomotive depot, and housed 'Royal Scot', 'Baby Scot' and 'Jubilee' locomotives to work the Wolverhampton, Birmingham and London Euston expresses. The timing from Birmingham to London was 1 hour 55 minutes, which was quite fast.

We had to clean the boilers, tenders, side-rods and wheels with paraffin, sandpaper the walking plates around the boiler, and wax the boiler and tender to bring them up to a high polish. The foreman cleaner, Frank Andrews, who had only one arm, would come round with a white sponge cloth when we had completed the work, and heaven help us if he got any dirt on his cloth. He would say, 'There's no need for me to climb the outside walkway - it should be that clean I can see it shining in the polish of the boiler.'

Bushbury depot on 5 October 1930 with a variety of former LNWR and Midland locomotives on view. *R. J. Essery collection*

We were employed at Bushbury from September until the week before Christmas, when we ex-Ryecroft lads received letters stating that from the first week in January 1940 we would be transferred to Alsager depot. We did not know where this was, but after numerous inquiries found out that it was on the former North Staffordshire Railway between Stoke-on-Trent and Crewe. So at the tender age of 17 Mr Hughes's question, 'Are you prepared to leave home?', came true, and I would have to live in lodgings.

— o —

At 9.00 am on the first Monday in January 1940 Ron Broadhurst (who was later to be best man at my wedding), Bernard Sweeney and I reported to the Chief Clerk at Ryecroft depot. The other three lads had resigned from the railway rather than move from home. We were issued with our rail tickets to Alsager and a letter for each of us to give to the Shedmaster there. He explained that as Bernard and I were under 18 we would receive a free travel home ticket each week to return to our parents.

We caught the train from Walsall at about 10.00 am and changed at Wolverhampton and Crewe, where we caught the train traversing the former North Staffordshire Railway to Stoke-on-Trent. Unfortunately, we did not know how many stations there were before our destination, and all station nameboards had been removed as a wartime precaution. Therefore it was not until we were leaving Alsager station, when we noticed a turntable and locomotive shed building on our right, that we realised we should have alighted there. At the next station, Harecastle, we alighted and had a long wait for the next train back to Alsager. We were about two hours late, and as we walked up the path from the station to the motive power depot with our suitcases, the shedmaster, Mr William Challinor, spotted us from his office window.

'I thought you weren't coming when you didn't arrive on the Crewe train.'

After we explained that we did not know where Alsager was, he took us into his office,

accepted our letters, and asked if we were passed cleaners. We replied 'No'.

He said, 'I needed more men for firing duties - you are no use to me.'

He then telephoned the Crewe local office and, after a long conversation, returned to us and said, 'You will have to be passed out as soon as possible.'

I spoke up for Bernard and myself, saying that we were 17, and 18 was the age to be available for firing duties. He went back on the phone again and, after another conversation, said that owing to the war the regulations had been relaxed, the railways could now allow boys of 17 to act as firemen on shunting locomotives.

He then produced a book containing the addresses of landladies who were willing to take lodgers, and told us to sort one out and report for work at 8.00 am next morning. One house was next to the depot in Audley Road, and another four doors away. We trooped to the first and knocked at the door of Mrs Baxter, who was the wife of a bricklayer who worked in the Harecastle Tunnel maintenance gang.

She invited us in and said, 'How long have you been travelling?'

We said, 'About seven hours', as it was now 4.10 pm.

She made us a cup of tea, then said, 'I have already got one lodger who is a fireman at the depot.' (His name we found out later was Alf Webb, who came from Willenhall, about 5 miles from Walsall.) She said that she could therefore only accommodate one of us.

We said, 'We have got another address, a Mrs Bourne.'

She said, 'One moment', and went out of the back door through the back yard. She reappeared in a couple of minutes with Mrs Bourne, saying, 'Mrs Bourne can take two of you.'

After a discussion, Bernard and I went with her and Ron stayed at Mrs Baxter's. She made us a meal, but when her husband came home from work he was surprised to see us, and told her she could not take lodgers. It was now 6.30 pm, and after a long argument between them they agreed that we could stay the night, but would have to find lodgings the next day.

Next morning Bernard and I took our suitcases to the depot and reported to Mr Challinor that we needed fresh lodgings. He looked in his book and came up with a Mrs Sherrat who lived in Talke Road, about 10 minutes walk away near the station level crossing. Again we picked up our luggage and found the new address. Mrs Sherrat was a widow; her son was in the Navy and daughter Joan lived at home, working in the ammunition factory that had recently opened at Radway Green, the next station on the line to Crewe.

She invited us in and asked us our names and where we came from, then showed us a back bedroom, where we dropped our suitcases. She said the rent would be 21 shillings a week. This was more than we could afford, so we said we would have to go and see the shedmaster. Back to the depot we went and explained to Mr Challinor about our financial predicament.

He said, 'Were you classed as redundant or on loan from Ryecroft?'

'Redundant.'

So once more he reached for his telephone. After speaking to two or three different people, he said, 'If you had been on loan you would have received 25 shillings a week comprising 7 shillings lodging allowance on top of your 18 shillings, but as you are redundant you cannot receive anything.' However, he went on to say, 'You will soon be passed out for firing duties, which will raise your pay considerably, so I will have to find you labouring duties, such as coaling locomotives, blowing tubes out, shed sweeping, and you will also work regular nights to get extra pay for the shift working.'

With that sorted out we returned to Mrs Sherrat to agree to her terms, change into overalls and report back, where we were told to start cleaning the only locomotive in the depot, which Ron had been engaged on while we had sorted out our place of abode. The shedmaster told us to book on at 4.00 am the next morning and then at midnight the rest of the week.

'We don't have an alarm clock,' said Bernard, 'and the boss said he would instruct the call man to wake us up at 3.00 am.'

When we got back to lodgings, we informed the landlady about the 3.00 am call and she accepted it, as she had accommodated railway workers before.

She was a homely lady who did cleaning for the local doctor and another large house in the village. Her house was one of eight in a terrace; it had one living room with a small kitchen and two bedrooms, together with quite a large garden where she grew vegetables, and where she also kept chickens and had a pigsty with two pigs. When I told her that my father had reared pigs for years, and also chickens, ducks and a goat, she exclaimed 'It's providence! With Percy being called up for the Navy, I was finding looking after pigs and the garden too much, and now you have arrived!'

She looked after us well, and although food rationing was in force, we always had eggs and bacon to supplement our rations, as well as the extra cheese allowance that railway personnel had for their shift workings.

The motive power depot consisted of a shed with four roads in it, holding about three engines each. It had no roof, as this had been taken down as unsafe some years before after a fire. There was an old-fashioned coaling stage where large buckets, holding about 5 cwt of coal, were filled from the wagons and winched on to the tender of the locomotive and unloaded. An ashpit was between this and the outside turntable. Again, it was not modernised and the clinker and ashes that accumulated had to be loaded manually with shovels into the empty coal wagons to be sent elsewhere. There was a large water tank covering a building that comprised a mess room and booking-on point, and notice-boards under the control of the shed driver who checked men coming to work. The other side of the building housed the fitters' stores and their messroom. There was only one senior fitter, Albert Wilson, and a mate employed there. They worked regular nights doing running repairs at the locomotives. For the big repairs, mileage examinations and boiler washing, they were sent to Crewe.

There were about 12 locomotives used at the depot, comprising three 0-6-0 tank shunters; two Class '3' tenders, ex-Midland freights; six Class '4' 0-6-0 Midland tenders; and one ex-LNWR 0-8-0 'Super D', which worked a colliery trip in the daytime and the night Birkenhead freight trains.

There were about 48 drivers and firemen and passed cleaners stationed at Alsager, while the goods guards booked on at the shunting yard and offices. The work at the depot consisted of colliery trips around the Stoke-on-Trent area, night freights to Garston, Liverpool, and an afternoon freight from Crewe North Staffs sidings to Derby, where the crew lodged and booked on around 9.00 am the next day to work the return train. There was also a night freight train to Birkenhead and back to Chester and Mold Junction, where the men lodged, returning with a train to Longport and Stoke.

There was a fairly large shunting yard adjacent to the loco depot where two shunting engines were continually employed from 4.30 am Monday to late on Saturday night. This was at the end of a branch line serving collieries and goods depots at Talke-on-the-Hill, Silverdale and Newcastle-under-Lyme. There was another line, about a mile east along the Crewe to Stoke main line at Lawton Junction, which led to Sandbach (where it crossed the Crewe to Manchester line), Middlewich and Northwich (where it joined up with the former Cheshire Lines Committee route between Warrington and Liverpool.

It was very rare to see an engine in the shed in the daytime, as most of them were employed in the morning and afternoons, returning in the evening to be prepared for the next day.

Alsager was a medium-sized village spread on either side of the Crewe road, 10 minutes walk from the station, about 8 miles from Crewe and 15 from Stoke-on-Trent. It had about two dozen shops, a church, two chapels and five public houses, including one on either side of the station level crossing. The Alsager Arms and the Railway Inn were two doors from my lodgings, with a Post Office opposite. There was a working men's club in a big house in its own grounds in Station Road; the secretary was Eddie Candliff, an engine driver, and most of the Committee were railwaymen. There was only one other firm in the village, the Settle Speakman Railway Wagon Works, whose owner, Mr Francis Joseph, lived in the nearby Alsager Hall overlooking the village. The opening of the government ordnance factory at Radway Green, some 2 miles away, brought a change of work to the area.

At this period of the war there was a complete blackout in operation, with no street, house or shop lights showing, and after being used to town life it was like living in a deserted island. We worked to a roster of a midnight to 8.00 am shift one week and 10.00 pm to 6.00 am the next week, and we were left instructions

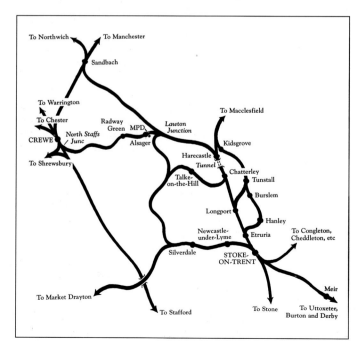

Map of the railways around Alsager and Stoke-on-Trent.

which engines to clean and which were to have their tubes and tube-plates cleaned. This was classed as labouring and commanded a higher rate of pay.

During this first winter of the war there was heavy snow and frosts, and one week I was instructed to stoke the frost fires under the water columns on the depot, in the shunting yard and at Lawton Junction about a mile away. At about 2.00 am one morning I went to the latter, poked the fire into life and put coal on, then proceeded to the other side of the line to the water column there. The poker I was using was a piece of signal rodding about 4 feet long. As I was using it, I glanced over my shoulder and saw what I thought was a monk standing behind me. I dropped the poker and prepared to run, but looking again, there was no one there. I picked the poker up again, and as I did so, with it silhouetted against the flames opposite, I could see the monk again. There was a large nut with two washers at the end of the rod and it gave the illusion of a monk's hat!

The shedmaster classed this work as cleaning, and we were only being paid 4 hours labouring rate, so our wages were only a few shillings above our lodging rent. One night we were talking to Albert Wilson, the leading fitter, and he said that stoking frost fires was labouring work, and told us to see our trade union secretary, who was one of our drivers. He advised us to put a claim in for labouring pay, but this was refused by Mr Challinor, so were advised to send a claim to the Crewe offices. After about a fortnight a letter came back conceding our claim; back money would be paid for the work for which we had been underpaid.

The shedmaster's job at Alsager was Mr Challinor's first managerial position, having recently been promoted from leading fitter at Chester depot. He put chalk marks inside the wagons that we put ashes in. He also tied the tube-cleaning lance to the brackets on the shed wall to see if we used it, so we cut the rope into small pieces. When he found what we had done he put chalk marks on the nozzle of the lance where it was put into the tubes, so one night we put some black axle grease on the handle after we had used it, so

that when he examined it he would get his hands dirty.

After a few weeks the blackout restrictions were relaxed and shaded lights were allowed to be used until air raid warnings were received. The only telephone was in the shedmaster's office, and the shed driver was the only one with the key to it. As he was mostly out in the shed yard or coaling plant he could not hear the telephone ringing, so as I was an ex-telephone attendant with a knowledge of railway telephone codes, I was entrusted with the key.

The first warning we received was 'air raid warning yellow', which indicated that an air raid was imminent. On receiving this I would operate the gas main shut-off cock three times to warn the staff working outside. On receiving 'air raid warning red', all lights had to be extinguished and no locomotive fires were to be thrown from fireboxes. On receiving the 'all clear', all lights would be operated normally. After we had finished our allocated work in the open shed it was nice to sit in the boss's office in the warm, making sure to tidy up afterwards. It was normal for the office fire to be lit at around 7.30 am before the end of the shift at 8.00 am, so the boss had a warm office when he arrived at 9.00 am, so we had the fire alight all night.

If there was an engine or wagon derailment in the shunting yard, Albert Wilson would instruct us to assist him in the re-railing process by carrying jacks and helping to put pieces of packing wood under the vehicle concerned, after the jack had lifted it, before slewing it back on to the rails. For this we were paid labouring rate and emergency breakdown pay.

After about eight weeks of this type of work, letters were received by Ron, Bernard, myself and a local lad, Alf Clark, telling us that we had to report to Derby medical centre on the following Monday for eyesight and medical examinations before being able to take up firemen's duties. Railway tickets from Alsager to Derby were enclosed.

We were told to book on duty at 7.45 am to catch the 8.05 am train, but as it was a weekend when Bernard and I were going home, we arranged to go from Walsall to

Derby and meet the others there at around 10.00 am. Unfortunately there was a heavy snowfall on the Saturday and Sunday, and when we arrived at Walsall station to catch the Derby train via Lichfield, we were told the line was blocked and no trains were running. We decided to go via Birmingham, then by the Tamworth route to Derby. When we got to Birmingham New Street, trains from the West Country to the North were running late, but we eventually got to Derby at around 1.00 pm. There was no sign of our mates so we thought they had already had their examinations and returned, so we reported to the doctor's office, and to our surprise she asked where the other two lads were, as no one had attended that morning. She said the doctor was at lunch and told us to come back at 2.00 pm; meanwhile we had a cup of tea and a sandwich in the cafe outside the station.

On our return, the doctor said, 'I'm glad someone has got here today.'

He then proceeded with the examination. I passed, but Bernard failed his colour vision test. The doctor said that this might be due to snow blindness, and went on to say that he would arrange for another examination when the snow had gone. Unfortunately he failed his next examination about a month afterwards and resigned from the railway. The last I heard of him, he had passed the army medical at the age of 18.

— o —

We arrived back at the depot at 4.30 pm on what we found was the first train to get through from Stoke. We reported to Mr Challinor, who said we had been placed absent without leave. We informed him where we had been, so he agreed to book us on duty for that day.

As I was the only one out of the four of us who had passed his medical, he said he would arrange for the footplate inspector to pass me out on rules and regulations to act as a fireman. He told me to book on at 8.00 am the next morning.

I had two days on the 8.00 am turn, and asked any driver and fireman in my vicinity what questions I would be asked by the footplate inspector. When I arrived for work on Thursday I was informed that Inspector Cadman was on his way from Crewe to pass me out. He duly arrived and I was called into the shedmaster's office.

He said, 'I normally pass out two together to save my time travelling here, but as there is no one else available, you will be on your own.'

He asked me my age, where I came from and what had brought me to Alsager. When I told him I was only 17 he said, 'I will ask you all aspects of fireman's duties, so when you become 18 you will automatically be available to work on the main line.'

He started by asking questions on the rules that applied to a fireman, and spent some time on Rule 55, which states that when a train is stopped at a signal, the fireman must go to the signal box to remind the signalman of the line on which the train is standing, and sign his block book with the time of signing; the signalman must acknowledge this by also signing and placing a collar on the signal lever to protect the train from another one running into its rear. (I found out afterwards that some signalmen are glad to see you in their lonely boxes; some offered a cup of tea if there was one in the pot, while others told you to wipe your feet, or would even bring the block book to the door to stop you dirtying the highly polished linoleum, and when the signing has been done send you back to your engine.)

Mr Cadman then asked about protection of the train after a derailment or an on-board fire. This rule instructs the fireman to go forward on the opposite line with a red flag, or a red light at night, placing detonators on the line, one at ¼ mile one at ½ mile and three 10 yards apart at ¾ mile, then proceed to the nearest signal box to inform the signalman of the nature of the incident.

He asked me about different stop signals and distant signals, shunting signals in goods yards and shunters' hand signals. He then referred to the locomotive and inquired how I would build up a fire. At that time, some of the local coal used produced a treacly type of clinker that ran between the fire-bars, thus blocking the air to the fire; the remedy was to throw a bucket of broken fire-bricks around the firebox, then gradually build the fire up in between doing other jobs in the preparation of the locomotive. He seemed impressed that I had taken the trouble to find that out.

He then asked about the procedure after booking on duty. I said that first you read any late notices, get your engine number, go to the stores for your shovel, bucket with hammer and chisel, spanners for the type of engine being used, a box of detonators with two red flags, and a hand brush. On climbing to the footplate, check the amount of water in the boiler, then the condition of the fire, the fire irons, clinker shovel, rake and dart; these would be from 4 to 7 feet long according to the length of the firebox. Next spread the fire and fire-bricks around the firebox, and put coal on, about 2 inches thick. While that is igniting, check that the smokebox door is tightly shut, and that there is plenty of sand in the sandboxes - if not, top them up. Put some more coal on the fire, take the head lamps and boiler gauge lamps to the stores to fill with paraffin, place them on the front and rear of the locomotive, then place the gauge glass in position and put some more coal on the fire. By now steam pressure would be building up, so test the water injectors that maintained the water in the boiler, and while these are working wash the footplate down and slacken the coal dust on the tender, especially if the locomotive had to go tender-first to collect the train. During this time the driver will be oiling the moving parts of the locomotive. The time allowed for this preparation was 45 minutes for small engines and 1 hour for larger types.

When everything is to the driver's satisfaction he will proceed out of the shed to the water column, fill the tank, then give the correct whistle code to inform the signalman where he needed to go for the train. At larger depots there was a phone provided to speak to the signalman.

Mr Cadman asked numerous questions on the running of trains and emphasised that safety was of major importance. After about 4 hours, he said, 'Go and have your food and I will see you in 20 minutes.'

Drivers and firemen did not have a proper food time. The regulations stated that shed and shunting train crews were allowed 20 minutes food time between the third and fifth hour, and main-line men when their duty allowed them a break.

After our break he took me across to the shunting yard and we climbed on to the shunting engine. He told the fireman to come back in a couple of hours and told me to carry on doing the firing; had I been over 18 he would have arranged for a trip on the main line on a freight train. After he had watched me for 2 hours firing and working the injectors to maintain the steam and water in the boiler, we went back to the depot and the shedmaster's office. He told me I had passed the exam and filled in the Board of Trade certificate stating that I was competent to carry out firing duties.

He then said, 'The shedmaster needs you firing on the shunter at 2.42 am, so make out a fireman's turn of duty sheet for today and book off at 2.40 pm so you can have 12 hours rest as the regulations allow. You will be paid fireman's rate of pay for today, and this is your first firing turn.'

I had to get 313 firing turns - equivalent to one year's firing (the 52 Sundays did not count) - to be paid the firing rate of pay, whether firing or cleaning, to be appointed as a regular fireman. Another important milestone associated with 313 turns was that you were then issued with a driver's and fireman's rough black jacket, and either an overcoat or mackintosh. These denoted that you were experienced; prior to this, when you mated up with a new driver, and he saw you were wearing a civilian jacket and mackintosh, he would immediately say, 'How long have you been firing?' and 'How many turns have you done?', and would treat you with suspicion until you could show him you could do your work properly.

2
FIRING
1940-41

At 1.40 am the next morning the call-man knocked at the door of my lodgings to wake me for work. He need not have done. I was wide awake with the excitement of going on my first firing turn. On arriving at the depot I inquired who my driver was. It was George Hood, a young man starting his own driving career.

First came the inevitable question: 'How long have you been firing?'

When I told him he said, 'Can you work a water injector?'

'Yes'

'Okay, let's walk across to the shunting yard and relieve the night crew.'

We shunted up and down until about 5.45 am when the night shunters stopped work; the day men took over at 6.00 am. This was our chance to have our food, washed down with cold tea from a bottle that had been warmed up on the boiler front (it was common practice for footplate men to acquire an empty 'Johnnie Walker' whisky bottle, as it was square and did not roll about with the lurching of the locomotive).

While we were eating our food, George said, 'You're doing all right, but you are too anxious. Try to keep the steam pressure 10 to 20 lbs below the 175 lbs blowing-off mark on the gauge for the tank engine we're working on, as it only annoys the shunters and the householders nearby. And try to keep the water in the boiler around halfway up the gauge, so that if we get a brief stoppage for signals you can use the water space to fill the boiler and keep the engine quiet.'

At 10.20 am the relief crew arrived to take over from us, and we walked back to the depot to sign off duty. On looking at the daily alteration sheet, I could see that I was firing on the same job again on the next day, Saturday. Three firing turns in the same week made me very happy, as the difference between the cleaning or labouring rate of pay and the firing rate was almost treble, from 18 shillings to 45 shillings per week.

The rostering of the drivers and firemen consisted of three links, as they were called, with 8 weeks' work in each, rotating round the 24 hours. Link 1 consisted of the top main-line work, working to Derby, Mold Junction, Garston, Macclesfield and Northwich. On the Derby and Mold Junction jobs the train crews lodged overnight before returning home. Link 2 worked around the Crewe and Stoke-on-Trent area serving the local collieries and factories. Link 3 was the shed and shunting link. As a passed cleaner I could be expected to be marked up for a week's work or placed on the daily alteration sheet from day to day. Drivers and firemen were mated together as their seniority directed.

On signing off duty at 10.40 am on the Saturday morning, I looked in vain for my name on the rosters; I was shown on my usual shift at 12.00 am cleaning. I was a bit disappointed, but I was able to go to my lodgings, wash and change and catch the 12.15 pm train via Crewe to Walsall to tell my parents that I had started firing, returning on the 6.25 pm from Walsall on Sunday night, ready to change for booking on at midnight.

On the Thursday I booked off duty at 8.00 am, and later in the day, while I was in bed, my landlady received a message instructing me to book on at 2.42 am for the yard shunter instead of 12.00 am cleaning. The daily alteration sheet did not appear until about 10.00 am so I had missed seeing it. I worked the shunting job on Friday, but on booking off I was not on the alteration sheet, so was back to 12.00 am cleaning on Saturday. This was a pattern I worked for about five months.

After about a month the other lads went for their medicals and passed them. They then had to see Mr Cadman, the footplate inspector, so they asked me about what questions they could expect. They passed, so we were put on three shifts, 6.00 am, 2.00 pm and 10.00 pm, to cover the 24 hours for spare firing turns.

I still received my weekly ticket to Walsall, but could not always go home because of the shifts. When I was booked on duty after 4.30 am I caught the 10.40 Sunday night train from Walsall, changing at Wolverhampton and arriving at Crewe around midnight. Then there was a long wait until 2.50 am for a train going up the North Staffs line; passengers wishing to alight at stations before Stoke-on-Trent had to inform the guard, and he in turn informed the driver.

During this wait we used to go into the refreshment rooms for a cup of tea and a sandwich or a pie, and as we travelled in these trains regularly we got to know the girls serving; if you said 'OCS' (On Company Service), you got the refreshments cheaper. During the war years there was a lot of shift work at Crewe, besides the railway's massive workforce. The Rolls-Royce factory was on war work and they also had to work shifts. The Picture Houses in the towns opened at 10.00 am, so we used to arrange to take the refreshment room girls there, catching the 9.15 am train from Alsager and meeting them outside the station. In turn, when we had our long wait at midnight, they would invite us into the kitchen, which was warmer than the public room.

The last train in the evening up the branch was at 9.25 pm, so if we wanted to go to the theatre or pictures, it had to be the first house. On two or three occasions we missed the train; the first time I was with Alf Webb who knew the way, so we had to walk the 8 miles home. The second time I was on my own and got hopelessly lost, as there were no road signs because of the war. I must have walked about 4 miles out of my way and arrived at my lodgings at about 1.40 am, as the call-man arrived to wake me to book on at 2.42 am.

We found it was better to go to Hanley for our entertainment, where there was a choice of three picture houses and a theatre; also, because of the heavy bombing of London and other cities, a lot of the stars of the day appeared there. The last train from Hanley was 11.15 pm to change at Etruria for the 11.35 train, stopping at all stations to Crewe, which got us to Alsager around midnight. Hanley lay on the 'loop line', as it was called, from Etruria to Kidsgrove serving Burslem and Tunstall. Kidsgrove was served by two stations, Harecastle (of tunnel fame) on the Crewe line, and Kidsgrove on the Manchester route. Alsager men used to work over the 'loop', and when I saw the small back-to-back houses, grimy from soot from the pottery kilns that overlooked them, I thought that they were worse than any I had seen in Birmingham and the West Midlands.

In the middle of one week I was working the 2.00 pm cleaning and labouring shift when the shed fireman injured his hand badly. He was throwing the fire out of a 'Super D', which entailed using a clinker shovel about 7 feet long, and the distance from the firehole door to the tender was rather limited, causing him to smash his hand on the hand-brake wheel. This was a lesson I learned: there was a 6-inch ring at the end of the clinker shovel, and apparently he had his hand on the outside of the ring. The safest method was to place your hand inside the ring so that it was protected. There were no industrial gloves in use at this time - the hot fire irons were held with a sponge cloth issued daily to drivers and firemen.

The shed driver instructed me to carry on in place of his fireman, and I had the job for the rest of the week. This afternoon shift was physically heavy for a fireman: there were eight locomotives arriving at the depot, and their fires had to be thrown out and ashpans and smokeboxes emptied, they had to be coaled and marshalled into the shed, and one locomotive prepared for the Birkenhead freight train. As a young chap it was extremely tiring for me, and the first few days I hardly had the strength to walk home, but slowly my muscles built up, and eventually I thought nothing of it.

On another week on the afternoon shift, I wanted to take the Saturday shift off duty, as there was a family wedding. Previous experience had shown me that if I applied for leave of absence it would be declined, so I decided I would report sick on this occasion. I must have mentioned it in the messroom, and this led to my undoing, as word must have got back to the shedmaster. My weekly ticket home used to arrive at the depot from Crewe on Thursday, but when I booked on duty on Friday it was not there, so I went to the shedmaster to enquire where it was. Mr Challinor said, 'I've got it and you will be given it when you finish duty on Saturday night.'

I was determined to go home, so on Saturday morning I went to the depot and reported to Mr Challinor that I was unfit for work, and asked for my ticket. He refused, saying, 'If you are ill you cannot travel home.'

'I have never changed my doctor and he is at Walsall', I protested, but it was to no avail and he would not give me my ticket.

I therefore went to Alsager station, bought a ticket and travelled home. I should have booked on at midnight on Sunday, but decided to be 'hung for a sheep', and had another day off, returning on Monday afternoon. I reported fit for work to Mr Challinor on Tuesday.

'Have you got a doctor's note?' he asked.

When I replied 'No', he said, 'You will hear more of this.'

About a week later there was a letter for me containing a 'Form 1' charging me with being 'absent without leave'. This form allowed me to explain the reason for the charge, or I could elect for a personal interview and could choose a union representative to accompany me. I chose the latter. When I joined the railway at Ryecroft I had joined the National Union of Railwaymen,

so I sent a letter to the secretary of my branch at Walsall explaining the charge against me, and asked for a representative. Surprisingly, I received a letter from him stating that there was a lot of absenteeism at that time and they could not spare a representative for me.

After another week I was given a date and time to see Mr Blackesley, the superintendent from Crewe, who would be visiting the depot to judge the charge against me.

There were three others waiting to see him on various charges, from passing signals at danger to derailing their locomotives or wagons. During a break in the proceedings Mr Bill Evans, the Associated Society of Locomotive Engineers and Firemen (ASLEF) representative, who later became general secretary of the union and who was attending to represent some of the others, asked me what I was there for. I explained my charge to him and he said, 'Have you a representative?'

I explained about the NUR and showed him the letter I had received.

'As long as you are in a trade union I will come in and represent you,' he said.

Mr Blackesley and Mr Challinor were sitting behind a desk in the office with papers in front of them. Bill Evans was told to sit down, while I remained standing. The charge was read out to me and I was asked for my explanation. I replied that I had reported sick 7 hours before my turn of duty and had reported ready for work 10 hours before my next shift.

Mr Challinor said, 'You went home that weekend.'

I agreed, saying that was where my doctor was. I explained that my doctor's surgery was not open on a Saturday afternoon and I returned to Alsager feeling better before the surgery opened on Monday morning.

Bill interrupted. 'He has only to produce a doctor's certificate after three days of sickness. Sunday is not part of the guaranteed working week.'

'How did you travel home on the Saturday?' asked Mr Blackesley.

I told him, and he telephoned the station to enquire if a ticket to Walsall had been issued for the 10.15 am train on that date.

They must have affirmed this because he said, 'I believe you.'

Bill again interjected. 'What happened to your weekly free ticket?'

I replied that Mr Challinor had retained it.

Bill exploded. 'That ticket is his property and no one else has the right to hold it, and we will be making an application for a refund of the money that Mr Alcock has paid out.'

Mr Blackesley said that he agreed and my money would be refunded.

Bill then enquired, 'How often do you manage to get home?'

'Sometimes once in two weeks,' I replied, 'or sometimes once in three weeks according to my shifts.'

Bill then said to the two bosses, 'The idea of this ticket every week is for this lad to go home and be in the environment of his parents.' He emphasised to Mr Challinor, 'You must arrange his shifts for him to be able to go home every week.'

We were then sent out of the room while they deliberated.

'They are in the wrong, not you,' said Bill, 'and if you're found guilty we will appeal.'

When we were invited back into the room, Mr Blackesley said, 'Passed Cleaner Alcock, you have been found not guilty of the charge against you. You will be refunded your fare home, your free ticket will not be kept from you again, and I have instructed Mr Challinor to ensure that you can go home every weekend.'

When we came out of the office I thanked Bill and said that I would join ASLEF. Thus began 45 years of membership, and eventually I became a trade union representative myself.

For the next few weeks Mr Challinor duly arranged my shifts to give me weekends off duty, but on 19 June I became 18 years of age; the weekly free ticket became a monthly one, and no provision was made for me to go home.

I was also now available for main-line firing, and I started by being booked to work on trains locally around the Stoke-on-Trent branch lines and colliery lines. Holidays were being taken by staff at the depot on a rota from May to September, so I was being booked for a week's work almost continually. The change in my wages was enormous, and I was able to send some money home for my mother and bought my first suit from Burtons at Hanley; I even started a Post Office savings account.

After September extra trains were being run for the war effort and I worked trains further afield to Chester, Stafford and Derby, where we lodged overnight, then gradually to the top link trains to Birkenhead and Mold Junction, where we lodged, and Garston docks near Liverpool.

On one occasion I was booked for a week's work on a day turn to Northwich via Sandbach and Middlewich. My driver was Owen Wilding, a senior driver who, like most North Staffs drivers, treated his fireman like an oil rag, and passed cleaners even worse. We were booked an ex-Midland Class '4' 0-6-0 tender engine. These were poor steaming locomotives even for experienced firemen, which I certainly was not. So I was struggling for steam most of the week and was being grumbled at by driver Wilding.

On booking off duty on the Friday afternoon I looked at the rosters and saw that I was booked with him again for the following week on the Birkenhead turn. As I was about to leave the depot, the shedmaster tapped his window and called me into his office. He said, 'Driver Wilding has been to me, complaining about having a passed cleaner on this job. I've told him that I have no other fireman to put with him so you will have to do your best.'

On Saturday, when we had eaten our food after turning the locomotive at Northwich, Mr Wilding said, 'Why don't you exchange next week's turn with an experienced fireman?'

'It's my proper turn and I'll do it if it kills me,' I replied.

I booked on at about 7.00 pm on the Monday night with my food bag packed with enough food for two days. I looked at the engine board to see that we had an 0-8-0 'Super D' allocated to us. Now I knew a little bit about these engines, and this type required a shallow fire and to be fired with six or eight shovelfuls every 2 minutes when working heavily. It was easy running to Crewe and when we left there, Mr Wilding said, 'Now we'll see what you're made of.'

I duly fired methodically every 2 minutes and the locomotive responded to it, keeping a full head of steam and boiler water to Chester, where we had come easy running around the back of the station. Then it was heavy working towards Port Sunlight and coasting into Birkenhead. On coming to a stand, my driver operated the firehole doors, looked into the firebox and remarked, 'You know how to fire these engines.'

We worked tender-first back to Chester and Mold Junction, where we left our locomotive on the locomotive depot and signed off duty at about 4.00 am. We then walked with the guard to the lodging barracks to have a good wash, some food and off to sleep with a smile on my face.

The barracks was a huge Victorian building with about 24 bedrooms, which were allocated to the lodgers by the steward on duty. Downstairs there was a large kitchen with about ten gas cookers for men to cook their own food (canteens were to come later). As we had to book on at 2.30 pm, the steward was left instructions to wake us at midday. On coming down I set about cooking my own breakfast. Mrs Sherrat, my landlady, had provided me with some home-cured bacon and an egg. Not knowing much about cooking, I heated the bacon in a pan; I did not realise that the bacon would provide enough fat to cook the egg, so I put it in a saucepan of water and boiled it. When I arrived at the table in the dining room my driver and guard were already eating their

food. Owen Wilding looked at my burned bacon, hard-boiled egg and dry bread and remarked, 'You'll have to learn to cook better than that or you'll starve', which I did, even to cooking on the shovel on a moving locomotive.

The guard offered me a cup of tea and we added our tea and sugar to make a large potful to fill our bottles. We then walked across to the depot to book on at 2.30 pm (when on a lodging turn we were allowed to book on duty after nine hours rest instead of the normal 12 hours).

We prepared our 'Super D', picked up our train for Stoke, and drew away from Mold Junction, through Chester and Crewe, then climbing about 15 miles past Alsager with a full head of steam and me with a big smile on my face. We climbed up to the summit at Harecastle, then it was easy running to Longport sidings, where we were released from our train, picked up another one, and returned to Alsager tender-first through Harecastle Tunnel, where water splashed on us from the roof. We deposited our train in the sidings, dropped the locomotive on our depot and signed off duty at around 11.30 pm. These workings were repeated for the rest of the week; with overtime of about an hour a day, night rate, and subsistence lodgings allowance, it made quite a profitable week.

The old drivers used to carry a wicker basket for their food and books, which was about 12 inches deep, 18 inches long and 6 inches wide, with a curved top and handle. I was using an army type of haversack, and some of the younger drivers and firemen carried a black tin box, slightly larger than the wicker basket, with a brass handle, lock and nameplate, and a place inside the lid for rule books, etc. These were advertised by a firm from Hull in the *Locomotive Journal*, the

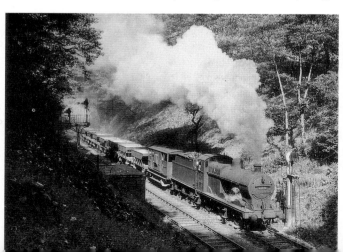

Midland Class '4' 0-6-0 No 44352 emerges into the sunlight between Harecastle Middle and South tunnels, between Kidsgrove and Stoke-on-Trent. *Michael Mensing*

ASLEF union publication, promising that they would keep food fresh. I sent off for one with a postal order representing about one week's wages, and about a week later I was the proud owner of a lodging box.

Pride has its fall, however, and for the next few weeks I was occupied firing on local turns. One was working up a branch line from Chatterley, at the south end of Harecastle Tunnel, to the Chatterley Whitfield Colliery (now a mining museum) about 2 miles away. We booked on around 6.00 am and prepared a Class '3' 0-6-0 tank engine (these were the largest allowed to work on this branch line), went light to Chatterley, shunted wagons for about an hour, made a train up of about 15 wagons and brake-van, and pulled them down the sidings near to the mouth of the tunnel. On being called by the guard from his van, we propelled the train, getting faster as we approached the start of the severe incline, and keeping a watch out for the guard's signals. We picked up the single-line staff up as we passed the shunters' buildings, and looked out for the guard to stop us when we arrived at the colliery. On some wet days the locomotive would start slipping on the wet rail, and despite the sanding equipment working properly, which was always checked as part of the preparation, eventually we would slip to a standstill. The driver would then reverse back down the branch, sanding the rail well, to the bottom of the sidings, then another attempt would be made.

During the war years, all colliery wagons were 'pooled' so that they could be used by any company. Previously they were loaded and sent to their destinations, then returned empty to their parent company. Now they could be used loaded in each direction, and it saved hours of shunting to separate the different companies' wagons for delivering home empty.

After a few weeks I was again booked on a lodging turn, an afternoon job to Derby. We booked on around 12.30 pm, prepared our locomotive, then went light engine tender-first to Crewe North Staffordshire sidings, or, if there was no locomotive available at Alsager, travel to Crewe South depot and get

an engine from there. We then worked a train stopping at Longport, Cockshut, alongside the huge gasworks at Etruria, to put wagons off and pick others up, then via Stoke station, climbing heavily for about 6 miles to Meir, followed by easy running to Blythe Bridge and Uttoxeter, where we again re-marshalled our train. Some more easy running through Tutbury brought us to Derby Chaddeston sidings, then light engine to Derby loco depot, and sign off duty around 9.00 pm. We would walk to the barracks near Derby station to lodge, then book on around 9.00 am next day to work back to Crewe.

The first time on this job I was booked with an elderly driver, Bill Higgins, who had recently remarried, and his wife would label his different packets of sandwiches in the order they were to be consumed over the 36 hours. We were allocated an ex-Midland Class '3' freight 0-6-0 tender locomotive. These were free-steaming engines, so I had no trouble maintaining steam pressure on the climb from Crewe to Harecastle summit. While we were shunting the train at Longport I used the coal pick to break some large lumps of coal, but on chucking it on to the top of the food cupboard on the tender end I smashed Bill's bottle of cold tea.

He cursed me for being so clumsy and said, 'When we get to Cockshut sidings, go across to the carriage sidings opposite the bottle bank and get two bottles, square ones if possi-

A panorama of Derby locomotive depot towards the end of steam in August 1966. *K. C. H. Fairey*

ble, wash them out with the hot water in the carriage cleaning sheds and bring me one back full of cold water and the other one empty.'

Rather perplexed, I did this, and when I returned Bill said, 'Give me your bottle of tea', which was about three-quarters full.

He put half of it in the empty bottle, then filled them both up with water, so we both had some rather weak tea for the rest of our journey. He said, 'We'll keep the spare bottle in case you smash another one.'

We climbed out of Stoke-on-Trent and had an uneventful trip to Chaddeston sidings, returning light engine to Derby locomotive depot where we signed off duty around 9.00 pm. We had about 15 minutes walk to the lodging barracks, and as we walked along Bill said, 'Do you drink beer?'

'I had a drink with the lads on my 18th birthday,' I replied.

'Right,' he said, 'we'll go and have a couple of pints in the Railway Institute opposite the station.'

When they closed at 10.00 pm he said, 'Do you like fish and chips?'

I said, 'I could eat a ton of them.'

So into a nearby fish and chip shop we went, getting a packet each and enjoying them in the barracks instead of our sandwiches.

Our waking up time of 7.00 am had been entered in the book for the day shift steward to call us; after a wash, we cooked our own breakfast, which I had learned to do reasonably well. When we signed on duty at the depot and looked at the engine board, we saw we had been allocated an ex-Midland Class '4' 0-6-0 tender locomotive. As I have mentioned before, these were a poor steaming engine, but I had asked other firemen at our depot the best way to fire them, and the conclusion I reached was that they needed a thick fire under the doors and in the back corners of the firebox, tapering towards the front end. On going light engine to Chaddeston sidings I built the fire up accordingly, and on the easy running to Stenson Junction on the Derby to Birmingham line I did all right.

Starting the climb towards Uttoxeter, Bill said, 'It's up to you to master this engine.'

I kept firing it heavily around the firehole door and hardly any up front, and the engine responded to it, the steam pressure remaining just under the blowing-off mark on the gauge. We stopped at Uttoxeter to re-marshal the train, and on departure with a heavy train, Bill said, 'It's heavy going for about 15 miles, so be prepared for a hard slog.'

The engine again responded to my method of firing and when we breasted the summit at Blythe Bridge with a full head of steam Bill said, 'Good lad, you've done well.'

This was praise indeed from Bill, and I had no doubts after that regarding firing the 'Midland Fours', although occasionally some of them would still be hard to maintain steam.

It was then fairly easy running to Crewe, where we left our train at the North Staffs sidings and returned light engine to Alsager, signing off duty at about 5.00 pm.

The natural way for most people to use a shovel is right-handed, which meant standing on the left-hand side of the footplate to shovel the coal from the tender to the firebox. However, most modern locomotives of the LMS were driven from the left-hand side, so the driver could see the signals, which were placed mainly on that side of the line. Consequently the firemen had to learn how to use the shovel left-handed, which was rather awkward at first, and a lot of coal was spilt on the footplate, to be brushed up immediately.

If you tried to fire right-handed the driver would say, 'Get over to your side of the footplate - you can't see the line, and platelayers are in danger if you can't see them and whistle to warn them of our approach.' One driver even kicked me up the behind to emphasise this. Eventually it became easy to me, swinging the shovel left-handed to place the coal to the front of the longest firebox, which was about 6 feet long.

The following afternoon we had another Class '3' freight locomotive to Derby, and the same procedure was followed on booking off duty, with two pints of beer and fish and chips on our way to the barracks.

On signing on duty the following day I was

rather pleased to see we had been allocated a Stanier 'Black Five' 4-6-0 tender locomotive. When we approached it in the roundhouse (most Midland sheds stabled their engines around the turntable in a shed on lines with pits underneath), we observed that it was brand new, having been recently sent out from Derby Locomotive Works; the '5A' on the smokebox indicated that it was allocated to Crewe North depot. I had no trouble maintaining steam on this trip, although the locomotive had a much larger and longer firebox, so my left-hand firing came in handy. On arrival at North Staffs sidings we were instructed to take the locomotive to Crewe North, at the far side of the station. On leaving it there we walked alongside the Class '8' 'Princess Coronation' 4-6-2 and Class '6' 'Royal Scot' 4-6-0 locomotives that were stationed there to work to London Euston, Glasgow and Perth. Little did I think that a few weeks later I would be firing one of these monsters.

We had worked the Birkenhead turn after there had been heavy bombing there, which delayed our arrival, and we did not sign off duty until 8.00 am, having been on duty over 12 hours. We lodged at Mold Junction barracks, and on booking on at 5.00 pm after our 9 hours rest, we were told that our train had been worked by another crew and we were instructed to travel to Chester depot to take a light engine to Crewe. Imagine my surprise when we were told we had engine number 6222, a Class '8' 4-6-2 named *Queen Mary*. It had still had its streamlined casing on, with the familiar blue with white stripes of the pre-war era; this had been removed from most of this Class owing to the locomotive being more difficult to maintain with it on.

We clambered on to the footplate and looked at all the working parts: the long

square firebox, which was carried on a pair of wheels, and the water injectors and dampers for me to work. When we left Chester I was as proud as a peacock as I leaned over the side, wishing we had an express train to work. On leaving it at Crewe we were instructed to travel home on the 9.05 pm train, so we booked off duty after working only 5½ hours, and 1½ hours before our normal time.

The Germans seemed to know when the shipping convoys would arrive in the River Mersey bound for Birkenhead and Liverpool Docks; there would be a quiet period, then when the convoys were due extra trains would run to load them, and that was the night the bombers would attack the docks.

I was booked to work a special train at 10.00 pm with a young passed fireman, Albert Smith, to Birkenhead. On arrival at Chester we were told that, owing to the bombing of the docks, we were to leave our train and turn our engine, a 'Super D', by traversing the triangle alongside the station to work a train back home.

We were running tender-first on the second part of the triangle, awaiting the clearance of the signal, when there was an 'air raid warning red' in operation, which necessitated hanging the tarpaulin sheet between the engine and tender and pulling down the side sheets, which were tied to the top sheet.

The top sheet was handy when working long distances tender-first in bad weather, but we did not like the side sheets down because they made the footplate unbearably hot. We could hear the droning of the bombers above us on their way to drop their

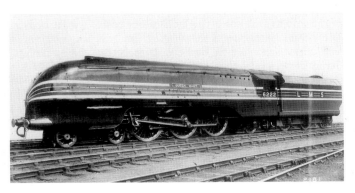

Streamlined 'Coronation' Class 'Pacific' No 6222 *Queen Mary*, which I unexpectedly had the opportunity to fire when we took her light engine from Chester and Crewe in 1940. *R. J. Essery collection*

bombs on the Mersey docks, and the rasping of the anti-aircraft guns operating from the nearby Chester race-course. We were anxious to leave the area, and peered from the corner of the sheets.

When the signal eventually cleared, Albert opened the regulator and we moved about 200 yards. Then we felt a bang and rumbled to a standstill; we realised that we had been derailed. I dashed to the signal box to inform the signalman of our predicament, but he already knew, coming to the top of the stairs as I approached, shouting, 'What did you move for? I didn't clear the signal.'

'You did,' I replied, 'or we wouldn't have moved.'

However, he continued to deny it. The breakdown train was sent for and we were eventually re-railed, but because he claimed we had passed a signal at danger we were relieved and sent home as passengers, the normal procedure when accused of this.

On the way home Albert asked me two or three times if I had seen the signal clear. I repeatedly said that I had and he said, 'I'll request you as a witness if I receive a Form 1.'

I did not see him again as he was put back on firing, but after a fortnight I received a letter instructing me to book on at 8.45 am to travel on the 9.15 am train to Crewe to attend a Form 1 enquiry as a witness.

Albert was at the depot waiting for me on the day in question, and we travelled together. He again asked me if I was sure I had seen the signal clear, and again I said I had. He said he had already been sent for an eyesight exam at Derby, and his eyes were all right.

We went into Mr Blackesley's office with our union representative, Bill Evans, to whom Albert had given the facts of our case. The charge of passing a signal at danger was read out. Albert said he had clearly seen the signal clear, and as we had stood there for some 7 or 8 minutes he would not have moved without clearance. I supported his statement.

The signalman was called into the room and he stated that he had not cleared the signal. A Signal & Telegraph linesman gave evidence that the signal could not be cleared with the points in the position they were

found. After 1½ hours of questioning we were told to leave the room.

'It looks as though the evidence is stacked against you,' Bill told Albert.

About 15 minutes later we were called back into the room. Mr Blackesley said, 'I have considered all aspects of this case and I find passed fireman Albert Smith guilty of the charge against you and I order you to be severely reprimanded, and it is to be recorded on your staff record card. He could have given him one, two or more days unpaid suspension from duty, and, in extreme cases, dismissal or relegation to labouring duties.

Mr Blackesley asked Bill to leave the room and told us to sit down. He gave us a lecture on the safety of the railways and ended by saying, 'Never be too anxious when waiting at a signal, even when an air raid is on, and don't move too quickly when a signal turns to green, as signalmen have been known to change their minds, but I have no proof this time. You are both young men in your driving and firing careers, so be very careful!'

We also worked night trains to Garston docks in Liverpool, and invariably the air raids would be on. We were often held back on the goods lines approaching Weaver Junction, south of Warrington, or on occasions were backed into the sidings at Birdswood at the top of the incline from Weaver Junction. From here we had a wonderful view over the River Mersey at Runcorn, Ditton and Liverpool, and could see the flashes of the bombs and guns erupting in the area.

One early morning after the 'all clear' had gone, we were running down the incline to Runcorn viaduct with a heavy coal train, with only the engine and guard's brake in operation, when my mate said to me, 'I hope they haven't blown the viaduct up.' As we crossed I looked down at the River Mersey a long way below us and was glad when we arrived on the other side!

We used to work trains of food or machinery back to Crewe or Stoke-on-Trent, and were sometimes on overtime before we left Garston, but it was part of the war effort and we were very often on duty 11 or 12 hours.

I used to ask my landlady to put some

extra food in my tin box. On one occasion, we booked on duty around 8.00 pm to work to Garston and arrived there at about 2.00 am after an air raid had finished. We were taking the locomotive to the turntable to turn it ready to work back home when another air raid started. Bombs and incendiary devices were falling around us and we tried to put the flames out by throwing ballast and ashes on them. After about 3 hours the 'all clear' sounded, and by this time there were about six engines waiting in the sidings. Daylight was breaking when the yard inspector came dashing towards us shouting, 'Move your engines into the locomotive depot across the main line. There's a land mine hanging by its parachute on the gasometers nearby!'

We arrived at the locomotive depot to find it in chaos. Locomotives that should have left the depot for the early morning trains were still there, and when our clutch of locomotives arrived there was no room for us to stable them, and it took about an hour to sort them out. We glanced repeatedly at the gasometers, wondering what the bomb disposal soldiers were doing and whether the land mine would explode at any minute. Eventually we were told to catch a local train at Allerton into Lime Street station and make our way home as passengers.

When we arrived there at about 8.00 am we found out there were no trains running to Crewe as the line had been damaged at Edge Hill near the locomotive depot, where the passenger locomotives were stabled. My mate knew of a workmen's cafe nearby, frequented by the station staff and taxi drivers, so we had some sausage sandwiches with mugs of strong tea.

Afterwards my mate rang Control to enquire how we could get home. They said they hoped to run a train around midday, so we tried to get a bit of sleep in a corner of the messroom. Around 12.30 pm a raft of coaches, which filled up with mostly women and children, with a few belongings, trying to escape the bombing of Liverpool.

At 2.00 pm we were still waiting to depart when the air raid sirens sounded. Most of the passengers evacuated the train and rushed to the air raid shelter, but my mate said, 'We'll stay on the train.'

Half an hour later a locomotive arrived and shortly afterwards we left, with the vast majority of passengers still in the air raid shelter. After a long tiring journey, with the train being continually stopped and diverted owing to bomb damage, we arrived at Crewe at 5.00 pm. We then caught the 5.35 pm up the branch to Alsager to sign off duty at 6.15 pm, having been 22¼ hours on duty. The shedmaster had gone home and the shed driver informed me that Mrs Sherrat, my landlady, had been to the depot twice asking what had happened to me. She knew I had gone to the Liverpool area, and had been told of severe bombing there that night. She made a fuss of me when I got home and produced a nice dinner, which I soon demolished!

We had to have our 12 hours rest, then we booked on at 6.15 am on the Saturday morning for our fifth turn of duty for the week. We were instructed to travel on the 7.00 am train to Stoke, then ask Control for instructions. When we did this, we were told to fetch a locomotive from the depot and work a freight train to Crewe.

At about 11.30 am we approached Alsager and my mate said, 'They will very likely relieve us so that we can book on before midnight for our sixth turn of duty.' To our amazement the signal cleared and we carried on to Crewe, leaving our locomotive on the South depot and travelling back passenger, arriving around 3.00 pm, so we were paid 8 hours for our sixth turn of duty because, with the 12 hours rest rule, we were unable to work it. A quick wash and change at my lodgings and I caught the 4.30 pm train via Stoke, Stone, Rugeley and Cannock to Walsall for an unexpected weekend at home.

A few weeks later we were again unable to book on for our sixth turn of duty owing to long hours on duty, but this time we were asked to book on duty on the Sunday at 7.15 am to work delayed freight to Garston. It was a pleasant change to travel over this route in the daylight without any difficulties and to see the gasometer at Garston still standing.

During this period the re-signalling at Crewe station, which had started before the outbreak of the war, was taking place. The huge gantries with dozens of semaphore signals were being replaced by a small amount of colour light signals with route indicators to show the line or platform for which each signal was cleared. On this Sunday we could see the work taking place, and later, when it was completed, all drivers and passed firemen were given maps showing all the new signals.

One day I was booked on the afternoon turn to Derby with Frank Barnett, and we arrived on the goods line outside Derby station at our normal time of 8.00 pm behind two other trains. After a long wait without any movement, Frank, who was a young driver, said he was going to walk up the line to London Road signal box. On his return half an hour later, he told me that the station had been bombed, people killed and severe damage done to the tracks and station buildings, and he did not know when we would be moved.

At about 11.30 pm a set of men clambered on to the footplate to relieve us. We booked off duty at midnight to lodge, too late for our fish and chips, but just right for our 9 hours rest before booking on at 9.00 am for our return train. However, when we arrived at the depot we were told that our train was not running owing to the bomb damage, and we would have to travel home as passengers. There was a bus service provided for passengers to Burton, where we then joined the 'Tutbury Flyer', a one-coach push-and-pull train, then another train to Stoke and Alsager.

The following day we worked our normal train from Crewe as far as Cockshut sidings, where a set of men were waiting to relieve us. They told us to call Control, who instructed us to travel as passengers to Derby for our return train the next day, as no freight was being received at Derby that day.

We signed off duty at about 6.30 pm and Frank suggested that we went to the pictures; I can still remember seeing Tommy Tinder in *The Foreman went to France*. Things were back to normal the next day and we worked our train back to Crewe.

During the summer of 1940 I asked my father, who was a lorry driver, to deliver my bicycle to his drop at Crewe, where I picked it up (while I could travel free on the train, on my weekends off duty I would have to pay for my cycle). This enabled me to see some of the countryside in the area. I had an aunt living at Sandbach about 15 miles away, and I used to visit her. I was invited to live with her, but the living within 2 miles of the depot rule was still in operation, so I could not do so. I also joined the Local Defence Volunteers, later known as the Home Guard. We trained with shunting poles and brake sticks as we had no rifles, and we were allocated nights to be on guard duty on bridges and signal boxes, being armed with fog detonators to place on the line in case of bridges being blown up.

I was firing on a regular basis in 1941, and one week I was booked on at 8.00 am for the Northwich train with a young driver, Tom Cookson, who was a local chapel preacher. We used to work down the branch from Lawton Junction to Sandbach, put traffic off there and at the nearby Foden motor works, then stop at Middlewich, where the local salt factory was serviced. (Occasionally, if a wife, or in my case a landlady, wanted salt, we could buy a block about 1 foot square and 3 ft 6 in long for a small price.) From there we carried on into Northwich, disposed of our train, turned the locomotive and returned, stopping at various places where the traffic was needed and arriving at Lawton Junction at about 3.00 pm, where a relief crew was waiting. We would then walk the 20 minutes to our depot to sign off duty. If we had bought a block of salt it would be weighing heavy by the time we got it home! On Saturdays, on the return trip, the salt factory and Foden motor works would be closed, so we came direct to Longport sidings, then light engine to the depot.

During the week Frank allowed me to drive the engine to the turntable and back to the sidings at Northwich. On the Saturday he said, 'Carry on driving - I'll see if you can handle a train,' This I did for the run of 2 hours or so.

When we arrived at Longport after passing through Harecastle Tunnel he said, 'I think you're doing all right, but when the guard comes up to ride home with us we'll ask him if you have knocked him about.' The guard reported that he had experienced a few snatches and a couple of bumps to begin with, but nothing out of the ordinary. I too was quite happy, having done my first bit of main-line train driving.

During one of my weekends at home in the spring of 1941 I met some of my old friends from Ryecroft depot, and was told that some new cleaners had started work, which surprised me, as we had been made redundant there and should have returned before anyone else was employed.

On returning to Alsager, I told Ron Broadhurst, who had also been made redundant, and we sent a letter requesting a return to our home depot as new entrants had been employed there. About a week later Crewe acknowledged the letter, but when Mr Challinor handed it to me he said, 'I can't spare you as I need all the firemen I can get. You'll return when I am ready.'

The following week I had 30 shillings extra in my pay packet, and when I enquired about it, Mr Challinor said, 'You are now on loan to us. That is a lodging allowance.' I protested at this as I had not volunteered to be on loan. Then the following week I received about six weeks back payment of lodging allowance, the period that the new entrants had been employed at Ryecroft. Nevertheless, Ron and I sent a letter to our union secretary, who replied that we had a good case to return to our home depot.

At the week starting Saturday 5 May 1941 I had 295 firing turns credited to me, 19 short of the 313 turns for regular payments as a fireman. On the 7th I received a letter informing me that I was to return to Ryecroft depot on the following Monday, 12 May.

When I saw Mr Challinor later that day he said sarcastically, 'Would you like to stay and complete your firing turns? You can volunteer to stay.'

'No thank you,' I replied, knowing that if I cancelled my redundancy I would remain at Alsager.

I carried on firing for the rest of the week, when I had 301 turns credited to me, just two weeks away from my goal.

I packed my suitcases (I had to buy another one for the extra clothes I had accumulated over the past 16 months), then took them and my bicycle to Crewe, where my father could pick them up. On the Saturday night I attended the local dance at the Church Hall and said a tearful goodbye to Peggy Dale, whom I had taken out a few times (her grandfather was a driver at the depot and her brother was a fireman at Stoke), promising to write to her.

On Sunday morning it was another tearful farewell to Mrs Sherrat and her daughter Joan, promising that I would return and visit them. I then caught the 10.00 am train to Crewe and Walsall, then home.

— o —

On Monday 12 May 1941 Ron and I reported to the Chief Clerk at Ryecroft locomotive depot. We showed him our transfer letters and when he produced our files he remarked, 'I see you are in the Home Guard. I am your captain and I will expect you on Wednesday evening for training. I also note that you are passed for firing duties, so I will inform the roster clerk to put you on his list.'

He then summoned a junior clerk to take us to the shedmaster, Mr White, who recognised us, then to the running shift foreman and finally to the foreman cleaner, who told us to book on at 8.00 am next day for cleaning duties, which we did for the rest of the week.

The following week I was on duty at 6.00 am doing three days labouring. When I received my wages for the first week at Ryecroft I was disappointed to see it was less than half what I had received at Alsager, but another transfer was imminent!

When we were first transferred to Alsager we were given a 'preference form' to fill in to indicate which depot we wished to be placed at as a fireman. Naturally I had put my home depot Ryecroft as first choice, then Bescot, Aston, Monument Lane and Saltley, to enable me to return to the Midlands. After three weeks at Ryecroft I was amazed to receive a letter stating that I had been made a fireman at Saltley, providing I passed a medical examination with the railway doctor.

I knew the whereabouts of the Aston, Bescot, and Monument Lane as they were ex-LNWR depots, but Saltley was an ex-Midland Railway depot and I did not know where it was situated. However, when I got home my father told me where it was and the route I would have to cycle, as his family originated from that area of Birmingham.

During the summer months the railway board's policy was to buy huge amounts of coal when it was cheap, and store it in large dumps, ready for the winter months when it became more expensive, so I spent the next few weeks unloading coal from the wagons and taking it in barrows to the site of the coal stacks. There was a bonus scheme operating for this work: 6¼ tons was classed as the basic amount to unload and stack, then for every ton over that we were paid an extra shilling. I can see from my diary that I moved 13½ tons on one occasion, giving me an extra 7 shillings for that day.

With only cleaning and labouring duties I got fed up with looking at the drivers' and firemen's daily alteration sheet without seeing my name on it for firing duties, but on one occasion I was surprised to see that I was rostered to book on at 9.35 am to work to Crewe. On booking on I asked driver George Nutt about the day's work, and he informed me that it was a special troop train from the West Country via Gloucester going to Liverpool docks. These trains were diverted away from Birmingham New Street station via Saltley and the ex-Midland line through Sutton Park to Ryecroft Junction. We relieved the train at Crewe at 10.00 am. It had Stanier 'Black Five' 4-6-0 number 5447 on the front, which I was used to firing, and had a good run to Crewe, operating the water scoop for the first time at Whitmore troughs. After about 40 minutes break we relieved another troop train coming from Holyhead behind three-cylinder Stanier 'Jubilee' Class 4-6-0 No 5618. I had never fired one of these, but although they were heavier on coal and water, they were capable of fast acceleration and higher speed with their three cylinders. We were booked via Walsall and Ryecroft Junction to Saltley, passing through the cutting near my family's small-

The first 'Jubilee' 4-6-0 I fired, No 45618 *New Hebrides*, seen many years later on 21 May 1956 near Millers Dale on the former Midland main line through the Peak, hauling the 2.25 pm St Pancras-Manchester. That occasion in 1941 was also the first passenger train I worked on, and my only firing turn from Ryecroft. *Michael Mensing*

holding. This was the first passenger train I worked on, and my only firing turn at my home depot of Ryecroft.

When we were relieved at Duddeston Road, we walked through Saltley locomotive depot to travel back to Walsall from Vauxhall & Duddeston station, and I had a quick look at the depot to which I was waiting to be transferred.

On 19 June, my birthday, I was instructed to travel to Derby on the 23rd for my medical examination, which I duly did and passed.

— o —

I reported to Saltley on Monday 7 July 1941 and was surprised at the large office with about 40 clerks working there, before being taken to the chief clerk, Mr Winfield. Saltley was the parent depot for five other depots: Bournville, Redditch, Kingsbury, Water Orton and Bromsgrove. At the latter were stationed the bank engines that pushed trains up the famous Lickey incline.

On looking at the files in front of him, Mr Winfield said, 'Where have you been since May 30th? That's the date you were registered as a fireman.'

I explained that I had been waiting for my medical examination.

Duddeston Road Junction, Saltley. Beyond the signal box in the middle distance in the coaling plant of Saltley shed, while on the left is Saltley gas works, served by the coal sidings on the right. *Derek Sharpe*

'What work have you been doing?' he asked.

'Labouring and cleaning - anything except firing,' I replied.

'Well, it's not your fault you've been delayed,' he said, 'so you will be paid for the last five weeks as a fireman.'

So I had got my 313 turns with a few to spare towards my second year's firing rate of pay, and I had quite a lot of back payment wages to come.

He told me my number at the depot and informed me that on pay day I would have to ask for a metal pay cheque from the time office and present it to the pay clerk for my wages. I still have it to this day.

Saltley depot and its sub-depots were overseen by a superintendent, Mr White (no relation to the Mr White of Ryecroft), an ex-army colonel. I was taken to his office by a junior clerk who carried my personal file. After I was introduced to him he looked at my papers.

'I see you have almost 12 months firing experience,' he remarked. 'We need as many firemen as possible for the extra freight and troop train traffic because of the war.'

I was then taken to the running shift foreman, who had an outside foreman to assist him with the marshalling of locomotives arriving at the depot for servicing; at times there were over 200 arriving and departing in 24 hours. In his office were three clerks, one booking on drivers and firemen, one booking on guards, and the other dealing with rosters, timetables, special train workings and notices.

I was asked for my address, and I said that I would be living at Walsall (the 2-mile rule had been abolished owing to the housing shortage and the number of men transferred

A general view of Saltley shed yard on 10 April 1949. From left to right are the ash pits and coal hopper, two departure roads, the entrance to No 2 roundhouse, seven stabling roads (including one incorporating the weighing machine), the roads to and from Nos 3 and 1 sheds, and two roads to the sand oven (the tall chimney on the right). Engines were stabled on the outside lines when the three sheds were full. *W. Potter*

to the depot). At that period there were over 50 drivers, firemen and guards travelling from Walsall. Of the 2,500 men working at Saltley, 1,000 were drivers and firemen, and 500 were guards.

The roster clerk took me to the roster boards which showed about 40 links made up of different passenger and freight workings, with approximately eight weeks work in each link, except the 'special' link and the 'Control' link, which each contained 52 weeks work, and the shed and shunting link, which contained over 100 drivers and firemen.

He showed me my link position in the 'Control relief' link. I should have been booking on at 9.00 pm, but he said, 'We'll keep you on day shifts this week for you to get used to the depot.'

He consulted with the locomotive-men's clerk and said, 'Book on at 10.30 am tomorrow.'

He pressed a button on his desk, and after about 3 minutes a young man walked into the booking-on hall dressed in footplate overalls. The roster clerk said to him, 'This is a new fireman to the depot.' He produced a key. 'Show him where his locker is, take him to the clothing store for his fireman's issue, then show him round the sheds and yard to familiarise him with them.'

It is a good job he did, as the place was massive. There were three roundhouses of the Midland pattern; two of them stabled 24 engines each around a central turntable, each road having a pit beneath, and No 3 shed housed about 30 passenger and heavy freight engines. In the corner of this was a huge furnace that dried the sand for the locomotive sand-boxes, and also served as a reservoir for lighting up the fireboxes of engines.

My guide then took me into the shed yard. Here there were about 24 straight roads, each holding about five to ten tender locomotives. There was a huge concrete coaling hopper where there were four coaling points, two on each road. One end produced best steam coal for the passenger end express freight locomotives, the other cheaper coal for normal freight and local work. These lines led to the ashpits, where three or four engines on each

could have their fires dropped and ashpans and smokeboxes cleaned, before being marshalled into the shed designated by the outside foreman. Finally, there was a small gas works in the corner of the yard alongside the canal, which provided gas for stations that still used it.

We returned to the buildings and the roster clerk took me to the clothing stores. This was another large room like a tailor's shop with hundreds of pieces of clothing. I was asked for my name and number, then the storeman looked at his papers and, when he found the appropriate one, said, 'Do you want a mackintosh or overcoat?'

I elected for the mackintosh, and he sorted one out.

'Try this one on for size.'

It was too big, but after three attempts one was found to fit me. The storeman then produced the magical black serge jacket that I had prized for so long, two sets of bib-and-brace overalls and two overall jackets.

'Sign for these.' he said. 'You'll receive overalls and serge jackets every 12 months and the choice of overcoat or mackintosh every two years.'

The young chap with me said, 'What about his uniform cap?' This was the familiar shiny topped locomotive-man's cap.

'Oh! I've forgotten that' said the storekeeper, and I tried two or three before I got one to fit.

My companion then took me to the locker rooms, which housed over 2,000 lockers, and found the one allocated to me, in which I placed my clothing. This was a luxury I had never had before, and having to cycle in from over 10 miles away, it would be handy to leave my heavy firing shoes and other items I needed at the depot.

'Do you fancy a cup of tea?' he asked.

We went to his locker and he produced a tea can and tea, sugar and milk. He then took me to the messroom where about 50 drivers and firemen were eating their food, some awaiting orders, 'foreign' men waiting to work back home, and shed drivers waiting for the outside foreman to give them instructions. He made the tea and said, 'Have you a can?'

Vauxhall & Duddeston station, on the former North Western line from New Street to Aston and Walsall, on 30 May 1959. Saltley shed was down the road to the right. *R. J. Essery collection*

'No,' I replied, 'I always carry a bottle of cold tea.'

'Not here!' he said. 'The fireman brings a tea can and makes the tea for his driver and himself.'

He borrowed a cup for me, and when we had emptied the tea can he took me to an ironmonger's near Vauxhall & Duddeston station, where I purchased one. I will have to bring tea, sugar and milk tomorrow, I thought.

During the afternoon my 'tutor' showed me the workings of the depot, how the locomotives were marshalled from the coaling plant and ashpits into the shed, and how they were taken on to the turntables and positioned over one of the radiating inspection pits. Nos 2 and 3 sheds had turntables powered from the vacuum pipe on the locomotive, while that in No 1 had a two-man-operated handle and, if this was too hard, long poles that could be reversed from the floor of the table, to protrude over the rim where the brickwork was alternated, so that a foothold could be attained to push the table round.

At 4.00 pm my new friend said that it was his time to book off duty; he took me back to the time office and informed the timekeeper that he had shown me all the workings at the depot. The timekeeper gave me a Daily Duty Statement to fill in, stating that I had transferred to the depot and had spent my time being trained in the working of the place.

I walked up to Vauxhall & Duddeston station to catch the train home via Aston and Great Barr. There was also a station at Saltley on the Birmingham to Derby line, where I could catch a train to Walsall via Castle Bromwich, but the journey was about 15 miles instead of the 8 by the other route. These two stations were the first stations outside Birmingham New Street, a couple of miles away.

3
THROUGH THE FREIGHT LINKS
1941-44

The following morning, before I caught the 9.45 am train from Walsall to Vauxhall & Duddeston to get me to work at 10.30 am, I had to purchase a three-monthly season ticket, on which I had a concession of a quarter of the fare, but I had to pay the full fare to take my bicycle with me.

From 5.45 am to 9.45 am there was a half-hourly service from Walsall and Birmingham via Aston, then it reverted to a 2-hourly service, except between 4.30 and 7.00 pm; the last train from Walsall was at 9.30 pm and the last one from Birmingham at 10.40 pm, but this might be delayed waiting for passengers if there was late running on the London, Crewe or Bristol services.

On arrival at the depot I asked for my time card and signed on duty at 10.30 am. I was told that my driver was Archie Cooke, and I went and introduced myself to him. (Later in the war he was awarded the George Medal for bravery during an air raid, when his train

Myself in the early 1940s.

was bombed and caught fire.) His first words were, 'Have you got a tea can?'

When I said 'Yes', he continued, 'Go and get it then.'

When I returned to him in the booking-on lobby he said, 'We're on Control relief, but there's nothing for us yet so we'll go to the messroom.'

The Cabin, as it was called, was half full of men. Periodically a bell rang and a spare fireman went to the booking-on point and returned with pieces of paper with instructions for different sets of men.

After about 45 minutes he returned from one of his trips and brought a message for Archie Cooke, who said to me, 'Here's some tea and sugar - make a can of tea, but don't put the milk in yet. We have to walk to Landor Street relief cabin to relieve a freight train coming from Gloucester and take it into Washwood Heath up sidings.'

When we boarded the engine, an ex-Midland Class '3' 0-6-0, he said, 'Now you can put the milk in the tea can. If we'd done it in the Cabin everyone would have liked a cup and there would be none left for us.'

The signal cleared and when Archie released the brake the weight of the train pushed us to the up Lawley Street goods line. From the next signal box, Duddeston Road, there were eight running lines to and from Washwood Heath sidings. We stopped behind another train at Saltley station, which was also waiting to go into Washwood Heath up arrival sidings.

It was about a couple of hours before we came light engine to the depot, where we coaled the tender, chucked the fire and clinker out of the firebox, emptied the ash-pan and smokebox of dust and marshalled the engine in No 2 shed. As we had been on duty for 4½ hours, Archie said, 'Make your tea - we'll have our food then report back to the time clerk for our next job.'

He told me to stay in the Cabin while he reported, and when he came back he said, 'Come on, we've got a bit of a walk to Bromford Bridge.'

The walking allowance was 40 minutes. As there was no relief cabin, we reported to Control at the signal box and waited, talking to the signalman for about 30 minutes until our train from Rotherham arrived behind an ex-Midland Class '4' 0-6-0 for us to work into Washwood Heath down sidings.

As we waited for an arrival road to become vacant, Archie said, 'Look around you at the signals.'

I looked, and there were hundreds.

'There's five signal boxes in these sidings,' he said, 'and you'll have to learn where every signal reads from and where it takes us to.'

On putting our train off, we went light engine to the depot as it was now after 7.00 pm.

'Pull the points over towards the back line,' said Archie. 'We'll leave this one for the shedman, as we're on overtime.'

When I booked off duty I was too late to catch the 7.12 train home, so I had to cycle the 10 miles.

For the rest of the week I booked on around 8.00 am, working with different drivers taking trains into Washwood Heath sidings. When I went to pick up my wages on the Friday evening after getting my pay cheque from the time clerk, the pay clerk told me that there was nothing for me.

'Have you just been transferred here?' he asked.

When I said I had, he continued, 'Evidently your wages have not yet been transferred here, so you'll have to wait until next week or go to your old depot for them.'

This I did, and lo and behold my wages were waiting for me at Ryecroft, and the clerk there said that he would ensure that all my future wages would be paid at Saltley.

On Saturday I booked on at 7.30 am and was mated with driver Arthur Hazeldine, who I had noticed alighting from the same train as myself at Vauxhall station. When I spoke to him to say I was his fireman, he asked me where I lived. When I told him, he remarked that he lived near Bescot. He had recently been transferred from there to get promotion to a driver.

We were sent to Landor Street to relieve a train coming from Bristol with a Class '8' 2-8-0 locomotive in front, to be worked into Washwood Heath. When the shunter booked us off the train, he told us to draw up to the inspector's office for instructions. Arthur was then told, 'Control want this engine at Bushbury Loco and I understand you sign the road there.'

We went along the old Midland route via Castle Bromwich, Sutton Park, Walsall and Darlaston, and on arrival at Bushbury we were told to leave the engine for their shed crews and travel home as passengers from Wolverhampton High Level, which was 45 minutes walk away.

It was around 2.00 pm when we arrived there, and on looking at the timetables we could see that we had an hour to wait for the next train.

'Could you manage a pint of beer?' Arthur asked.

I replied that I could, so we had a couple of drinks before the closing time of the local pub at 2.30 pm. This started a long friendship of over 35 years.

We caught the next train home via Dudley Port, then another to Vauxhall & Duddeston, booked off duty at around 4.30 pm, and travelled home together.

The following week I was booked on at midnight on Sunday for shed marshalling of locomotives. Over the weekend there would be over 200 locomotives stabled at the depot, and as the roundhouses would only hold about 75 locomotives, the rest were stabled on the straight lines outside. On this first full working day of the week there were about two dozen extra sets of men, besides the regular shed crews. About eight sets would be allocated to each shed; two crews would be working the turntables, and the rest would be bringing the engines in from outside. As the locomotives were oiled and prepared, they were taken out to the departure roads, to be replaced by the ones outside. These would very often be low on steam, having been lit up only a few hours previously, so they could not create the 21 inches of vacuum to operate the turntable motor, so the windlass had to be used. Some locomotives had no steam at all, and they were propelled into the shed by another locomotive; once turned to an empty pit road, the locomotive opposite would be used to push the dead one off the turntable. As it would have no steam brake, the hand brake was used to stop it at the end of the pit. This entailed about 20 turns of a wheel, and at times the engine or tender might overshoot and hit the shed wall, damaging it as well as the buffers or buffer beams. If this happened, the driver in charge of the locomotive concerned would have to make out an incident report for the main foreman, and he would be disciplined at some later date. This was a continuous operation, so cans of tea and sandwiches were taken on the turntables.

I had cycled the 10 miles from home, leaving at 11.00 pm for this shift, as the last train on a Sunday evening from Walsall was at 9.25 pm, and I could hardly push the pedals round when I signed off duty at 8.00 am, to cycle up to Vauxhall & Duddeston to catch the 8.15 am train home.

I had looked at the Daily Alteration Sheet and could see that instead of booking on at 12.00 am for Control relief, I was shown to book on at 12.20 am to work to Nottingham. When I came for this turn I was shown to Driver Willingham, who took me to the engine board to see that we had an ex-Midland Class '4' 0-6-0 freight locomotive, which was stabled in No 2 shed. We prepared it and informed the outside foreman's clerk at 1.05 am that we were ready to leave for Water Orton sidings, some 12 miles away, for our train.

On arrival, the guard who rode with us from the depot got off and walked along our train, and returned after about 30 minutes to tell us how any wagons we had behind us. We departed at around 2.20 am, detached some vehicles at Burton and arrived at Nottingham at around 4.30 am, where we

were relieved. After having our sandwiches, we relieved another Class '4' freight engine on a train coming from Lincoln to work back home.

Because of the war effort there was heavy freight traffic about and the yards were congested, so on approaching Water Orton the signal diverted us along the down goods line. As we passed the signal box the signalman came to the window to show us a green flag, which my driver acknowledged, to indicate that there was another train in front of us. We would then have to take our turn behind about ten or a dozen trains to get into Washwood Heath, taking about 3 or 4 hours.

At Washwood Heath junction a set of Control relief men relieved us and we walked the 30 minutes to the depot, where we booked off around 10.30 am. This happened all the week; one day we were on duty over 11 hours.

On Bank Holiday Saturday, 2 August, I was rostered on a special passenger train to Bath, a relief train to the 'Pines Express'. The 'Pines' ran from Manchester to Bournemouth via Birmingham New Street, but relief trains were directed via Walsall to ease the traffic going through New Street.

We were allocated a Stanier 'Black Five' 4-6-0 and went tender-first to Walsall via Sutton Park, where we took over the train and worked through to Bath Green Park station, stopping only once at Gloucester South away from the station to put water in the tank. When we arrived at the Bath terminus we uncoupled from our train while another locomotive came on the other end to work it to Bournemouth over the old Somerset & Dorset line.

When the train departed we followed it to the end of the platform and were turned into the locomotive depot to turn the engine, clean the fire of clinker, pull coal forward from the back of the tender, make the fire up again, then have a quick cup of tea and eat our sandwiches while we waited for our return train to Birmingham.

There was a mileage bonus scheme operating whereby working 140 miles was classed as equivalent to 8 hours work, and every additional 15 miles or part thereof was classed as

'2P' 4-4-0 No 40396 on pilot duties stands on the through road between platforms 3 and 4 at New Street on 5 March 1958. This was a handy place to await duties, giving ready access to the various platform roads. *Michael Mensing*

1 hour extra payment. Bath was about 90 miles from Birmingham and Walsall 15 miles from Saltley, so the mileage on this job came to approximately 210 miles, and we were paid 5 hours extra.

A few weeks later I was booked on at around 2.30 pm for the West Pilot, an engine located in New Street ready to assist trains that were overloaded for the climb out of the station, about 2 miles through three tunnels, or to hook on to the front to Blackwell at the summit of the Lickey incline, or even as far as Bristol.

We were on an ex-Midland Compound Class '4' 4-4-0 passenger locomotive one afternoon when at about 3.45 pm the station foreman came to us and said that the engine on the Leeds to Bristol express due to depart at 4.18 was doing badly for steam and they needed us to assist as far as Bristol. When it ran in we hooked on the front and away we went, stopping at Cheltenham and Gloucester, arriving at Bristol at about 6.30 pm.

My driver arranged with the station foreman to get us back to Barrow Road depot to turn the locomotive, and couple to the 7.40 pm mail train to return home. After leaving Cheltenham this train was booked to go via

Worcester, so that put extra mileage on our journey. We arrived at New Street at 9.45 pm and took our locomotive to the depot; my mate reckoned that we had clocked up over 190 miles, giving us 4 hours mileage payment.

These were, however, highlights in an otherwise mundane period of my firing career. I was mostly employed relieving trains working into Washwood Heath, walking to Bromford Bridge 40 minutes away, or even Castle Bromwich, a further 30 minutes walk. One day we walked all the way to Water Orton looking for the train we had been instructed to relieve, among the dozen or so trains standing along the goods line. On arrival there without having found our train, my mate telephoned Control and said sarcastically, 'Which way do you want us to walk, fast line to Kingsbury or slow line via Whitacre?'

Control replied by saying that they could not understand why our train was not amongst the ones on the goods line, and they would ring us back. I made a cup of tea from the signalman's kettle and shared it with him while we had a mouthful of food. Eventually Control rang back to tell us that our train had not left Toton some 40 miles away, and gave us another train to relieve.

One day, after a night of heavy bombing in the Midlands, we were sent as passenger to Kings Norton to relieve a train coming from Cardiff. We found it to be third on the goods line and took over from the Gloucester crew, who had been on duty over 12 hours. We realised we were at least 13 trains away from Washwood Heath, as there would be a train standing at every signal box along the Camp Hill line, which was now being used mainly as a freight line. After a long boring day looking at the guard's van of the train in front of us, we were on overtime ourselves, and were relieved, having been on the engine over 8 hours without turning a wheel. By the time we returned to our depot we had been on duty for over 10 hours.

Toton train crews used to work heavy coal trains into Washwood Heath and return with mixed freights. One day we were instructed by Control to relieve one such crew, as they

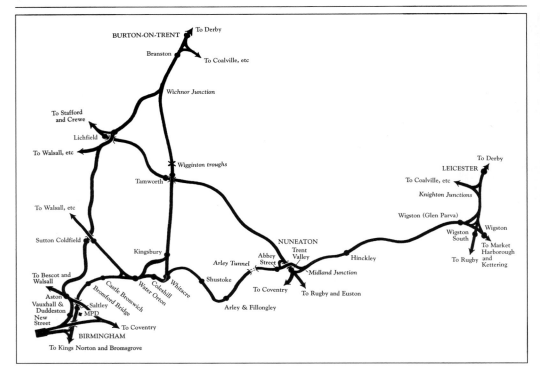

Lines from Birmingham to Burton, Nuneaton and Leicester.

were on overtime just working into the area, and work their train to Toton. There was an ashpit, water column and turntable at the Bromford Bridge end of Washwood Heath up sidings, and a set of men worked on each shift to service these locomotives. The locomotive we relieved was number 7974, a Garratt-type locomotive. These 2-6-0 + 0-6-2 engines had been built to work the heavy coal trains of over 100 wagons from the Nottingham coalfields to London, replacing the two locomotives that used to work them. They had a huge boiler slung between a water tank at one end and a rotary coal bunker at the other, carried on two separate sets of wheels, each with cylinders driving the six coupled wheels. The rotary bunker was worked by a small steam motor that could be operated from the footplate; it was situated in the centre of the locomotive to bring the coal from the back of the tender instead of the fireman having to shovel it forward.

We relieved the Toton men at Washwood Heath down junction and, after taking the train to Duddeston Gas Works sidings, we arrived at Bromford Bridge servicing depot, where the shedmen quickly cleaned the fire while I filled the water tank and rotated the bunker. We eventually backed on to our train in Washwood Heath up sidings. The guard was already waiting for us to tell my driver that we had 100 wagons; this was the limit for the stretch of line over which we would be running because of the length of the siding into which we could be put to allow passenger trains to pass us.

We drew out of the sidings and it seemed ages before the guard's van came into view in order for me to exchange hand signals with him, denoting that the train was complete. We travelled along the up goods line, and this enabled me to build up a good fire in the massive firebox. These locomotives were not called 'The Collier's Friend' for nothing!

Two passenger trains overtook us on the

Wigginton troughs, north of Tamworth, in Midland Railway days; 4-4-0 No 761 picks up water. *Derek Sharpe collection*

main line and when we approached the end of the goods line at Water Orton, the signal cleared for us to go via the fast line and we knew that we had to go to Burton before we could get off the main line. I worked the water scoop at Wigginton troughs, north of Tamworth, to fill the water tank, and at Branston Junction, approaching Burton, we were directed to the up goods line around the station. An express passenger passed us giving the derisory whistle of one long and one short blast, indicating that we had delayed them, the fireman leaning over the side of his footplate with two fingers to denote 2 minutes delay.

By the time we had reached Horninglow Bridge signal box the express had cleared the section in front at Repton & Willington, so we were turned out on to the main line again. At Stenson Junction we were diverted over the Nottingham branch line to Trent and Toton sidings, where we left our train to go over the modern shunting hump while we left our locomotive at the depot. As we were on overtime we travelled home as passenger via Derby.

Working in the Control relief link was quite haphazard. It was rare to have the same driver two days consecutively. Some days it meant 'walking the track', as it was called, relieving as many as three trains a day and bringing their locomotives to the shed. In the winter months, walking for 30 or 45 min-

utes in rain and snow after booking on at 2.00 or 3.00 am was most discouraging. Some days a freight train going through the area to Gloucester, Sheffield or Leicester, for example, would be running late, so we would be sent to relieve it and work it to its destination. This often meant working overtime. Occasionally a fireman would report sick; I would then be told to work his turn on a passenger or freight job. On each Sunday that I was available I would be booked to work.

My social life was therefore in tatters, as I could not make definite arrangements with my friends, and I was looking forward to being booked with a regular mate in a proper link, but this was to be some years away.

— o —

In May 1942 I graduated to the special link which consisted of 52 weeks' work. 'Special' men booked on duty every half-hour round the clock, with two sets booking on together at busy periods. There were no 'special paper' workings as there had been on the ex-North Western. We covered holidays and sickness for a week's work, and special trains on a day-to-day basis, with a trade union agreement of a 2-hour movement from the booked time.

There were a lot of freight trains working to the West Country, Avonmouth Docks and South Wales, which we used to work as far as Gloucester. The lines were heavily congested, and we would languish up the goods line for the 6 miles between Kings Norton and Barnt Green for hours on end, awaiting our turn to descend the Lickey incline. Trains arriving at the summit at Blackwell were stopped while the brakesman and guard would consult as to how many brakes to pin down on the wagons according to the weight of the train. Normally there was only the locomotive brake and that of the guard's van to stop the train. By the time the train had been pulled over the summit at a slow speed to allow the brakes to be pinned down, it would have been delayed for about half an hour. Having arrived safely, sometimes trains would run away.

At Bromsgrove, at the foot of the incline, water would be taken while the wagons were

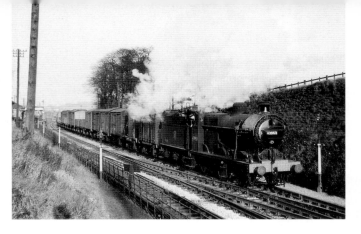

Goods trains not fitted with a continuous brake arriving at the top of the Lickey Incline at Blackwell stopped for the brakesman and guard to pin down a number of wagon brakes according to the weight of the train. This 'fitted' freight behind '4F' 0-6-0 No 43959, easing its way on to the incline in November 1956, will not have suffered that delay. *Michael Mensing*

examined and the brakes taken off. Very often we would have been on duty for eight hours or more, but as there were no relief crews at Bromsgrove, we would be asked to carry on to Gloucester. If this happened, we were allowed to go to the depot and purchase a tin of corned beef or Spam, and two large hard biscuits the size of a saucer, to sustain us. I used to keep a couple of tins of Irish stew or McKonichies dinners in my lodging tin, which could be heated on the boiler front, and take the cold meat to my mother, as it was on ration.

Bromsgrove Loco serviced five 0-6-0 tank engines, and a 2-10-0 tender engine, the only one designed by the ex-Midland Railway and nicknamed 'Big Bertha', which banked both passenger and freight trains up the 1 in 37 climb to Blackwell.

The shedmaster was Mr Tug Wilson, who I got to know better a few years later when he became foreman fitter at Bescot in charge of the breakdown train there, where my future father-in-law was employed. On the day shift there was a beautiful blonde girl in the booking office dishing out the tins of food to us, and after hours up the goods line looking at your old driver it did your eyes good to see her.

On leaving Bromsgrove the line fell to Ashchurch, then there was a climb to Cheltenham; from there to Gloucester the Great Western line from Stratford-upon-Avon joined the former Midland route, and as there was only a double line, long delays occurred, hours being spent in sidings awaiting our turn.

Eventually we would arrive at Gloucester with 12 or more hours on duty, the journey home as passengers making about 16 or 18

hours on duty. Eventually there were four lines built to take the extra traffic, but I saw them reduced to two again during the Beeching cuts.

On one occasion we signed on at 4.00 am to work to Gloucester, and at 8.00 pm we had been shunted into a siding at Spetchley, near Worcester, for a couple of hours or more. Our food, tea and sugar had all been consumed, so we went to the signal box where my mate asked if there was anywhere we could get something to eat. The signalman pointed us in the direction of the local pub, 'about a mile away'. Indeed it was a country mile; it took us half an hour to get there and we were disappointed to find that there was no food and no beer, only rough local cider. We had two pints of this lethal mixture and walked back to our train, hungrier than ever. My mate had words with Control and they agreed for us to stable the train and return light engine to Saltley, where we arrived showing about 20 hours on duty. The Ministry of Transport regulation of 11 hours responsibility was ignored.

We normally worked three shifts: day, afternoon and night. If we started at 8.00 am on Monday, for example, worked 16 hours, booked off at midnight and had 12 hours rest (another MOT regulation), we booked on next at 12.00 noon and gradually went later on duty as the week progressed, so no social plans could be made.

When we started on the night turns, it was almost impossible to get in your six turns of duty for the week. Regularly we were paid the sixth turn for nothing, having booked off after noon on Saturday after our fifth turn.

Meanwhile, the firemen on the local passenger trains were working their normal

8 hours a day, and were glad of some over-time, so we could make out a mutual exchange form for the week whereby he did your work while we did his.

One Saturday evening I signed on at 4.00 pm with driver Bob Gibson, who liked over-time; we worked a train to Rotherham, arriving at about 9.30 pm, and relieved another at about 10.00 pm to work home. It started to snow heavily and at Ambergate Junction we were diverted along the goods line to Broadholme at about 2.00 am. We came to a stand in an exposed position; despite the air raid sheets placed between the engine and tender, the wind and snow were blowing in on us. The River Derwent was below us on the one side and ran under a bridge in front of us just beyond the signal box. (One night a Saltley crew ran past the goods line signal, smashed through the stop blocks, and finished up in the river.)

At 8.00 am we were still there; the signalman should have closed the box at 6.00 am as it was Sunday, but could not clear the points to release us out on to the main line. Platelayers arrived at about 10.00 am to release us; they had been busy clearing points on the triangular junction at Ambergate station. We went as far as Derby St Mary's, where we left the train about midday, then took the engine to Derby Loco. There was a new canteen there, so we had a good meal, and walked over to the station to catch to 2.00 pm train home. Owing to the heavy snow, this train arrived about 3 hours late, so we arrived at New Street at about 6.30 pm and caught the train to Vauxhall & Duddeston, 10 minutes walk from our depot, showing over 27 hours on duty. During this time one set of Saltley men had over 32 hours on duty.

When I started working these long hours of duty, my mother used to worry as Birmingham was being bombed at the time. She even walked to the nearest telephone box, about 20 minutes away, to ring the depot to enquire what had happened to me. I tried to console her by saying that if anything happened to me the railway company would tell her, even if they had to wake her up at 3 o'clock in the morning!

We also covered firemen on holidays or sickness. If a man was sick you stayed with his driver until his return to work, if the driver was satisfied with you. I had a month with driver Arthur Tabener in the top passenger link, working to Sheffield, 80 miles away. This was equal to 10 hours on the mileage rate, and Bristol, 90 miles away, equalled 11 hours for 8 hours work.

The 12.15 pm from New Street reached Bristol Temple Meads at around 2.30 pm, terminating in the dead end of the old Midland station. After the train had been taken off, we went light engine to the Midland depot at Barrow Road, left the engine under the coaling plant, had our food, prepared our return engine, usually a 'Jubilee' 4-6-0, and watched our ten coaches being pulled into the station by a shunting engine. If we had any more than ten, we knew we had a hard run in front of us, and would need an extra bank engine at Bromsgrove. We would follow the coaches into the station where the shunter would be waiting to couple us up, the guard would tell us the loading, usually '10 for 330 tons', and we would depart at 5.00 pm.

We were due in New Street at 7.08 pm and there was a Walsall train departing at 7.12 pm and stopping at Vauxhall & Duddeston. On the first day of this job, Arthur asked, 'Do you want to catch the 7.12 pm train home?'

Naturally I said 'Yes'.

'So do I,' he said, 'so do your best for steam - we need to be in about 7.05.'

Cheltenham was our last station before New Street. We got the train smartly away, got up to a really good speed on the falling gradient to Ashchurch, and kept the momentum going up to Stoke Works Junction, where he whistled one long, two short, to indicate that we required two bank engines at Bromsgrove. If we required an extra banker it was one long, three short, and so on; 'Big Bertha' was classed as two bankers.

We came to a flying stop at Bromsgrove, whistled a 'crow' to indicate that we were ready to leave, listened for the bank engines to whistle two 'crows', letting us know that they were ready behind us, and away we went

Top and above 'Black Five' 4-6-0 No 45264 rolls into Bromsgrove station with a northbound express in 1955. In the second view, taken the following year, another northbound passenger train gets away up the Incline with the assistance of two 'Jinty' 0-6-0Ts, Nos 47425 and 47305. *Michael Mensing/T. J. Edgington*

Above According to this 1947 *Standard Code of Whistles* booklet produced by Saltley driver George Wilkins, later Mayor of Walsall, the whistle code at Stoke Works Junction for two bankers at Bromsgrove was 'one short, two short', but an initial long whistle, or even a 'crow', was employed by enginemen to be sure of attracting the signalman's attention.

working heavily up the incline. At the summit at Blackwell they dropped away from us and we thundered through Barnt Green.

At Northfield Arthur shut the regulator and started braking for the 30 mph speed restriction round the curve between Kings Norton and Lifford, then at Bourneville he opened up again. The line runs between Birmingham University and the Queen Elizabeth Hospital, each with a clock on their towers. We looked to see the time - about 6.58 or earlier (drivers were not issued with watches, but most bought their own).

Arthur then shut the regulator and started braking for the 30 mph outside Five Ways station and through the tunnels, reducing to 5 mph into New Street station.

I had brushed the footplate clean and washed it down with the slacking pipe on the run in, got our food tins and tea can ready, coats were put on, and as we came to a stand at Platform 9, we jumped on to the platform, met the Sheffield relief crew, told them the loading and how the engine was steaming,

climbed the stairs two at a time across the footbridge to platform 2, and were in time for the 7.12 pm train.

Arthur got off at Vauxhall & Duddeston, telling me to carry on home as he would sign me off duty, so I was in Walsall at 7.40 pm, the time we were booked to sign off duty, and we were getting 11 hours mileage bonus payment.

After about four weeks I looked for my name with Arthur on the roster, but his mate had reported fit for duty, and I looked in the lower links to see that I was booked on a local tripper working from Washwood Heath to Bromford Tubes, Dunlop, Castle Bromwich and Water Orton, trundling along at about 10-15 mph watching the expresses go flying by.

Then one Saturday I was surprised to see that I was booked on the big job at the depot - the afternoon Carlisle via the Settle route. We would lodge at Carlisle overnight, and the mileage for this job was 226, which equalled 14 hours payment.

The trade unions had an agreement with the railway management to share this work out, so in the week we worked four days and had two off, but even then we had 56 hours payment plus night rate and lodging allowances.

I was booked on at 3.52 pm Monday, returning from Carlisle on Tuesday afternoon at 3.45 pm, day off on Wednesday, then on duty again at 3.52 pm Thursday, return on Friday, and another day off on Saturday. Other train crews would work the Sunday, Monday, Wednesday, Thursday and Saturday/Sunday turns.

The locomotive was prepared for us, but it was to my advantage to arrive at work about three-quarters of an hour before time to check the fire irons and shovel, put about a ton of coal in the firebox, then shunt under the coaling plant to top up the tender; this saved a lot of work later on. I then cleaned the footplate, boiler front, gauge glasses and windows, ready for the driver to step on. He, in turn, would look around the springs and essential parts of the locomotive for his own satisfaction.

My driver was Alf Reading, a big man, about 60 years of age, who had been a boxer in his younger days; he was a nice quiet man, and a good engineman who used to work the locomotive as light as possible.

'Have you worked to Carlisle before?' he asked.

When I said that I had not, he said, 'I'll keep my eye on you and will only tell you what to do when I think you need to know. I've been having a drink with Arthur Tabener over the weekend, and he's spoken well of you.'

We were booked to leave the Loco at 4.07 pm with 'Black Five' 4-6-0 No 5276, coupled to two other engines for Water Orton sidings. Our guard, who incidentally was not paid the mileage bonus, rode on the engine with us while we backed on to our train, coupled up and connected the vacuum pipes for the brakes. After about half an hour, when he had examined his train, prepared his brake-van and lit his fire, the guard would return to us with his loading form to tell us the amount of vans and wagons - 45 was the

limit - the weight of the train and the number of the vehicles with the vacuum brake working; the latter number had to be over one-third of the total. He usually asked me for a couple of big lumps of coal for his stove, then told the driver to whistle up to show that we were ready to depart.

At 4.45 the foreman shunter called us out when the yard signalman was ready for us. Alf started the train slowly, and while it stretched out behind us we moved down the goods line to Water Orton station. I looked back to see the guard's signal indicating that he was on his van, and the train was complete.

At Water Orton the signals cleared for us to go over on to the fast line, with only two booked stops before Carlisle. After getting up to 30 mph, Alf wound the reversing lever up gradually to use steam economically until we were proceeding along at 45-50 mph on the mostly level track.

At Wigginton troughs, north of Tamworth, I put the water scoop down, filling the tender with 4,500 gallons of water. Approaching Derby we looked anxiously for signals to see if we would be on our booked route through the station or, if they were busy, via the goods lines to Derby North Junction, which would delay us about 15 minutes. Leaving Derby we started to climb to Belper and Ambergate, then heavier working to Clay Cross Tunnel, through which we coasted, then over Clay Cross Junction with light running to Chesterfield, where in daylight there was a wonderful view of the famous twisted spire.

At Tapton Junction, where George Stephenson's old house could be seen through the trees, we were signalled via Staveley to Rotherham, bypassing Sheffield. We were booked to stop at Rotherham for 12 minutes for the train to be examined for broken springs or hot axle-boxes. I filled the tank, and if the fire was clinkered I took out as much as time would allow. Meanwhile, the driver looked round the engine and made a can of tea in the carriage & wagon examiner's cabin. If any wagon was found to be defective it would have to be shunted off the train, which would cause about 15 to 20 minutes delay before we continued our journey towards Leeds and our next booked stop at Skipton.

This was my first trip beyond Rotherham and it was winter, so it was dark when we left Water Orton. Approaching Leeds I could see a lot of signals and it seemed as though I had been at work for ages. I said to Alf, jokingly, 'Are we there'?

He laughed and said, 'We're about half way. We need to get a move on to Shipley Junction to make sure we get in front of the local passenger train from Bradford.'

This accomplished, we had a good run to Skipton where the same procedure of examination, fire cleaning and taking water was followed. The guard came up and asked for another couple of lumps of coal, which was now halfway down the tender, and he and the driver filled the tea cans up again.

On getting the 'all clear' to proceed, Alf said, 'This is where we start work.'

We climbed steadily to Hellifield and had a spell of fast running to Settle Junction, then we were on the 'Long Drag' of the Settle & Carlisle line to Ribblehead and Blea Moor. In between firing the engine with six or eight shovelfuls of coal every 2 minutes, I was in the tender scraping coal forward ready for the next firing, and working the boiler water injector to keep the steam pressure at around the 225 lbs per square inch mark.

This climb took over an hour, and as we passed Ribblehead signal box we could indicate by whistling if we needed to go into the goods line at Blea Moor for water, or if some of the sheets on the wagons needed fastening, having blown loose on the high ground in prevailing strong winds.

Alf looked at the tender water gauge and decided that we had enough to get us to Garsdale troughs, the highest in Britain, some 5 miles away. We passed through the 2 miles of Blea Moor Tunnel, gaining speed on the level running towards Dent Head, with old sleepers made into a fence above us to stop the snow drifting from the embankment on to the line. On the other side in daylight we would be able to see the village of Dent in the valley down below.

We took water over the troughs, passed the stockaded turntable at Garsdale where the assisting engines from Carlisle turned before returning, then passed the site of the train disaster of Christmas Eve 1900 at Aisgill, where just past the signal box a sign proclaimed 'Aisgill Summit 1169 feet above sea level'. This is almost 200 feet higher that Shap Summit on the Crewe/Carlisle route.

Alf then closed the regulator and I gave a sigh of relief after 2½ hours of continual firing, swept the footplate clean and slacked the coal so that the dust did not blow about on the fast running to come. After a few minutes I had to look for the distant signals for Kirkby Stephen and Crosby Garrett, which I would see first on my side, then get some coal from the back of the tender for the short climb outside Carlisle. Through Appleby we coasted, along the lovely Eden Valley, following the river that in daylight we could see rising above Kirkby Stephen.

The gradient started to rise from Armathwaite, so Alf opened up again, climbed to Cumwhinton, which was where the coal from the back of tender came in. He then shut off and we coasted again into Durran Hill sidings, about 2 miles outside Carlisle, hooked off the train and left the engine on Durran Hill Loco at about midnight. We had traversed 19 viaducts and 14 tunnels on this amazing line from Settle.

We were now joined by our guard and walked for about 20 minutes to the modern railway barracks, where there were baths and a canteen providing hot meals 24 hours a day. Men from Crewe, Wigan, Liverpool, Manchester, Glasgow and Edinburgh also lodged here. By the time we had seen to our personal needs it was about 2.00 am. The stewards told us our room number and we informed him of the time we wanted to be wakened up.

On waking we had a cooked breakfast. All the meals we had were signed for, and the cost was deducted from the lodging allowance we received in our wages a week later. Carlisle was a nice town to walk around, either along the riverside or among the shops. The markets provided some delicacies such as rabbit, farmhouse cheese and offal to take home and help out with our food ration.

We had a couple of pints of Carlisle beer, which had been nationalised in the 1914-18 war to try to overcome drunkenness and absenteeism from work, then had lunch at about 2.00 pm. I was told jokingly by the guard to have the roly-poly pudding, for if there was a strong wind blowing on the mountain it would save me from being blown off the footplate.

We booked on at 3.30 pm for our return trip, picked our engine up at Durran Hill Loco, usually the same one we had brought up, checked that our tools and fire irons had not been changed, and went over to the up sidings where our guard was waiting with our train loading and brake power.

We departed at 4.25 pm. I had built my fire up coming from the depot, as we had 2 hours of climbing in front of us. There was a steep gradient to Cumwhinton, which tested the fire, then a short bit of easy running that gave me the opportunity of putting the fire right and filling up the boiler, ready for the heavy working to Aisgill.

Approaching Appleby Alf checked the amount of water in the tender. Although we were booked for water at Garsdale troughs, if we had an engine heavy on water, or a heavy train, he could indicate at Long Marton signal box by whistling that we would be stopping at Appleby.

From there the gradient became more severe, reducing us to 5-10 mph over the summit at Aisgill, then we accelerated to 45-50 mph because the faster we were running the more water we picked up over Garsdale troughs.

Alf told me to look out for the distant signal for Blea Moor outside the tunnel, which was visible to me first. We were booked right away here, but if there were any special passenger or troop trains catching us up, we would be put in the goods line until they had passed.

After easy running over Ribblehead Viaduct, Alf closed the regulator for about 25 minutes coasting, an ideal time to eat a sandwich, then there was a slight rise from Settle Junction to Hellifield before coasting again for another 20 minutes to Skipton. This gave me a chance to look at the fire and, if it was clinkered, to run it down ready for cleaning

during the 12-minute stop for water and examination. More tea having been made, we had easy running, which gave me a chance to build the fire up again for the fast running to Leeds.

After leaving Leeds we were in coal-mining areas, with a lot of speed restrictions because of subsidence, all the way to Rotherham, where the train was examined again and water taken. Leaving Rotherham we still had colliery subsidence to Chesterfield and Clay Cross Tunnel, then some fast running could be done to Ambergate, where a 30 mph speed restriction was in force through the tunnel and round the sharp curve where the Matlock line joined ours. Then some more fast running to Derby and Washwood Heath sidings. If we had lost time *en route* this was an ideal run to pull it back.

After hooking off the train, the guard clambered on to the footplate and on the 5-minute run to the depot he and Alf swapped comments regarding the run. Then we left the engine for the shed men to service and booked off at about midnight.

As we walked to our lockers, Alf said to me, 'For your first trip on the Carlisle route, you've done all right; my mate has been scalded and looks like being off sick for a long time, so I'll ask the foreman for you to stop with me.'

Although I had a 10-mile cycle ride home, Alf's remarks made my pedals go round very well.

I had about three months with Alf. One memorable afternoon, because of the war, all the Class '5' locomotives were being used on extra troop trains, so we were allocated a Class '8' 2-8-0. When I approached it I could see that it was brand new. These engines had small driving wheels to make them good at pulling, but were no good for speed.

On leaving Water Orton with a full train of 45 vehicles, Alf got the train moving smartly as usual, but after taking water at Wigginton troughs, Alf said, 'Can you smell anything burning?'

I said I could detect the aroma of hot oil, and he said, 'We'll have to look at this at Burton.'

Passing Wichnor Junction we whistled that we would be stopping at Burton for examination. At Branston we were turned on to the goods line to Leicester Junction, just outside Burton Loco. On stopping we clambered down and smelled our way to the left-hand big-end; Alf tried to put the back of his hand (never the palm) on it, but it was so hot he dared not touch it.

'Go to the signal box,' he said, 'and tell the signalman to advise Control we need a fresh engine.'

After a telephone consultation Control told us to uncouple the engine, put it on the Loco, and get another one there.

When we reported to the shed foreman, he said that he had only a Class '4' 0-6-0 ex-Midland freight engine for us, and that had just arrived on the ashpits, so there would be a long wait for it to be prepared.

Alf protested, saying that we had a Class '5' load, but the foreman replied that there was no other engine available. After about an hour and a half he called us to say that it was now ready for us. On getting on the footplate we could see that it had no tender doors and Alf said that on no account was I to climb over the tender end to get coal. A few months previously a Saltley firemen had been killed on the Stockport train, having been hit by an overbridge when getting into the tender.

We had lost about 2 hours, and when we got going we could not maintain the running speed of the train and lost about 45 minutes to Rotherham.

'I'll go and have a talk with Control,' said Alf. 'This engine will be no good beyond Skipton.'

He came back after about 10 minutes and said, 'They're going to bring us a bigger engine from Canklow Loco.'

After about an hour's wait, a Class '7' 2-8-0 ex-Ministry of Munitions engine built during the 1914-18 war arrived. I made some derogatory remark, but Alf said, 'Don't worry, we won't be going beyond Leeds tonight.' I had not realised that we had now been on duty for about 7 hours.

At Leeds we were put along the goods line to Whitehall Junction. Near the Loco another set of men stepped on to relieve us and we walked to the booking-off point. At about 12.30 am we were told that we would be advised what time to book on next day.

There was an old barracks in the depot yard near the coal hopper; it had no bathing facilities, but at least there was a canteen. We were allocated sleeping berths in an old camping coach nearby. 'It's better than the barracks,' said Alf. 'It's too noisy there.'

Next morning when we arrived for breakfast we were told to book on at our normal time of 3.30 pm to work our own train. Alf said, 'We'll have to wait until 8.00 pm for it, unless they start from Carlisle earlier.'

We went for a walk around the town, and had a few pints of ale. I was amused to see the amount of servicemen - English, American, Canadian and French - in the pubs with girls, drinking pints of beer. The guard said, 'Do we drink quarts?'

While we were enjoying our drink a young lady came up to us and enquired if we wanted a good time. Alf said, 'We're already having one', and she went away.

We returned to the barracks, had our lunch, booked on at 3.30 pm and prepared to wait for our train until 8.00 pm as Alf had predicted. On relieving the Carlisle men, I was not happy with the fire we had, so on the easy running to Rotherham I worked on it until it was to my satisfaction for the rest of the trip home.

I was told afterwards that another set of Saltley men had a similar trip, and approaching Leeds at about 1.00 am the driver had wanted to carry on to Carlisle, but his old hand fireman had had enough, and threatened to throw the firing shovel off the engine if the driver did not stop, saying, 'We'll see how far we go then.' There were still men over 45 years of age firing, and there was a trade union agreement that these men would not be booked on these jobs.

Eventually Alf's regular mate came back to work and I was back in the special link. The difference in driving techniques was highlighted to me a few weeks later when I was booked for a week's work on the Carlisle route with a driver nicknamed Rhubarb Roberts, whose mate was on holiday.

I had the normal fire as required for Alf Reading on leaving Water Orton, but the Rhubarb method of working the locomotive was totally different. Over that fast line to Kingsbury the regulator was put right over on full and the reversing gear hardly wound up. Sparks were coming out of the chimney so high that they were coming down as icicles, and I was struggling for steam.

We arrived at Derby about 10 minutes before time, and we had to wait for our booked 'path' through the station. This gave me a chance to get a good thick fire. On leaving there it was the same procedure, but I was now ready and coped with the heavy working all the way to Carlisle, nearly emptying the tender in the process. As we walked to the barracks the guard winked and said to me, 'Shall I carry your lodging box?' He knew of Rhubarb's enginemanship.

The rest of the week I maintained a thick fire for him, and was glad that his mate had only a week's holiday!

— o —

The war and the blitz were now at their height, and when I had to book on in the early hours of the morning I would cycle over Barr Beacon, a local beauty spot and the highest point in the area, from where I could see all over Birmingham and the West Midlands. If there was an air raid in progress I had a bird's eye view of the flashes of anti-aircraft guns and bombs going off, and would think that I would be amongst it in 10 or 15 minutes time.

One summer morning, when daylight was breaking and the 'all clear' had sounded, I was cycling near Aston Villa football ground when I came across bomb damage to a block of terraced houses, which partially blocked the

road. I had to dismount from my cycle to walk around the bricks and rubble. I could see the rescue squad working, so I paused to look as they carried a dead woman out of the wreckage, followed by a man carrying a dead baby, only a few months old. The thought of the killing of innocent women and babies haunted me for a long time.

On a few occasions I worked Red Cross ambulance trains. We would go light engine to Worcester and turn on the triangle at Rainbow Hill Junction to go tender-first with a conductor-driver to show my mate the route to Malvern Wells, where there was an American Military hospital.

The train of about 10 coaches would be waiting for us, loaded up with wounded men on stretchers or in wheelchairs, and even a group of American servicewomen carrying babies. I was amazed to see white girls carrying black babies, which was strange in those days. We worked this train to Liverpool, and my driver was an ex-Aston man, Horace Edmunds, who knew the road. When we arrived at Garston a shunting engine was waiting to take the train into the docks alongside the hospital ship. After hooking off the train we took the locomotive to Edge Hill depot and caught a lift on a light engine going to Lime Street station to travel home as passengers.

About two months later I worked a similar train with another ex-Aston driver, Arthur Kendrick, who allowed me to drive the train from Worcester to Crewe via Walsall, after the conductor-driver had left us. As I passed

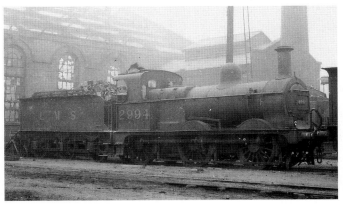

Considerable air raid damage to Saltley No 3 shed is evident in this 14 December 1947 view of old ex-Midland '2F' 0-6-0 No 2994 standing in front of the sand oven house, with its tall chimney. *Derek Sharpe*

our home I gave a good 'tootle' on the whistle. On this occasion, when we arrived at Edge Hill another locomotive was waiting for us to pick up the empty train and work it back to Crewe, where we were relieved. The mileage for this was over 210 miles, equal to 13 hours pay, but we were on duty over 12 hours, so we did not get too much out of a heavy day's work!

Saltley drivers were generally more friendly than the Alsager men, and when they had assessed your work and experience, would allow you to drive. Some of the younger men would work a day about, him driving one day and you the other. After about 18 months of special link working I was again promoted (if that is the right word!) to the local trips link. We would work trains to the local factories, collieries and the ex-Great Western yards at Bordesley. At least I had my first regular driver, George Gilbey, one of the travellers from Walsall, who had transferred from Bescot some years before.

There were two of these links and I was in the one that worked to the Austin motor factory at Longbridge, and further up the Old Hill branch line to Rubery. We would also go into the Bournville factory at Cadbury's, where on a Friday you were allowed to buy chocolate misshapes cheaply. To the north of Saltley we worked into the Dunlop tyre factory and to Kingsbury sidings and along the branch line to Hall End and Baddesley collieries.

After 18 months of long-distance work this was a bit tedious, but George did not do much driving. He was quite happy to teach me the finer arts of driving, which was invaluable experience. We were standing on the goods line one afternoon awaiting our turn into Washwood Heath, opposite the Dunlop factory, when an aeroplane came out of the sky above us and dropped a cluster of bombs, which fortunately fell on the Bromford racecourse. We jumped off the engine and sheltered underneath it, while the plane made another run so low that we could see the swastika markings on it as it machine-gunned along the standing trains. I heard a shout from George and thought he had been hit, but some scalding hot water had dripped on to his neck.

'I don't know what's worse,' he said, 'being scalded or being shot.'

The air raid sirens then started to sound.

'A bit late,' commented George, as the German plane had already departed from the area. Next to the Dunlop site was a factory making parts for Spitfires, which were completed and tested at the nearby Castle Bromwich aerodrome on the other side of the road. We guessed that this was what the lone bomber was after.

One night, when an 'air raid warning red' was in operation, we were standing near the canal, known locally as Saltley Docks, waiting to get on to the arrival roads at Washwood Heath, when a stick of about two dozen incendiary bombs fell on and alongside our train. We dashed along the ballast with the clinker and firing shovels, picking the flaming incendiaries up and throwing them into the canal. Some had lodged on the sheeted wagons and I had to climb and try to dislodge them with the long clinker shovel.

During this period driver Archie Cooke, for whom I fired on my first day at Saltley, and fireman George Simkins were involved in a similar incident when their train of bombs and army ammunition caught fire. They were in the cutting at St Andrew's Junction alongside Birmingham City football ground. The guard came and uncoupled the blazing vehicles, secured the rest of the train and told them to take them forward. They were directed into Lawley Street sidings where they managed to get some fire hoses to put the flames out before the bombs exploded. For this action they were both awarded George Medals and went to Buckingham Palace to receive them from the King. The guard, who was just as brave, unfortunately got no recognition for his deeds.

As already mentioned, there were over 50 drivers, firemen and guards travelling from Walsall to Saltley depot, and driver George Wilkins, who was to become Mayor of Walsall, ran a sickness or injury club whereby if anyone was off work owing to ill health, accident at work or bomb damage to his house, he would receive a sum of money collected by George at 1 shilling a call.

In the early hours of one morning, one of

our travellers, fireman Stan Webster, was walking with his mate along a path to Saltley station when he was knocked down by a bank pilot engine returning light to its sidings. He was badly injured and had to have both of his legs amputated. George Wilkins left notes for us all in his sickness club calling us to a meeting at Walsall station on Sunday morning. About two dozen of us turned up; some were naturally at work.

George told us that he had visited Stan in hospital, as had Mr Spencer, our depot supervisor, who had said to him, 'Don't worry about your job, there'll always be one for you on the railway.'

George went on to say that our 1 shilling a week would not be enough, so we would have to do something more. We formed a committee, which I joined (the first of many committee posts for me). As it was about six weeks from Christmas we decided to run a Christmas raffle. We approached the local traders in the Saltley area and they gave us prizes of whisky, wine, joints of meat, greengrocery and confectionery. My father donated one of his ducks, and when at Cadbury's Bournville depot buying our reject chocolate, I mentioned the raffle to the warehouse manager, explaining Stan's circumstances, and he gave us two boxes of good chocolates and said, 'When you have your raffle books printed, send me some here and I'll get them sold for you.'

We sent books of tickets to all the union branches in the Midlands, explaining the circumstances, and they responded marvellously, so that we made over £200 for Stan.

In the New Year we decided to put on a dance at Walsall Town Hall, with the proceeds going to Stan. We approached Mr Spencer and informed him of our plans, and explained that the last train from Walsall to Birmingham left at 9.25 pm, and the dance did not finish until midnight. He responded by saying that he would arrange a special train to run from Walsall at around 12.30 am. This helped us immensely, as we could sell tickets to rail staff living in Birmingham, guaranteeing a service home.

We had to apply for a special drinks licence, and I accompanied George, who was a town

councillor and a solicitor, to put our application to the town magistrates. The solicitor explained that it was a charity dance to raise money for our injured workmate. They were sympathetic for us and agreed for the licence in the names of George and myself, which we signed to agree to the conditions laid down. The dance was a huge success and Stan was able to attend in a wheelchair. He thanked us for our efforts, which raised another £300 for him. When he recovered from his injuries he was given a job as a clerk in the offices at Bescot depot near his home.

There was a lot of damage done to the railway lines because of the bombing, with locomotives and wagons being blown up. During one raid at Washwood Heath the driver and fireman left their shunting engine and went to the air raid shelter. When the 'all clear' went they returned to where they had left their engine to find a massive hole with their charge at the bottom of it; they could only look down on to the cab roof!

The Saltley breakdown gang were kept busy under Mr Bill Thorley, the foreman fitter. I was often a fireman on the locomotive pulling this train and its huge steam crane to places where damage had been done. When the crane was being used to pick up vehicles, Bill had a code of whistles for the crane driver to hear above the noise of the machinery. One night we were working in New Street station on a derailed locomotive when there was a conflict of whistles because the shunter also had a code for when shunting engines were out of sight inside the tunnels. Bill stopped all work and said to the station inspector, 'Stop your shunters working until I have finished this job or there'll be another accident.'

Bill was a boss who looked after his men regarding food and drink, and one evening we took his train to Water Orton sidings, arriving at about 7.00 pm. It was a big derailment and a couple of hours later he came to us and said, 'My men have been on duty since 2.00 pm on their normal work at the depot and they need some refreshments. Where is the nearest pub?'

We told him that it would be the Dog at Water Orton station.

'Will you take my messroom attendant there?' he asked.

We carried four large enamel jugs holding about a gallon each to be filled up with ale for his men and us, which we drank out of our teacups.

Bill Thorley was later to become superintendent at the GWR's Old Oak Common locomotive depot, which served Paddington station, then was promoted to the British Railways Board. He also wrote a book, of which I read the first volume, but he died before the second could be published.

— o —

Every May the summer timetables appeared, and this was also the changeover time for firemen at the depot. In May 1943 I found myself placed in the Gloucester freight link with Reg Roberts, an ex-Walsall man, who had returned to the Midlands from Bristol depot. It was back to the long hours at work, as there was a lot of delay owing to the congestion of traffic towards the West Country and South Wales.

We had eight weeks work, including an afternoon train working via Redditch, Evesham and Ashchurch to Gloucester, putting off and picking up traffic at all the local stations and sidings. We were booked to lodge at Gloucester in private lodgings where we had to cook our own food and slept together in a double bed.

As food rationing was getting tighter, the trade unions eventually got these conditions changed, and some old camping coaches and dining and kitchen coaches were stabled in the sidings near the locomotive depot where meals were prepared for us, but for which we had to pay out of our next week's wages.

The following day we would return via Evesham again. On joining the main line at Barnt Green it would be around 10.00 pm and we were invariably sent along the goods lines in the queue towards Kings Norton. When we came to a stand behind other trains Reg went to the signal box to ask Control for relief as we had no extra food after lodging (although we had managed to buy rabbits, etc, from Gloucester market).

Under the trade union lodging agreement we had priority for relief, and eventually a set of men would clamber on to the footplate and we would have to scrounge a ride to Saltley. Even then we would very often have been on duty for 11 or 12 hours!

Reg lived just outside Perry Barr and he used to accompany me for part of my cycle home. We were cycling along one early afternoon and joined the Aldridge Road from Wellhead Lane when we saw crowds of people on either side of the road with a few policemen standing in front of them. We carried on as far as the Boars Head pub, where a police officer stepped in front of us and said, 'Where do you think you are going?'

We said, 'Home', and he replied, 'You'll have to stay here, the King and Queen are coming along shortly.'

We waited there and had a good view of them as they drove by! They had come to Birmingham to see the damage the blitz had done and to lift the morale of the people.

The Boars Head pub was also the scene of another memorable event. We were cycling home at about 9.00 pm on a quiet evening when Reg suggested that we stopped and had a pint of beer. We were drinking our second one when the air raid sirens sounded. Most of the customers emptied their drinks and disappeared, leaving about a dozen of us in the bar. Shortly afterwards there were some huge bangs, as though bombs had exploded nearby. Everyone disappeared, including the bar staff.

When we finished our drinks, Reg said, 'If we've got to be blown up we may as well die happy.'

He picked up our glasses, went behind the bar and pulled a couple of pints.

'It's like having a pub of our own,' said Reg.

We stayed there until around midnight replenishing our glasses a number of times. Eventually, although the air raid was still on, we could not drink any more, so we decided to carry on cycling home, although the steering was a bit hazy. It was a good job there was no other traffic on the road.

When we booked on duty the following day, Reg said that he had found the reason for the continual heavy bangs of the previous evening. Evidently some new rocket guns had been stationed in the nearby park and they sent about four or five rockets up simultaneously at the enemy aircraft.

Despite the long hours being worked and the air raids we were enduring, I still had to report for Home Guard duty for training and guarding railway installations around Walsall. We were told to apply for leave from work at certain weekends to attend training camps, where we were taught battlecraft and did shooting practice with the different rifles and guns available to us.

One winter's night I and Ron Broadhurst (who had also come to Saltley for promotion about six months after me) attended night guard duty wearing our army overcoats, and were surprised to see that we were the only ones wearing them. The sergeant in charge asked where we had got them from.

'We were issued them at Alsager where we came under the Cheshire Regiment,' I replied.

Evidently the South Staffordshire Regiment had not issued any to their Home Guard units.

Early one June morning, when it was just getting daylight, we were working a freight train to Gloucester alongside the wartime aerodrome at Defford when we could see the huge British and American bombers landing after their air raid duties in Germany. As we passed along the perimeter for about a couple of miles, there must have been two dozen aircraft touching down. My mate remarked, 'I hope they've done the damage to Germany that we have had to put up with here.'

Promotion through the lower links was rapid, as more freight trains were being worked and extra footplatemen came into the depot. It was said at that time that there was only one depot in Great Britain with more men booking on duty over the 24 hours, and that was Polmadie in Glasgow.

When the winter workings commenced in October I was moved to the lower Peterborough link. There was a senior link that lodged at Peterborough six weeks out of eight, but in the lower link we lodged two weeks out of the eight. We also worked to the Leicester, Wigston and Nuneaton area.

For the Peterborough lodging turn we booked on at 11.30 am to work from Whitacre sidings with a Class '8F' 2-8-0 freight locomotive, but with delays to engines getting to the depot owing to the bottleneck at Washwood Heath sidings, we had almost any locomotive available allocated to us, and sometimes we would have to wait a couple of hours or more for one.

Albert Randle was my new mate, and if we were still waiting at 12.30 pm, he would inquire of the foreman how long it would be. On getting a negative response, he would tell the foreman that we wanted to eke out our lodging food, so we would go and get a meal at the Orange Tree pub, commonly known as the Wack, about 5 minutes walk from the depot.

Mrs Swift, the landlady, served cooked meals from 12.30 to 1.30 pm, and we would have a couple of pints of beer to wash it down. During that hour she would also serve the best beer at 1 shilling a pint, instead of the wartime ale at tenpence a pint.

Very often we would be over 2 hours late departing from Whitacre, going via Arley Tunnel, the heaviest part of our route, Nuneaton, Hinckley, Leicester, Melton Mowbray and Oakham. Instead of arriving at Peterborough at 7.00 to 7.30 pm, it was often 10.00 pm or later.

We lodged in railway barracks and the hard water of the area meant that our soap would not lather as it did at home, and when making a pot of tea only half the amount of tea was needed compared with the Midlands soft water, or it would turn out very strong.

We were supposed to book on at 5.15 am to assist our senior link men by double-heading their train home, but owing to the late booking-off time the previous night, we could not show our 9 hours off duty, and we would book on around 7.30 am and work a special train to Leicester or Birmingham. Occasionally, if there was no train or no locomotive to work with, we would travel home as passengers via Rugby.

Another turn of duty where food was involved was booking on at about 9.00 am to work to Arley Colliery or Stockingford sidings with empty coal wagons, bringing loaded

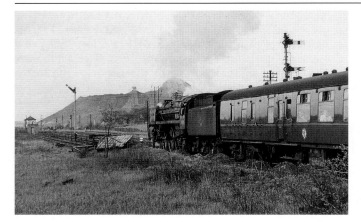

Beyond No 70000 *Britannia* and its Nuneaton-bound train in this 1964 view can be seen Arley Colliery Sidings signal box and the slag heaps of the colliery itself on the opposite side of the line. In 1943 Albert Randle and I used to enjoy a huge lunch at the miners' canteen here - the Government certainly looked after the miners!
Michael Mensing

coal back form Arley to Washwood Heath. Again we would be waiting for a locomotive, and if things got very late Albert would volunteer to take one not serviced, with a dirty fire and coal at the back of the tender. The reason for this was that we wanted to be at Arley Colliery at around lunchtime, certainly not after 1.30 pm, so we could have a cooked meal in the miners' canteen. These meals were huge!

One day our guard remarked, 'I'm ashamed to be eating all this meat on my plate! There's more than my wife is allowed on ration to last the two of us for a week!'

We could also buy soap, sweets or chocolates, which were normally rationed. As Albert remarked once, 'The government certainly looks after the miners.'

One Saturday we arrived at Arley rather early, around 11.30 am, and Albert said, 'You've been trying to go down the mine - now's your chance.'

He spoke to the yard foreman who took me to the lamp room where they rigged me up with a miner's helmet and lamp, then put me in the lift cage, which descended rather sharply, leaving my stomach somewhere above. On reaching the bottom I was put into a small horse-drawn truck and we travelled for what seemed to be miles to the coal

face, where miners, stripped to the waist, were loading coal in the trucks. I was hot and sweating as I was wearing my normal overalls, and I could understand why the miners worked half naked. After being shown around the coal face we returned to the lift, riding on wagons full of coal.

When we arrived at the top, I remarked to our guide, 'I wouldn't want to work down there!'

He responded by saying, 'I was given a ride on the footplate of a passenger train once and wouldn't want to do it again. I don't know how you can go along at speed at night without any headlights to see your road.'

We were booked to depart at around 2.00 pm and would join the queue along the goods line awaiting our turn into Washwood Heath, and it was very often 7.00 or 8.00 pm before we arrived at the depot. I used to bring my shaving tackle and have a wash and shave in a bucket of hot water to facilitate my going out at night.

Now and again, when delays were particularly bad, we would be relieved along the goods line. Albert bought cuts of pit props from the colliery once a week to use on his house fire. One evening, after such a purchase, we were relieved when we were standing third back from Bromford Bridge, which meant that we would have to carry a 1 cwt bag of wood cuts about 3 miles to the depot before he could put it on his cycle to take home!

4
PASSENGER AND
TOP LINK FREIGHT WORK
1944-50

The next promotion I had was in 1944 into the local passenger link, and my first driver was Sid Dutton, another fellow traveller from Walsall. He had lived in the Aston area, but his house had been demolished in a bombing raid and he and his wife had returned to live with his family in Walsall. The work entailed firing on Class '3' or '4' tank engines working to Redditch, Evesham and Ashchurch, and into the Austin motor factory at Longbridge. We also worked on Class '2' 4-4-0 passenger tender engines and Class '4' 4-4-0 ex-Midland Compounds to Worcester and Gloucester. I joined him in the winter months, and lights on stations were not allowed to be very bright so as not to attract the attention of the German aircraft.

The first train I worked with Sid was the 5.08 pm from New Street to Ashchurch, traversing the single line from Barnt Green to our destination. It was the fireman's duty to catch the single-line staff from the signalman, which was our authority to be the only train on that stretch of line. At Redditch there was a stretch of double line between the two signal boxes into the platforms, and from there another staff was required to Studley, where staffs were exchanged for the journey to Alcester.

I had to make the exchange while travelling at around 10 miles per hour. I leaned over the side of the footplate, bracing my legs so that I did not fall off, then looked out in the dim light for the hoop to which the staff was attached, being held out by the signalman. I put my arm through the hoop while holding the other staff low, hoop outermost,

so that the signalman could do the same. Having completed this manoeuvre successfully the train would carry on to stop at the station platform.

One night I missed the staff and shouted to Sid, who immediately stopped the train before the station for me to clamber down on to the ballast and go back for it. The passengers, thinking that we had arrived at the station, started opening doors to alight, and I had to shout to them to stay in the train as there was no platform there.

There was no signal box or signals at Coughton station. One November night we stopped there and I could not see anything. Sid said, 'There's a platform your side.'

The lonely station at Coughton on the Barnt Green-Ashchurch line. There was no signal box and no signals, so it was particularly difficult to locate in the dark, although Sid managed through experience and knowledge of the road. Here '4F' 0-6-0 No 44406 passes with the 4.20 pm Ashchurch-Birmingham train. *R. J. Essery collection*

An early postcard view of Ashchurch station, looking north. The line to the left is the Tewkesbury branch, straight ahead is the main line to Bromsgrove and Birmingham, while the Evesham, Alcester and Barnt Green line curves away to the right, linked to the Tewkesbury line by the third side of triangular layout, which crossed the main line on the level. We used the triangle to turn the engine rather than having to travel back to Birmingham bunker-first. *R. J. Essery collection*

I looked out again and thought 'He's wrong', then a glimmer of light appeared as a porter came out of the booking hall; then the guard appeared with his hand lamp to close the doors before signalling to me the 'right away'.

I thought, 'How did Sid find this station in the dark, without any lights to guide him?'

I found out afterwards that about a quarter of a mile from the platform there was a crossover road with points leading into the small sidings, which were operated by the single line staff when freight trains called. Coming in the other direction there was an overbridge prior to the platform to act as a guide.

On arriving at Ashchurch I would uncouple the engine, go forward to fill the water tank, turn the engine the triangle of the Tewkesbury and Gloucester lines, and re-couple to the coaches.

We were booked to wait and connect with a train coming from Gloucester. One summer's evening two young ladies about 20 years of age came over the footbridge towards our train. I could see them in conversation with our guard, and said to Sid, 'These girls are going to Coughton Court, and we're not

booked to stop at Coughton with this train. It means they'll have to get off at Alcester or Studley. Will you stop there for them?'

Sid agreed. 'We can pick up the time lost before Redditch.'

We duly stopped at Coughton and the girls alighted, waving their hands in thanks. However, the porter, who was working in his garden at the station house, came to the hedge and waved his fork threateningly at us. The guard waved his green flag and we got smartly away. The next evening on our out-ward trip the porter came up to Sid to complain about us making the special stop. He told us it was wrong, and if he was to report it both Sid and the guard would be in trouble.

Redditch tunnel was a bad one to go through as it was a single line, which made it narrow and low, with a sharp curve in the line in the centre. Approaching it from Studley, we climbed to within 200 yards, then the line dipped sharply towards the tunnel mouth. When the driver closed the regulator, I had to put the steam blower on to blow the smoke and fumes up the chimney and close all dampers under the firebox. If this procedure was not carried out, there would be a 'blow-back', and flames and fumes would come through the firehole doors. I knew of one such accident where a driver had all his clothes burned off and only his leather belt and boots were left on him. Fortunately he lived, but spent over a year in hospital having skin grafts.

A 1962 view from the platform end at Redditch station, showing the mouth of the notoriously restricted tunnel. If the signals were not clear for a goods train to run through the station, it would be held at the far end of the platform in order to get a run at the tunnel. Of course, under such circumstances the fireman had to be sure to make a clean single-line token exchange, because if he dropped it and the train had to reverse, the driver might be less than pleased. . .! *Michael Mensing*

On one occasion a Saltley train crew, driver Ginger Haines and fireman Bert Smith, were working a freight train from Redditch up the heavy gradient into the tunnel with a Class '8' 2-8-0 freight engine. These locomotives had a ventilation plate about 2 feet square in the cab roof, which could be slid open or shut. They were working the locomotive heavily, and the wheels started to slip on the wet rails, and eventually came to a stand. The steam pressure in the boiler was high and the safety valve operated, throwing scalding steam on the roof of the tunnel, which rebounded it through the ventilator, filling the cab and scalding both men badly.

Ginger Haines managed to reverse the locomotive and backed the train out of the tunnel, but they had to be rushed to hospital, also for skin grafts over a number of months. Ginger never worked on the main line again, working on shunting locomotives for the rest of his career.

When arriving at Redditch with the return train, we would always fill the water tank with about 2,000 gallons of water, for as Sid remarked, 'We may need it later.'

After arriving in New Street Station at around 10.30 pm we would take the empty coaches to Saltley carriage sidings, then go light engine to the depot to pick up the Derby stores van and take it to New Street station and leave it there. To save the shunter hooking us off then hooking the shunting engine on, he would invariably ask us to wait until the Bristol to Derby parcels ran in and we would place it on the rear of the train; when it departed we would follow it along the platform, and after it cleared the section of the line to Proof House Junction we would carry on back to the depot. This meant about an hour's overtime, plus night rate, which was very acceptable as both were in short supply in the local passenger links, compared with the long hours on duty in the freight links.

I cycled home, but Sid was too old for this. Instead, he would walk to Curzon Street goods depot, between Vauxhall and New Street, and catch a freight train to Bescot station, then walk home.

Sid was the man who introduced me to the fish market near New Street station, where there were about a dozen stalls selling a good variety of fish, which was not rationed. If we had half an hour to spare between working trains he would take me there to purchase some for his wife and my mother. I still did this for my wife years after retirement!

We were only booked to work on two Sundays of the eight-week rotation of the link, but as there were a lot of extra Sunday freight workings at this time, we would volunteer to work those weekends that we were available.

One Sunday we had been told to book on duty at 7.10 am for a freight train, and Sid signed the route to Stratford-on-Avon via Redditch. When we were given the workings we could see that it entailed two sets of drivers and firemen and a guard taking two Class '8' freight locomotives light to Stratford (the former SMJ station), turning them *en route* on the Broom Junction triangle, where the Gloucester, Birmingham and Stratford lines met, then proceeding tender-first to Stratford. There a conductor-driver would take us for about an hour's run to army sidings at Kineton, where a train of 50 vans loaded with bombs was waiting for us.

It was a very heavy train, hence the two large locomotives, and we had to have a bank engine at the rear to push us from Redditch to Barnt Green. We took this train to Washwood Heath and returned to our depot with the two locomotives.

One June morning we were working a parcels train past Defford aerodrome at around 4.00 am, and could see a lot of activity. We were used to seeing aircraft departing around 8.00 to 10.00 pm and returning at dawn, but this was an unusual time of day. My mate said, 'Something's going on.'

When we booked off duty later in the day we found out that the invasion of Europe was taking place.

We used to work a local passenger train from New Street at about 8.00 pm stopping at all stations via Worcester to Gloucester with a Class '2' 4-4-0 tender passenger engine. The last station we stopped at before Gloucester was Churchdown, where we were booked to stop for 12 minutes for the guard to collect tickets as it was a non-corridor train. As soon as we came to a stand, Sid would jump off the engine and dash up the station steps to the Welcombe Hotel, just outside the station buildings, to down a quick pint of ale. He would always bring me a bottle of beer back to have with my food at Gloucester, telling me to save the bottle for the next night to take back, as there was a deposit of twopence on it.

While the tickets were being collected, the porter would bring two empty coal buckets to fill with our hard coal. Churchdown was an ex-GWR station, but he said that their locomotives used the soft Welsh coal, which would not burn on his stove. In return he would give me once a week a lettuce or tomatoes or cauliflower from his garden.

We were on this job in the early May of 1945, and on the 18th it was he who told us of the end of the war in Europe. After giving me the empty buckets he produced a bottle of home-made wine. I had only a cup to drink it with, but it went down very well, so that was how we celebrated the end of the war.

We used to work a parcels train back to New Street, arriving at about 3.30 am, when we were relieved. We were allowed 40 minutes walking time to our depot, but Sid would catch the 3.45 am newspaper train to Walsall and I would book us both off duty and cycle home.

This was my last week firing for him as it was May, the time for the annual changeover of firemen.

— o —

I was placed in the number two passenger link, covering Derby, Nottingham and Walsall via Aldridge. My new driver was Tom Pulley whose grandson, John Bloor, later became a fireman for me and is now a driver at Inverness, Scotland. Tom had recently transferred to Saltley from a depot on the old North Staffordshire Railway and had just been promoted to this link himself.

We worked ex-Midland Class '4' 4-4-0 three-cylinder Compound engines, of which he had no experience. When starting a train the engine was operated in 'simple' mode,

which meant that only the single high-pressure cylinder was being used. When the train had gained a good momentum the regulator was opened wide, which in turn operated a valve that sent the exhaust steam from the high-pressure cylinder into the two low-pressure cylinders, thus using only two-thirds of the steam. The reversing lever could then be wound up, and these engines, with their 6-foot driving wheels, could manage express timings with a seven- or eight-coach load.

We worked an all-stations train to Derby, and on the first occasion that we had a Compound I noticed that Tom did not open the regulator wide between Saltley and Castle Bromwich, and I was having a job to keep steam pressure up or fire in the firebox. The same occurred on the journey to Water Orton. We were booked over the fast line to Kingsbury, and I thought he would get the engine compounding on this stretch of line, but no, he carried on the same way. I'd had enough of this, so while we stood at Kingsbury station I said, 'Why don't you open the regulator wide when we get the train on the move?'

He replied, 'But you can't keep steam up when it's only half way open.'

I explained to him the principle of the compound locomotive, and when we got up to about 20 mph I shouted, 'Shove it wide open.'

Ex-Midland Railway Compound 4-4-0 No 1001 moving from the ash pit towards the dead end of Saltley shed yard; the GEC factory can be seen in the background. Once the technique of driving them was mastered, these Compounds could manage express timings with a reasonably sized passenger train. *Derek Sharpe*

Immediately the rhythm of the locomotive changed and we picked up speed towards Tamworth. On the long run to Burton we did the same, with steam pressure high, and when we stopped he exclaimed, 'Well, I would never have believed it!'

We had no further trouble with Compounds after that.

Tom had two daughters working in the canteen that had opened about two years earlier because of the shortage of food and amount of overtime being worked. If one of them was on duty when we were ready to ring off the depot, Tom would give me a half-crown coin (worth 2s 6d) to buy a can of tea and a bacon or cheese sandwich, according to the time of day. Invariably I would be given 2s 6d change! One of Tom's daughters married a fireman, and John Bloor is their son.

We had an unusual Sunday working once every eight weeks. We would book on duty at around 7.00 am, walk to Saltley station and relieve men on a Class '2' 4-4-0 tender engine to work to Leicester, stopping at all stations. After disposing of the coaches we went to Leicester depot, where we were relieved, and signed off with less than 3 hours on duty. As there were no barracks we killed time in the messroom or had a stroll along the closed shops in the town. We would book on again at 3.00 pm and work back to Saltley with the same locomotive, and get relieved at around 5.30, signing off duty at 5.50 pm. The reason for this working was the Board of Trade regulation that would not allow train crews to be diagrammed for more than nine hours on duty (although we had done more than double that on duty during the war, undiagrammed). As we were booked off at Leicester for less than 9 hours, we were paid continuous duty, which meant that we had about 10¾ hours at Sunday rate.

I was in this link for about six months, until the winter passenger workings came into operation in October 1945, and with the war over, extra passenger work was started and I was placed in the top passenger link with driver Bill Taylor.

The work in this link entailed working express and Royal Mail trains to Bristol and

Sheffield. These were mostly mileage turns of duty, with Class '5X' 'Jubilee' or 'Black Five' 4-6-0s. During the war years these locomotives had been used extensively without regular heavy maintenance, and we were having some rough riding and poor steaming trips. Gradually they were taken to Derby or Crewe workshops to be overhauled, and it was then a pleasure to have one of these.

On one rough day in particular we worked the 4.15 pm from New Street to Bristol with a 'Jubilee', relieving Sheffield men who said that they had not been able to maintain steam pressure. On the climb to Kings Norton and Blackwell I repeatedly had to use the fire irons to liven the fire up and try to get some more heat, and Bill remarked that we had lost 5 minutes. Down the Lickey incline to Bromsgrove he let her have some fast running, but the big-ends were knocking badly and they loosened the floorboards of the cab when we were running at high speed. I tried to replace them by using the coal pick, and dust from underneath was blowing everywhere, but Bill pushed on relentlessly. We pulled back the 5 minutes to Ashchurch, but lost another couple to Cheltenham. On the climb from Gloucester Midland station I struggled for steam again with the coal in the back of the tender, which I was having to shovel twice. Despite our efforts we arrived at Bristol 10 minutes late. When we left the locomotive at Barrow Road depot, Bill filled in two repair cards stating the defects.

We were booked to work a Royal Mail parcels train back to Birmingham at about 8.30 pm, and were pleased to see that we had been allocated a refurbished 'Black Five', so we looked forward to a comfortable trip home. However, fate had other ideas!

We were booked to stop at a small station called Stonehouse to pick up vans from the former Midland branch to Stroud. Being about a quarter of a mile beyond the signal box, the points from the main line into the sidings were worked from a ground frame by the shunter. They had evidently not been set correctly, because when we reversed the train over them, there was a rumble and we came to a sudden halt.

I could see from my side of the footplate

that some of the vans had fouled the opposite line, so I told Bill and picked up the box of detonators and the hand lamp and dashed along the line, placing a detonator at a quarter of a mile, one at half a mile and three, 3 yards apart, at three-quarters of a mile. I had to do this while waving a red light as per the rule book to prevent a train coming in the opposite direction from running into the derailed vehicles. I then carried on to Standish Junction signal box another couple of miles away.

On arriving, the signalman said that he already knew of the incident as the Stonehouse signalman had given him 'Obstruction danger' on the block telegraph after the shunter had informed him from the ground frame.

The Standish man told me that the breakdown train had been ordered from Gloucester and I should stay with him to take it to the site of the derailment. We enjoyed a cup of tea, then about an hour later the breakdown train arrived. It took them about another hour to re-rail the vans, then we had to take them at caution speed to be detached at Gloucester. We arrived at Landor Street Junction about 3 hours late, so our 3 hours mileage was lost, having been on duty about 11½ hours.

On another occasion I volunteered for an extra Sunday turn of duty and was told to book on at 5.50 am. When I arrived I was instructed to mate up with driver Bob Gibson, a special link man, to work to Rotherham.

'It's a troop train that we're working,' he informed me, 'and we're booked to stay over an hour at Derby.'

This was most unusual. We relieved the Bristol men at Landor Street and worked to Derby, arriving at about 7.00 am. While I was on top of the tender putting water in the tank and pushing coal forward, I heard the sound of a bugle blowing 'Reveille', and I saw soldiers emerging from the coaches. Sergeants were barking orders, lining the men up and marching them to the centre of the platform, where army field kitchens had been set up to feed them.

After a while a young lieutenant came to us and spoke to Bob, asking if we could put some more heat in the train as it was a cold winter's morning and these men had just come back from Singapore (the war against Japan having recently finished) for demobilising at Catterick. I was already putting 50 lbs steam pressure into the coaches, but I increased it to 70 lbs, the maximum.

He then said, 'Would you like some breakfast?'

We naturally said 'Yes', and he took us to the field kitchen, where they gave us bacon, sausage and eggs.

While we were enjoying this luxury he remarked, 'I've always wanted to ride on the footplate of a locomotive.'

'Just before we're due to depart come up and you can ride with us,' Bob replied.

During our wait the officer in charge of the train, a major, came to us and asked, 'Everything all right, men?'

'Yes,' Bob replied. 'We're sorry we didn't give you sufficient heat but we've rectified it now.'

'I know nothing about this!' exclaimed the major.

Bob explained about the other officer. The major snorted and said, 'Shut the bloody heat off. They have to get acclimatised some time.'

Bob explained that he could not do this as railway regulations stated that all passenger trains had to be heated from October to May.

As the platform staff's whistles were blowing, signalling all doors to be closed, the young lieutenant came and joined us on the footplate. It was daylight by now, and I told him to sit on my wooden seat as I would be too busy to use it for about 30 minutes until we got to Clay Cross.

When I could, I pointed out landmarks and explained different peculiarities of the line and signals. He was startled when we plunged into the darkness of the tunnel outside Belper, then the same at Ambergate. Approaching Clay Cross Tunnel we had gained speed, and as this one was a lot longer, I warned him beforehand. In the firelight I could see him holding the side of the cab tightly. Then came the noise of the brakes being applied by Bob for the 30 mph speed restriction around the curve at Clay Cross Junction.

On the easier but faster running I offered him a cup of tea, which he tried to drink out of the tea can lid. I told him to stand up and flex his legs to allow for the oscillation of the footplate.

Bob opened the regulator wide to have a run at the climb towards Dronfield. At the top we approached Bradway Tunnel and I again warned him as the brakes would be applied half way through it for the 25 mph speed restriction at Dore & Totley Junctions. We then had about 10 minutes of fast running on the descent towards Sheffield station, which we ran through at 15 mph on a line away from the platforms, carrying on to Rotherham where we stopped for water and relief.

As he climbed down from the footplate and returned to the train he thanked us and remarked, 'I see you both smoke pipes.'

We handed over to the relief crew, and as we walked along the train he leaned out of the window and gave Bob a 2-ounce tin of tobacco, which we shared.

We were then booked to travel into Sheffield to work a train to Birmingham New Street, and we booked off duty in just 8 hours, but we had 10 hours mileage at Sunday rate, a free breakfast and tobacco, so it was a good day.

On 1 January 1946 there was a tragic accident at Lichfield Trent Valley on the Crewe to Euston line, in which 20 passengers were killed and 21 were injured. My future father-in-law, Jim Wakelin, who was an ex-fitter at Bescot depot, served on the breakdown gang that worked on the smash. Tug Wilson, who used to be the Bromsgrove shedmaster, was the foreman fitter, and they later told me that it was the worst damage to a train they had ever seen. The coaches were constructed of wood on steel chassis and were smashed to matchwood, causing horrific injuries to the passengers. I have recently read the Ministry of Transport's report and I can understand why the trade unions thought the findings by Lieutenant Colonel E. Woodhouse RE were controversial! Briefly, the 6.08 pm local passenger train from Stafford to Nuneaton with

a 'Prince of Wales' tender locomotive with four coaches was standing in the platform when the 2.50 pm fish train from Fleetwood to London with a Stanier 'Black Five', seven vans and a guard's brake-van, which should have gone along the through line between the platforms, crashed into the rear of it.

The driver of the fish train insisted that he had seen the outer distant signal, a colour light, at green, and the inner distant also at clear. Six other witnesses, including the signalman at Lichfield No 2 signal box (the accident occurred under Lichfield No 1's control) gave evidence of buckled rodding controlling the points, and the signalman at No 1 said that he had cleared the through road for the fish train. Despite this, the blame was placed on the shoulders of the driver of the fish train and the signalman at No 1 box.

The Saltley breakdown gang also attended, and my future father-in-law commented on the difference between the conditions of the two gangs. He said that the Bescot men had to rely on corned beef and biscuits, whereas the Saltley gang had hot meals provided by the railway's Midland Hotel in Birmingham, delivered by vans on the orders of Bill Thorley, their foreman.

One of the most gruelling week's work I found in this link was working the early morning mail from New Street to Bristol. We would book on at 1.50 am, after having cycled 10 miles from home. We would then walk the 40 minutes to New Street and relieve the Sheffield men at 2.40 am. We departed at 2.42 am and, as the 'Jubilee' locomotive had come through from Newcastle, the coal was in the back of the tender and the fire clinkered. We were booked to stop at Worcester, Cheltenham and Gloucester, arriving in Bristol Temple Meads around 6.00 am. We had our food while waiting for the mails to be unloaded and the coaches taken away to allow us to go light engine to Barrow Hill depot.

We then took over another 'Jubilee' that was prepared for us, but I would have a busy time building the fire up for the heavy climb out of Bristol towards Mangotsfield. We would follow our train of North Eastern coaches, usually 12 or 14, which was heavier than our LMS ones, into the station to be coupled on. We went non-stop to Gloucester, then stopped at Cheltenham before a fast run to Bromsgrove, where we stopped for two or three bankers according to the weight of our train. We arrived at New Street at around 10.00 am and, after being relieved, caught the 10.12 passenger train to Vauxhall to book off duty at 10.40. (As our mileage bonus came to 11 hours we were actually doing 50 minutes work for nothing.) I would then cycle home, arriving about 12.00 noon, and go to bed until 7.00 pm to enable me to see my girlfriend or play snooker, come home at about 11.00 pm or midnight to get ready to go to work.

We did this duty for six days, and on the Saturday morning after breasting the Lickey incline at Blackwell I would sit on my seat for the easy running to New Street, thankful that the week's work was over. It was harder than the Carlisle work as it was six days work, whereas Carlisle was only four.

— o —

May 1946 saw the annual changeover of firemen and I was promoted to the top freight links, which stood senior to the passenger links for firemen. Drivers, when their seniority took them to the top of junior freight links, had a choice of whether to move to the passenger links and work through to the top, or go into one of the top freight links, where they would remain until retirement or move to shunting or bank pilot work if they suffered ill health or defective eyesight.

There were eight of these freight links with eight weeks work in each, covering Bath, Bristol, Peterborough, London, Sheffield, Bradford, Lincoln and Carlisle. The firemen moved around them every 12 months, to enable them to have a good knowledge of the routes at the depot when they were passed out for driving duties.

I found myself in the old Bath link with driver Bill Whittal, but the lodging turns had been abolished during the war years, except to Carlisle with its modern barracks and canteen facilities. As the delays of the war years

on this route had been eliminated with the opening of four lines between Cheltenham and Gloucester, we worked trains only as far as Gloucester and Worcester, instead of going through to Bath, and worked back to Washwood Heath.

Trains had also been re-timed to run faster. Some worked with a minimum of one-third of the vehicles fitted with vacuum brakes, operated from the locomotive. We worked these trains mainly with the old Midland Class '4' 0-6-0 freight locomotives, which were steam-shy and many were still run down following the war. To work these 'fitted' trains, as they were called, the engine had to maintain 21 inches of vacuum to keep the brakes off, and if the steam pressure was reduced by about 40 lbs, the vacuum would be reduced, causing the brakes to go on and bring us to a stand.

During the spring of 1946 my father had died at the age of 47, so I was left to look after our smallholding, with pigs, ducks, chickens and a goat to sustain. It was a good job my mother, who was a farmer's daughter, could milk the goat, as although I tried on many occasions, I failed hopelessly. I was glad that the lodging turns had been cut out so I could look after the flock.

Between February and March of 1947 we had heavy snow, with hard frosts at night, and our hamlet was almost cut off with snowdrifts. The coal merchants could not get to us, but the local canal, which ran alongside our fields, was frozen solid with up to a foot of ice. Because of the coal shortage we would cut a hole in the ice like Eskimos and use a pole with a cage of chicken wire on the end to draw up coal that had fallen off barges. Occasionally we would spend about an hour making the hole to find that there was no coal underneath, so we got to know the likely places on bends or near narrow bridges where the barges would bump the side of the canal.

The local policeman would come along most days to assess the thickness of the ice for our safety and to check that we were not working on the aqueduct where the canal crossed the railway line on the other side of our smallholding.

One Sunday afternoon my girlfriend came

to our house for tea and when my mother said that I was getting coal out of the canal, she stared in disbelief, until my mother took her across the field to where I was working. Not only did we need coal for the house, but we also needed it for boiling the pigs' food.

Some of the snowdrifts were still about when I got married on 5 April; Ron Broadhurst was my best man. My new wife, May, was the daughter of Jim Wakelin, who I have already mentioned. He was a fitter and member of the breakdown gang at Bescot, so she was used to the vagaries of railway work. As there was a housing shortage we lived for a few years with my mother, and May helped out with the animals until we were allocated a council house.

As railway shift workers regularly took sandwiches to work we were allowed an extra cheese allowance during the war years and even in 1947 some rationing was still in being, so we still had the extra cheese. One morning May was being served at the Rushall Co-op alongside a man, and when she collected her shopping from the serving counter she picked up a large piece of cheese, thinking it was our allowance. The man said, 'Excuse me, but I think you've taken my cheese.'

'It's mine!' protested May. 'My husband is a fireman on the railway and we're allowed extra.'

'I'm a driver on the railway and I also get extra,' he replied.

Evidently the shop assistant had only cut one piece. When this had been sorted out, the man concerned, Frank Smith, our local councillor, asked May who her husband was, and when she told him, he said, 'I know him well. He's at Saltley, the same depot as me.'

When May told me of the incident later in the day I remarked, 'Don't pinch Frank Smith's cheese - he's our local councillor and we're waiting for a council house, so we have to keep well in with him!'

The next link I went into was the old London link, but we worked only as far as Wellingborough or Wigston, just south of Leicester. My driver was Bernard Ingram, who was aged 62 and had been in this link about 20 years, having worked through to Cricklewood via Bedford and St Albans and lodged at London. He told me of an incident when he returned during the war after lodging away overnight. When he cycled over the railway bridge in Pelham Road, he saw a pile of bricks and wreckage where his house should have been! He inquired from the air raid precautions man, who had been working in the area, if his family was safe, and they directed him to the local school where all survivors had been taken. When he arrived there he found his wife and daughter quite well; as his wife said to him, 'You're never at home when you're needed!'

He was a very methodical driver and when I got used to his methods I could tell within a few yards where he would open and close the regulator, but as with most methodical drivers he expected his fireman to do the same. He wanted maximum steam pressure when it was needed for heavy work, but on light running or coasting he loathed the engine to be blowing off from the safety valves, saying that it was a waste of water.

One of our turns of duty was the night London fitted freight train. We booked on at 7.15 pm, with our locomotive prepared, usually a Hughes Class '5P/4F' 'Crab' 2-6-0 or an ex-Midland Class '4' 0-6-0, departing from the depot at 7.30 pm into Lawley Street, where our guard, Bill Dailey, was waiting. This was when the guards had eight weeks work in the links so we would get the same one on each job. He was a good experienced man, and after giving us our loading, usually about 20 vehicles, he mentioned any new temporary speed restrictions. This was a good safety measure in case we had missed any during our 10-minute perusal of the notices when booking on duty.

We left at about 8.10 pm for Water Orton, and Bernard showed me a way of improving the steaming qualities of the Class '4' locomotives. This involved taking a bucket of sand on to the footplate when leaving the shed; on passing Bromford Bridge racecourse I removed the baffle plate from the mouth of the fire box and filled my shovel with sand, then Bernard would open the regulator wide and put the reversing lever full down, while I threw the sand towards the tubeplate and tubes. This resulted in a black plume of soot issuing from the chimney towards the race-course. We would do this two or three times until no soot was emitted, then we knew that the tubes were clean.

At Water Orton sidings the shunters would make our train up to 40 vehicles, or 45 if we had a 'Crab', and we would depart at about 9.00 pm via Whitacre Junction, then heavy working to just outside Arley tunnel, through which we coasted down to Nuneaton Abbey Street. After crossing the Trent Valley line, it was heavy working to Hinckley, where we stopped to pick up vehicles, then easy running to Wigston sidings and relief. We had about half an hour break for our food and my can of tea (Bernard always carried a bottle of cold water) before our return train arrived for us to relieve.

My first job was to put water into the tank, then get the fire irons down and clean the clinker out of the fire before the climb back up to Hinckley. We would arrive at Washwood Heath around 2.30 am and sign off duty around 3.15 am.

On another turn we booked on at 12.15 am for a London train to Wigston. For this shift I would sleep in the daytime, then cycle to work for 11.30 pm. We were booked to prepare our own locomotive, so while I was doing my own work I would oil and inspect the locomotive, so that by the time Bernard arrived we had only to take it out of the roundhouse to the departure roads and 'ring off' the shed into Lawley Street sidings.

On the return train from Wigston we were usually sent along the goods line from Water Orton, waiting our turn to enter Washwood Heath sidings. There was a train from Saltley to Aldridge at 8.15 am, which gave me only a 5-minute cycle home, and if we arrived at the

depot at the right time I would be able to catch it. If, however, the goods lines were full and we were delayed, Bernard would tell me to catch my train at Castle Bromwich station. 'I can look after this on my own into Washwood Heath.'

The last week I had with Bernard we were on the night Wigston turn and my wife was expecting our first child. On Saturday 8 May, on nearing home at around 4.00 am, I was surprised to see a car near my mother's house, and on entering I was further surprised to see the midwife and doctor enjoying a cup of tea. My son had been born about an hour earlier. My younger brother Edgar, who had returned home from the army, had called them out to attend at the birth, so they in turn were surprised to see me, thinking Edgar was the father.

May 1948 took me into the Sheffield and Rotherham link with driver Jack Butler, working Bristol to York trains from Landor Street Junction, or from Lawley Street to York as far as Masborough, just outside Rotherham, and from Lawley Street to Sheffield Queens Road. Jack was a comical man, an inventor who had his own metal lathe he had bought in Sheffield; he had made his own washing machine and had put his own central heating in his home. He used to go to the British Industries Fair at Castle Bromwich each year for new ideas; because of his enthusiastic questioning and examination of the goods on show, one of the exhibitors, thinking he was a Japanese spy, had told him to clear off.

For one week's work we booked on duty at 8.15 pm for a fully fitted train from Lawley Street to York. This was booked non-stop to Masborough with a 'Black Five' or a 'Crab', but when we arrived at the prepared locomotive road in the dark we saw that it was a LNER-type engine, which at first we thought was a 'B1'. On reaching the footplate we could see in the firelight that the operating handles were totally different from what we expected.

'Crab' 2-6-0 No 42822 (fitted with Caprotti valve-gear) with a parcels train on the up Camp Hill line at Duddeston Road. H. F. Wheeller, R. S. Carpenter collection

Jack looked for the reversing lever and could not find one. He said to me, 'I'll go and find someone who knows about these engines.'

While he was away I found out how to open the firehole doors. Instead of two doors sliding open, this one worked on a ratchet and opened into the firebox, a 'baker's oven' door as I later found out it was called. I looked into the firebox and it seemed about 10 feet long; I practised to see if I could reach the front of it by bouncing the coal off the shovel on the mouth of the firebox. When I could do this satisfactorily, I started to build the fire up. By the time Jack came back the fire was burning bright, giving us more light on the footplate. He arrived with the shift foreman fitter and the driver who had prepared the locomotive, and they explained the positions of the valves working the injectors, the whistle and the brake, and explained that the reversing lever was steam-operated.

By the time this was sorted out, we left the shed with the mystery engine about 30 minutes late, in turn leaving Lawley Street at about 9.30 pm. As we ran down the goods line to Saltley station, I could see that the signalman had stopped a Birmingham to Derby local passenger train to turn us out on the main line in front of it. The passenger train was worked by Saltley men, and the driver, Bert Matthews, one of Jack's neighbours, gave us a derisory whistle as we passed.

When Jack had got speed up to about 30 mph around Bromford Bridge, he tried to work the engine economically by notching up the reversing gear, but instead of winding it up as on our engines, he had to use the steam valve, but instead of staying in forward gear, it went into reverse, stopping us sharply, and the train came together with a clatter of buffers.

Jack said, 'Go back and check if the vans have become derailed and see if we've hurt the guard.'

The train was all right, but the guard used some bad language. When I inquired how he was, he said, 'Is he trying to kill me?'

I explained about the reversing gear and advised him to hold on tight for the rest of the journey. We restarted and were put along the goods line at Water Orton West for the local passenger to pass us, with another derisory whistle, on its way via Whitacre.

We were then turned on to the fast line and Jack remarked, 'I'll open the regulator wide to see if we can get some speed up like that.'

When he did there was a great roar from the chimney and I expected to see the fire bars come out of the chimney along with the fire that came out! Jack said, 'We can't work like that', so he reduced the power from the regulator and we just chugged along slowly. As we approached Kingsbury Junction I could see that the local passenger train was standing on the slow line from Whitacre.

Jack remarked, 'Control are persevering with us, as we're an important train.'

We received another rude whistle from Bert Matthews as we carried on in front of him. Over the water troughs at Wigginton I tried to drop the scoop to fill the tank, but there was no tender gauge to see how much water we had gathered. I found out later that there was a handle that opened tiny holes through which water came out, indicating the level of water in the tank.

Jack was not satisfied with how much water we had, so on passing Wychnor Junction he indicated by whistling that we would be stopping at Burton to fill up. At Branston Junction we were placed along the goods line to Leicester Junction, where we stopped at the water column. I was on the back of the tender when the local passenger again passed us, to more whistles and fingers raised, to show us how many minutes we had delayed them.

We arrived at Derby about 2 hours late and were relieved by a set of ex-LNER men from Canklow depot, who understood these locomotives. We waited for our return train and on signing off duty we were informed that the running shift foreman wanted to see us in his office.

'Control have been going mad about the delay to this train,' he said.

'I've never seen one of these engines before,' Jack replied, 'and to expect us to take over one at night when we can't see our equipment was ridiculous.'

'Make out a detailed report,' retorted the foreman.

Jack took about 20 minutes doing this, and he showed it to me for confirmation. I smiled when I read the last sentence: 'On arriving at Derby we were relieved and I was quite glad to get off what I think was a travelling menagerie.'

We used to work the 8.10 am express passenger train from Birmingham to York as far as Derby, then work a freight train from Chaddeston sidings back to Washwood Heath. A few weeks later, when we were relieved at Derby, a Mr Shorto, who had been assistant superintendent at Saltley and was now stationed at Derby, alighted from the train and came and spoke to us, as he usually did. Jack mentioned our experiences on the unusual locomotive, and Mr Shorto asked was its number was.

Jack informed him. On the following morning he approached us with a photograph and asked, 'Was this your mystery locomotive?'

We agreed that it was.

'It's a Raven three-cylinder 4-6-2 express passenger engine built around 1920 for the NER,' he said.

As I remarked earlier, Jack was very comical and one summer evening we relieved the Bristol to York fully fitted express freight at Landor Street Junction at around 7.00 pm with a 'Crab' in front, with the coal in the back of the tender. After passing Clay Cross Junction we had the distant signal for Avenue Crossing against us. On stopping I took the opportunity to go into the tender and shovel coal forward to the firing plate. To my amazement Jack shouted, 'Do you fancy an ice-cream?'

'I could manage a pint of beer better,' I replied.

There was a few minutes silence, then Jack came back on to the footplate saying, 'Here you are.'

He handed me an ice-cream cornet, while eating one himself. When we proceeded over the level crossing I could see an ice-cream van standing there.

On another occasion we had terminated our train at Burton at around 7.00 pm and we had to wait until 8.25 pm for a train to travel home. Jack suggested that we should have a couple of pints at the station hotel bar. While quaffing these, two ladies came in. One waved in our direction, then they came over to us with their two half pints of best Burton ale. These were placed in front of us, and the lady said 'Hello, driver Butler' to Jack, and 'Sorry, I don't remember your name' to me.

Jack then recognised her as Mrs Chappel, the manageress of the railway barracks at Sheffield, where he had lodged before it had been stopped, and she was waiting for a train home at 8.15 pm. She reminded us of the incident when we were lodging at Sheffield with train crews from Bescot and Newcastle-on-Tyne. The Bescot fireman was listening to the conversation and remarked to his driver in his Black Country accent, "ark at 'im calling werter (water) watter!'

When our glasses were empty Jack went to the bar for four half pints, then later nudged me to do the same. The ladies said goodbye to us at around 8.05 pm, and on the way out purchased something at the bar. When we finally finished our drinks and prepared to leave, the barman said, 'There's two pints of bitter paid for you here.'

'We'll have to drink them,' said Jack, 'because we don't know when we'll be in here again.'

We gulped them down and rushed on to the platform to see our train home departing! The next direct train to Birmingham was the 12.30 am mail. However, there was a train for Walsall leaving in 5 minutes, so we dashed up to the bay line and just scrambled aboard. Burton was famous for its beer and had a local byelaw that they would not sell beer below a specific gravity, and Burton's was stronger than ordinary beer.

We had drank 3½ pints of it in about an hour and we became a bit merry during the run to Walsall. The train terminated there, and there was another leaving for Birmingham shortly afterwards. There were a few Saltley men waiting for it, so I asked them to look after Jack because of the merry mood he was in. I could then catch the bus home to save me travelling to Saltley to book off duty.

5
THE 'BRADFORD' AND CARLISLE LINKS 1950-54

May 1950 saw me in the old 'Bradford' link, as it was still called, but we no longer went to Bradford, as extra Carlisle work had come to the depot, and with lodging stopped at Bradford the Carlisle work had been placed in this link, but the title Bradford link had been retained to differentiate it from the original Carlisle link.

The new train left Water Orton at 4.15 am and we worked most of these jobs with one week on the afternoon train, while the Carlisle link had one week on the early morning plus their normal afternoon work. The 4.15 am departure enabled me to see parts of the line that were in darkness on the afternoon trains.

My driver was Harry Birks, an ex-Crewe man, a rather fiery tempered man who was liable to explode if we were having a bad run. One day on the return run we were delayed by signals and were stopped at Goose Hill Junction, Normanton, where the signal lowered to take us along the goods line. Harry jumped off the footplate and rushed up the signal box steps two at a time. From the footplate I could see him gesticulating to the signalman, then he put his hands around his throat. I dashed to the box to separate them.

'I've been ordered by Control to divert you off the main line as there's a special express train behind you,' the signalman croaked.

Harry calmed down, and we proceeded along the goods line, where the express passed us, returning to the main line at West Riding Junction.

I had by now learned the art of cooking on the firing shovel when the locomotive was at a standstill, but Harry gave me an extension to my cooking skills. We bought bacon, eggs and sausage and a loaf of bread at Carlisle, then departed on the return run at 4.00 am, working hard on the incline to Aisgill and Blea Moor for 2½ hours. On the subsequent downhill run of about 20 minutes to Settle, I would scald the firing shovel with the boiling water from the slacking pipe, put the bacon and sausage on it, and place it in the fire hole door where the fire was high up in the firebox glowing red. It took a matter of minutes to cook the meat, then I placed a couple of eggs in the fat that was in the shovel, and if there was any fat left I placed two pieces of bread to fry. This concoction smelled lovely in the early morning air. I then dished it out on a newspaper on our seats and we tucked into it on our run to Skipton.

On the outward daytime journey we would arrive at Carlisle at about midday. Harry was a darts enthusiast and we would go to the local pub with the guard and play darts for a couple of hours. After having cycled for an hour to book on duty at 3.15 am and standing up firing on a rocking footplate, very often my legs were aching when we thankfully returned to the barracks to go to bed, until being woken at 1.30 am to book on at 3.00 am.

I recall one of these sessions. Wiping a glass, the barmaid remarked, 'I can't tell the driver from the fireman or guard.'

Our guard replied quite seriously, 'I am the guard, I work the train; Harry is the driver, he works the engine; and Bill is the fireman, he works his balls off.'

The barmaid laughed so much she dropped the glass on the floor, where it smashed.

One lunchtime, when we left our locomotive at Durran Hill depot just outside Carlisle, I recognised a man in a nice suit, but could not think where I had seen him before. It was in fact Bill Challinor, who had been the shedmaster at Alsager some ten years earlier, and was now assistant supervisor at Carlisle. We spoke for a few moments about the old days and he said he was glad I had made the grade as a long-distance fireman.

On one northbound afternoon turn, we were coming to a stop at Skipton and I dropped off the footplate at the water column to take water quickly, but as the engine stopped with a lurch, the boiler water injector flew off, spraying steam and boiling water around my feet. I clambered on to the back of the tender to put the pipe into the tank and felt a sharp pain around my left ankle. Hobbling on to the footplate I pulled my sock down and could see a large blister forming. Harry took me to the signal box where there was an ambulance box; there was no first aid man on duty, but some ointment was smeared on the blister and a bandage wrapped around it. The pain had now subsided and I thought that there was no use in stopping at Skipton, so I decided to carry on firing to Carlisle. When we arrived at the barracks we undid the bandage and discovered that the blister was now the size of a Jaffa orange. The Carlisle depot first aid man was sent for.

'You'll have to go to hospital!' he exclaimed, and arranged for a railway van to take me there. At the casualty department the doctor burst the blister to drain the fluid out and asked me what my work was. After placing a dressing on the wound he said, 'No work for you for some time - I don't want any dirt or coal dust in this.'

Back at the barracks the first aid man telephoned the depot, repeating what the doctor had said. After 15 minutes wait the telephone rang and they informed me to lodge in the normal way and travel home passenger on the 12.15 pm from Carlisle to Birmingham. It was now around 2.00 am. I had a meal in the canteen and spoke to Harry, who was playing cards with some of his old compatriots from Crewe, to tell him that he would have a Carlisle fireman on the return trip. He afterwards told me that he had, in fact, three firemen to complete the journey!

I duly caught the Glasgow to Birmingham train at 12.15 pm and at about 1.30 pm a waiter came along the train calling passengers for last lunch in the dining car. I asked him if I could get a cup of tea, as I had left the tea can with Harry. He asked, 'What are you doing travelling passenger?'

I explained that I had scalded my ankle and was going home.

'Come with me to the kitchen car,' he said.

He gave me a cup of tea, and after three-quarters of an hour, when the rush of serving food was over, the chef came to me saying, 'Have you got any food?'

'I've a few cheese sandwiches left over for our return journey,' I replied.

He told me to hang on and returned with a plate of roast beef and vegetables, then a pudding. After leaving Crewe at around 4.15 pm the waiter brought me another cup of tea and a slice of fruit cake. On arriving at New Street at 5.15 pm I telephoned our depot and informed them of my predicament, and the time clerk said that he would fill in a time sheet in for and told me to go straight home. He told me to bring a doctor's certificate to the depot when I had seen my own doctor.

The following day I attended our local surgery and was passed to the doctor's assistant, who was a lady. She examined the injury, placed a piece of gauze that had been dipped in a yellow ointment on the ankle, and bandaged it up. She gave me a chemist's prescription for a tin of the yellow gauze and a certificate to take to work describing my injury, and told me to go back and see her in a week's time.

When I returned to see her she asked how my ankle was and I replied that it was all right and I had no pain. I said, 'I'll be all right to go to work at 3.15 am tomorrow.'

She smiled ruefully and remarked, 'You won't want to got to work when I've finished dealing with that wound. All the dead skin has to be removed before it will heal properly.'

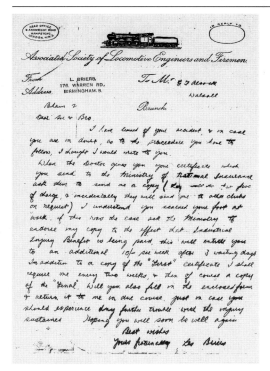

A letter from the ASLEF Saltley Branch Secretary, Les Briers, advising me of procedures, Industrial Injury Benefit, etc, following the scalding of my foot at Skipton. He was a highly respected union officer, gaining the BEM for his work, and when he died a plaque was erected in his memory at Saltley depot.

She then proceeded to do just that, exposing red raw flesh, and, after placing a dressing on it, said, 'See me in a week and keep your foot up on a stool when sitting down.'

When I attempted to walk I felt excruciating pain in my foot and could hardly move. I staggered out of the surgery and should have had a 10-minute walk home, but across the road was a working men's club whose steward was Ken Sutton, who had been a fireman at Saltley. I hobbled in there, and when Ken saw me he exclaimed, 'What's happened to you? You look like death warmed up!'

I explained while he poured me a glass of brandy.

'Have this on me,' he said. 'The club's secretary will be here shortly and he has a car. I'll get him to take you home.'

I was off duty for over two months. My little son was now at the crawling stage and would pull himself up on anything, including my foot that was resting on a stool, despite the pain I felt.

One Friday morning about a fortnight before Christmas I reported to the doctor again; although I was receiving accident payment from work, it was only about half of my basic wage, so I was anxious to get back to work. I explained this to the doctor and she said, 'Are you sure? I will give you a certificate for another fortnight.'

'No, I'd sooner go back to work,' I replied.

'Very well,' she said, 'but bathe the wound in salt water to harden the skin, because if it breaks you'll be off duty longer.'

I reported to the depot that afternoon stating that I was right for work for the 3.15 am to Carlisle on Monday morning. The timekeeper asked if I wanted to come to work on Sunday. As I was short of money I agreed, and he gave me a job booking on at 2.00 am for a platelayer's ballast train, which was quite easy work.

On Christmas Day we were booked on duty at 8.00 am standby, and at about 9.30 am I was instructed to go to New Street station and go with a Derby driver to Bristol, as his fireman had injured himself (this was Derby's top job). When the train arrived at New Street, the fireman was taken to hospital with a smashed foot caused by a heavy lump of coal falling from the tender on to it.

We worked to Bristol, arriving at about 12.15 pm, and were relieved. We had a quick sandwich and a can of tea and departed again at 12.45, arriving at New Street around 3.00 pm, where I was expecting relief, but to my dismay there was none. As I was had been on duty less than 7 hours I could not refuse to carry on to Derby. We arrived there about 4.00 pm, where the Derby driver walked over to the depot to book off duty, leaving me on the platform. I inquired about a train home and was told that the next one to Birmingham was at 8.00 pm! I telephoned Control for an earlier service, such as a freight train, but they said that there was nothing going towards Birmingham, so I spent Christmas afternoon in the messroom on my own. I eventually arrived at New

Street at 9.15, travelled to Saltley and booked off duty at 10.00 pm. I had been on duty for 14 hours, and my mileage was 230 miles, equal to 14 hours bonus payment, so one cancelled out the other.

I arrived home at about 11.00 pm. My wife had been worried about me, and I had not seen my family on Christmas Day, missing seeing my young son opening his presents. My dinner had dried up in the oven and I vowed never to work another Christmas Day, even if it meant applying for leave and losing a day's pay.

During the early months of the new year we were on the early morning train from Carlisle. Our guard was 'Tat' Carter, one of our fellow travellers from Walsall. The reason for his nickname was supposed to be that he was one of triplets and there was no tit for Tat! We backed on our train and Tat gave us our loading of 45 vans, and added, 'You'll find them heavy. They're Scottish seed potatoes.'

He was not joking! Pulling out of the sidings up the incline to Cumwhinton was like pulling a coal train, and we eventually got the train moving towards Armathwaite. Approaching Long Marton, Harry looked at the tank water gauge and, seeing that we had used a lot, decided that we did not have enough to get us to Garsdale troughs, so he whistled to indicate that we would be stopping at Appleby. On arrival there the signalman leaned out of the window of his box and indicated he wanted us to shunt our train on to the branch line to allow another train to pass, as we were losing time. We filled the tank and I built up a good thick fire for the heavier climb ahead.

After 30 minutes delay we had the 'right away' signal and started moving again. On the climb towards Kirkby Stephen we had the regulator wide open and the gear lever fully down, and we were barely moving. I was having to work both boiler water injectors to maintain the water in the boiler. After a long struggle we got over the summit at Aisgill with some easier running to give us some speed to pick water up at Garsdale troughs. I looked for the distant signal for Blea Moor, which was at caution, and we were directed on to the goods loop. I cooked our breakfast standing still for a

change, and we departed after a passenger train passed us. Harry said that we were now about 2 hours late. We ran easy to Skipton, then struggled to get some speed up towards Rotherham Masborough, where I had to clean the fire of clinker and shovel some coal forward from the back of the tender.

After some 30 minutes we were ready to carry on. At Wingfield Sidings signal box between Clay Cross and Ambergate we were stopped again and instructed to shunt on to the other line for a train to pass us, as there were not enough sidings to hold our train. As we were making this movement, I said to Harry, 'There's not enough coal to get us home.'

'I'll go to the box to carry out the protection duty and ask for a fresh locomotive,' he replied.

We had now been on duty for about 10 hours. While we waited for the express to pass us, I shovelled the remainder of the coal to the front of the tender and estimated that we had only about 15 cwt left. Harry, being short in stature, always placed a lump of coal about 3 feet wide by 1 foot high in front of his seat to rest his feet on, and jokingly I broke it up and put it in the firebox.

When we reached Derby we were surprised to see a set of men waiting to relieve us.

'You should have brought a fresh engine,' said Harry.

'Why?' they asked.

Harry pointed to the tender where there was only about 5 cwt of coal left. The Derby driver remarked, 'I've never seen a tender so empty', and turning to me said, 'You must have burned over 10 tons of coal.'

We left them arranging to take the locomotive to the Derby depot to be replenished.

Whenever I met Tat Carter afterwards he would invariably ask if I had planted any seed potatoes. To add insult to injury, about a fortnight later Harry received a letter from management asking for his explanation for the late running of the train. He wrote back scathingly, stating that seed potatoes weighed about 20 tons per van and should not be put on express freight trains and the Traffic Department should monitor the labelling of vans better.

During this period British Railways was building more Stanier 'Black Five' locomotives, with modern features such as Timken roller axle bearings, which made for freer running, rocker fire grates, so that clinker could be broken up on the run when coasting, ashpans that would open underneath, which saved having to rake the ashes out, self-cleaning smokeboxes, and on some even steam-operated sand guns to clean the tubes and tubeplate, shades of us throwing sand into the firebox at Bromford Bridge!

There was also an exchange of locomotives with other regions. The ex-LNER 'B1s' were supposed to be more economical than Stanier's 'Black Fives', but they were not popular with the ex-LMS men. They were very dirty, with dust blowing around the footplate from the ashpan. There was only a front damper, which, when open at speed, caused air to rush through towards the footplate, whereas the 'Black Fives' had a front and back damper and would steam efficiently with only the back dampers open. I found the footplate awkward to work on, and the tender had only a small aperture to shovel the coal from, whereas the 'Black Fives' had a large shovelling plate plus large doors that could be opened to gain access when the coal became out of reach. The firehole door on the 'B1s' was called a 'baker's oven' door; it opened inwards, which meant a burnt behind every time I fired! I was glad I never had one on the Carlisle job, and I heard stories of

them having to be replaced at Leeds owing to the fact that the fireman could not reach the coal in the tender.

I also had experience of the ex-GWR 'Hall' and 'County' Class locomotives. These were also very dusty and used too much of our hard coal, as they were designed for the softer Welsh coal.

— o —

The annual merry-go-round of firemen came round again in May. However, in the recent Wages and Conditions Agreement the unions and British Railways had agreed to a reduction from a 48-hour to a 44-hour week. This was achieved by the provision of a 'rest day' once a fortnight, worked on a Monday to Saturday rotation. This meant links of 12 weeks instead of eight, and instead of eight top freight links there became five.

The result of this changeover was that I found myself back in the Masborough and Sheffield link with Jack Butler. Some extra work had been added; we now worked the Stockport trains to Rowsley, north of Matlock. One was a night turn and another a day turn, which gave me a view of the beauty of this line.

Jack was as eccentric as ever. He told me he was working on a compound to put on the soles and heels of boots and shoes that would wear out pavements and roads but not his footwear. He also mentioned that his pear-tree would not bear fruit. Someone had suggested that he move it around his garden to find a suitable place. He retorted, 'I've moved it that often I've fastened a pair of wheels on it to make it easier.'

One day we were working the 8.10 am New Street-York express to Derby when between Elford and Wichnor a cloud of feathers went up in the air, indicating that we had hit a bird. When running into Burton station (where the platform was on the fireman's side) I noticed a porter look at the front of the engine and point, so as we came to a stand I dashed to the front and saw a pheasant lying there. Jack told me to take it home for my wife to cook. The following day, after we relieved the Bournville men at New

The ex-LNER 'B1s' were supposed to be more economical than Stanier's 'Black Fives', but they were not popular with the ex-LMS men. Here is No 61318 simmering in Saltley No 3 shed in about 1950. *H. F. Wheeller, R. S. Carpenter collection*

Street, I went to the front of the locomotive to alter the headlamp code from empty stock to express passenger. Jack handed me a handful of corn.

'This should attract the birds.'

I had a happy 12 months with Jack, then in 1952 the annual changeover occurred and I was placed in the London link again with Bernard Ingram. Extra work had also been put in this link to make it up to a 12-week roster, with trains now being worked to Coalville and Evesham.

We booked on around 7.00 pm for the London train, only to be told that defects had been found in the walls of Arley Tunnel between Whitacre Junction and Nuneaton. In order to gain the ex-Midland main line at Bedford, we were therefore being diverted via Redditch to the old SMJR route from Broom Junction via Stratford-upon-Avon, crossing the ex-GWR line south of Banbury at Fenny Compton, the ex-GCR line at Woodford and the West Coast Main Line near Roade; three

On 17 July 1957 '4F' 0-6-0 No 43873 rumbles along the single line of the old Stratford on Avon & Midland Junction Railway with a goods train, having just crossed the West Coast Main Line near Roade. *K. C. H. Fairey*

of our passed firemen had transferred to become drivers at Woodford shed.

We caught single-line tokens at signal boxes I had never seen before. They seemed to be at the bottom of gradients, which meant braking the train to walking pace, then working the locomotive hard to climb the next gradient. We were near Bedford before we found our return train, which was being worked by an ex-Midland Class '4' 0-6-0. We had to top up with coal at Stratford, and eventually arrived back at Landor Street Junction, where we were relieved. We then walked to our depot to book off after over 16 hours on duty. I was dead tired; I had been on duty at other times longer than this, but we had usually languished along a goods line. On this occasion we had been at work almost continually.

When Bernard spoke to the foreman to tell him that we would miss our next turn of duty by over 4 hours, owing to the 12-hour-rest condition of service rule, the foreman asked, 'Where have you been?'

'A place called Ravenstone Wood Junction.'

'Where's that?' asked the foreman.

'About 60 miles from Stratford,' Bernard answered. 'Uphill both ways.'

On booking on next day, Bernard remarked, 'We'll take our time tonight. The earlier we are the further we'll go before we meet our train. That'll mean extra work for both of us.'

We eventually met the return train at Woodford Junction and we again had to go to Stratford loco for more coal and fire cleaning, and this meant another 16 hours on duty; we therefore missed our booked turns on the Thursday evening. On the Friday night we were again diverted, and I noticed that Bernard was not in any hurry on our return train, telling me not to rush the fire cleaning and to make a good job of it. This in turn meant the fire was a long time relighting, and I became a bit anxious, but Bernard said, 'Don't worry, I'll answer any reports we may have.' Eventually we restarted our train and arrived at Landor Street at 12.30 pm on Saturday lunchtime, booking off at 12.50 pm.

Bernard said to the foreman, 'We need our

12 hours rest so we can't book on before 12.50 am on Sunday.'

This meant that we could not get our sixth turn of duty in for this week, so we were paid eight hours for nothing. I was therefore awarded some compensation for the hard work I had done that week. No wonder Bernard was in no hurry that night!

Arley Tunnel remained closed at nights for some months while repairs were carried out. The midnight London train was diverted via Burton, Coalville and Leicester, while night trains to Wellingborough and Bedford, as well as the evening London train, went via Stratford. To cut out the overtime we were now being relieved at Stratford on the outgoing train, and returned with the first return train.

For one train we booked on around 10.00 am and worked from Washwood Heath to Wellingborough, via Arley Tunnel. We were surprised to see a Garratt locomotive allocated to us, and on approaching the tunnel, where a 5 mph speed restriction was in force, we were stopped at the temporary signal box controlling the single line that had been placed in the centre of the tunnel. One of the chief engineers approached us demanding to know what we had brought this massive locomotive for, as the tunnel was in a dangerous condition.

'We have to work the locomotive allocated to us,' Bernard replied. 'If you don't want this type through the tunnel you should ban them, but it's too late now, we can't go back.'

'Wait there,' the engineer retorted. 'I'm fetching my men out while you go through. I don't want them killed through falling masonry.'

When he had cleared his men out he instructed us to proceed at walking speed. Bernard remarked to me, 'They're not concerned about us.'

A story went round the depot that one of our drivers, named Taylor, was working a return train from Peterborough and was stopped at the cattle sidings just outside Leicester. He was told that two vans of pigs on the train had got to be put off. The guard walked up to do this and said, 'These are labelled to Camp Hill, Birmingham.'

'Control state that they have to go via Coalville and Burton,' the signalman said, 'as it's not safe for them through Arley Tunnel.'

On hearing this driver Taylor exploded, and telephoned Control, saying, 'What about us?'

'It's all right - you are insured!' came the reply.

He was known as 'Piggy Taylor' from then on.

I had an unusual job one Sunday on a track renewal job between Whitacre Junction and Shustoke station. We booked on at 11.00 am and travelled by the depot bus to the site, and I was surprised to see that our locomotive was an 0-6-0 diesel shunter. These had been replacing the steam shunters at Washwood Heath and Lawley Street for some time. The platelayers were involved with prefabricated relaying, which meant using ready-assembled 60-foot lengths of track loaded on to long flat wagons. Our locomotive was on the opposite line attached to a long double-jibbed crane. This picked up the lengths of track and we took them to the appropriate place indicated by the inspector in charge of operations. The old rails and ballast had been removed earlier in the day, and we placed the new track on the new ballast.

With no shovelling to be done, I was quite happy. All my work consisted of was watching for any signals from the ground staff, which were visible from my side of the locomotive. There was an electric stove and cooking tin in the cab and I was able to cook our food and boil the water in the tea can in comfort.

At the end of the day, when we were laying the last length of track, there was some commotion because the rails were about a foot too long to fit into the vacant length. The 2 miles of track we were relaying consisted of three curves, and someone had measured it incorrectly. Some petrol-driven power saws were sent for and it took about an hour to cut through the hard steel to enable it to fit.

'It's a good job it wasn't a foot short!' one of the bosses remarked.

On 6 August my daughter was born. I was on an early morning shift and was at home in the afternoon, when my wife told me to get the doctor and midwife. The doctor I found at home, but the midwife was elusive, as she was doing her rounds looking after other young mothers. After cycling around the village for three-quarters of an hour I found her. I was panicking by then, but she remained calm, saying, 'I'll come shortly.'

The baby was born in the early evening. I telephoned the depot from the local phone box requesting leave for the rest of the week, and they were very understanding and asked me if I could come on duty at 2.00 pm for shed duties so that I could be at home in the mornings when I was needed. I thanked the roster clerk for this and duly reported at 2.00 pm. As I had no driver allocated to me I could not work on the 'six and right away' system, as it was unofficially called. This was a local working that had been started during the war years by the outside foremen, and was designed to encourage the quick-turn round of locomotives arriving at the depot when queues were waiting to have their fires, ashpans and smokeboxes emptied after coaling. The locomotives were then marshalled into the roundhouses. When the driver and fireman had attended to six locomotives, the foreman would allow them to go home. As disposing time for a locomotive was an hour and marshalling time 20 minutes, six equalled 8 hours work, but by men working hard together, sometimes one on each engine, it could be done in about 4 hours!

When I reported to George Sturmy, the outside foreman, he found me work raising steam on locomotives standing on the outgoing roads ready prepared for their crews. I was busy doing this at about 5.30 pm when someone told me that the outside foreman wanted a word with me.

'Why didn't you tell me your wife has just had a baby?' he said. 'I wondered what a main-line fireman was doing on shed work, and I've had to find out for myself. Clear off home - I'll sign you off duty at 10.00 pm. You'll do more good there changing nappies! And come and see me at this time for the rest of the week and I'll see if I can spare you to send you home.'

At the end of September we were informed that we had been allocated a council house on a new estate about 2 miles on the opposite side of Aldridge. On Thursday 2 October, my rest day, we moved into our first home, leaving my two younger brothers to look after the smallholding with my mother.

The following week we were on the 8.00 pm Lawley Street to London train, which was now running over its proper route as the repair work in Arley Tunnel had been completed. On the Monday evening Mr Bates, the footplate inspector, was waiting for us when we booked on duty at 7.15 pm to tell us that he was riding with us to check the running of the train.

'Carry on normally as though I'm not here,' he said. He then asked me, 'What side of the footplate do you fire from?'

'Any side,' I replied.

We had been allocated a 'Crab' 2-6-0, so I suggested he sat on my seat. We were booked to pick up traffic at Hinckley; as we left there one of the boiler water gauge glasses burst, spurting steam and water over us until the safety plugs worked. We always carried two spare glasses in our locker and as we were coasting towards Elmesthorpe I set about changing it. After about 10 minutes I had completed the job.

When we arrived at Wigston sidings some

The work on Arley Tunnel involved removing a section and opening out the west end to form a deep open cutting; the new cutting is seen here some years later, in 1966, with English Electric Type 4 No D215 on a Birmingham-bound train. *Michael Mensing*

10 minutes later, just before we were relieved by the Leicester crew Jack Bates tapped me on the shoulder and said, 'Well done, fireman, you saved some delay waiting for fitters to do that job. I'll make a note of it on the train timekeeping report.'

He carried on to London and was on the return train when we relieved it at Wigston the following night. He again rode with us on the outward train on the Wednesday evening, 8 October 1952, which was the day the Harrow & Wealdstone disaster occurred; when we arrived at Nuneaton we were delayed because express passenger trains were being diverted via our route through Wigston to London, so we were about 2 hours late arriving. Our return train was also delayed and we were on duty over 13 hours, thus missing our job the next evening. I wonder what Jack Bates put on his timekeeping report.

— o —

May came round again, and in 1953 it was all change in many ways. I was placed in the original Carlisle link and should have mated George Austin, but because of his age he had elected to finish his years on shunters. Jim Richardson should have taken his place, but he had domestic difficulties and could not stop overnight lodging at Carlisle, so he made a mutual exchange with driver Ernie Guy. He was a man over 60 years of age and had been in the London link for a number of years. This entailed many months of road learning, as he did not sign the route beyond Derby.

This meant that I had a string of young special link drivers being booked with me on a weekly basis. When they realised that I was experienced (I was now the second senior fireman at the depot) they allowed me to drive over part of the journey. One driver, one of our Walsall travellers, was Arthur Thomas, who virtually taught me the route to Carlisle.

When we were travelling along he would say, 'What's the name of the next signal box?' When I answered he would invariably say, 'What is unusual about the signals

there?' I would have to tell him of distant or stop signals on my side of the track. The sequence of signals at junctions was important in that we could be turned along goods lines. If I could not remember the name of a signal box he would say, 'Don't look as we go by it - see how long it takes you to remember.' He would select a third of the run to allow me to drive, for example Derby to Leeds, Rotherham to Skipton or Skipton to Carlisle, while he fired the locomotive.

In this link we worked the afternoon trains to Carlisle and just one week on the 4.00 am train from Water Orton. The old early morning return train had been replaced by a train of fully fitted vehicles, leaving around midnight and running non-stop from Carlisle to Rotherham Masborough. One Saturday morning I had driver Jack Dennis as a mate, and when we passed through Skipton he said, 'Come over here and let me see you drive while I fire it', which I was glad to do.

Approaching Leeds we ran into thick fog. I said, 'Do you want to take over?'

'Stay there,' he replied. 'Now's the time to find out if you know the road, but if you're not sure of anything give me a shout.'

We duly arrived at Rotherham and it was still foggy, and after I had filled the water tank and taken some clinker out of the fire while the train was examined, I expected him to take over, but he said, 'Carry on - you're doing all right.'

We arrived at Washwood Heath at the right time despite the persistent fog. We were booked to be relieved there, and the front half of the train was British Road Services (BRS) traffic for Lawley Street, guaranteed to be there before 8.00 am or a heavy fine would have to be paid by British Railways to BRS. We rode on the footplate to Duddeston Road signal box at the entrance to Lawley Street sidings, and Jack, pointing to me, remarked to the Control relief driver, 'He's been driving from Skipton and done a good job in the fog, getting us here at the right time.' I gracefully blushed at the praise.

On summer Saturdays 'Starlight Specials' ran from Scotland to London, and we were booked into the goods loop at Blea Moor from about 2.15 am to 2.25 am to allow one to pass us. We took this opportunity to top up the water tank and cook our breakfast. One morning I was looking for the Blea Moor distant signal, which appeared on my side, expecting it to be at caution, when to my surprise it was clear. I shouted to Arthur Thomas, 'We're right away.'

He glanced at the water tank gauge to check that it was fairly full (I had taken a good amount over the troughs at Garsdale) and said, 'Good, but what about our breakfast?'

'I've got a certificate for mobile catering!' I replied.

On the downhill run from Ribblehead to Hellifield I showed him how it was done.

'That's the first time I've seen that,' he remarked.

We had one of the modern 'Black Fives' and, running down to Skipton, I gave the fire a rocking to break up the clinker, expecting to be put into the goods line to allow the 'Starlight' to pass us, where I could drop the clinker out of the ashpan. However, once again we saw clear signals.

'The special must be well down,' said Arthur.

We carried on expecting to be 'put inside' somewhere, but approaching Leeds the signals were again green.

'We shan't see him now,' said Arthur. 'He's booked to stop at Leeds. Come over here, I'll do the firing.'

We stopped at Rotherham for our only booked examination, having run about 140 miles non-stop. I managed to get the clinker out of the ashpan, and after our 12 minutes booked time we were away again, with me still driving. We eventually arrived at Washwood Heath about an hour before time, too early for our relief.

Ted Rogers, the yard inspector, asked us if we would take the BRS traffic to Lawley Street. Arthur replied, 'We'll take them to Duddeston Road - our relief should be starting to walk to us by then. Tell them to wait there.' This they did and, on climbing on the footplate, they said, 'Have you come across the fields this morning?'

It was 15 November before Ernie Guy completed his road learning. He had ridden

with us on a few occasions and I had spoken to him at Carlisle barracks where he stayed for a few weeks, when completing the last part of the route from Hellifield.

He was used to slower running in the London link, and I was surprised how lightly he worked the engine. Once or twice I had to tell him that we were losing time, for which he thanked me.

'You are more used to this type of train, so always inform me if we are going too slow. But I don't like to knock a fireman about by working too heavy.'

He never carried a watch, remarking, 'When British Rail provide one I'll wear it', so I got used to spotting the station and signal box clocks that I could see from my side, passing the time on to Ernie and commenting whether we were early or late. As he had just learned the road I used to assist by calling out the signals to him, and he remarked one day, 'When you get passed out for driving you'll be able to sign the road to Carlisle with confidence.'

About a fortnight before Christmas we had worked up to Carlisle on the Sunday afternoon, and on the Monday morning our guard, Charlie Kett, said, 'I need a typewriter as a present for my daughter. There are a couple of auction rooms operating in the town on Mondays, so I'll go and see if there's anything there.'

I agreed to go with him. We looked in at a couple of auctions but saw nothing, then at the third there was a typewriter in good condition. There was also a Hornby Dublo model train set with two locomotives, about ten coaches, and a dozen wagons and vans, rails and an electric transformer in a big wicker washing basket. My son had been asking for one for Christmas and I had contemplated buying him a new one, but the ones I had seen had only one locomotive, just a few coaches and were on a smaller gauge.

We waited for the auction to start. The typewriter came up for sale but the price rose out of Charlie's range. Then the train set came up. I made a bid at £1, and it rose to £1 5s. I bid £1 7s 6d, but it went against me again at £1 10s. I said £1 11s and was surprised when no other bid came, and it was knocked down to me. When Charlie and I arrived at the barracks with the basket, Ernie exclaimed 'I didn't know you were going to buy a train set!'

'I didn't know myself until Charlie took me to the auction rooms.' I replied.

Ernie was secretary of the Birmingham Model Engineers' Club and, although used to bigger gauges, cast his professional eye over my purchase.

After lunch we carried it again to Durran Hill Loco, struggled to get it on the footplate, and tied it on the tender in the well where the fire irons were stored (it was a rocker-grate locomotive and we hoped that the fire irons would not be needed).

On arriving at Saltley at about midnight we unloaded the basket from the footplate. Quite a few men came and looked at it and passed comments - you would not have thought that they worked on trains all their life! I had a carrier on the back of my cycle, to which I tied the basket, sideways on - like an 'out of gauge' load - and proceeded to cycle the 12 miles or so home. I was stopped by a policeman at Perry Barr who wanted to know what I had got; fortunately I had the receipt for it.

When I awoke at around 10.00 am my son was at school, so I laid the rails in the lounge and tested it, and it worked satisfactorily. I needed a headlight bulb for one of the locomotives and a guard's van for the goods vehicles. My wife looked into the room.

'I can see who'll be playing with it,' she remarked.

'Don't be sarcastic,' I said, 'or you won't be getting the washing basket for *your* Christmas present.'

'Black Five' 4-6-0 No 44659, the engine aboard which we were blown to a standstill on the Settle & Carlisle line in January 1954. Four years later it was photographed passing Saltley station with a down (Birmingham-bound) freight. Nechells Gas Works is seen in the distance, and on the right is the noxious chemical works; metal railings beside the line corroded away in the emissions! *Michael Mensing*

On Friday 15 January 1954 we worked the early morning Carlisle train with a new locomotive, No 44659, which had all the modern innovations installed on it. It was a day of gales, and we had climbed the 'Long Drag' from Settle to Ribblehead with a good head of steam. Ribblehead viaduct was very exposed - it was said that there was nothing higher between it and the Irish Sea at Morecambe Bay. When we were about a quarter of the way along it we started to slow down considerably, and the spring-held doors between the engine and tender on my mate's side blew open. I tried to shut them but the wind was too strong. Ernie opened the regulator fully and dropped the reversing lever down to its extreme. As we were hardly moving the wheels of the locomotive started to spin, and we came to a stand about three-quarters of the way over the viaduct. I looked backwards along the train from my side and saw about half a dozen wagon tarpaulins blowing loose.

'Go back to the guard and tell him we need an assisting engine to push us away,' Ernie said. 'The tripper was in the sidings at Ribblehead as we passed.'

I climbed down on to the ballast, and as I walked between the tender and the first van of the train I was almost blown over. I had to hold on to the wall of the viaduct. On passing the sheets that were blowing across the other line, I cut the remaining ropes and they went over the moor like big balloons. I met

the guard, Tiny Hart, who weighed about 18 stone, walking towards me.

'Some farmer will have some free sheets for his hayrick.' he said.

'The way they're going it'll very likely be a Dutch farmer!' I replied.

I told him about the engine at Ribblehead sidings, and after about 30 minutes it buffered up behind us. We listened for the banking whistle, but the wind was blowing the sound away from us, so Ernie opened the regulator and we started moving gradually. We were placed in the goods loop at Blea Moor signal box, where men were ready to re-sheet the train - this was a regular practice during the winter months. After about an hour we proceeded, arriving at Carlisle about 4 hours late.

As we did not book off until 3.00 pm we could not book on again until about midnight, so we did not leave until about 1.00 am, about an hour late. Ernie told me that the Birmingham Model Engineers' Club had its open day that Saturday, so he said that he was going to try to pull back the late start. I knew we had a good locomotive, so I said, 'Go for it, Ernie! See if you can beat me for steam!'

We had a marvellous run, and as we were late we did not go into Blea Moor loop as booked for the sleeper train, and had another non-stop run to Rotherham, where the rocker grate and opening ashpan came in handy. We arrived at Washwood Heath right on time.

One of the members of the Model Engineers' Club was a stockbroker with a very large house and his own small railway around his grounds. He would travel up to Carlisle on a Saturday and stay overnight in a hotel, then meet us on the Sunday afternoon every 12 weeks to ride with us on the return train. Ernie provided him with a set of overalls and a footplateman's cap.

On the first occasion Ernie introduced me to him, instructing me to look after him, and added, 'If he offers you some cash, don't refuse it - he's a millionaire. That will be yours - I get my reward in other ways!'

I placed our visitor on my seat, remarking, 'I shan't be using it for a couple of hours or so.'

During the coasting down to Hellifield he stood behind Ernie watching him working the train while I had a sandwich. On the easier running between Leeds and Rotherham I gave him a chance to fire the engine, after showing him the correct way. As we ran light engine from Washwood Heath to the depot around 1.00 am he pressed a note in my hand, saying, 'It's been the most enjoyable day of my life.'

I thought it must be a 10 shilling note, but when I looked in the locker room it was two pound notes! I remarked to Ernie afterwards, 'He can come with us every day at that price.'

His chauffeur-driven Bentley was waiting at the depot, and he was taking Ernie home to Stechford. He said to me, 'Can we give you a ride?'

'I've got my cycle,' I replied, 'and I'll need it to come to work tomorrow.'

He asked where I lived and was amazed when I said, 'Aldridge'.

'How do you do it after a day's work?' he asked.

'I do it every day,' I answered. 'I often say that's where I start work.'

Once every 12 weeks we worked the Sunday evening express to Sheffield, and a parcels train on the return run. Occasionally we would have an ex-LNER 'B1' locomotive, and would also have our millionaire riding with us. On one of these occasions, while we were having our food break at Sheffield, he followed me to the toilet and remarked, 'As you know, Ernie hasn't got a model locomotive, his role in the engineering club being of an administrative and technical nature, but the members have built a 4-4-0 model of the ex-Midland Class "2" passenger tender locomotive, and we are going to surprise him by presenting it to him at the annual dinner. But we need a name to be put on it.'

'That type of locomotive didn't have names,' I replied.

'We know,' he answered, 'but we can use poetic licence.'

I could not think of a name then, but on the journey home a flash of inspiration came to me. I thought of 'Ais Gill', which was not only the summit of the Carlisle run but the summit of Ernie's career, as he had only a few more years to work.

While we were waiting for the railway bus to take us from New Street station to the depot around 2.00 am, I drew our guest on one side and told him of my thoughts, with which he agreed. He pressed something into my hand when we arrived at the depot; this time it was a five pound note.

Some months later, when Ernie came to work on the Monday after the dinner, he told me about it and said, 'After dinner they presented me with my own locomotive. What do you think they've named it?'

I answered innocently, '"Ais Gill".'

'You devil, how long have you known about it?' he retorted.

'Months,' I replied. 'I suggested the name to your friend, who decided what to call it.'

When Ernie retired he was employed at the stockbroker's house, looking after the locomotives and track there, and after his death his locomotive, *Ais Gill*, was put on show in the shop window of Powell's cycle shop at Six Ways, Aston, where his son was manager.

I had another 12 months with Ernie, as his next fireman did not like the Carlisle work and asked me to make a mutual exchange for the year, which I was glad to do.

There was a voluntary organisation, the Mutual Improvement Class, at the depot, teaching budding drivers the technicalities of the job. This was done in the men's spare time by drivers, fitters, etc, who explained the different working parts on various locomotives.

They used to have an annual trip to railway workshops or important junction signal boxes and stations to further the education of the men. This particular year they arranged to go to Brighton locomotive works on the old Southern Railway. I travelled to Euston from New Street with Ernie, his friend the stockbroker and Mr Thorley, the foreman fitter and breakdown train boss.

Ernie asked me if I could manage a British Railways breakfast. I laughed and replied, 'It will make a change from cooking my own on the shovel.'

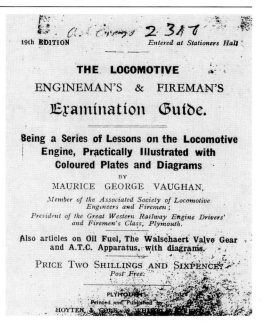

The title page of my much-thumbed copy of *The Locomotive Engineman's & Fireman's Examination Guide* written by a member of an MIC class at Plymouth.

The four of us adjourned to the dining car. Ernie was a small eater and he had cereals and toast, but I and the other three ordered the full meal of cereals, followed by bacon, sausage, egg, tomatoes, kidneys and fried bread, then toast and marmalade to finish off. We were near Euston by the time the meal was over. We then caught the underground train to Waterloo to catch the Brighton train, where we arrived at 11.00 am. A guide met the 50 or so of us and showed us around the workshops where locomotives were in different states of repair and all working parts could be seen more easily.

At about 1.00 pm he took us to the Staff Association Club where a buffet meal was laid out for us, after which we were taken on a tour of the station and signal boxes before making our way home.

In later years the MIC annual trip took members to Switzerland, Germany, France and Austria to broaden their knowledge.

6
PASSED OUT FOR DRIVING
1954-56

At the annual May changeover in 1954 I looked for my name in the Bath and Bristol link, where it should have been, but could not find it. I searched in the other top links to no avail, so I inquired of the roster clerk if he had forgotten me. He answered, 'You and nine other senior fireman have been placed in the special link ready for passing out as drivers, so you had better start swotting up on your rules and regulations.'

He need not have bothered telling me that, as I had stood second behind Jack Siggs for two years waiting to be passed out. Besides the Saltley Mutual Improvement Class we had attended our own class at Walsall run by George Wilkins for about ten years. If you recall, he was the man who got me on my first committee.

On Monday 24 May Jack Siggs and I reported to the chief footplate inspector, Mr Bates, to be examined on our abilities to become drivers. He welcomed us by saying, 'I have ridden with you on numerous occasions and know you are good firemen, and these two days will decide if you have the makings of a driver.' He went on to ask, 'Have you had your medicals?'

When we said we had not, he exploded, saying, 'What's the use of having two days with me and then failing your medical through no fault of your own? I'll get this sorted out.'

He gave us some strands of wool and trimming wire and said, 'Make a little-end trimming.' This was the woollen oil-plug that fed oil to the bearings, and we had practised making them many times. In the meantime he telephoned the chief clerk about the medicals. When that was sorted out, he looked at our efforts and tested them for size in a gauge.

Satisfied, he said to me, 'What are the duties of a driver when working on the main line?'

'To observe and obey all signals,' I answered. 'On starting a train receive a green signal from the guard, see that the station signal is clear, ensure that the fireman looks back until the train clears the platform and that he looks back frequently to see that the train is travelling safely.'

'Right,' he said. Then turning his gaze to Jack Siggs, he asked, 'When do you use the whistle?'

Jack gave about ten different occasions for doing this. We carried on answering questions on all the aspects of the rule book with the accent on the safety of trains and the staff on the lineside.

Mr Bates then placed four Wrong Line Order forms on his blackboard and gave us different failures of train on the main line, asking us which we needed to use: driver to signalman, guard to signalman, signalman to driver, or signalman to guard.

After about 4 hours of answering questions on the rule book and the regulations of the General Appendix, he said, 'Go and get your food, then come back in half an hour and I'll find out what you know about locomotives.'

After lunch he drew a set of locomotive wheels with the side rods showing on the blackboard and said to Jack, 'This represents an ex-Midland Class "4" freight locomotive in fore gear. Bearing in mind the position of the side rod, where is the steam entering the cylinder?'

Jack explained that the big-end was opposite the side rod, which in turn showed where the piston was within the cylinder, so it could be deduced at which end of the cylinder steam was being admitted.

Mr Bates then turned his attention to me and asked, 'Where is the other big-end, and where is steam being admitted in reverse gear?' I answered his question successfully.

We then went on to all aspects of the design of valve gears and motions including Joy, Stephenson, Allen and the modern Walschaerts. He asked questions on how we would take a damaged side of the motion down and work on one cylinder, and set up engines to examine defective pistons and irregular flows from the chimney to detect a worn out or damaged piston valve.

After 3½ hours he beamed and said, 'Good lads', and, turning to Jack, said, 'You are the senior man, so I'll take you on the main line tomorrow.' To me he said, 'I'll take you on the following day. Book on duty at 7.00 am and meet me at New Street station to work the 7.50 am local passenger train to Derby. Don't forget to bring your weekly notices and study them for any temporary speed restrictions on the route.'

I stayed spare in the depot the next day and spoke to Jack when he signed off duty. He said he had passed and told me, 'Don't forget to give the routing whistle at Kingsbury because I didn't and he told me off.'

The next day I met Mr Bates at New Street station. He told the driver to travel in the train. We had ex-Midland Class '2' 0-6-0 tender engine No 463, which was right-hand drive, so all the platforms except Saltley and Burton would be on the fireman's side. We received the 'right away' signal from the

guard and left on time, travelling through the tunnel to Proof House Junction. Then I shut the regulator and started braking for the 30 mph restriction around the curve at Landor Street Junction.

As there was no speedometer, speed had to be judged by the driver. I stopped the train of four coaches at Saltley, and when I received the green flag from the guard, I proceeded. Kingsbury station was an awkward place to stop at with a right-hand drive locomotive because the platforms were not opposite one another. I had been shown a manhole cover between the two main lines as a guide as to where to stop, and did this successfully.

At Wigginton water troughs I instructed the fireman to operate the water scoop to fill the tank. He knew all about it, but on this day a driver had to show authority. We completed the journey to Derby where Mr Bates said, 'Have your food, I'll see you shortly.'

After about three-quarters of an hour he looked into the messroom and called me out saying, 'There's a coal train for Saltley Gasworks coming along the goods line - we'll work that back home.'

No 4173, an ex-Midland Class '4' 0-6-0 freight locomotive, rolled up in front of 40 wagons of coal. Jack instructed the Derby driver to ride in the guard's van as he was passing me out, and he would be responsible for me. The fireman was a lot older than me, and while Mr Bates was talking to the driver, I said to him, 'I know you know your job, but today I've got to show I'm boss so don't take it too hard if I tell you what to do.'

He smiled and replied, 'I understand. I'm waiting to be passed out myself.'

The appropriate signal on the gantry cleared and I started to move the train, instructing the fireman to look for the guard's

'4F' 0-6-0 No 44158, sister engine to No (4)4173 which I drove back from Derby to Birmingham with a freight when I was being examined by Mr Bates. The fireman called me 'Driver', the first time I'd been called that! Later that day Mr Bates passed me out. *H. F. Wheeller, R. S. Carpenter collection*

signal on his side to indicate that the train was complete. At London Road signal box we were routed via the main line, and had a good run to Burton, Leicester Junction, where we were placed along the goods line to Branston Junction. I stopped the train in the correct position for us to take water, and while the fireman was doing this I walked around the locomotive examining springs and feeling the axle-boxes and the big- and little-ends for any hot points, but everything was all right. After an express passenger train had passed us, we were turned out on the main line again. I once more instructed the fireman to look for the guard's signal.

On approaching Wigginton troughs we had only used about 500 gallons of our 3,500, so I said, 'There's no need to dip for water, we don't want the footplate flooded.'

He knew, but answered, 'Right-o, driver.'

That was the first time I had been called 'Driver'!

On passing Kingsbury Junction, with our signals indicating that we were routed fast line, I whistled three long and one 'crow' to indicate that we were going to Duddeston Sidings. Mr Bates remarked, 'The signalman knows where we are destined today.'

At Water Orton we were directed again along the main line, then through Washwood Heath Sidings to Washwood Heath No 1 signal box, where we were stopped while a train came by on the up main line. The signal was then lowered for the down Lawley Street goods line to take us to Duddeston Sidings. After we had come to a stand to await the shunting engine to take the wagons off us, the Derby driver walked up to us and remarked that it had been 'a nice smooth run'. Whether he meant it for my or Mr Bates's benefit, I never found out, but it made me feel happy.

We walked across to our depot and Mr Bates instructed me to go and prepare the locomotive for the afternoon's Carlisle run, and to return to him when I had finished it, so he could inspect it.

I looked at the engine board and saw that 'Black Five' No 44966 was the booked locomotive. I took the oil-can to the stores for the ration of 1 gallon of oil, filled the feeder, oiled every moving part and inspected them. I spotted that one of the sanding pipes was broken, so I made out a repair card and took it to the shift foreman fitter. While I was working on the locomotive the driver who was booked to prepare it came by and asked what I was doing. When I explained, he said, 'Good, that's one less for me to do.' His day's work was to prepare seven locomotives and marshal them out of the roundhouses to the departure roads.

After I had satisfied myself that everything was done, I reported to Mr Bates that I had prepared No 44966 in No 3 shed.

'Was there anything wrong with it?' he asked.

I explained about the sandpipe and that I had filled in a repair card.

'Good' he said. 'I wondered if you would spot it. I won't bother to examine it.'

He shook my oily hand, saying, 'You've done very well - I'm passing you out. I liked your confidence by declining to get water over Wigginton troughs - we would all have got our feet wet.'

Mr Bates sat at his desk, produced the Ministry of Transport certificate and proceeded to fill it in with my name and other particulars of my railway career. He remarked that this had to go to British Railways headquarters, and the locomotive superintendent would be interviewing me. Then I would be available for driving duties, pending passing my medical at Derby. He said that he hoped I would, and that the other potential drivers had gone there today. I later found out that they had all passed, but Mr Bates had failed one in his examination of the locomotives.

He told me to make out a driver's duty sheet, and the test would count as my first driving turn. The 313 turns representing a year's driving had now been reduced to 287 because of the rest days we now enjoyed.

The following Monday Jack Siggs and I travelled to Derby for our medical examination, which we passed, and came out of the offices around 12.30 pm.

I said to Jack, 'We haven't got a tea can - we'd better have a pint of beer to celebrate.'

So we went across the road to the Derby Railwaymen's Institute, where I had gone with Bill Higgins 12 or 13 years before when I was a passed cleaner at Alsager.

Jack later became a deputy foreman at our depot, then was promoted to the Control offices, and eventually became a running shift foreman at Nuneaton. I used to see him every 12 weeks when he continued to pay me his trade union contributions. Sadly, he died in his middle 40s.

On Tuesday 15 June 1954 I was instructed to report to Mr Talbot, the depot superintendent. On entering his office he congratulated me on passing out as a driver and went on to say, 'You have done extremely well - yours are the second highest marks I've seen in the seven years I've been in this position. We can do with men like you in management.'

I thanked him, but my path was to go along the trade union way.

He instructed me to go to the roster clerk to fill in my route card, another Ministry of Trade regulation, which I signed stating that I knew every signal, bridge, cutting and permanent speed restrictions that I had initialled. Ernie Guy had told me that I knew the route to Carlisle, so I signed for that route via Staveley and Rotherham, and from Chesterfield into Sheffield, but not the few miles from Sheffield into Rotherham, as I had not worked frequently over it. I also signed the route to Bristol via Redditch and Worcester, and to Leicester and Walsall via Sutton Park and Aston - a total of over 400

miles of railway. The Ministry of Trade regulations stated that this had to be re-signed every 12 months, and if we did not go over a route for six months we could ask for a refresher, or cross off the route.

The roster clerk issued me with about a dozen passenger and freight timetables for the routes I had signed, and about half a dozen General Appendices and their supplements. I was almost weighed down with paperwork to put in my locker. As well as these we were issued with two weekly notices containing temporary speed restrictions, signal and track alterations, and amendments to the rules and General Appendix regulations.

I then waited for my second driving job - but it was quite a long wait!

— o —

It was not until Sunday 15 August 1954 that I started my driving career. Arley tunnel was found to be unsafe again and it had been decided by railway engineers to dismantle about 200 yards of it at the Birmingham end, which meant severe alterations to trains. There was a shuttle service from New Street as far as Arley & Fillongly station, where a bus service carried passengers to Stockingford station to continue their journey to Leicester and beyond.

I booked on at 7.35 am to work a special passenger service making two trips between New Street and Arley & Fillongley, and was

On Sunday 15 August 1954 I started my driving career at the regulator of Class '4' 2-6-0 No 43013, a recently built BR 'Doodlebug'. In this photograph she is seen in 1960 at Alvechurch, between Barnt Green and Alcester. *Michael Mensing*

informed that Jack Beaman was my fireman (Jack is now a footplate inspector on the Severn Valley Railway). Our locomotive was Class '4' 2-6-0 No 43013, a modern engine recently built by British Railways. They were nicknamed 'Doodlebugs', owing to their ugly appearance. However, to our advantage it had a cab that totally covered the footplate at both ends, giving plenty of shelter when travelling tender-first.

We prepared the engine and went light engine to Saltley carriage sidings where we picked up four coaches and went empty to Arley & Fillongley. There we ran round the coaches to work a stopping train to New Street. We then returned with empty coaches to Arley & Fillongly and worked an express train into New Street, then a stopping train back, then empty coaches back to Saltley carriage sidings. It was a busy day's work, especially for Jack, having to uncouple and re-couple the locomotive at each end. I have a copy of my driver's ticket to this day!

There was a local union agreement with management that all special Sunday work would be worked by Passed Firemen to give them experience, so it was not surprising that my next driving turn was also on a Sunday.

My driver's ticket for that first driving duty.

We booked on around 11.00 am and travelled into New Street to relieve a special passenger train from Newcastle-upon-Tyne and take it to Bournville for Cadbury's chocolate factory. While we waited on the platform Inspector Jack Bates came along, having been instructed to ensure the smooth working of this train as it was a party of Dutch trade people. The train arrived with ex-LNER 'B1' No 61143 heading ten 1st Class dining and kitchen coaches. We worked to Bournville where a gaggle of hostesses were waiting to take the visitors on a tour of the factory. We took the coaches to Kings Norton for cleaning, then went light to Bournville loco depot to coal and service the locomotive before turning it ready for the return trip. As we were booked there about 4 hours and were not due off the shed until 5.30 pm, Jack Bates, who lived close by, said, 'I'll go home and have my Sunday lunch.'

At the appropriate time Jack reappeared and we returned to Kings Norton to pick up our train and take it to Bournville station. Jack took a walk along the train and returned with three boxes of Cadbury's presentation parcels containing a selection of chocolate biscuits, cocoa and other of their products. He smiled, saying, 'The hostesses had some to spare so we might as well sample them.' We departed at about 6.15 pm for New Street where we were relieved by Sheffield men.

Another interesting job, again on a Sunday at the end of the year, was booking on around 8.00 am to work a freight train to Toton as far as Leicester via Arley Tunnel, work having by then been completed on the repairs. We had a Class '8F' 2-8-0 locomotive and we met with some delay, so we changed over trains at Narborough. The second train had a Garrett-type locomotive on front, and I noticed that the water level was rather low; it was doubtful whether there was enough to get us to Nuneaton station, our booked water stop.

I therefore decided to stop at Elmesthorpe, so I whistled at Croft signal box to indicate this, but on stopping at Elmesthorpe I realised that both signal boxes were closed! I said to my mate Bob Roberts, 'While you fill the tank I'll go back to the guard to tell him to protect the rear of the train with detonators as we are virtually stopped in the middle of the section. The next signal box to be open will be Nuneaton Midland Junction.'

After filling up, we proceeded to Nuneaton Abbey Street, and as we had no need to stop and we had clear signals, we had a good run for the climb to Arley Tunnel.

About a fortnight later I received a letter telling me to see Mr Tom Wood, the assistant footplate inspector, who asked me why I had stopped out of course at Elmesthorpe.

'I didn't think I had enough water to get us to Nuneaton,' I replied.

'You knew that Elmesthorpe signal box was closed.'

'Yes,' I replied. 'I instructed the guard to protect the train as per the rule book.' I gave him the guard's name for verification, and he seemed satisfied with my explanation as I heard no more about it.

Driving turns were slow in coming and by the end of the year I had only nine to my credit. The rest of my time I spent firing in the special or shed links so that I could be handy if a driving turn came up in an emergency. I was not only doing dirty jobs (my wife remarked, 'I thought you'd got promotion, but looking at the state of your overalls I doubt it'), but I was also working a bare 8 hours, so I was receiving less wages than when firing in the top links.

May had good cause to remark on the state of my overalls. When I was on shed duties I would coal the tenders or bunkers before throwing the fire out of the firebox, clearing the ash out of the ashpans, and shovelling char out of the smokeboxes, then marshalling the engines into the roundhouses. Disposing of six engines constituted a day's work.

When on the preparing shifts two pairs of overalls were worn, as we had to oil eight engines. As my driver was just a few years senior to me we would do four each. The fireman's duties consisted of building the fire up and filling sandboxes, head and gauge lamps, as well as climbing into the entrails of the motion, as it was called, to oil the big- and little-ends, the eccentrics that controlled the valves admitting steam to the cylinders, and the outside side rods.

Each oiling point had an oil cup capped by a cork, which had to be removed before oil could be poured in, then screwed tightly in again. The number of corks varied between 20 and 26 according to whether it was a two- or three-cylinder engine. Our only light to see the oiling points was a rape oil torch, which consisted of a long feeder with about a dozen woollen strips protruding from the nozzle end, which burned the rape oil with a smoky flame. Great care was needed when clambering inside the engine with a torch in one hand and an oil feeder in the other. If you tilted one too much you had either thick oil or hot rape oil running down your arms.

One of our drivers, Harry Watts, who had done a fortnight's preparing, estimated that he had pulled out over 1,000 corks in that period. When he sat down to lunch on the final Saturday, his wife had cooked fish and chips and she asked Harry to pull the cork out of a new bottle of vinegar. He looked at the bottle and said, 'No thanks, I'll eat my chips without vinegar.'

After we had completed the oiling and built up the steam pressure we took the engines out of the roundhouse to fill the water tanks and marshal them in the appropriate order on the prepared engine line.

By the end of the week overalls were soaked in oil and ingrained with ash and coal dust. May would have to soak them in washing powder solution for a couple of days before attempting to wash them!

On 23 January 1955, which was a Sunday, there was a serious accident at Sutton Coldfield station where 17 people, including the Burton driver and Gloucester fireman, were killed. The train was the York to Bristol express with No 45274, a Bristol 'Black Five', on front. This had been a Saltley locomotive before going into the workshops, and I had travelled many a mile on it. The train had been diverted from Wichnor via the ex-LNWR line to New Street, owing to permanent way work on the Midland main line via Tamworth.

A Burton Horninglow Bridge depot driver was conducting the Gloucester train crew, and the estimated speed of the train was 55 to 60 mph instead of the 30 mph allowed for the curve into Sutton Coldfield station, where

On 23 January 1955 there was a serious accident at Sutton Coldfield. The train exceeded the speed limit for the curve into the station and became derailed, smashing into the opposite platform and station buildings. This is the scene the following July, showing the sharpness of the bend through the platforms, and the foundations of the demolished buildings in the foreground. Class '3' 2-6-2T No 40080 calls with the 6.26 pm Lichfield-Birmingham service. *T. J. Edgington*

the train became derailed, smashing into the opposite platform and station buildings. The Gloucester driver should have stood behind the Burton driver, who was working the train, but the heavy knocking of the engine trailing axleboxes causing his legs to ache, so he rode in the train from Lichfield, despite Rule 127, which states briefly, 'In every case the train driver must study signals, speed restrictions, etc, for that part of the line over which he is being conducted.'

He was heavily censured by Lt-Col G. R. S. Wilson, who conducted the inquiry into the accident, although he could not have done anything to prevent it as he was not conversant with the route.

The inquiry inspector had two test trains run with 'Black Fives' and ten coaches, including a dynamometer car operating a speedometer, which the crash locomotive did not have. The time allowance of 15 minutes from Lichfield Trent Valley to Sutton Coldfield was criticised, as one test run took 21 minutes and the other 16 minutes, despite running at 52 mph on the 40 mph restriction from Four Oaks to the Sutton Coldfield tunnel.

Arthur Attenborough, a ticket collector,

and fireman W. Smith, who were travelling to work, were both praised for their efforts in stopping another express coming on the other line between Chester Road station and Sutton Coldfield, thus preventing a larger disaster occurring. Arthur Attenborough was presented afterwards with a gold pocket watch suitably inscribed by the grateful Railway Board.

The blame for the accident was placed on the dead Burton driver, but no reason for the excessive speed was found, and part of the blame was directed at the conductor guard for not applying his brake fully. The condition of the axleboxes of the locomotive was examined and, although there was some play in them, it was considered that it did not contribute to the derailment. The Gloucester driver was removed from his job for his violation of Rule 127, and spent the rest of his railway years as a shed labourer. The inquiry inspector also recommended that permanent speed restriction cut-out boards be placed at the commencement of speed restrictions to remind drivers and to assist men learning routes that included these restrictions.

My father-in-law, Jim Wakelin, attended the accident on the Bescot breakdown train, along with gangs from Saltley and Rugby. The following Monday and Tuesday I fired on a special train going empty from Saltley carriage sidings to Sutton Park station on the old Midland line to work a commuter train to take passengers into Birmingham who would normally have travelled via the ex-LNWR route.

I used to make a mutual exchange with firemen booked on Carlisle and Bristol jobs who did not like the work, to enable me to keep the route on my card. One week we were working the 4.15 pm New Street to Bristol and returning with the 7.40 pm from Temple Meads, which was a Royal Mail train going to Newcastle. At this time two ex-LMS 4-6-0 'Patriot' locomotives, which we called 'Baby Scots', were stationed at Midland depots: No 45509 *The Derbyshire Yeomanry* of Derby (17A) and No 45538 *Giggleswick* of Leeds (20A). Midland firemen were not happy with

One of the 'Baby Scots' stationed at Midland depots, Derby's No 45509 *The Derbyshire Yeomanry*. Midland firemen found them hard to fire, but I tried firing it in the LNWR manner, with a thin fire. It was harder work, but the result was good. No 45509 is seen here descending the Lickey Incline in 1957. *Michael Mensing*

these locomotives as they could not maintain steam pressure.

On the Monday return job we had No 45509 allocated to us, so I thought I would try firing it, as other LNWR locomotives, with a thin fire instead of the thick Midland fire. It was harder work, but the result was good, with full steam pressure when we needed it. My mate Victor Searle congratulated me, saying, 'My regular mate can't do that!'

The next night we were allocated No 45538 and I was full of confidence of maintaining steam, but I was greatly disappointed. On the climb out of Bristol I was struggling, and was glad of the stop at Mangotsfield for the mails to be loaded; I then managed to revive the steam and boiler water on the easier running to Gloucester. After leaving Cheltenham, Victor got plenty of speed towards Ashchurch, then we had the long climb to Bromsgrove and I was struggling again to retain steam pressure.

Because the tenders on these locomotives only held 3,500 gallons of water we had to fill the tank, and instead of stopping for a couple of minutes at Bromsgrove for the bank engines, we stopped for 7 or 8 minutes, giving

me a chance to revive the boiler water and steam pressure for the climb up the Lickey incline. Before we had got to the summit at Blackwell I had sacrificed water to maintain steam, then on the easier running from Barnt Green to New Street I managed to get the gauges looking respectable again. I informed the Sheffield fireman of the poor steaming, but he said he already knew about it.

The next night we had *The Derbyshire Yeomanry*, and again I fired it thinly successfully. Other nights we had our normal 4-6-0 'Jubilees', then on the Saturday we were allocated *Giggleswick* again.

'I might as well be an idle fireman as a busy one,' I remarked to Victor, and at Barrow Hill depot filled the firebox with as much coal as I could get into it. We did no better for steam and I struggled again.

As we stood at Bromsgrove, I asked Victor, 'Where does the name "Giggleswick" come from?'

'I think it's a town in North Yorkshire,' he replied.

'Then they ought to keep it there,' I retorted.

From the spring of 1955 the railway trade unions and the Railway Board had been in conflict over rates of pay, and it came to a head when our union, ASLEF, called all locomotive men out on strike. From Whit Monday, 30 June, I was on strike for 16 days. A small percentage of drivers belonged to the NUR, and were not called out, but several at our depot joined us, including George Wilkins, who was one of the NUR's local committee men.

The 50 or so men who travelled from Walsall to Saltley had a meeting and agreed to assist with the picketing at Ryecroft and Bescot depots, which were largely NUR-dominated. Bescot, which normally worked freight trains, had Bushbury's 'Jubilee' passenger engines stationed there, and worked the Euston trains instead of the Bushbury and Monument Lane men, who were mainly ASLEF members.

During this period I had gone to the strike meetings held at Highfield Road Club at Saltley and listened to the arguments being aired, and joined in with them. After the

A letter that I wrote to the local paper after the 1955 strike. I considered myself very brave to have done such a thing, and it marked the start of my involvement in trade union matters.

strike was called off, not very successfully for the unions, I became involved in trade union activities.

On Friday 27 August I had my first mid-week driving turn, a passenger relief train to Sheffield with No 44813. I had Len Biss, a Passed Fireman, as my mate; he was senior in service to me but did not sign the route beyond Derby. At Sheffield we turned the locomotive and were booked to double-head a return train. I offered Len the job of driving, as I had been offered many a time, but he declined, saying, 'It's your driving job.' We booked off in under 8 hours, but were paid for 10 with the mileage bonus - my first driving mileage turn.

On booking off duty I looked at the daily alteration sheet and found that I was rostered to book on at 9.12 am the following day, driving on the regular 10.12 am from New Street to Sheffield, a top passenger link job with a young fireman, not the regular one!

When I stepped on to the footplate of No 45572 at New Street, Vic Searle, for whom I had fired for a few weeks previously on the notorious *Giggleswick* and who had worked the train from Bristol, exclaimed, 'Where's your driver?'

'I'm the driver,' I replied.

He said, 'Haven't they got a proper driver?'

I felt a bit insulted. He went on, 'This is a top link job', and proceeded to tell me of some temporary speed restrictions on the route. I listened patiently but did not tell him that I had driven over the route the preceding day. I thought, 'He'd rather have carried on to Sheffield than let a Passed Fireman do it.'

Leaving New Street, our first stop was at Derby, which we did all right. The next stop was Sheffield, and on the climb to Clay Cross my young fireman was struggling for steam. The water and steam gauges were going lower and lower and we were both glad to close the regulator to get through the tunnel at Clay Cross. I looked at my watch (which my wife had bought me when I passed out as a driver) in the firelight, and could see that we had lost 3 minutes. When we emerged from the tunnel and braked for the 30 mph speed restriction at Clay Cross Junction, I opened the firehole doors and could see that my mate had been too anxious and had over-fired it, and there was a lot of black unburnt coal.

I said, 'Leave it alone, I'll try and brighten it up for you.'

This was a trick I had seen other drivers do. I notched the reversing gear up to almost mid-gear, then opened the regulator fully and dropped the gear down to 75 per cent. There was a terrific roar from the blast-pipe and thick black smoke emitted from the chimney.

'That should clean the tubes as well,' I remarked.

I shut off for the temporary speed restriction at Hasland and the steam pressure immediately started to rise. My mate went to fire it again. I said, 'Leave it alone until I tell you.'

Over the speed restriction I opened the regulator to have a run through Chesterfield for the climb to Dronfield. When we were halfway up the bank I shouted to my mate, 'Right, you can fire it now.'

The steam pressure was maintained to the top of the bank, where I had to close the regulator to coast through Bradway Tunnel. As we passed around Dore & Totley curve at the regulation speed of 30 mph, I again looked at my watch, to find that we were still about 2

'Jubilee' 4-6-0 No 45572 *Eire*, which I drove in August 1955 on the regular 10.12 am from New Street to Sheffield, a top passenger link job, with a young fireman. This was one of my first mid-week driving turns. She is seen here arriving at Tamworth High Level on 21 June 1959 with the Sunday 2.10 pm Bristol-Bradford train. *Michael Mensing*

minutes behind. I got a good momentum going through Beauchief; we had no speedometer on the engines then, but when they were fitted later we found out it was possible to reach 90 mph down the bank before shutting off power and braking for the 15 mph run into Sheffield station. We arrived at the right time, and as we walked along the platform after being relieved the station inspector said to me, 'We had you reported 3 minutes late at Clay Cross. Control must have been mistaken.' Nevertheless, about a fortnight later I had a letter from management asking about the 3 minutes late passing Clay Cross, this being the boundary of the Midland and North Eastern Regions.

On the return journey I had to tell my mate to hold back on firing the locomotive and to watch the chimney until the smoke had cleared before putting more coal into the firebox; as a result we did quite well keeping time throughout the journey. Two driving turns and another mileage bonus in

the same week meant that things were looking up!

On Friday 21 August I was firing on the shed, disposing of locomotives on the 6.00 am shift, when at around 8.00 am I and fireman Gordon Bennett walked together to the coaling stage to service two locomotives. Gordon took the first, a Class '8' freight, and I climbed on to the one behind it, a 'Black Five'. He coaled his and took it to the ashpit, and I followed behind. About 20 minutes later, while I was busy throwing clinker out, I noticed the shed shunting engine taking empty coal wagons along the next line away from the coaling plant. I then heard a lot of shouting and saw men running towards the engine in front. I jumped off mine and was surprised to see Gordon lying underneath the wagons with one of his legs outside. Cyril Payne, who was a First Aid man, crawled underneath to put a tourniquet on his thigh to stop the bleeding.

An ambulance and the fire brigade soon arrived, and the firemen had to dig out the ashes from between the rails to make enough room to slide a stretcher underneath Gordon. They then slid it out, and put him in the ambulance to take him to the accident hospital. As he was taken away I thought, 'There but for the grace of God could go I. It could have been me on the first engine.'

He survived the accident, although losing a leg, and as I write I have been informed that he is now a signalman in the Saltley power box.

ASLEF went to the High Court in Birmingham to try and get compensation for him. They produced photographs showing the amount of spent ashes lying about at the time, causing a hazard. These, however, were rejected by the Judge because they had been taken without British Railways' permission! The site had been cleaned up by the time the investigating team looked at it. He did not get any compensation because the Judge said he had contributed to the accident by walking on to the line without looking for moving vehicles.

A few weeks later I changed for a week's work on the afternoon Carlisle run with a driver reputed to be the most idle at Saltley - he would not budge from his seat from Water

Orton to Carlisle. When we were getting water during the train examination at Rotherham Masborough on the first trip, I was busy getting clinker out of the fire when he shouted to me, 'The tank is running over, Bill.' He wouldn't climb down and turn it off.

The guard used to walk up and make our tea, as well as his own. My driver used to smoke a pipe and there would be a half circle of tobacco ash around him, but he would not allow me to wash his side of the footplate down, as he claimed it caused rheumatism, so periodically I had to sweep his area with the hand brush.

On our last trip back from Carlisle that week, our 'Black Five' had gone astray and we were allocated a 'Crab' 2-6-0. The driver remarked to me, 'You've got some hard work in front of you today.'

On leaving the sidings with a full train he shoved the regulator wide open, then gradually notched up to 50 per cent, and left it there. As the tender tank held only 3,500 gallons of water we had to stop at Appleby, but she was a good steaming engine even when I had to use the two water injectors to maintain the boiler. My mate hammered the engine when the signals were at clear and we arrived at Washwood Heath on time with the tender nearly devoid of coal. As we ran light engine to the depot, he said to me 'You want to change with my mate regularly. He wouldn't have kept steam up as you've done today.'

I thought, 'No, thank you.'

I also did a mutual exchange to do a week's firing on the early morning Carlisle with driver Harold Godfrey, who was entirely different. He worked the locomotive very light and still managed to keep time, and was helpful to the fireman when he could. We left Water Orton sidings at 4.15 am and had only been on the road about 15 minutes when one of the boiler water gauge glasses burst, throwing scalding water and steam about the footplate. The safety valves, which should have shut off and stopped the rush of steam and water, did not operate, and Harold stopped the train at Tamworth while he went to the signal box to explain our sudden halt.

I took my mackintosh out of the locker and placed it in front of my face and body, managed to locate the manual shut-off cocks, and stopped the escape. I then lit the boiler water gauge lamp, which had been extinguished, and placed it on the other gauge glass to see if we still had about half a boiler of water. Harold rejoined me to restart the train, saying, 'I've requested fitters to meet us at Derby to replace the gauge glass.'

'Don't worry,' I replied. 'I should have it done myself if everything goes all right.'

I successfully replaced it in between firing the locomotive on the light running to Derby. We were stopped in Derby station by signals, and a fitter and his mate approached us, and when we informed them it had been done they were most surprised. Harold said to them, 'We'll take the new glass off you in case it happens again.' Thankfully it did not, and we arrived at Carlisle only about 30 minutes late.

— o —

The beginning of 1956 saw heavy snowfalls and frost, and early in February I looked at the weekly roster to see that I had been booked to drive on the three afternoon trips to Carlisle. This was the best-paid week's work at the depot, with two Sundays and six days extra mileage payment.

On the first Sunday, with Bob Roberts as my mate, we had a good trip to Skipton, where we arrived on time, but when we tried to get water while the train was examined, we found that the water column was frozen solid, the frost fire underneath having gone out. I went and had a word with the signalman and we agreed that when the train examiners had completed their work, we would draw up into the station to fill the tank there, but found that one was also frozen. I found a telephone on the platform and had a few sharp words with Control for allowing this to happen.

I was told to unhook the locomotive from the train and go on to Skipton loco, where they assured me there was water available. We were directed by the shed staff through the coal stage, and after obtaining our water, I said to Bob, 'We'll borrow some of their coal to save you going into the back of the tender on the "Long Drag".'

It was not a modern coaling plant, coal being trundled by big buckets holding about half a ton of coal. We found about four buckets already full so we dumped the contents into our tender, then rejoined our train. This had delayed us about an hour and a half, and we arrived at Carlisle about 2 hours late and booked off duty at 2.15 am.

When we awoke and went to breakfast the steward came to us and said, 'Control has spoken to me to tell you that your return train has been cancelled owing to snowdrifts on the line. You have to travel home as passenger on the 12.15 from Citadel station.' I was disappointed as I was looking forward to my first run back as a driver.

We duly caught the Glasgow to Birmingham express, and when the waiter came along near Penrith calling customers for second lunch, I asked for a can of tea, as I had when I travelled home on the same train when I had scalded my foot. Unfortunately it was a different dining car crew. They gave me some tea, but no food was forthcoming! Our guard was Joe Littlewood, a senior hand, who was very meticulous and carried his own gallon bottle of water from Birmingham, as he said that other water upset him. We booked off around 6.00 pm, thinking that normally we would have been approaching Aisgill at that time. We were booked to have two days off duty (Tuesday and Friday) on this week's work, and as this was classed as a contract mileage bonus, we were still paid our 14 hours for travelling home passenger and booking off in 6½ hours.

The Wednesday and Thursday trips were worked in heavy snow, and I found out why my regular drivers used to bring sacks to wrap around their legs in cold weather; it was quite cold sitting for 8 hours on the driver's side of the footplate. I watched Bob doing his work efficiently, so on the next outward trip I told him to do the driving from Rotherham to Skipton, which kept me warm for part of the journey.

On the Sunday return train I offered Bob the chance of driving from Skipton to Rotherham, but at Normanton Goose Hill Junction we were diverted via the goods line, owing to permanent way work on the main line, and as he was not sure about the signals he asked me to take over again. We lost about 30 minutes as we could not maintain our normal speed through speed restrictions, and we arrived at Washwood Heath around 12.30 am.

As we travelled light engine to the depot, Joe Littlewood said to me, 'Considering this is your first week driving on this route you've done very well. I haven't had any snatches or bumps through braking too heavy, which is more than I can say about some of the regular drivers.'

'I've fired for many different men and have tried to pick the best techniques.' I replied.

Bob joined in. 'You work the engine too light.'

'We've still kept time,' I said.

The snow lasted well into March, and when it thawed it caused heavy flooding on the Settle line. I had changed for firing on the same week's work with my old mate Ernie Guy. On the Saturday afternoon outward trip we were stopped at Hellifield and a conductor driver climbed on, saying that owing to parts of the ballast being washed away, we were to be diverted from Settle Junction to Tebay and via Shap to Carlisle. This route took us via Low Gill, and as we went through a dimly lit station I saw the name Giggleswick. I cried out to Ernie, 'This is where that so and so engine should be stabled!'

We arrived at Carlisle about an hour and a half late. Again, when we came down to breakfast on the Sunday morning we were informed that our return train was cancelled because of the state of the line, and we travelled home as passengers.

I was on my regular turn of duty, booking on at midnight on the Monday morning for shed duties, when at about 2.00 am I was informed that the running shift foreman wanted to see me in his office. I wondered what I had done wrong. As I entered Mr Smart's office the timekeeper, Jack Prestridge, followed me in.

The foreman asked me, 'If I sign you off duty now have you transport to get you home?'

'Why are you signing me off duty?' I asked.

Jack Prestridge explained. 'We've had a new freight train diagrammed to the depot which entails booking on at 3.07 pm to work to Leeds and lodge there.'

'Yes,' I replied, 'I can cycle home all right and come for it this afternoon if you're short of a fireman.'

'It's a driver we're short of,' said Mr Smart. 'You'll be it.'

They were looking ahead for themselves because they would be working 10.00 pm to 6.00 am, then on Monday would book on at 2.00 pm to 10.00 pm, and would be on duty for the working of this train. The timekeeper signed me off duty at 2.30 am, but because of the guaranteed day I would be paid 8 hours.

When I booked on at 3.07 pm I looked at the workings and noticed that we were booked to go via Sheffield to Rotherham to detach vehicles at the station yard. I told Mr Smart that I did not sign for the bit of the route between Sheffield and Rotherham, but he knew and a conductor had been wired to Sheffield for me.

We had a 'Crab' 2-6-0 allocated to us, which we prepared and ran coupled to the Carlisle engine to Water Orton for our train. We then followed the Carlisle train out of the sidings to the station, and after a pause of about 7 minutes while it cleared Kingsbury Junction, we were signalled to follow it over the fast line.

We were booked to stop at Derby St Mary's to detach and attach traffic, then continued on our journey. I had never driven a freight train between Chesterfield and Sheffield and was surprised how the heavy train slowed us down compared with a passenger train. My conductor driver was waiting at the end of the platform at Sheffield, but he left us at Rotherham while we detached vehicles, and we continued to Leeds Stourton sidings where we were relieved. When we booked off at the offices there, we were told that a taxi was waiting for us to take us to Farnley barracks, which was an ex-LNER lodging house, more modern than our old barracks at Holbeck.

We were diagrammed to book on again at 9.30 am, and a taxi was waiting at 9.00 am to take us to Holbeck. We prepared a 'Black Five' and went light engine to Stourton sidings to await a fully fitted freight coming from Glasgow; we changed locomotives and worked non-stop to Washwood Heath. it was a change to have a fresh engine for this part of the route, with coal at hand and a new fire.

With new lodging turns now being introduced, the trade unions had negotiated new agreements; one was that when diagrammed train work had been completed after lodging, no further work was to be done.

When I instructed my fireman to pull the points to take us to the left engine queue, he said, 'Aren't we going to dispose of it?'

'Not today,' I replied.

When I reported the engine on the shed and stated my booking on time, as was always done, the outside foreman said, 'What have you left it there for? You have 2 hours to do, plenty of time to dispose of it.'

I referred him to the new agreement, but he argued that it did not refer to shed work.

'It says "No further work",' I replied, 'and that means train or shed work.'

'You won't be paid for the 2 hours that you're short,' he said.

'We'll see,' I replied, and walked to the signing-off point.

When I looked at the daily alteration sheet I could see that I was on the same job on Wednesday, so I left a letter for the secretary of the local Departmental Committee, our union's shop stewards, stating what the outside foreman had said regarding the agreements and lodging turns, and my understanding of them.

When I booked on duty on Wednesday afternoon there was a letter from him waiting for me, stating that he had spoken to management and they agreed that I was right, adding that he was glad that I had taken that stand as it was the first time it had cropped up, and if I had disposed of my locomotive it might have created a precedent!

When we arrived at the depot on Thursday afternoon there was no argument regarding disposing of the engine, and on signing off duty I could see that I had been allocated 8 hours pay for Tuesday. The timekeeper said, 'Mr Smart wants to see you.'

'You've already got five turns in for this week,' he said, 'having booked on twice on Monday, so you can't do that job again this week. Book on at 8.00 am in the morning and all next week, and learn the road between Sheffield and Rotherham.

I worked this train quite often in the next few months and it was quite nice to book off duty at around 3.30 pm, 24 hours after booking on for an afternoon turn. It was eventually placed in the Bradford and Carlisle link.

I was virtually the only Passed Fireman on my shift over this route signing beyond Rotherham. On the other shifts there were two senior men who did: Cliff Fletcher, who was later to become a footplate inspector, and Tom Wooton, who jokingly threatened to change shifts as they were not getting many jobs beyond Rotherham.

During the bad winter of 1956/57 I frequently had to walk over Barr Beacon to Kingstanding, because the road was blocked with snowdrifts. This was about 6 miles away, where there was an hourly bus service into Birmingham throughout the night. My wife therefore decided that we should live nearer to my work, but I did not want to live in Birmingham itself, having been brought up in a country area. When my wife went to the Aldridge post office she spotted a postcard from someone living in Kitts Green, on the south side of Birmingham, who wanted a house exchange as her husband was working in one of the new factories in Aldridge. We got in touch with them and went to look at their house. I had been told by one of our Saltley men, who lived nearby at Stechford, to be careful as it was a rough area.

The house itself was nice, although small compared with ours, but when I looked at the garden I was surprised to see that the fence between the gardens was partly down and the garden itself looked like a rubbish dump, so we declined it.

One of my mates, Charles Lindley, lived at Great Barr, which was at the end of the countryside near Barr Beacon, and he informed me that there was an all-night bus service from there. My wife and a friend went to look at the area, and she placed a postcard in the local newsagent's requesting a house

exchange in the area. This was on Easter Monday, 2 April. We had a letter the following Thursday from a couple asking if they could come and look at our house on the Saturday. They liked ours, which was only about two years old - I had got the garden in good condition, using my rest days every two weeks and two days of duty when working on the Carlisle turns.

We went to look at their house on Sunday, and liked it too. It had been built only about 12 months previously, and although the garden was in a bit of a mess, I could see that the soil was quite light and sandy, compared to our heavy clay.

We therefore agreed to the exchange and, as both houses belonged to Aldridge Urban District Council, we both made letters out, with each of us signing them, and I said I would take them to the council offices the following day. When I handed them in on the Monday the lady clerk, with whom I had been at school, remarked, 'You're not leaving us?'

'Only to the other side of the Beacon.'

She smiled and said, 'There's a council meeting tonight. I'll put your exchange on the agenda.'

On Wednesday we both received letters agreeing to the house exchange. We met on Thursday and arranged to change over on the following Saturday, so within a fortnight we were living in Great Barr.

Unfortunately we were soon to find out why they had been in a hurry to move out, when local traders came knocking at the door asking for bills to be paid. We had to tell them where the previous occupants had moved to.

Some years later we were offered the opportunity to buy the house from the council. As it was a well-built place in a quiet area, which suited my sleeping habits in the daytime because of my shifts, we agreed to do so, and we are still there some 35 years later!

At the end of April it was 12 weeks after the previous three trips driving to Carlisle, and as Bob Roberts's driver was still off duty, I was booked to work the same week's work again with him as my fireman, and Joe Littlewood as guard. We had quite a good week, with Bob doing a bit of driving. On the second Sunday return working I had read in the weekly notice that the up line between Ribblehead and Settle was blocked by relaying work, and single-line working would be in operation on the down line.

We were booked to depart from Carlisle around 1.00 pm, some 3 hours earlier than usual. Because of this we arrived at Ribblehead at about 3.30 pm, where we were stopped by signals. Bob went to the signal box to sign Rule 55, and on his return informed me that there was an express coming through in about 30 minutes, and the pilotman was on it.

Alas! When this train came through he was not on it; he had sent it through the section, as he was allowed to do. I went to the signal box and telephoned Control to find out what was going on. They replied that they would get in touch with him, saying, 'He has got a car at his disposal and could be driven to you.'

Two other trains came through in the next 3 hours, and the pilotman eventually came through on the ballast train with the papers to re-open the line, as the work had finished! When he clambered on to the footplate we told him in no uncertain terms what we thought of his performance in delaying the train by 3 hours.

He laughed and said, 'Look at the extra Sunday money you'll be getting.'

'We're on mileage bonus,' I replied, 'so we'll get nothing extra.'

We duly dropped him off at Settle with our complaints ringing in his ears. When we arrived at Washwood Heath, Joe Littlewood joined us on the engine to the depot and remarked, 'A nice 3 hours overtime.' Guards were not on the mileage bonus!

'There's none for us yet,' I said, 'but I'll try to get some.'

On the Monday I put in a claim for the 3-hour delay, which was equal to 5¼ actual hours with the Sunday rate of pay. A few days later the chief clerk, Mr Winfield, called me into his office to ask what had happened. I gave him a detailed explanation, stating that the pilotman could have ridden on three trains to come through to us and there was

plenty of time interval for us to use the single line. When I mentioned that he also had a car for his use, the clerk asked, 'How long would it take you to run between Ribblehead and Settle Junction?'

'About 15 minutes.'

'You could have gone through before the first express if he had been at Ribblehead?'

'Certainly.'

'Leave this to me,' said Mr Winfield. 'I hate inefficiency and delay to freight traffic.'

About ten days later I received a letter stating that management had agreed to my claim and we would be paid the 5¼ hours money. I saw Bob a few weeks later and he offered to buy me a pint, as he had not expected to get any extra payment.

Although I tried to teach him to work a locomotive lightly and economically, when he became a driver some years later he was one of the heaviest and maddest at the depot!

On 9 May I worked my 287th driving turn, which put me on the second years' rate of pay when driving; this had taken one year and 11 months to attain.

Another afternoon turn I worked occasionally, which finished on the day shift on alternate days, was conducting Bristol men to Leeds. They worked the 'Devonian' express from Bristol to Bradford as far as Leeds, and lodged there overnight, returning to work the 8.30 am from Leeds the next day. Because those lodging turns had recently been reinstated, some of the drivers did not know the route beyond Birmingham.

I booked on at 3.30 pm to travel to New Street to conduct them on the 4.15 pm departure, and we arrived at Leeds at about 7.30 pm. As Leeds was a terminus we had to wait for the coaches to be taken off us to carry on to Bradford, then follow them to Whitehall Junction and be turned on to Holbeck Loco, booking off around 8.30 pm.

Next morning we booked on at 7.15 am and prepared the locomotive, usually a 'Jubilee'. When our train came past Whitehall Junction from Bradford, we would follow it into the station and depart around 8.30, arriving at New Street at 11.40; I would then travel to Saltley and book off duty around 12.30.

One driving turn of note was when two crews took two Class '8' freight locomotives light engine to Broom, where we turned them on the triangle. We then picked up a conductor driver to take us via Stratford-upon-Avon into the Warwickshire countryside to Kineton, to pick up a train of vans loaded with bombs. We had No 48336 allocated to us, and we worked via Redditch, where we had a bank engine as far as Barnt Green into Washwood Heath sidings. This was an identical job to one I had worked as a fireman during the war, but this time the bombs were going for disposal, not war!

The Metro Cammell company at Washwood Heath was building coaches for Brazil, and as they were wider than ours, they had to be transported to Liverpool Docks on Saturday nights and Sundays on special bogies. I worked these trains quite often, usually as far as Bushbury or Stafford. One Saturday evening I booked on at 7.15 pm to prepare No 44226 and go into Washwood Heath West End to pick up our train, which comprised of three beautiful blue coaches, two wagons carrying the coaches' bogies, a staff coach and a guard's van. The train had to be turned at Water Orton for unloading at the docks, so we had to run tender-first there, then run around the train, coupling up to the staff coach.

A traffic inspector rode on the train supervising the slewing of the coaches through certain bridges and platforms. On this particular night we had a new inspector, full of his own self-importance. He greeted us with the words, 'Have you got steam heater pipes on the engine as the staff need to be kept warm.'

'I've worked these trains before,' I replied. 'I know what's needed.'

We could not couple to the staff coach until we got to Water Orton, but when the shunter was coupling up there he said, 'There's no heater pipe on the coach.'

The inspector clambered down and dashed to the other end of the coach, hoping to find one there, but to no avail. During the summer months they were removed for refurbishing, and I had to have them put on our locomotive before we left our depot. There was no Carriage & Wagon staff on duty to put some on, and after a conference it was decided to telephone Walsall for staff to put pipes on there. We started to go up Sutton Bank and the inspector decided to ride on the footplate, although I assured him that I knew the bridges at which we had to stop.

When I stopped at the bridge over the A38 at Penns, he said, 'There's no bridge here.'

'There's an underbridge,' I replied.

'We don't stop at underbridges,' he snorted.

'At this one we do,' I pointed out. 'There are buttresses in the centre of the tracks and the foreign coaches have to be jacked up to go over them.'

The staff had already got down on to the ballast to start work.

This obstacle negotiated, we carried on to Penns station, where the coaches had to be slewed about a foot off centre to enable us to pass the platform; while we were doing this, no trains were allowed to come the other way because of us fouling them.

We then carried on to the short tunnel at Sutton Park. The inspector was shining his torch on the bridge numbers and checking his papers, but got confused because he could not see the underbridges, and was surprised when I stopped for the tunnel. At Streetly station we had to be slewed again, and at the bridge over the A452 at Chester Road the train had to be jacked up once more. We proceeded through Aldridge and Lichfield Road Junction, stopping repeatedly until we arrived at Walsall. There the Carriage & Wagon staff were waiting for us to put the heater pipes on, and we could then dispense some heat to their coach.

On the curve between Pleck Junction and Darlaston there was a temporary speed restriction warning sign about 3 feet wide and 4 feet high, carrying two yellow lights and a white '15 mph' sign. I stopped at it and said to the inspector, 'These are what you have to be aware of.'

He looked at it and said, 'Carry on, we should clear it.'

I moved on cautiously, looking back as the train approached it, and saw the back lights of the sign go up in the air. I stopped quickly and said, 'We've hit it and knocked it over.'

He climbed down to have a look, but returned to report that the board had snapped, breaking the upright, and that we could not replace it.

'We'll have to stop at Darlaston Junction signal box,' I said, 'and inform the signalman so he can tell the Pleck Junction signalman to warn other drivers that there is no speed warning board.'

We eventually arrived at Bushbury Junction at about 5.00 am, having taken about 8 hours to travel the short distance. When we were relieved I remarked to the Bushbury driver, 'Watch this inspector, he doesn't know much about this work for all his bluster.'

We had to walk to Wolverhampton station to catch the train to Birmingham, booking off duty at 8.20 am, having been on duty 12 hours and 5 minutes. I often wondered how long it took the train to get to Liverpool, and what was the cost to Metro Cammell to get it there. Then there was the cost of shipping the coaches to Brazil!

In February of 1956 diesel multiple units (DMUs) had been introduced to the old North Western side of Birmingham for the commuter trains, and Monument Lane depot, just north of New Street station, had a lot stationed there. In the January vacancy list 21 drivers were needed for training, and about a dozen Passed Firemen at Saltley had successfully applied, including several junior to me. I had not applied because I had a good road card and did not want to throw it away by going to another depot.

However, in the vacancy list of April and July, further vacancies were declared (one fireman from Saltley had to be passed out as a driver to go there), but again I resisted the opportunity.

In October there were three vacancies declared, and as I was doing mainly firing duties on the shed, as all holidays at the depot had finished, I finally decided to apply.

After about a week's wait I was informed that I had been allocated as a driver at Monument Lane depot. I was lucky to get in; the other two vacancies were taken by senior men, one from Saltley, the other from Stafford.

The method of applying for the vacancies adopted by most men was to apply to be made a driver at their home depot as a first preference. Then their second preference was the depot where the vacancy existed. They would then return to their home depot when a vacancy for their seniority date came up.

I was informed to transfer there on 15 October 1956 at 9.00 am, but before I could take this up I was delayed slightly. When I booked off duty on Saturday 13 October I remarked to the timekeeper, 'I'll see you in a couple of years time', being the period I estimated I would be away.

'Not so fast,' he said. 'You're booked on duty tomorrow at 3.30 pm to conduct the Bristol men to Leeds.

'I can't,' I replied. 'That's a lodging turn and I'll be booking on at Leeds on Monday instead of Monument Lane.'

'You're the only one available for the job,' he said, 'and it's been arranged that you'll return as passenger when you arrive at Leeds on Sunday night.'

I therefore worked the train and travelled home on the 10.30 pm mail, arriving at New Street at 1.30 am, booking off duty at 2.30 am. I informed the timekeeper that I would not be able to book on at my new depot until 2.30 pm, and asked him if he would inform them of this.

So, at the age of 34 and with over 19 years of apprenticeship, I had achieved my ambition to be an engine driver!

7
MONUMENT LANE
1956-58

At 2.30 pm on 15 October 1956 I duly reported to the shedmaster at Monument Lane, Mr Lowe, who shook hands with me and said, 'Didn't they want to let you go? The other two were here at 9.00 am.'

I explained about having to work to Leeds on the Sunday afternoon, then he said, 'Come with me', and took me to the running shift foreman, Bert Preston, whom I knew as he was a fellow traveller from Walsall. He had also been at school with my father-in-law. He produced a route card and asked me to fill in the routes I knew.

I said, 'I don't suppose they will be much use here.'

'Put them all in - they may come in handy one day,' Bert replied.

He then gave me the General Appendix and its supplements for the ex-LNWR area, asked the timekeeper for my locker key, and told me where the locker room was.

'You have today for transferring to this depot,' he told me. 'Book on at 8.00 am in the morning to learn the road to Crewe.'

Even after 19 years of apprenticeship I had not finished learning, by any means!

The following day I teamed up with Sid Bounds, the other Saltley man to be appointed to the same vacancy list. A man from Stafford, Harry Bosson, was the third, but he was sent to learn the road to Rugby via Coventry as he already knew the Crewe route. We walked to New Street station to ride on the footplate of the locomotive working the 9.10 am to Liverpool. The train crew were Monument Lane men who worked to Liverpool Lime Street, returned as far as Crewe, and lodged there overnight.

It was a foggy morning and I stood at the fireman's side of the 'Royal Scot' engine while Sid stood behind the driver. Within a minute of departing we entered Monument Lane Tunnel, where we were shrouded in steam and smoke for about 5 minutes until we emerged just outside the loco depot. Through the fog we dashed along, stopping at Dudley Port and Wolverhampton High Level stations, where we alighted.

'What do you think of that?' Sid exclaimed. 'We'll be months learning that bit!'

'There's only one signal,' I said, 'and that's the one we stood under at Dudley Port.'

'Don't be daft,' he shouted. 'There's hundreds of them!' (Sid was a very serious man.)

The distance from Birmingham New Street to Wolverhampton High Level was about 16 miles, and a 25-minute run with an express train. Along this Stour Valley route, as it was known, were ten stations and 20 signal boxes, and as the sections were short there was a distant signal for the next signal box under every stop signal. In places such as Soho, Smethwick, Dudley Port, Tipton and Catchmans Corner, the distant signals read for two boxes in advance.

The fog had lifted for our return trip, and we rode in the cab of one of the new diesel multiple units (DMUs), and with no steam and smoke around us we had a good view of Sid's 'hundreds of signals'. This train stopped at all the stations and the Bushbury driver had time to explain some of the junction signals at Bloomfield, Tipton and Soho Soap Works. This run took us about 45 minutes,

When learning the route from New Street to Wolverhampton we decided to ride on the DMUs whenever possible because of the better view and extra comfort for writing notes as we went along. This two-car Metro Cammell set is approaching Tipton with the 7.00 pm Coventry-Stafford service on 7 July 1959. *Michael Mensing*

and on returning at New Street we adjourned to the mess room to make a few notes and have a cup of tea. We decided as far as possible to ride on the DMUs because of the better view, and it was handier to write notes of the route.

We caught another train to Wolverhampton, then spent a couple of hours walking around the station looking at the different platform signals, and another hour in the station signal box, where one of the signalmen explained some of the movements he could do and pointed them out on his track diagram.

We returned to Birmingham again in the afternoon and the sun was shining on the steelworks, glassworks, gasworks, chemical works and all sorts of industrial complexes, churning out smoke, soot and all the impurities of the industrial West Midlands.

Monument Lane locomotive depot was situated in a triangular piece of land just outside the northern portals of the tunnel from New Street station. It was a typical LNWR shed with a modern concrete coal hopper and ashpits, together with four straight roads in the shed, each holding about five tender locomotives. There were three other roads outside the shed on a higher elevation, called The Parade, and a turntable situated on the main-line side of the administration buildings. The latter comprised the shedmaster's office, from whose windows there was a good view of the shed yard; the general office, with a chief clerk and four other staff; and the

running shift foreman's office, manned 24 hours a day by the foreman and timekeeper. Locker rooms, stores and a mess room completed the buildings along No 1 shed road. Along the stop-block ends were the fitters' workshops and foreman fitter's office. He was an ex-Ryecroft man, Frank Rigby, whom I had known in 1937. There was a steep footpath leading into Sheepcote Street, alongside which we later built a Staff Association Club.

The DMUs were stabled in the carriage sheds, 10 minutes walk away on the far side of Monument Lane station. These sheds consisted of six roads, each capable of holding eight coaches or four twin-set units, with a fuelling pump at the entrance of each road, and examination and repair pits inside. A foreman fitter, George Whitaker, was in charge of about five fitters and an electrician on the night shift, with two fitters on the other shifts. Carriage cleaners, Carriage & Wagon examiners, and a shunter on each shift, completed the staff. There were about 100 drivers and 50 firemen at the depot; the big reduction in firemen was because the DMUs were single-manned.

The roster links consisted of the No 1 link, which worked to London Euston and Manchester; the next link also worked to

Monument Lane depot, looking north in about 1959; the main line running down through the tunnels to New Street is over to the right. The sidings in the foreground were known as The Parade; at a slightly higher level than the rest of the shed yard, they were used for the storage of engines awaiting repair, etc. *R. J. Essery collection*

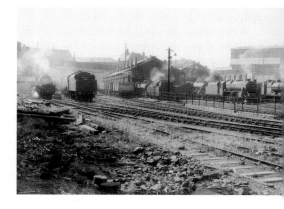

Euston and Liverpool. Below came the few steam-operated local passenger turns, and the freight and shunting links. There were three DMU links, filled by volunteer drivers because of the new type of single-man operation, and a special link, which covered holidays and sickness.

The locomotive complement consisted of three 'Black Fives', two ex-Midland Compounds, which were used mainly for double-heading express trains to Euston and return, one 'Super D' 0-8-0, two ex-Midland Class '4' tender freight engines, two ex-Midland Class '2' 0-6-0 tenders, two Class '2' 2-6-0 modern passenger tanks and two 0-6-0 shunting tanks, one of which was always at the out-station at Tipton, where a set of men were stationed.

The DMU fleet consisted of 25 Derby-built two-car 'lightweight' units, comprising a power car, with two bus-type diesel engines slung underneath, and a trailer car. Each set had driving cabs at both ends, and up to four sets could be coupled together and driven from one cab.

I was placed in the special link, and Sid, being senior to me, was given the choice of going into the steam or DMU links. He chose the latter, so he only had to learn the local passenger routes, while I had to learn most of the routes at the depot.

To start with we concentrated on the route from New Street to Wolverhampton, and the frequent DMU service enabled us to make three or four return trips each day. Some days we would alight at Oldbury, Tipton or Deepfields to walk about the shunting yards and see the ground shunting signals therein.

After three weeks we decided to extend our learning to Stafford and Crewe, which took another three weeks, then we carried on from Stafford to Rugeley Trent

Valley, Walsall and into Birmingham via Bescot, Perry Barr and Aston. When we were conversant with these lines we concentrated on the Lichfield line from Aston, which was a busy commuter line and included the line to Wichnor Junction, which joined with our Midland routes to Derby. When we had completed these routes, we signed our route cards and Sid took his place in the links.

However, the running shift foreman instructed me to learn the route from New Street to Rugby via Coventry and Leamington. There was a return working from Leamington at 7.40 am, which bypassed Coventry, taking the Kenilworth to Berkswell loop, but the only train to get us to Leamington departed from New Street at 4.30 am. I was accompanied on this route by Harry Bosson, and we decided that 4.30 was a bit too early on a winter's morning, so we booked on at our usual time of 8.00 am and travelled to Coventry and Kenilworth, where we alighted and set out to walk the 5 miles or so of the loop to Berkswell.

We found out that we had chosen the wrong direction, as it was uphill most of the way, with only the last three-quarters of a mile downhill. The sun came out after a night of frost; wearing our heavy overcoats, we were perspiring heavily when we approached the signal box at Berkswell just after 2.00 pm.

I remarked to Harry, 'I could manage a pint at the station pub.'

He agreed, and we made to walk past the signal box when the signalman appeared on his balcony.

'What are you pair doing?' he shouted. 'I've seen you in the distance for the last half hour.'

We told him that we were road learning and were going for a pint.

Monument Lane had a DMU fleet of 25 two-car Derby-built 'lightweight' units, comprising power car and trailer car. This brand new set was photographed approaching Walsall station in about 1956. *R. S. Carpenter*

'Hard luck,' he retorted. 'They close at 2.00 pm, not 2.30 pm as they do in Birmingham!'

However, he took pity on us and made us a cup of tea while we rested our weary feet before catching the local train back home.

I also had a few runs to Crewe to refresh my knowledge of a few months earlier, because the station signals were very complicated. I travelled home on the locomotive coming off the North shed to work the 3.45 pm to Birmingham. This was the train from Glasgow, on which I had travelled home from Carlisle as a passenger a few times.

This was interesting for anyone road learning, as the locomotive would be signalled to go over the South Junction and reverse into one of the bays to pick up a parcels van; then, when the Glasgow train ran in, its locomotive was hooked off and sent to the depot. We in turn would go again over the junction and back on to the train. There were about four different ways these movements could be made, and it gave me a good opportunity to observe the dwarf shunting signals. On the second day the Crewe driver invited me to drive off the shed, which I was glad to do on the 'Royal Scot' engine to get the feel of the shunting movements.

When we backed on to the train, I offered the controls back to him, but he said, 'Stay there.'

We were booked first stop Wolverhampton. I intended to get off there to go into the train and have a wash before arriving at Birmingham, as I was fully conversant with that part of the route.

It was dark and misty at Wolverhampton, and when I offered him the controls again, he said, 'Stay there. I sign the route to Euston this way and via Nuneaton, but this is the worst piece of the route for signals. I don't like it.'

So I carried on driving to New Street. I thanked him on my departure and he said, 'Come again tomorrow.'

I eventually completed my road learning in February 1957, taking 12 weeks to do so. During this period we had ridden with a Monument Lane driver, Dick Lloyd, a pleasant 60-year-old bachelor. One evening he was involved in a collision while working a DMU from Lichfield to New Street. Two light steam engines left Aston Loco around 5.00 pm, one for New Street and the other for Exchange Sidings, and stopped to uncouple at Proof House Junction. It was a foggy night and the signalman forgot the engine that should have reversed towards Exchange Sidings. When the engine for New Street arrived at his box he cleared the section and pulled the signals off for Dick Lloyd's train to go into New Street. He hit the light engine at about 20 mph (the speed over the junction) and smashed the front of his cab. Dick was trapped by his legs and it was about an hour and a half before he was freed and taken to hospital.

The following day we looked at the damaged coach, which had been taken to Monument Lane carriage sidings, and Sid remarked, 'That could have happened to us had we been in the cab with him.' It was said that the steam engine was not damaged.

After a couple of days no one at the depot knew what was happening to Dick Lloyd, so we decided to go to the accident hospital to find out.

'Are you workmates of his?' asked the ward sister when arrived and made enquiries.

When we answered, 'Yes', she said, 'You can go in and see him. Railway officials have tried to interview him but the doctor will not allow it.' Evidently his legs would be saved, but were badly injured.

He cheered up immediately on seeing us, saying, 'You're the first visitors I've had.'

We explained what the sister had said and inquired if he needed anything. He asked us to go to his landlady for his pyjamas and shaving tackle, and to get him an ounce of his favourite tobacco, as he rolled his own cigarettes. This we did, but after a couple of days the other patients in the ward complained to us. Evidently he smoked a strong shag tobacco.

'What did you bring that tobacco for - he's nearly smoke-dried us!'

Towards the end of the week he gave us a letter asking the pay clerk to pay his wages to us on the Friday pay day, and told us to take his rent to his landlady and bring the remainder to him.

I had been attending the monthly ASLEF trade union meetings, and on the following Sunday I spoke to the branch secretary, Taffy Hughes, and he was surprised that we had seen Dick in hospital.

'I've tried to see him to get a statement regarding the accident,' He said, 'but they won't let anyone see him.'

'Don't go as an official,' I suggested. 'Go in your railway clothes as a workmate.'

Dick was about two months in hospital, and we visited him frequently. Then he was off duty for another three months while the injuries to his legs healed, but he was never to drive main-line trains again and was confined to shunters.

— o —

In the special link I was involved in a large variety of work covering other men and working special trains. One turn I had on the afternoon shift was conducting the 'Midlander' express. Camden men worked this train from Euston to Wolverhampton with a 'Royal Scot' locomotive, and it was routed from New Street via Soho Junction, Perry Barr and Bescot to Wolverhampton, instead of the normal route via Dudley Port.

A lot of Camden men did not sign this route and I would meet the train on arrival around 7.30 pm and conduct the driver. At Wolverhampton we would take the coaches to the carriage sidings, then go light engine to Bushbury depot where the Camden train crew lodged overnight to return to London the next day.

One foggy evening the brakes of the engine and train went on, bringing us to a sudden halt between Darlaston station and Darlaston Green signal box. I looked at the vacuum gauge to find that we had only 10 inches of vacuum instead of the normal 21 inches.

I said to the Camden man, 'It looks as if someone has pulled the communication cord.'

The fireman and myself climbed down on to the track to meet the guard and inform him of the situation. As the fireman did not know the area I said I would go back to Darlaston station with detonators to protect the train, while he and the guard sorted out in which coach the cord had been pulled, and the reason.

As I walked back in the heavy fog I placed one detonator about a quarter of a mile from the train, then arriving at Darlaston station signal box placed three detonators on the track.

I climbed into the signal box where the signalman rushed to the door exclaiming, 'What's gone wrong? I've been expecting the Green to signal the train out of section for a few minutes now!'

After about 10 minutes I heard the engine whistle being sounded, so I set off to rejoin the train, speaking to the guard on the way, who informed me that he had found the coach with the communication cord pulled and a door open as though someone had jumped out. (A similar event happened outside Crewe during the war years and another train smashed into the stationary train with fatal results.)

We carried on with our journey and, on arriving at Bushbury Loco, the running shift foreman said, 'Control want a word with the driver about the incident.'

The Camden man said to me, 'You'd better speak to them - you know the area where we stopped.'

Control informed me that the guard had spoken to them at Wolverhampton, when asked about the late arrival, and they needed our information as to what had happened. After I had given them a full account, they said, 'Tell the Camden driver to make out a report, and you also sign it.' (This was standard procedure.)

I had to tell the Camden driver the names of the signal boxes involved, and by the time we had finished I had missed my ride on a light engine to Wolverhampton, so I had a 45-minute walk in the fog.

A new job came to the depot, involving booking on duty at 10.55 am, preparing a Class '4' 2-6-4 tank engine, going light to Kings Norton, bringing six empty coaches into New Street, then working an all-stations train to Coventry at about 1.30 pm. On arrival at Coventry we took the coaches into the sidings, then turned the engine and filled the water tank at the locomotive depot. We then worked another stopping train to Wolverhampton, ran round the train and worked back to New Street, where we were relieved.

Other work took us up the Harbourne line with a local freight train with a Class '2' 0-6-0 tender engine, taking traffic to Rotton Park Road, where we detached vans for Mitchells & Butler's brewery; their own engine took them on to Cape Hill in Smethwick. We then carried on to Hagley Road sidings, where coal wagons were detached, then on to Harbourne where we shunted the yard for about an hour before returning tender-first towards Monument Lane sidings. At Hagley Road we shunted out empty wagons, then proceeded to Rotton Park to pick up the M&B traffic. The brewery men would leave a stone jar for us near the points of the ground frame to enjoy a drop of their product.

There was an early morning train departing at 6.00 am, and on another turn we relieved the morning men around midday. The procedure when picking up traffic at Rotton Park was for the guard to unhook his brake-van, come to the engine and take the signal-line staff from us to open the ground frame, then we would draw the train forward clear of the points. He would open the points and call us back on to the wagons or vans waiting for us. He would hook them on to the train, inform us how many vehicles we had and instruct us to draw forward clear of the points. He would then reverse the points, lock the frame and take the staff with him to his van. As we were on a severe down gradient, to save us struggling to push the train on to the brake-van, he would roll the van on to us.

One day we completed this movement with Harry Hughes, our guard, and I felt the brake-van buffer up to the train. My mate, Bill Stacksy, who had been looking for the guard's signal, said, 'Right away, Bill.'

I released the brake and we rolled down the branch line, stopping the train at the signals on the canal bridge at Harbourne Junction on the main line. It was about 5.30 pm with the rush-hour at its peak, so we expected to wait awhile until the signalman could get a break in the main-line traffic to operate about seven pairs of points to put us on to the Monument Lane up goods line.

After standing there for about 10 minutes my mate looked back along the train and shouted to me, 'We haven't got the brake-van!'

I stepped across the footplate to look over his side. He was right - there was no van to be seen. I put the engine into forward gear and started propelling the train back up the branch line.

Bill said, 'Where are you going?'

'To fetch the brake-van and guard,' I replied. 'He has our single-line staff and it's a crime for us to be without it.'

After about a mile we saw Harry walking to meet us. When we picked him up he exploded, saying, 'What did you go for? I hadn't hooked on the van - it bounced away from the train about a foot.'

'You gave me the right away signal,' Bill retorted.

'I was calling you to come back on to it,' Harry replied.

We picked up the errant van, the staff was returned to its rightful place on the footplate and we returned to Harbourne Junction. We had been away for about 30 minutes, and after 5 minutes the signal cleared for us to go into Monument Lane freight yard.

As we approached the signal box, Arthur Trueman came on to his verandah holding a red flag. I stopped near him.

'Put my mind at rest,' he shouted. 'Were you standing at the signals half an hour ago?'

'No,' I replied, 'we've only just arrived.'

'I must be going mad,' he said. 'I thought I'd seen you there, pulled all the levers over and waited for you to come over the junction, but when I looked there was no train there!'

We both started laughing and drew into the sidings. On arrival, the guard walked up to us and I told him what Arthur had said. We decided to telephone him from the shunter's cabin to explain what had transpired.

'Thank you for telling me,' he said. 'It's put my mind at rest. I was beginning to think I was seeing extra trains!'

On another freight turn we booked on at 7.30 am to find a 'Super D' prepared for us to

A 'Super D' 0-6-0, No 48964, backing down into Monument Lane Tunnel, which led into New Street station. These locomotives were used for shunting in the Soho yards. *6201 Princess Elizabeth Society Ltd*

go light engine for shunting duties at Soho Pool sidings, a big freight yard within a mile of Birmingham city centre. It had once been a pool, which had been drained; it comprised over 30 lines, each holding over 100 wagons, and was at the bottom of a steep gradient from Soho Road signal box, worked by a single-line staff. The yard handled coal, cement, bricks, petrol, scrap metal, sweets and biscuits. There were two warehouses that handled the light goods, and four petrol storage tanks. A large locomotive was needed to shunt the heavy strings of wagons out of the sidings. We were relieved at 3.00 pm to walk the 30 minutes to the depot to sign off duty. The afternoon shift shunted until around 8.00 pm, then worked a train to Bescot sidings, then one to Aston goods depot, and from there to Monument Lane sidings.

There were two level crossings in the yard for lorries and vans, and these were controlled by a flagman. Unfortunately, he could not be in two places at once, especially when long rafts of wagons were being manoeuvred; lorries and three-wheeled Scammell 'mechanical horses' were always dodging about. One day, when my mate, Les Riddle, was driving, we were drawing out a raft and the flagman was protecting the traffic at the top crossing. The shunter stopped us as we cleared the bottom crossing, and a scrap

metal lorry tried to cross behind our wagons. However, its driver did not allow for the rebound of the wagons after they had buffered up; the result was that the last wagon's buffers ripped out the side of the driver's cab and the body of the lorry.

There were some hard words spoken between the injured lorry driver and the flagman and shunter. About a week later I was asked for a report of the incident, but I stated that we were about 70 wagons away and could not see what had happened.

The yard was unmanned after the 8.00 pm train to Bescot left, but a freight train was booked into the yard around 4.00 am, leaving traffic for the day shift to handle. The biscuit warehouse would work an occasional night shift at busy periods such as Christmas and Easter, unloading railway vans and loading their lorries. The unloading bay held about three vans, and one night there were six to be unloaded, so when they had unloaded the first three they decided to push them out of the warehouse and roll the others into their place. What they did not know was that there was a slight falling gradient into the dip at the bottom of the branch line, so the vans rolled gently on to this line without anyone being aware.

The early morning train loaded with coal, cement, bricks, etc, duly arrived hauled by a 'Super D' 0-8-0. The driver picked up the staff at the signal box, which indicated to him that he should be the only train on the branch line, and headed into Soho Pool in the darkness. He crashed into the vans at the bottom of the dip and the weight of the train behind the heavy locomotive smashed them to pieces.

When we arrived at 8.00 am to enter the sidings, the signalman at Soho Road box explained to us that the line was blocked at the bottom by wrecked vans. The train and locomotive had been dragged clear, but we could only go down as far as the damage to await the Bescot breakdown train. It has just broken daylight and we were amazed to see a group of women and children from the nearby houses with buckets and bowls picking up biscuits, chocolate bars and sweets. We joined them, filling the footplate lockers with goodies.

The breakdown train arrived at 9.00 am and we took our engine to couple up to it. While my mate was doing this, I spoke to the train driver about the situation. Tug Wilson, the breakdown train boss, looked out of the staff coach window. When he saw me he shouted, 'Morning Bill, everything all right?'

'Nothing you can't put right,' I replied.

He then called my father-in-law, Jim Wakelin, to the window.

I shouted, 'Do you want any broken biscuits to complement your staff rations?'

It took them about 4 hours to clear the line of smashed vans, broken axles and wheels, so we did not do much shunting that day.

One afternoon I relieved driver Bob Clarke, another man promoted from Saltley, and I could see he was a bit upset. When I inquired what was wrong he told me that he had been involved in an incident on the bottom level crossing, similar to mine. Evidently he was propelling a raft of wagons into the sidings, with the crossing keeper at the top crossing, when he felt a slight bump. He stopped immediately and could see men running towards the bottom crossing. He climbed off the footplate and joined the crowd. A three-wheel Scammell tractor was flattened beneath the wagons. The shunter climbed under the vehicles to see if he could rescue the driver, but could not see him. He ordered Bob to pull the train clear, but having done so there was still no sign of the driver in the wreckage. The man was found some minutes later walking dazedly behind the stop blocks at the end of the yard, having been thrown clear through the windscreen by the impact.

'I thought I'd killed him,' said Bob. 'No one could have lived in that wreckage.'

One Saturday morning I booked on around 7.30 am as a spare driver. The foreman informed me that he had a Class '2' 4-4-0 ex-Midland passenger engine to go to Derby, but the 9.10 am New Street to Liverpool was overloaded, as it was Grand National day, and I was to assist it to Wolverhampton. We arrived at New Street and coupled up to a 'Royal Scot' at the head the train. I spoke to Charlie Jackson, a Monument Lane driver, regarding braking arrangements; the proce-

dure of double-heading meant that the driver on the leading engine did the braking for signals and speed restrictions, and the driver of the train engine braked and stopped the train at stations.

We proceeded into the blackness of Monument Lane Tunnel, which was made worse by two lots of steam and smoke being emitted from the chimneys of the locomotives and bouncing off the roof. We could hear the eight exhaust beats to each turn of the 'Royal Scot's' wheels and the four beats of our larger wheels. I shouted to my mate in the firelight, 'I reckon he's going faster then us. I believe he's passed us.'

My fireman looked nonplussed. 'I'll be glad to get out of here,' he said.

Eventually we cleared the tunnel and were glad to get some fresh air into our lungs. We stopped at Dudley Port and Wolverhampton, where we unhooked and went tender-first to Bescot to turn our engine on the triangle; we then proceeded chimney-first towards Walsall and Lichfield to Derby.

The procedure at Monument Lane for covering sickness and holidays with special link men was totally different from the procedure at Saltley. If a man was off duty in the top link, the senior man in the second link would fill this position, then the senior man in the third link would take his place and so on, until the special link man took the last vacancy. This sometimes meant six or seven men moving because of one man being off duty. During holiday periods from April to September, when our holidays were staggered, the senior man in any link would be continually changing links, which sometimes meant four or five weeks on early morning shifts or the same amount of time on afternoon shifts.

I thought this was unsatisfactory and, after speaking to some of the drivers concerned, passed on the opinions I had received at our trade union branch meeting. I suggested that we adopt the Saltley system, whereby special link men took the vacancy, wherever it was in the links, which meant only one man having to move to fill one vacancy. The special link driver whose time was nearest to the vacancy would be the one to move.

However, some of the senior drivers were aghast at the thought of young special link men working in the top links. I tried to show them that it would save some of them moving up and down links like yo-yos, and that they could plan their home life better knowing what shift they would be on. I made no progress at this meeting, but gave notice that I would attempt to get a petition of men and ask for a special branch meeting. This was done, and I proposed that special link drivers should cover any holiday and sickness vacancies according to the shift they were on. Another junior driver, my friend Ron Broadhurst, seconded the proposition, and I presented the petition showing that 75 per cent of the men were in agreement.

The senior drivers, two of whom were on the local departmental committee (LDC), similar to shop stewards in outside industries, opposed the proposition, but after a 2-hour debate it was carried. It was also agreed that it would be put into operation at the next timetable changeover in October.

At the December branch meeting, where there was voting for the LDC positions and branch committee posts for the coming year, I was voted in as an LDC man, so I had started my trade union career.

If a special link driver had no week's work to cover, he would book on spare at his allotted time, and cover any day-to-day work. If there were no jobs to work he would stand spare at the depot. If running shift foreman Bert Preston was on duty he would ask the spare man if there was any route he needed to refresh, and would invariably make out a road learning form so that he could take a run over the route. This arrangement enabled me to retain my knowledge of the routes between Bristol and Carlisle.

Bert was quite an exceptional man on locomotive and train crew diagrams, and during the 1955 strike had been seconded to Crewe Control to assist them to get the most from the train crews available. He was later to become a drivers' inspector.

During August 1957 the World Scouts Jubilee took place in Sutton Park. When it finished I booked on around 10.00 am, prepared a 'Black Five' and went light engine to

Saltley carriage sidings, where I picked up two luggage vans and eight coaches. I took them to Sutton Park, loaded up with scouts and their belongings, carried on to the specially built wooden platform near Streetly station to load more equipment, then worked via Walsall Portobello Junction, Stafford and Crewe, where we were relieved for the train to carry on to Liverpool docks.

— o —

At the start of the winter timetables in October 1957 I was promoted to the bottom DMU link, so I had to be trained to drive them and have a working knowledge of the mechanical operation of these new trains.

One Monday I booked on at 7.30 am with instructor Walter Beech, who provided me with books and diagrams of the units. We travelled in the cab of a DMU to Four Oaks, where I observed how the driver changed gear and worked the brake - totally different from driving steam engines. At Four Oaks the unit was stabled for about 3 hours, which gave Wally time to show me around this new form of rail transport. He showed me the two diesel engines slung under the framework of the power cars and instructed me how to isolate the final drive if an engine failed. He then took me into the cab, showing me the driving controls, the air and vacuum gauges, the speedometer and the tachometer, which showed the revolution of the engines and indicated when to change gear, as the engines could not be heard. The only indication that the engines were working was a row of lights, two for each power car, for up to four power cars. Each one also had a final drive light, which indicated that it was engaged. Thus a driver could drive four two-car units from the one cab.

We then started the engines from the floor. They could also be started from the cab, but needed 50 lbs of air pressure to operate the hand throttle, which could be done manually on the floor. When the air pressure had attained 70 lbs he showed me how to change the final drive to the direction we wished to travel. He also showed me the operation of the vacuum brake. This had 'off'

Switches to be Closed before Engines can be Started Locally

Main Battery Switch, Control Isolating Switch, Engine Isolation Switch. If this is switched off fitters must be seen for reason Control Isolating Switch, when Mains Battery Switch is closed gives through control currents throughout train.
Reverser makes desk alive and selects direction, enabling currents through control currents from Cab.
Deadman's (throttle) must be engaged, as this in turn energises the Gear Selector.

Preparing Car

Collect satchel from foreman. Proceed to cab which is to be driven from, see hand brake is on, flags and detonators, hand lamp, and two fire extinguishers are intact, see that deadman's valve is not isolated, no keys left in panel. A.T.C. flag in use.
Place tools on desk then insert and turn C.I.S., place reverser in pocket, proceed down No. 2 side Subs. and Gloucester C.C., No. 1 side Swindon C.C., and turn on battery switch. On Leyland engines, examine sump first, then pull out throttle control and press start button, five seconds after engine fires, release start button, and gradually reduce throttle till engine ticks over. Examine belts, fuel, fire bottle connections, springs, brakes, final drive isolating bolts, jumpers, vacuum hoses and air pipes, whilst walking round to No. 1 engine. Start engine, then walk down car examining as before, then switch on other battery switch, and start up. Climb into rear cab and examine, take off brake. and isolate A.T.C., also see no other keys left in desk, lock all doors then start other engine. Walk down to first engine, examine for leaks, then, if in the shed, stop by the stop button, if outside, stop by testing the fire alarm test switch. On A.E.C. engines test sump, stop other engines the same. When passing guard's van notice if isolating fork is there.
Air pressure should now be 75 p.s.i., proceed to cab and insert reverser, engage Deadman's, press start buttons individually and start engines. If necessary open throttle slightly to assist.
Create vacuum and see if it stands at 20"-21" with valve in lap, destroy 5" to test I.R. glands, release Deadman's to see if it operates. Give Guard vacuum test.
Take handbrake off, create 15" of vacuum, select No. 1 gear, then immediately blow brake off, and when car moves open throttle.

3

A page from *Questions and Answers on Multiple Unit Diesels and Diesel Electric Shunts* produced and published by S. E. Webb, instructor of the Stourbridge Improvement Class, 1947-58.

and 'on' positions, and a 'lap' position, which was unusual for a steam man; this held the brake operation with the reduction of vacuum at a set amount.

Wally asked me to sit in the driving seat in the rear cab, and move the unit towards the stop block, about eight coach lengths away. I did this slowly; we then changed cabs, reversed the final drive and ran towards the signal at the entrance to the sidings. We made these movements three or four times, then the booked driver arrived to work the train into New Street.

Wally said to him, 'You can sit in the train. I'll be instructing Bill driving into Birmingham.'

We shunted the unit from the sidings into the platform and prepared to depart.

'Don't forget you have a lightweight train,' warned Wally, 'not a heavy steam locomotive. If you brake too hard the wheels will lock and you can slide through the station!'

The guard signalled me to start by sounding two buzzers. I put the unit into first gear,

then gradually moved up the gears to the fourth and top gear. I stopped satisfactorily at Sutton Coldfield station because I had had to reduce speed to 30 mph at the speed restrictions approaching the tunnel before the station. I also stopped at Wylde Green and Erdington quite well, but as we approached Gravelly Hill we had attained 70 mph on the falling gradient and I had a job to stop, taking the two coaches the full length of the station, which held about eight coaches.

We arrived safely at New Street and had a cup of tea and our food, then we formed up into a three-unit train of six coaches, working to Lichfield City. Wally again instructed the driver to ride in the train and told me to drive it. I soon found out when stopping at Vauxhall & Duddeston that a bigger brake application was required to destroy the vacuum in six vacuum chambers.

Gradually I got used to the brake. The hand throttle incorporated the 'dead man's' device, which applied the brake if released for any reason, and my wrist was aching after holding the spring-operated device down for over an hour. We did the return journey safely and my first day's DMU training was over.

The following morning we walked up to the carriage sidings, where there were two units on the pit roads, and went underneath with our hand-lamps. Wally showed me the driving belts from the engines to the compressors, exhausters, cooling fans and dynamos. He also showed me the final drive and how to operate it manually, and the oil dip-sticks showing the oil levels in the different components. We spent the morning looking at these parts and the handbooks with diagrams of working parts, trying to identify them. After lunch I again worked the three units to Lichfield City.

The following day I drove all day, going to Lichfield and Coventry. On Thursday we booked on at 6.30 am to work to Stafford, then along the Trent Valley line to Rugeley and over the branch line to Walsall and Birmingham. Wally explained that this was the route the driver's inspector would very likely take me on the next day. The last couple of hours Wally spent asking me questions about the units and how to keep them going when certain parts failed.

The following morning we arrived at the inspector's office at New Street at 7.00 am, where Jack Allen was seated. I knew him by sight as he also lived at Great Barr and I had noticed him travelling to work.

We joined the 7.15 am to Stafford, which consisted of a pair of units, and the driver was again told to ride in the train while I worked it, stopping at all stations to Stafford. There we shunted the unit into a bay line and during the half-hour wait Wally went and made a can of tea while Jack asked me a few questions regarding the units; I had studied the handbook regarding failures and remedies and knew most of the answers (although when failures occurred in later years, they were not always in the handbook).

By the time we had had a cup of tea and a sandwich it was time to depart for our first stop at Rugeley Trent Valley. This gave me the opportunity to attain the 75 mph maximum speed of the units, but not exceed it. I worked the train through to New Street where we arrived around 11.30 am. We adjourned to the inspector's office where Jack produced some diagrams and asked me to identify different parts of the unit. He stressed to me the importance of sounding the horn; evidently I had not used it enough. He pointed out that these trains were a lot quieter than steam locomotives, and platelayers and staff along the line could not always hear their approach.

He then produced a Board of Trade certificate, asked me my full name, which he copied on to the form, and said, 'You are now a DMU driver.'

This, after five days' training, meant that I had moved from a steam man to a diesel man, but I still had a lot to learn and experience to gain. We would sit in the diesel driver's mess room on No 6 platform at New Street during our break periods, listening to drivers talking of failures they had experienced and how they had overcome them. We were virtually learning as we went along. It was to be about 18 months before I went to a diesel drivers' mobile school, and another

two years before I attended the school at Derby.

On the following Monday I was booked on duty at 7.30 am to travel on the 8.10 am train to Derby to fetch a new BR-built DMU to Monument Lane carriage sidings. It was No 79125 and it was strange being alone in the cab with no one to talk to or pass a cup of tea. There was a high wind blowing and Jack Allen's warning of blowing the horn came to me. As we approached Lichfield Trent Valley station there was a group of platelayers working on the line. I sounded the horn about four or five times, and as I was about to apply the brake they evidently heard me and dashed out of the way at the last moment!

On the Friday I was again booked to go to Derby carriage works to fetch another DMU. When I reported to the foreman he informed me that it was No 79146 on No 4 road, and when I climbed aboard I could see that a side window was broken. I went to the fitters' office to report it and they said that they would send someone to replace it.

While I was waiting for this to be done I saw two tea chests full of carriage door keys and ignition keys.

'We can't get any of those,' I remarked to the foreman fitter. 'We have to wait for a driver to book off duty and use his.'

'Help yourself,' he said. 'We've plenty here.'

I found a couple of heavy paper bags and put about 50 in each. When I arrived at Monument Lane carriage sidings I gave some to the drivers who were there, and when I arrived at the Loco booking-on office, Bert Preston was the foreman on duty, and I presented the remainder to him.

'Where did you get those from?' he exclaimed.

When I told him he said, 'Hang on', and telephoned Mr Lowe, the shedmaster, who appeared from the general office door. He looked at the keys and said, 'I've sent about a dozen orders in for these without success. We have enough here to issue each DMU driver with his own. You can go to Derby any time to get stuff for us.'

The following week I was on duty at 11.00

am, working three twin units to Coventry and return, then a run to Four Oaks and back, and, to finish the day, to Lichfield and return. Before the arrival of the DMUs at Monument Lane a set of steam men would have prepared a locomotive to go light engine to the carriage sidings to work five or six empty coaches into New Street. They would then have worked a local passenger train to Lichfield and return to New Street, taken the coaches back to the carriage sidings and returned the engine, which they would have disposed of to complete their day's work. A DMU driver was very often booked to work three trips to Lichfield and back, so the saving in manpower between two men doing one trip and one driver doing three trips was terrific.

When the DMUs were first introduced they were much faster between stations and had time to spare, but after about 12 months the Railway Board timekeepers took notice and cut the timings down so that as much as 10 to 12 minutes was saved on the Lichfield City run.

One Saturday evening I had my first engine failure on unit No 79132. I had two sets on a New Street to Wolverhampton and Walsall turn, and at Dudley Port I noticed that one of the engine lights was out. I started it from the cab control, but it stopped again before we arrived at Wolverhampton. We had about 20 minutes before departure, so I climbed on to the ballast to look at the engine concerned. I tried to start it manually but noticed that it gradually slowed down with the hand throttle fully open. I diagnosed fuel starvation, and as we had plenty of fuel in the tanks I thought it might be an airlock in the fuel line. As I had been taught, I opened the locking screw with a coin and pumped the fuel through manually for a few minutes until I could see it running freely. I then locked up the screw and started the engine, and was relieved to see it worked properly. I was becoming experienced!

The one rough job we had was booking on at 3.00 am to walk to the carriage sheds to prepare and start about 30 units. After examination, each unit had to be started from the hand throttles on the floor. Then, when the

air pressure had built up to over 50 lbs, we closed them down and climbed into the cab to restart them from there and test the reversal of the final drive, and check that all engine lights and final drive light bulbs were working satisfactorily. The clambering underneath and climbing into the cabs made my legs ache considerably. If anything was found amiss I had to go to the bottom end of the shed to alert the fitters or electricians of the malfunction. I had to decide which department the fault came under: if it was lighting or heating or brake blocks it was the Carriage & Wagon Department; if it was engines or the operation of the brakes it came under the Loco Department. As their offices were at the opposite ends of the sheds I did not want to walk about unnecessarily.

Most of the units had departed by 8.00 am except those being repaired or on mileage examinations. At about 9.00 am units started to return, and these needed fuelling and marshalling into the shed roads. When my relief arrived at 10.40 am my legs were so tired I could hardly walk back to the depot to book off duty, but after a few weeks my muscles got used to it.

At the December union meeting I was elected as a collector of dues. This meant standing near the pay office on pay days and taking the weekly payments from the members. It was cold and draughty at the end of the steam shed, and after standing there for 2 or 3 hours I would adjourn to the new Staff Association Club and have a couple of pints of draught Guinness, which I could feel warming me. This draught Guinness had recently come into Birmingham via the Monument Lane goods depot across the road, and the brewery representative experimented with it at our club.

There were still a few steam jobs in this link. One entailed booking on at 1.45 am, preparing two locomotives, then our own, usually a 'Royal Scot', and going light engine into New Street to work a passenger train around 4.30 am to Leamington via Coventry. We then went light engine to Warwick Milverton Loco, turned the locomotive on the turntable, topped up the tender with coal, filled the tank and cleaned the fire of clinker.

Mont Lane Branch   C. Alcock Collector.

2

INSERT MEMBER'S NAME ON RULED LINE BELOW	CONTRIBUTIONS				
	Society Funds	D. & R. Fund	Orphan Fund	Political Fund	Assurance Fund
Cliff Jones	21/8	1/1		6	
M. R. Nevitt	21/8				
S. Williams	21/8	1/1		6	
B. Forbes	21/8	1/1		6	13/0
R. Nichols	21/8	1/1		6	6/6
R. Hodgetts	13/0	1/1		6	
S. Baker	21/8	1/1		6	
Les Jones	21/8	1/1		6	
K. Green	15/0				
D. Bowen	1/2				
B. Gibbons	1/3				
P. Boyle	2/0				
T. Trumph	2/6				
F. Carter	3/9				
T. Turner	21/8	1/1		6	
A. Bowyer	18/0				
H. Hughes	21/8	1/1		6	
C. Ellis	2/6				
M. Mason	4/0				
R. Hope	3/2				
TOTAL	**£13-1-0**	**9/9**		**4/0**	**19/7**

RECEIVED from Collector as above the sum of £ **14 : 14 : 6**

A. G. Long .... Branch Secretary.
(Signature)

Date 19 . 27 . 1959   T.C.V.–F

A page from my ASLEF dues Collector's Book of 1959, with which I hovered near the pay office. The Society Funds were compulsory, while the others, including the 'D & R' (Death & Retirement) Fund, were optional. Note that the book's printing dates back to the 1930s.

We then backed on to 10 coaches to work the 7.30 am local train via Kenilworth and the Berkswell loop to New Street, arriving at 9.10 am. This train then formed the 9.15 am express to Liverpool, where we were relieved by our men for us to walk to the depot. You can imagine how dirty our overalls had become by the end of the week.

One Saturday morning, as we walked from New Street to our depot at about 9.30 am, we passed the Civic Centre and the Register Office. A lone woman of about 30 years of age stopped my mate Ron Judge and asked him if we would be witnesses at her wedding in half an hour's time. Ron declined, saying, 'We have to work another train.'

I remarked to Ron afterwards, 'I couldn't see a man with her - you may have finished being married to her.'

Another steam job entailed preparing a Class '4' tank engine or tender engine and working a local train around 8.00 am to Rugeley Trent Valley via Walsall. On arriving there, we turned the locomotive, then took a raft of wagons containing steel, cement and bricks, etc, into the new Lea Hall Colliery and Electricity Power Station that was being built. This was to be a showpiece place with the coal mined at the site of the power station. However, as I write the colliery has just closed down after only 30 years, when most collieries last over a century.

When I was at Saltley there used to be an excursion train to Hull, which ran every six or eight weeks. It was steam-hauled, but I was never available to work it. It was booked for a conductor driver at Swinton Junction, north of Masborough. In the spring of 1958 I was road-learning from Stafford to Stoke-on-Trent, and when I booked off duty on Thursday, Bert Preston called me into his office and said, 'Do you still sign the road to Carlisle?'

I thought he was going to tell me of a Carlisle job, but he went on to say, 'There's a job to Hull on Sunday with DMUs diagrammed on it. It's been allocated to Saltley, but I intend claiming it as our job, as it starts and finishes at Monument Lane carriage sidings and I can say we have men who sign the road.' (Actually, he had only two, Bill Austen and myself.)

When I booked off duty on Friday Bert was waiting for me. 'We've got the Hull job!' he exclaimed. 'You're working it. Mr Lowe wants a word with you.'

I went to the shedmaster's office and he asked me if I was fully conversant with DMUs.

I replied, 'As well as I can be, having only four months working on them.'

'Well,' he continued, 'there's no fitting staff with knowledge of them beyond Derby, so if anything goes wrong with them you will have to put it right yourself.'

On Sunday 23 March I booked on at 8.45 am with a second man, Sid Rushden; he was booked with me because I would be on duty over 5 hours without a 'physical need' break. We walked to the carriage sidings to find that we had been allocated four twin units. I had a quick look around them for my own satisfaction, although they had been prepared

MONUMENT LANE	*G Allcock*	5 4 ?		
SUNDAY 23RD MARCH 58			a m	p m.
			8.45 2.54	5 ?
DIESEL DRIVER & SECOND MAN'S WORKINGS				
	Mont Lane	9.20am	Quad Empty	
9.25am	New St.	9.35	Quad M9?4	
2.24pm	Hull			
	SHORT REST			
SUNDAY 23RD MARCH			p m	p m
			6.15 11.41	5.26
	Hull	6.45pm	Quad M9?4	
10.56pm	New St.	11. 1	Quad Empty	
11. 6	Mont Lane			54?

ERegion Conductor Driver Rotherham Mexboro
to Hull and Hull to Rotherham Mexboro'

My day's workings for the Hull run on 23 March 1958.

for me. We went empty into New Street and departed at 9.35 am, stopping at Derby, Chesterfield, Sheffield, Rotherham, Doncaster and Goole. I should have picked up my North Eastern Region conductor at Swinton Junction, but he was on the platform at Rotherham and informed me that he had caught a train from Mexborough, his home depot, to save him walking the 2 miles or so to Swinton Junction. He had never seen a DMU before, so I had to carry on driving while he kept me informed of signals and speed restrictions. We had an uneventful run and arrived at Hull some 10 minutes before time at 2.24 pm.

I shut the engines down and instructed Sid to put the handbrakes on in each driving cab. Because they would remain in the dead-end platform until our return at 6.45 pm, we locked all cab doors, as railwaymen and the general public were flocking around them as though they were something from outer space.

We were classed as 'short rest', as we had booked off duty in less than 9 hours, so we would be paid continuous duty for our day's work. We had our food in the loco men's mess room, then we had a stroll in the town and along the docks.

We booked on again at 6.15 to work back at 6.50 pm. My mate was only a fireman and was not even passed out to drive steam engines, but he was willing and assisted me in topping up the coolant water and examining the oil levels of the eight engines. We departed on time and had a trouble-free run. I told the Mexborough conductor that he could drop off again near to his depot as there were only four signals between there and Swinton Junction. We were booked about 5 minutes at Sheffield, and as there

was no way we could boil water I showed Sid where he could dash and make a can of tea in the mess room.

We arrived at New Street at 10.45, 11 minutes early, giving our passengers the chance to catch the last regular buses at 11.00 pm instead of waiting for the night buses at 11.30 or midnight. When we arrived at the carriage sidings, George Whitaker, the diesel foreman fitter, was waiting to speak to me.

'Any trouble, Bill?' he said.

'No complaints' I replied.

When we had finished a day with a steam locomotive or a DMU we were compelled to fill in a repair card or, if there was nothing wrong, a 'no repairs' card; these units all had the latter made out for them.

We booked off duty at 11.45, which was 15 hours on duty at the Sunday rate of time and three quarters, and the mileage bonus brought our total pay to 30½ hours. As there was not much overtime or night rate at Monument Lane, this was a good start to the week.

About six weeks later I had another trip to Hull. On the return journey we stopped at Goole and our guard came up to the cab and said, 'There's a lot of smoke and fumes coming out of one of the power cars.'

I walked back along the platform to the centre of the train and looked at the engine concerned. It appeared to be ticking over all right, but when I operated the hand throttle, heavy smoke emitted from the exhaust pipe between the engine manifold and the silencer box. I shut the engine down and isolated it from the final drive, and asked the platform foreman to telephone for someone to meet us at Doncaster with some Jubilee clips, as the exhaust pipe had become uncoupled. This caused us some 20 minutes delay.

At Doncaster a Carriage & Wagon fitter met us and quickly effected the repair. I reconnected the final drive, started the engine up and tested it with the hand throttle; it seemed all right. The fitter gave me a couple of Jubilee clips in case we might need them, but I had no screwdriver or spanner to do any repairs; it was about three years before we were provided with a kit of tools.

Our delay was now over 30 minutes, but we arrived at New Street only 15 minutes late. On arrival at the carriage shed, George Whitaker was again waiting for a verbal report. When I told him of the engine trouble and of our makeshift repair, he said, 'A Carriage & Wagon man? It's not his job repairing engines.'

'I was glad of anyone,' I retorted. 'I needed that engine for the heavy climb out of Sheffield.'

While at Hull I had spoken to a man from the Commercial Office of British Railways, Birmingham, who had come on the trip. I remarked that it was an unusual place to run an excursion train, and that they usually go to seaside resorts such as Blackpool, Llandudno or Weston-super-Mare.

'When unemployment was high in the 1930s,' he explained, 'a lot of people moved from this area into the Midlands to find work, and this train is always well subscribed.'

Bill Austin, who was on the opposite shift to me, was the only other driver to sign the road beyond Sheffield, so we had the monopoly of this Hull work.

The DMUs were very popular with the travelling public, and during the summer excursions were run to Weston-super-Mare, Matlock, Rhyl, Llandudno, Blackpool and Southport. I worked these trains to Weston and Matlock, and was able to take my wife and two children with me. I used to wear some nice trousers under my overalls, which were still our official issue, and take a blazer, so I could become one of the crowd when walking with the family after I had disposed of my train. It was the first time that they had been able see me at work, as I used to save a couple of seats in the coach behind my driving cab.

Metro Cammell at Washwood Heath had also been building some DMUs. These were three-car sets, two power cars and a trailer car, as well as some twin sets with one power and one trailer car. I had worked a few jobs taking them from Saltley to Derby workshops

for examination before acceptance for service, then taking them to Four Oaks sidings for storage, to await the changeover from the Derby 'lightweights', as they were called. The new units were heavier and the cabs more comfortable to drive from. The only drawback was that only two units could be coupled together, as there were only six banks of engine and final drive lights.

On Sunday 1 June 1958 the changeover took place, with our depot being allocated 18 triple sets and six twin sets. On the Monday and the following Tuesday I took four of our old twin sets to Allerton on the Liverpool to Warrington line, where they had been transferred. On the Wednesday I took another four twins to Carlisle via the Settle line. It seemed a long journey, although the actual time of driving was about 5½ hours instead of the 8 or so on the Saltley freight working. I tried to explain the different aspects of the line and the scenery, which could be seen better from the windows of a DMU, to my young second man. This was to be the last time I worked a train over this beautiful line.

During the Birmingham industrial workers' holiday in August, the railway commercial office introduced a weekly excursion ticket for the 'City of Birmingham Holiday Express', which went to a different resort every day of the week. It was a steam-hauled train of 10 or 12 coaches according to the bookings. The locomotive was usually a 'Black Five' in good condition.

On August Bank Holiday Monday I worked this train with No 44837, and as it was not a Sunday, 'short rest' working did not apply. We worked to Blackpool and travelled home passenger, and another set of men travelled there to work the train home at night. A few weeks later I was asked to go to the shedmaster's office, where he showed me three postcard-size black and white photographs taken of the train emerging from the short tunnel between Birdswood and Preston Brook near Warrington. The photographer had found out which depot had worked this train and had sent them to us. The shedmaster gave me one, another was given to Walter Gee, who worked the return train, and the other was framed for his office.

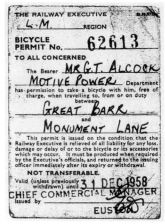

Above One of the three photographs taken of the 'City of Birmingham Holiday Express'. The photographer had found out which depot had worked the train and had sent us the pictures. I was given this one, and later had a painting done of the scene, which is reproduced on the back cover of this book.

Right My 1958 permit to take my bicycle by train free of charge.

Some 20 years later I went to an exhibition of oil paintings by Dick Potts, an ex-Tyseley driver now at Saltley. He had a lot of steam locomotive works on show as well as aircraft, the City of Birmingham Town Hall with the Symphony Orchestra playing, and some portraits. I asked him if he could paint one for me in colour from the black and white photograph taken some 20 years before. He replied, 'Bring it to me to look at and I'll see what I can do.'

Some three years later my wife and I collected the finished painting, which now has pride of place on the mantelpiece of our dining room; it is also reproduced on the back cover this book.

On the following Thursday I worked this train again, with the same locomotive, as far as Bristol, before being relieved for it to go on to Weston-super-Mare. We then worked a 'Jubilee'-hauled Plymouth to Sheffield relief train back to Birmingham.

One night in October I worked to Stoke-on-Trent and back, booking off duty around 1.00 am. I went to the cycle shed to go home but could not find my cycle. It was only about three months old, a Powell's own make from the shop of the son of my old mate, Ernie Guy in Aston. I returned to the time office to report the theft to the railway police, then had to walk into town to catch the 2.00 am night bus home. I was glad we had come to live nearer as the bus terminus was only about 10 minutes walk from my home.

When I booked on duty next day there was a city policewoman to interview me. She needed to know what time I had left my cycle, whether it been locked up and its general description, number and make. I remarked that I had left cycles at Saltley for over 15 years without as much as a pump being stolen.

A week later I received a letter to go to Steelhouse Lane police station. I thought they had found it, but they took me to a storeroom with literally hundreds of cycles in, all recovered by the police. The constable said, 'Is yours among these?'

If it had been a Hercules or a Raleigh I could easily have said, 'Yes' but as there was no Powell there I had to say 'No'. I visited two or three times afterwards, but to no avail.

After about a month of travelling to and fro from work by train in one direction, and by night bus in the other, I bought myself a second-hand motor cycle. Having halved my journey by moving house, I was now motorised, and my travelling time was again halved to 15 minutes.

At the December union meeting I was elected Vice Chairman under the Chairman, Walter Beech, my diesel instructor, and had my first taste of chairing at the January 1959 meeting. I was slowly moving up the trade union ladder.

8
BACK TO SCHOOL
1959-63

In January 1959, after I had been driving DMUs for 17 months, I and five other Monument Lane drivers, with others from Ryecroft and Bushbury depots, had a week's schooling at a mobile school for DMU driving. This consisted of two coaches stabled at Bescot Station; one was set up as a classroom with blackboards and screens for the showing of photographic slides of brakes, gear boxes, fluid flywheels and the operation of the diesel engine, while the other held an exhibition of all parts of the DMU.

The converted coach serving as the DMU training school at Bescot in January 1959. In the front row are Ernie Jones and Steenie Morris (who was one of the older men who still found DMUs 'boxes of mystery'); I am sitting behind Steenie. *Author's collection*

The Ryecroft and Bushbury men had just started using DMUs, but some of the Monument Lane men had been driving them for over two years, so we were able to ask pertinent questions about failures that were not contained in the faults and remedy book with which we had been issued. I complained that we had changed from the Derby 'lightweights' to the 'Met' sets, as we called them, without any further training, even though the throttle handle and the gear change lever were entirely different.

When we finished the course on the Friday evening I spoke to an old Ryecroft driver, Steenie Morris, who was in his 60s.

'They're still boxes of mystery to me,' he remarked.

DMUs had one drawback: they did not have a coupling to enable parcel vehicles to be attached, so special parcel trains had to be run. We used to work a Class '4' tank locomotive with three or four parcel vans from Birmingham to Walsall, run round them, then, after unloading and loading had taken place, work them to Wolverhampton, then to Birmingham, stopping at Ettingshall Road for Bilston, Tipton, Dudley Port and Smethwick. After more trans-shipping of parcels we carried on to Coventry, then returned, to be released from the vans to go light engine to the depot. After a couple of years diesel parcel vans were built; they had their own engines and could be coupled to the passenger units or run alone.

One morning we were working one of the steam-hauled parcel trains from Wolverhampton and had stopped at Ettingshall Road, where the platform was full of parcels waiting

A Gloucester RC&W diesel parcels unit attached to the rear of two three-car Western Region suburban DMUs near Smethwick on 15 October 1966. *Michael Mensing*

to be loaded. We stood there for about 15 minutes, then were signalled along the goods line to Coseley & Deepfields to allow an express passenger train to pass us.

I had a driver, Ginger Whitehouse, learning the road with me, and while we stood at Coseley he decided to eat his sandwiches. After the express had dashed passed us we departed, and on approaching Bloomfield Junction we could see a crowd of people on the track, including police officers, who flagged us down. One shouted, 'Go steady, someone has just committed suicide.'

As we passed we could see a body in the centre of the track, and someone held a human head up by its hair. My road learner was sick into the coal bunker and threw the rest of his sandwiches into the fire.

'It's a good job we had to wait behind the express,' I said, 'or it could have been us who killed the victim, which would've entailed police statements and attendances at inquests.'

Such accidents were reported to our union, and representatives were sent to assist our members at inquests.

Working three trips to Lichfield and back was a regular day's work, and at LDC level I repeatedly asked the railway management to vary the work as men were getting bored stopping and starting at 10 or 11 stations, six times a day. I suggested a run to Coventry or Wolverhampton in between the Lichfield run for the safety aspect, but could get nothing done.

On one occasion, when arriving at New Street from Lichfield, my guard Arthur Attenborough, the hero of the Sutton Coldfield disaster, remarked to me about a man running to catch the train at Chester Road station. I thought for a moment, then answered, 'I can't remember stopping there.'

'Don't be daft,' he said. 'Of course you did.'

I had stopped there automatically.

On another occasion we worked a train from the bay platform at Four Oaks at around 8.30 am. We followed a train that came on the main line from Lichfield to Birmingham and ran non-stop from Sutton Coldfield to New Street. This particular day, when the signals cleared for us, we ran towards Sutton Coldfield and I had the distant signal at caution. As we approached the home signal, it slowly cleared and I ran through the short tunnel into the platform and stopped.

When I received the guard's 'right away' buzzer, I looked and could see the starting signal at the end of the platform clear, so I proceeded. There was an advanced starting signal some 100 yards further on, and I did not remember seeing it. The signals at Wylde Green station were controlled by Sutton signal box and the distant signal was at caution; the stop signal was at the end of the platform and was at red. I stopped there, thinking that it was unusual, as the previous train should be half way to Birmingham.

I tried to think if I had seen the advanced starting signal at Sutton Coldfield, but no matter how I tried I could not remember. When I received the guard's 'right away', the signal was still at danger, so I climbed down to telephone the signalman to inquire of the delay. I fully expected him to castigate me for passing his signal at danger, so was pleased when he said, 'There's a failure at that signal - pass it at danger. You have the road to Erdington.' It showed how boring the work was when you could not remember important things like signals and stations.

At the April union meeting I was elected as delegate to the Birmingham Trades Council. This was where all the trade union delegates met once a month, and where all aspects of trade unionism were discussed.

In June we took our annual holidays at Bournemouth and it worked out cheaper than I had anticipated. When May was talking about sandwiches for the return journey, I said, 'We're catching the "Pines Express", which has a restaurant coach on it - we'll have lunch on it. It'll make a change from cooking on a shovel!'

This train went via Templecombe on the old Somerset & Dorset line to Bath, where Saltley men took it forward to Birmingham, as I had done many times. Just before arrival at Bath we were invited to take our seats in the dining car. We commenced our meal with soup, then we had the fish course, and when we received the meat course Elaine, my 5-year-old daughter, piped up for all the coach to hear, 'Look Dad, another dinner.' The sweet and cheese and biscuits took us to Bromsgrove, just in time for us to take our seats prior to arriving at Birmingham. This was the first of many meals on trains in this country and in Europe, as well as on railway-owned ships going to the Channel Isles, and on cross-Channel ferries to France and Belgium.

At the September union meeting it was decided to form a welfare and entertainment sub-committee to raise funds to make payments for men off duty through sickness, and to make retirement grants. I was elected secretary, and this started over 25 years of welfare work.

On 5 December we had our first dance, and three men received retirement grants. We had a couple of men with long-term illnesses. One of them, Harry Wilkes, never worked on the footplate again, and I used to see him toilet cleaning at New Street station. I would have a chat with him, thinking how unkind fate could be that because of an illness he could not follow his chosen profession.

The single manning of DMUs caused other troubles for drivers. The railway medical officer became very strict at the five-yearly (or yearly if over 60 years of age) examinations. He was issuing men that he considered overweight with diet sheets and ordering them to lose weight, then calling them back to the surgery after three or six months to see if they had been successful.

The Birmingham railway medical centre was in Queens Drive, which separated the old Midland and London & North Western sides of New Street station between platforms 6 and 7, and was immediately above our diesel drivers' mess room, where they took their 20 minutes break.

One morning a Crewe fireman inquired whether we had a cooking stove or a frying pan to lend him to cook some bacon. Bob Jones, an elderly driver, who was one of the victims of the diet sheet, exclaimed, 'If him above could hear you talk of frying pans and bacon he would strike you down.'

The fireman was dumb-struck, thinking that Bob was referring to the Lord.

I said, 'Have you never used your shovel? It tastes better cooked on that.'

A DMU driver was allowed a break of 20 minutes between the third and fifth hour, but a guard was not. After a couple of years, when the driver and guard stayed together as a crew all day, some economist in the diagram office decided that as guards were not allowed a break, 20 minutes a day could be saved. In October new diagrams were introduced, and instead of a guard having a break with his driver he carried on with another driver.

In November we had a few weeks of heavy fog with trains running late, which disrupted the now tight timetable workings and the running of the DMUs. Drivers arrived to work trains to find that their guard was delayed on another train, and the same applied to guards awaiting drivers. It was an expensive way of saving 20 minutes, as I informed our bosses at an LDC meeting.

'If a driver and guard are always together you have a train crew to work a train.'

The boss agreed, but answered, 'The whizkids are only interested in economy, not working trains.'

How right he was in years to come.

Monument Lane had three lodging turns of duty. One was a night parcels train to Euston and the other two lodged at Crewe, about an hour's running from home. The latter were both steam locomotive turns. One booked on at 8.30 am to work to Liverpool at 9.10 am, returning to Crewe at around 3.45

pm and booking off there at 4.15 pm. The Manchester turn booked on at 11.35 am to work the 12.15 to Manchester, and returned to Crewe, booking off around 7.30 pm. The economists found a way of getting around the lodging agreement, where no further work could be done on arrival at the home station. The men who had lodged after working the Liverpool turn were rostered to book on at 1.30 am to work on a shunt engine until it was time to work the 7.15 train to Birmingham, arriving around 8.30 am. The same applied to the Manchester train crew. It seemed ridiculous that men were booked to lodge away from home, and be paid lodging allowances, to save some 30 minutes over-time if they worked direct home, as the two trains were both Birmingham-bound.

As an LDC representative I raised this item on numerous occasions at our meetings with management, but to no avail. The economist reigned supreme.

At the turn of the year I and Ron Nichols, who was later to die from leukaemia, were sent to learn the route to Northampton via Rugby and via Leamington. These were notorious places for semaphore signals. At Northampton there was a sharp right-hand curve when arriving from the Birmingham direction, and a lot of signals were placed on the right-hand side of the track, away from the driver's left-hand driving position, with short distances between the signal boxes.

Rugby still had its huge signal gantries. One on the up line carried 58 signals, and a driver had to be able to read his particular signal as he ran towards it on the different approach lines. It took us three weeks before we were happy to sign as knowing the road, and the following Sunday I booked on duty at 11.25 pm to work two triple units via Coventry and Rugby to Northampton at 12.15 am, then returning to Rugby and tak-ing the line to Leamington, where I stabled the units and travelled home passenger on the 6.30 am train.

At the beginning of February my wife had to go into hospital for an operation and it was estimated that she would be in for about 10 days, so I applied for my two weeks annual holiday, which should have been in July, to

be brought forward so I could be at home to look after our two children. I handed my application to the shift foreman, Taffy Hughes, who had been our union secretary, and explained the circumstances.

'Your wife is going to need your attention when she gets home,' he said. 'You're down to learn the route from Coventry to Nuneaton, which should take a couple of weeks. What if I put you down to do it when she goes into hospital? You can arrange the times to suit your children's schooling. You can then take your holidays when she comes home.'

I thanked him for his thoughtfulness and arranged my times as he suggested.

The line from Coventry to Nuneaton was similar to the New Street to Wolverhampton line, with about a dozen signal boxes and eight stations, and numerous collieries along 10 miles of railway. I completed this in the two weeks and was glad to take my holiday when May arrived home.

On Easter Sunday 1960 I had a DMU excursion to Weston-super-Mare, a short rest turn involving being on duty for around 12 hours with a 4-hour break at Weston. I arranged for my wife and two children to travel in the coach behind me; I made a can of tea when I changed ends at New Street, so they had the dubious pleasure of drinking railway tea, drivers' fashion, from the tea can! We were still being issued with overalls at this time, so I could take them off and leave them in the guard's locker and become another tourist after I had stabled the units.

In July I had another DMU excursion, involving two drivers. I drove two triple units to Kings Norton, from where the train start-ed, picking up passengers at Bournville, Selly Oak and New Street. We were then directed via Saltley, Sutton Park and Aldridge to Walsall, where we changed cabs to reverse the train.

I had arranged for my family to travel by bus to Walsall, as it was nearer than travel-ling into Birmingham, and I instructed them to stop at the rear of the platform so that they could sit behind the cab when I changed ends. I then worked the train via Bloxwich and Rugeley Trent Valley to

Stafford. My co-driver, Cliff Wall, did not sign for this route, which is why I was required; he then took over and worked the train to Rhyl over the route from Crewe, which I did not know. I was thus able to join the family in the train and enjoy sandwiches and tea from a flask, offering Cliff some, plus pieces of home-made cake. We had a good 4 or 5 hours at Rhyl, and worked the same procedure home. I dropped my family off at Walsall around 10.00 pm, but it was around midnight before I signed off duty, and my family pulled my leg the next day, accusing me of not working very hard.

On August Bank Holiday Monday I was booked to sign on duty at 8.10 am to take two triple units into New Street, then work an excursion to Bournemouth via Gloucester, Mangotsfield and Bath Green Park, where I was relieved; the train went on via Templecombe over the old S&D line. We were booked home as passenger from Green Park on a train some 2 hours later, but I suggested to the guard that we could get home more quickly by walking to the Western Region station, where the service was more frequent to Bristol Temple Meads and we could get a quicker service home.

One morning in October I was working two triple sets from Lichfield City to Birmingham. When I arrived at New Street station at around 8.45 am, prior to taking the units to the carriage sidings, I was approached by a man who showed his identity card, stating that he was a City of Birmingham smoke inspector. He informed me that he had ridden on my train from Sutton Coldfield and would be reporting me for allowing heavy smoke from three of the eight engines. He went on to say that his report would start from Chester Road station, the first after crossing the Birmingham boundary.

'I can't see any engines,' I replied. 'My only knowledge is these engine lights, which tell me if they're working or not.' I then started to smile.

'What do you find amusing?' he said.

'I was a steam engine fireman for about 18 years,' I replied, thinking of the smoke I churned out then, and was now being booked for it on diesel engines!

When I arrived at the carriage shed sidings I had the shunt driver move the units towards the fuelling pumps so I could identify the erring engines. I made out a repair card stating which were emitting heavy smoke and took it to the fitters. They laughed at first, but when I informed them of the smoke inspector they took it more seriously. I was then booked to walk to New Street to work a train to Wolverhampton and Walsall before returning to New Street to sign off duty at 12.45 pm, when I made out a report stating the facts.

When I booked off duty the next day at the same time, Bert Preston said, 'The shedmaster wants to see you, but he's gone to lunch.'

'I've signed off duty now,' I said.

'Well book on duty again,' Bert replied. 'You'll be paid overtime while you wait.'

When he returned, Mr Eanson, the new shedmaster, asked me what had taken place. When I explained he said, 'I've had a telephone call from the City of Birmingham Environment Department informing me that they are considering prosecuting us.'

He went on to explain that the excessive smoke was caused by the fuel injectors getting worn and putting too much fuel into the cylinders.

Having been a steam engineman for so many years, I was amused to be 'booked' in the autumn of 1960 for making smoke on a DMU! Here a Redditch-bound DMU pollutes the New Street atmosphere at platform 11 in 1962. Note the fine ex-LNWR signals still in use, and the diesel shunter in the sidings on the left. *Michael Mensing*

'I can't do anything about that,' I replied. 'I only drive them.'

At the next union meeting other drivers complained of similar clashes with the smoke inspector and the matter was debated. The question 'Who would be responsible in the event of prosecution?' was asked, and it was decided that the LDC should remonstrate with the management regarding the poor maintenance of the engines. The chairman added, smiling to me, 'We'll come and visit you in prison.'

A few weeks later I received a letter from Mr Eanson stating that the Railway Board had received a severe warning from the City of Birmingham.

For some months diesel shunting locomotives had been gradually introduced into the depot to replace the steam shunters. In November three of us, Ron Nichols, Fred Massey and myself, were booked to travel to Saltley for training on them, and at the end of the week Mr Locke, the assistant footplate inspector, passed us out to drive them. They were booked on the Monument Lane freight yard shunting Soho Road, Tipton (which was a residential depot) and New Street. They certainly made shunting easier, and on the New Street turn, when banking of trains through the north tunnel was needed, the windows could be kept closed to keep out the smoke of the train's locomotive, which normally choked you. The previous summer I had been off duty ill with bronchitis after working on the Soho Pool turn with a 'Super D' steam locomotive. It had been a particularly hot week and we worked in the basin surrounded by factories and houses, sweating profusely on the hot and dusty locomotive, so the diesel shunters were a godsend.

— o —

At the December 1960 union meeting I was nominated as LDC representative, with driver Ernie Bennet, for the coming year's ballot at the depot. We were both elected, together with George Sharret, an NUR member.

One of our first meetings was the proposal by management for the partial closure of the depot. Our meeting place was at New Street station where we were shown plans for the Oldbury and Soho Soap Works, and the Albion and Soho Pool shunting yards, now dieselised, to be worked independently from Monument Lane with men booking on and off duty at the individual depots.

The first two locations entailed three-shift working, and the others two shifts. Tipton already had one set of men stationed there, with the steam shunter being taken out and brought back to our depot daily. This was to become a two-shift depot with the new diesel shunters, which could be shut down and stabled at the different yards for about a fortnight before returning to our depot for fuelling and servicing.

We said that we would look at these proposals and reply within a week. We sent copies of the proposals to the District Sectional Council (full-time trade union representatives for the Midlands region). Their secretary was Les Briers, who used to be the Saltley branch secretary and who I knew quite well. He advised me to find as many objections as possible to the scheme and he would call for a Sectional Council meeting with management to consider their plans. A week or so later we attended a full Sectional Council meeting with top railway management and union representatives present.

I had been elected as chairman of our group and gave a list of things that would have to be provided, such as mess rooms with lockers and drying rooms for clothes, and inspection pits to be built to enable the drivers to examine the locomotives daily, as per the railway instructions. I also requested a travelling allowance for the men who transferred from Monument Lane to cover these stations. Different ideas were put forward, and the meeting was adjourned until the following day.

During the following morning no progress was made and we adjourned for lunch at New Street station's Queen's Hotel. While we were there, Mr Talbot, the superintendent at Saltley and our depot, came and shook hands with me. He reminded me of his advice when I became a driver to apply for managerial jobs, and asked if I had done so. I replied that

I was now interested in trade union activities. Later on in the lunch hour one of the management representatives broke away from his group and said to me, 'If you will agree to Soho Pool being an outside depot we will give way on all the others.'

The working there at that time was that a driver booked on at Monument Lane at 7.00 am and walked for 30 minutes to Soho Pool to start work, and the same happened on the afternoon turn, with drivers finishing their shift having to walk back to the depot to sign off duty at 10.30 pm. There were no buses, so in bad weather they arrived for their day's work wet through.

I had a consultation with my colleagues and Les Briers said, 'If you're happy with it, what about the mess room and inspection pits?'

'There's plenty of old buildings that can easily be turned into a mess room,' I replied, 'and there's already an ashpit there provided for the steam locomotives, which management must have missed.'

After lunch the meeting was brief - management cancelled all their proposals except Soho Pool. I then asked for a further consideration. I proposed that instead of Soho Pool being classed as an outside depot, the turns would remain rostered at Monument Lane and the men on these rosters would book on and off at Soho Pool, thus saving a travelling allowance. Management considered this for a few minutes and consented.

When we reported back at our next union meeting the members were quite happy with our negotiations, as a lot of the men concerned lived near Soho Pool, and it would save them going to Monument Lane then walking back.

There was an LDC agreement that the paying out of wages would be from 1.00 pm to 4.30 pm on Friday, and any unclaimed would be taken to the booking office at Monument Lane station, where men could get their wages until 9.00 pm and from 9.00 am until 12.00 pm on the Saturday. There was an exception to this, as the men who booked on at 11.30 am to work to Manchester and lodge at Crewe did not book off duty until around 2.00 pm on the

Saturday, so could not get their wages. It was agreed that they could receive their wages when they booked on at 11.30 am.

With rest days now being worked at the depot, we had men finishing their week's work around 11.00 am to 12.00 pm and having rest days on Saturday, so they also could not draw their wages. I went and had a quiet word with the pay clerk, Miss Maggie Salt, a woman of about 50 years of age noted for her blunt way of speaking. I told her the situation and asked if she was prepared to pay these men before 1.00 pm on Friday.

'Not likely!' she exclaimed, point blank. 'The agreement states that it is the Manchester men only who have this concession and I take care to look at the rosters to ascertain who they are.'

At the next LDC meeting I put this item on the agenda, asking for longer hours of wages payment at the depot. I quoted the times of payment at Saltley, from 1.00 to 9.00 pm on Fridays and 8.00 am to 1.00 pm on Saturdays. I stressed the inconvenience caused for men having to walk to Monument Lane station when booking on or signing off duty after 4.30 pm on Fridays. I also pointed out the men who had rest days on Saturdays and that the cash arrived at the depot from the bank at 9.30 am. After a long discussion we got the agreement altered so that the rest day men could get their wages from 11.00 am if they applied in writing to the pay clerk by Thursday afternoon, and wages would be paid until 5.30 pm at the depot and 9.00 pm at Monument Lane station.

For the new workings of the outside depots with diesel shunting engines, the Oldbury men were booked to travel out by train, and the Soho Soap Works and Albion men by Corporation bus. The fare was paid by vouchers issued from the time office and exchanged for a ticket from the bus conductor. All these turns started at 6.00 am on Monday morning, so the men booked on around 5.15 am to travel there. However, the man for Oldbury was shown to book on at 4.10 am. When I spotted this while looking through the new diagrammed workings I asked for a meeting with the shedmaster to complain about it.

'You can't expect a man over 60 years of age, some suffering with arthritis and other ailments for which they have been placed in the shunting links, to walk that far in the early hours of the morning,' I said.

'It's nothing to do with me,' he replied. 'The Crewe diagram office have made these workings out.'

'It is to do with you!' I retorted. 'You are supposed to look after the welfare of the men under you, not shrug your shoulders and disclaim anything to do with it.'

'If I don't get any satisfaction from you,' I continued, 'I'll ask for a recall Sectional Council meeting.'

With this his attitude changed and he asked, 'How would you propose to get the man to Oldbury?'

This was what I needed, as I had been looking and found a way. 'There's an empty DMU that leaves the carriage sidings at 5.20 am for Wolverhampton,' I explained. 'If you made out a special stop order for Oldbury that would get him there for 5.30 am, in time for him to examine and start the locomotive for his day's work at 6.00 am.'

After some consideration he agreed to do this. I explained that most drivers and guards would stop to drop the driver off, but the occasional awkward man would quote the rule book and refuse to stop, but with a proper stop order he would have to do it.

There was one awkward running shift foreman who had recently been promoted from a driver, who was trying to make a name for himself management-wise. On one occasion I was in the time office talking to Mr Eanson, the shedmaster, when I heard the foreman fitter, Frank Rigby, say to this foreman, 'I need the Oldbury engine changing for its fortnightly servicing.'

The other replied, 'Is there any hurry as we can change the engine over when the relief man books on duty in one and a half hours' time?' Then he added, 'That'll stop them going out on their push-bikes or motor bikes.'

I rounded on him and said, 'At the last LDC meeting you complained of the non-co-operation of staff. Now you have two sets of men standing spare in the mess room who could do the changeover within an hour, and

if men make their own way to Oldbury, they are saving the bus fare for the railway company.'

Mr Eanson just smiled, and it was obvious that I would get no support from him, so shortly afterwards I went to the foreman fitter's office and spoke to Frank Rigby, whom I had known over 20 years, and put him in the picture.

'OK, Bill,' he said, 'I'll ask for the engine to be changed immediately.'

A few weeks later I was on a turn that arrived at the depot around 1.00 am with a steam locomotive. The awkward foreman was on duty when I booked off. When I booked on duty the next day I could see that my time card had been altered and 2 minutes - yes, 2 minutes - deducted from the time I had shown.

When I booked off the following morning I said to the timekeeper, 'Who altered my time card yesterday?'

He pointed to the foreman, so I asked him, 'Why?'

'You are only allowed 3 minutes after passing Sheepcote Lane signal box,' he replied, 'and you took 5.'

'Whatever time I took I can account for,' I replied, 'as I had to change points to stable our locomotives on the coal stage road, and you have no business altering my time card as it is my responsibility. If you are not satisfied you must report it.'

'There is a company rule,' I carried on, 'that engines in steam must not be left unmanned, and as the shed train crew are busy disposing of another engine, I've left my fireman on our locomotive and I'm going back to join him until we can be relieved.'

It was about another 30 minutes before I booked off duty.

Before the next LDC meeting I dug out old working agreements and found out that the 3 minutes from passing the signal box had been agreed some 20 years previously, when there were three sets of shed men on duty. Now, because of the fewer number of steam locomotives at the depot and the increase in DMUs, there was only one set of shed men.

I put this item on the agenda for our LDC

meeting. We now had a new shedmaster, Mr Tudge, a young man of about 25 to 30 years of age who had just come from the railway college. I outlined our case for this 3-minute rule to be rescinded as locomotives could not be left unattended when the shed men were occupied elsewhere. After a long discussion, when the foreman was sent for to explain his part in altering not only mine but also other men's time cards, it was agreed that the old agreement was to be scrapped and men would book off duty after being relieved by the shed men.

The Railway Board had been experimenting with main-line diesels for a few years, with the pioneer ex-LMS diesel-electrics Nos 10000 and 10001 being worked occasionally from our depot on Euston trains. It was about 18 months before the Board made up its minds to order a fleet of 2,000 hp English Electric and 1,160 hp Sulzer diesel locomotives.

In September 1961 I was booked on duty at 11.30 am for training on the English Electric locomotives. Ken Beasley was my instructor and, after providing me with a bundle of instruction books, he said we would travel on the 12.15 pm to Rugby, where we were sure of a locomotive to look over. No D341 was on the front of the train, so we rode with the Bushbury men and Ken showed me the power controller, brake and

One of the Sulzer 1,160 hp diesel-electric locomotives in the D5000 series (later Class 24) introduced in 1958 waiting to leave platform 3 at New Street with the 3.58 pm to Norwich via Market Harborough on 19 November 1960. This was a regular diesel working by this time. *Michael Mensing*

the deadman's valve, which was a treadle held down by the weight of the feet. At Rugby we found a locomotive in for servicing and he took me into the massive engine room, showing me the huge engine, generator, auxiliary generation, exhausters and compressor. He also showed me the cooling water and fan equipment and the traction motors around the axle-boxes. After spending about 6 hours there we rode back home on another example, No D221.

On another day we again caught the 12.15 pm and Ken asked the Bushbury driver if I could drive if he were to take responsibility. He agreed, so I took D342 with 10 coaches out of New Street, the first stop being at Coventry in 18 minutes, then on to Rugby, where we alighted for another day around a stationary locomotive. On the return train home Ken again asked the Camden driver if I could gain experience by driving the train.

The training carried on all week and on Saturday we booked on duty at 8.30 and I drove the 9.15 am through to London Euston with D221 on the front, returning with D312.

The following Monday I was rostered at 9.30 am to travel on the 10.15 am to Rugby for training on the 1,160 hp Sulzer locomotives. Ken had some difficulty getting me the appropriate books for this locomotive type, so we arrived at New Street at the last minute to catch our train. As we dashed along the platform looking for some seats we could see Inspector Locke calling us towards the front of the train. There were two locomotives on the train, D297 and D299.

'Come on!' he shouted, pointing to me. 'I want to see you drive.'

As we jumped into the cab the Bushbury men jumped off, saying that they would ride on the rear engine to Rugby. I sat in the driving seat, still wearing my mackintosh, as the guard waved his green flag. After negotiating the 20 mph speed restriction to Grand Junction, I opened the power handle fully, and was amazed at the power I had bringing the 10 coaches quickly up to 75 mph. The distant signal for Stechford was at caution, so I shut the power off and started to apply the brake gradually. It did not seem to be having

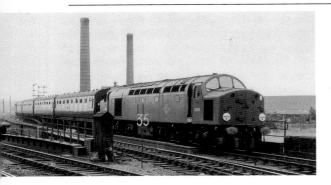

D299, one of the English Electric Type 4 diesel-electrics (later Class 40) on which I trained in 1961. She is seen here bringing the 4.35 pm Euston-Wolverhampton train round the sharp curve into Northampton station on 17 June of that year. *Michael Mensing*

much effect, so I put it on full. We could see the home signal at danger racing up towards us and we came to a shuddering stop within a couple of feet of it.

Ken laughed and said, 'How's that for a stop?'

Mr Locke replied, 'I won't need any Andrew's liver salts for a month.' (Had we passed the signal at danger he would have had to answer any reports on it.)

'The brake didn't seem to have any effect,' I said, 'until I put it on full.'

Ken then went to sit with the Bushbury men. When we ran into Coventry the brake was quite different and I made a comfortable stop. The same applied at Rugby. The three of us alighted and Mr Locke spent the day with us asking me questions on the English Electric locomotives. At the end of the day he passed me out and, as he resided at Rugby, he said that he would not be coming to Birmingham with us.

After he left us Ken said, 'When I went back to the rear engine I found that the exhausters that should have been isolated were still working, so when you were destroying the vacuum to operate the brake, they were recreating it. I didn't say anything because Mr Locke would report his own grandmother, let alone the Bushbury driver. If you had passed the signal at danger, I would have to have said something; evidently Mr Locke didn't know what was happening.'

The rest of the week we travelled to Rugby to find a Sulzer locomotive; they were nicknamed 'one-armed bandits' because of the driving panel. The following week I should have been on an afternoon shift, but was rostered on the Monday to book on at 9.30 am to pass out on the Sulzers. However, I was rostered on duty the previous day at 3.45 pm. I spoke to the foreman, pointing out that if I worked this turn I would not sign off duty until 11.45 and, with 12 hours rest, I could not book on until 11.45 on the Monday.

'You can book on with 9 hours rest for passing out,' he replied.

'I can't,' I said, 'because I shall be expected to drive.'

'I'm not changing it,' he said.

I duly booked off duty at 12.05 am and informed the foreman on duty that I would be coming on duty at 12.05 pm. When I arrived, it was the awkward foreman on duty again. He said, 'I told you to book on in 9 hours. Mr Locke is in New Street fuming, having to wait for you.'

'I told you on Saturday I would have 12 hours rest,' I replied, 'and you refused to alter my Sunday turn.'

On arriving at Mr Locke's office I was greeted with the words, 'Are you frightened to pass out with me?'

'I'm not frightened of you or anyone else,' I replied. 'I've already passed out with you once on the English Electric.'

I explained about the 12 hours rest and of the foreman's refusal to change my turn of duty, and went on to say, 'Am I to be victimised for obeying a Board of Trade regulation because of the inefficiency of the staff at Monument Lane? If so, I may as well book off duty now, and in my opinion this training programme of one week on each locomotive is insufficient to change from a steam engine driver to a diesel driver.'

He tried to calm me down by saying, 'We'll have a cup of tea and catch the 1.10 pm to Rugby.'

It was after 2.00 pm when we got there; on the way he had asked a lot of questions regarding the 'one-armed bandits'. We found one in the shed and climbed on to it; he asked me to name the various parts in the engine room and their operations. Around 4.00 pm he said, 'I'm passing you out. Give me your name, etc, for the MOT certificate. I shan't be coming back with you.'

So I had an early finish!

Towards the end of 1961 the Railway Board and the trade unions agreed on a 42-hour week. This entailed three rest days off duty in four weeks. When we attended the LDC meeting, Mr Tudge, our new shedmaster, remarked, 'I've had a course in working rosters at the Derby college and this is how I think they should be', and showed us his efforts. We looked at the rosters and could see that he had put the best work in the top links (ie both the Manchester and Liverpool jobs were in the same link regardless of times and rest day coverage). He was showing men as being five weeks on an afternoon shift, then seven weeks on early morning turns. We rejected them, saying that it was our prerogative to make them out to suit the men as well as the management.

It took Ernie Bennet and myself the rest of the week to get the rosters workable (George Sharret had conveniently reported sick). We decided that each link would cover its own rest days. For every one week in 12 a man would start his weeks at around 6.00 pm, then 4.00 pm the next day, then 2.00 pm on the third day. Then, as the depot had a lot of early morning shifts, we had to give a rest day in the middle of the week to enable the 6.00 am and 4.00 am shifts to be covered, showing 12 hours rest. Once in every link we made a Saturday rest day followed by a Monday rest day, with most of them finishing after an early morning shift around midday or so on Friday, and the Tuesday shift started on a late afternoon turn. We did not roster the men to work on the intervening Sunday, so this gave them a long weekend off duty.

At the LDC meeting to implement these links, Mr Talbot, the area superintendent from Saltley, was chairman for management and I was chairman for the footplatemen. He congratulated us on completing the links, as other depots had not completed theirs, having difficulties balancing the 42 hours a week. I explained that one week of six days work of 48 hours must appear in the same

place over the 12 weeks work; for example, two weeks of 40 hours, then a week of 48 hours with no rest day, then another week of 40 hours. This was repeated three times to make a link of 12 weeks. For payment, the 40-hour weeks had 2 hours added to them, and the 48 hour week had 6 deducted. I explained about not rostering anyone on duty on the Sunday of the long weekend, but Mr Talbot was not happy with this, as we wanted a written agreement that management would not roster a man to work on that weekend on Sunday special work. Mr Talbot was reluctant to give us this, but we insisted, stating that it would only affect 12 drivers and four firemen each weekend.

After a full day's argument we eventually got the agreement we wanted and the proposed links were posted at the depot for a week for the men to consider them. We had no complaints at that time, but after the workings had been in operation for three weeks, a couple of drivers of the overtime breed asked at the monthly union meeting why they could not work on the Sunday of the long weekend. I explained the agreement for which we had fought, saying that 'All your railway life you have been at the beck and call of the railway management. You are still at their beck and call for 11 weekends, but the 12th is now yours to go away on holiday, paint your house, dig the garden, or whatever. You can plan in advance knowing you have that weekend every 12 weeks.'

After a debate it was accepted by a big majority of the members. However, I was not to enjoy these workings for very long!

— o —

Because of the 42-hour week, extra men were needed to cover the rest days, and on the 1962 January vacancies sheet I spotted that I had been re-allocated to Saltley, thus taking up my proper driver's position at the depot after five years away. I had expected to be away for a couple of years, and I later found out that over 100 drivers had retired or died in that period, with no vacancies being needed, and staff had been reduced owing to the efficiency of the DMUs and main-line diesel locomotives.

I reported at Saltley at 8.00 am on Monday 22 January, with another returned ex-Saltley man, Jack Heron, who had been at Bescot. We were given our new lockers and filled in our route cards. I could see that I was placed in the special link and, as we were allowed a day to transfer, was instructed to book on at 8.00 am for route learning the following day. For the next three weeks we refreshed our knowledge of roads we had not been over in the last six months. On Monday, when we asked Harold Evans, the running shift foreman on duty, to sign our road learning sheet, he said to us, 'Go and learn the Kingsbury branch line to Baddesley. Everybody wants to sign for the main line, but few sign for this colliery branch line.'

In February I attended the Saltley union branch meeting where I was greeted by David Salt, a passed fireman and LDC man, with the words, 'What have you returned for? You've prevented me from getting my driver's position.'

'There are vacancies being declared at Aston and Monument Lane,' I retorted. 'There's nothing stopping you from applying for one of them, like I and a good many more Saltley men have done.'

I was warmly greeted by other branch members and was appointed collector of members' dues. The first Sunday I worked was 5.00 pm shed, which meant disposing of six locomotives with a young fireman. As I was throwing hot fire out of a Class '8' freight locomotive I realised how easy I had had it for the last couple of years on the DMUs and diesel locomotives. I was sweating profusely and my hands, which had become soft, were sore (no one wore gloves then), and I wondered if I had done the right thing returning to this type of work. However, after a few weeks I got back into my stride!

In March I was rostered to book on at 8.00 am for main-line diesel training on the 2,500 hp Sulzer/Crompton Parkinson locomotives, familiarly known as 'Peaks' from the names of the first ten. Saltley had a more professional approach to training, with a locomotive at the depot and a classroom with blackboards and diagrams to peruse. Two drivers were under the wings of two instructors, Len

Sulzer/Crompton Parkinson 2,500 hp Type 4 diesel-electric (later Class 45) No D72 standing outside No 3 shed at Saltley some time in the early 1960s. Compare this photograph with the 1947 view on page 49 to see progress on refurbishing the dilapidated roundhouse! *Derek Sharpe*

Stokes, who later emigrated to Kenya, and Arthur Thomas, one of my Carlisle special link drivers.

The first morning was spent in the classroom where each instructor in turn showed us the main parts of the locomotive on the blackboard. In the afternoon we were shown over the locomotives and eventually started the engine and did various tests and examinations. The following morning and the rest of the week we prepared the locomotive and took it to Saltley carriage sidings to take a train over the Sutton Park branch line to Aldridge and Lichfield Road Junction, near my old home where my mother and younger brother still resided.

The instructors taught us how to drive and stop efficiently on our two or three return trips a day, and later in the week arranged faults, which either stopped the engine or train, for us to rectify. It was more intensive training than we had enjoyed at Monument Lane. At the end of the week inspector Jack Bates accompanied us to watch us drive and ask a host of questions regarding the locomotive, eventually passing us out as qualified to drive them. The following week we were trained on the Brush Sulzer 2,500 hp locomotives with a similar training procedure, and were again passed to drive them.

An interesting job came up one evening

around 8.00 pm. The breakdown train had been called to re-rail some vehicles at Soho Soap Works sidings, and as I was one of the few Saltley men to sign the road, I was instructed to take them there. We were only about an hour picking up the wagons and putting them back on the rails with the steam crane, and on completion it was decided to propel the train for the short distance to Soho East Junction and return via Winson Green station, thus turning the train. As we were doing this manoeuvre I heard some shouting and could see the crane driver waving his arms about - some of the wheels of the crane had become derailed on the sharp curve. I remarked jokingly to Tommy Mackintosh, the breakdown foreman, 'What do we do now? Send for the Bescot crew?'

'Not bloody likely!' he replied, and shouted to his men, 'Get the jacks and packing, we'll do this ourselves.'

It took longer to complete than the original mishap, and we were also blocking the main line!

In May I had further training on the named 'Peaks'. These were all stationed at the Toton depot near Nottingham, but as a special link driver I had to be available to relieve them and work back to Toton if any late running took place. Again I had Arthur Thomas as my instructor on D6, named *Whernside*, and was duly passed out with inspector Jack Bates. Further diesel training

The Saltley breakdown train in Washwood Heath up sidings behind '8F' 2-8-0 No 48646. The Nechells gasholder is in the background. *Derek Sharpe*

took place in June. Six of us were detailed to travel to Tyseley to train on the Brush 2,750 hp locomotive; ex-GWR drivers and fitters were also being trained on one there, which had just been delivered from the Brush works at Loughborough. We had a week's training, but as the locomotive parts were dismantled for the fitters' benefit, we never even started the engine, let alone drove it, and it would be over 12 months before I would drive one.

The following week the same six of us were detailed to sign on duty at 7.15 am to travel to Derby to attend the new diesel training school. One of the lecturers was Jack Allen, the ex-New Street footplate inspector who passed me out on my first DMU. He lived near me so we travelled together for the week from Great Barr station. The school time was from 9.00 am to 5.00 pm, so by the time we arrived back at our depot we had 12 hours on duty.

Men from Crewe, Sheffield, Nottingham and Leeds (who lodged at Derby for the week) attended. Canteen facilities were made available to us at Derby loco depot for lunch, and tea or coffee was brought round to us mid-morning and mid-afternoon. It was like being in heaven compared with our normal way of eating our sandwiches on the footplate or in the mess room. This schooling was highly intensified, but at the end of the week we were more conversant with our locomotives.

On 20 June 1962 I had to take a medical examination at Derby, having attained 40 years of age the previous day. I expected to be told to lose weight but, unlike the New Street doctor, the Derby one said I was all right and he would see me again in five years time.

Amongst all the diesel training, steam traction was still going on. One Sunday in July I was rostered to work a steam-hauled excursion to Rhyl. We booked on at 6.50 am and were allocated 'Jubilee' 4-6-0 No 45690 *Leander*. This was prepared for us, but my fireman, Brian Phillips, brought to my attention that there was no mouthpiece shield and baffle-plate in the firing hole of the firebox. These were protectors for the firing ring and for the depletion of air under the brick, to mix with the fire gases. I made out a repair card and gave it to the fitters, stating that we were now due off the depot. Another fitter arrived about 10 minutes later to say that they did not have any. I immediately went to the running shift foreman and explained the position. He shrugged his shoulders, saying, 'If he hasn't got any you'll have to do without.'

'If you think I'm taking an engine off the shed in that condition and it will be my responsibility, you're mistaken,' I replied. 'If they haven't got the parts we'll have another engine.'

Having been provided with the missing parts, we left the depot 35 minutes late and went light engine to Kings Norton, picked up 12 coaches weighing 368 tons, took them to Northfield, where we ran around the train, then proceeded on our journey, stopping at Kings Norton, Bournville, Selly Oak and New Street. We departed via Aston, Bescot, Bushbury and Crewe. As I did not sign the road from there, a conductor driver climbed on our footplate.

I said to my mate, 'If you want to ride in the train I'll fire it from here, but bring me a bottle of beer when we arrive at Rhyl, as there are no pubs open on a Sunday there.'

The conductor driver worked the locomotive far heavier than I would have done on a fairly level road, and on arriving at Rhyl around 12.45 pm I was glad of the bottle of beer. By the time we had stabled the coaches and taken the engine to the depot it was around 1.30 pm. After we had consumed our sandwiches we took a walk along the seafront towards the Kimnel Bay end where they were experimenting with the new hovercrafts.

We were sitting on the sea wall watching them, Brian in his new black fireman's jacket, when a seagull flew over and dropped his load over Brian's jacket. I laughed as he tried to wipe the mess off, saying 'That bird has flown all along the seashore to find the only Saltley fireman here today.'

We booked on around 6.00 pm to work the return train at 7.00 pm. I again fired the engine to Crewe, where Brian rejoined me, again with a bottle of beer, although I hadn't asked for one this time. We booked off duty around 1.00 am, which was equal to over 31

hours pay. Brian left the railway about a year later, but after a couple of years came back as a guard, and I often pulled his leg about the seagull.

The following Friday I booked on at 1.40 pm to work a summer special passenger train from Torquay to Sheffield with 'Black Five' No 44852 and fireman John Burke. When we arrived at Sheffield we were booked to take the coaches to Heeley carriage sidings, then to take the engine to Canklow loco depot near Rotherham. We met with some delay and it was around 7.00 pm when we left our engine at the depot. I inquired of the foreman, 'Have you a service home for us to get to Sheffield to catch our booked train at 7.30 pm?'

He replied that he hadn't and gave us vouchers to travel on a Corporation bus. We missed our train by half an hour, which meant a long wait until 11.00 pm for the next train home, the Newcastle to Bristol Mail. In the meantime we adjourned to the railway club and had a couple of pints and fish and chips before catching the Mail, booking off duty around 1.45 am.

It had been a very hot day and I decided to have a shower in the new amenity block. As I started up my motor cycle there was a flash of lightning and a roll of thunder, followed by heavy rain. I decided to carry on, but more heavy rain poured down. As I passed Aston Hall Park near Aston Villa football ground, flood water was running across the road. As the motor cycle splashed through it, the engine stopped. I tried to kick-start it a few times, but to no avail. I pushed it to Perry Barr, where there was a little downhill run, and tried to start it, but again it would not, so I pushed it up the hill to Great Barr and home. It was now around 4.00 am, and as I was wearing my leggings and mackintosh I was wet outside and inside with perspiration. As I opened the door to the house my wife came to the top of the stairs and shouted, 'Is that you Bill? I was worried about you being so late.'

'Don't worry,' I replied. 'I'm now at Saltley again, and hours and overtime are different from Monument Lane. Throw me a couple of bath towels as I'm going to have another bath!'

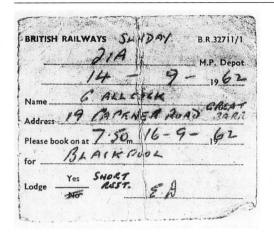

BRITISH RAILWAYS SUNDAY B.R.32711/1

21A

14 - 9 - 19 62 M.P. Depot

Name G. ALLCOCK

Address 19 CARTNER ROAD GREAT BARR

Please book on at 7.50 m 16-9- 19 62

for BLACKPOOL

Lodge Yes SHORT
       No   REST.   E.A.

The train ticket for our trip to Blackpool on 16 September 1962. This would have been delivered to me by a messenger or call-boy the day before, instructing me of the duty and when to book on.

One Sunday later in the month I had to sign on duty at 7.50 am for a short rest job to Blackpool. When I booked on I could see the reason for me having the job. We were booked to go light engine to Kings Norton, where the special started, then come into New Street station via the Camp Hill line. We left New Street via the Monument Lane Tunnel to Dudley Port, where we picked up further passengers. We then carried on to Tipton, where we were diverted via the Prince's End line owing to permanent way work on the Bushbury to Stafford line. This took us to Wednesbury and Walsall, then via the Cannock line, joining the Crewe line at Rugeley Trent Valley.

We had No 45575 and we had been on duty some 2½ hours when we stopped for water at Walsall, where my mate remarked, 'Is this all the distance we have come in this time? I thought we'd be halfway to Blackpool by now.'

'Give me the tea can,' I replied. 'I'll make another brew while you get water. It's going to be a long day.'

We eventually arrived at the seaside around 1.00 pm, but by the time the coaches had been taken off us and we took the engine to the depot, it was about 2.30 pm when we signed off duty.

There was a railway barracks there and after having a wash and taking our food, we had a stroll along the front and the Pleasure Beach. We booked on duty again at 9.00 pm to work back at 10.30. We were diagrammed to travel along our normal route from Stafford to Wolverhampton, as the permanent way work had been completed, but it was 4.35 am on Monday before we signed off duty, and as my week's rostered duty began around 11.00 am, and I had to have my 12 hours rest, I booked on at 4.35 pm. It was Wednesday before I could book on for my proper shift. These jobs would normally have been worked by Monument Lane or Aston men, but after Monument Lane had claimed the Hull job some years earlier, because they were starting from there, Saltley was doing the same. There were about a dozen drivers who had returned to Saltley from Monument Lane who signed the route to Crewe; about four of us signed for Blackpool or Llandudno, so I was getting the benefits of both depots.

The following week I was on the 4.00 pm shift, and when booking on at that time on the Thursday, the timekeeper said, 'The roster clerk wants to see you.' I went to Norman Beckett's office (he had been a fireman but owing to ill health had to come off footplate duties and had been found a clerical position). He said, 'I want you to book on at 12.00 pm on Friday so that you can sign off duty at 8.00 pm, then I need you to book on at 8.00 am on Saturday morning for a short rest job to Blackpool, then book on again on Saturday night for an extra turn of duty.'

He showed me the workings of the train and I could see that it was shown to stop at Great Barr station (now called Hamstead). I asked him, 'Can you do me a good turn - can you get one of my free travel passes for my wife and two children for them to travel to Blackpool?' The proper procedure was to give a week's notice when applying for travel passes.

'I'll see the chief clerk and tell him you are doing us a good turn,' he replied. When I signed on duty on the Friday my family's pass was waiting for me.

I duly booked on duty at 8.07 am with 'Jubilee' No 45660 *Rooke* and fireman Jack

Gregory to go light engine to Kings Norton. As Jack hooked up, I told the guard that my family would be joining us at Great Barr; he said that he would put three reserved tickets for them in the coach nearest to the engine. We took the empty coaches to Northfield, where we ran round, then departed, stopping at Kings Norton, Bournville, Selly Oak, New Street, Aston, Perry Barr and Great Barr. Unfortunately my family would not have as good a view of the line or my work as they had when travelling in the DMUs.

We arrived at Blackpool around 1.00 pm and one of the first passengers to alight, a middle-aged lady, came up to us and gave me a half-crown, saying, 'Have a drink with me.' That was the only tip I ever received in 48 years of railway work.

We left Blackpool at 11.30 pm, and were diverted via Ormskirk and St Helens to Crewe, so I had a Wigan driver to conduct me. He was a small fellow wearing clogs, and with a scarf round his neck.

I said to Jack, 'You can get in the train to Crewe - I'll put a bit of coal on.'

I afterwards wished that I had not volunteered, for although the driver was small in stature, it did not stop him opening the regulator fully. I did not mind that, as that was the way I worked 'Jubilees', but he hardly wound the reversing lever up to the 50 per cent mark, whereas I would have brought it back to 30 per cent or even 25. He certainly kept me busy to Crewe, where he alighted, and Jack came up with a welcome bottle of ale, saying, 'How are you? I could see the sparks going up like rockets.'

'A bit warm,' I replied.

As we went along in the cool night air I could feel the sweat going cold around my back, so I had to put my coat on. I duly dropped my family at Great Barr at around 3.30 am for the half-hour walk home.

While I had been away at Monument Lane, Saltley had acquired about 20 of the new Class '9F' 2-10-0 freight locomotives. Some were fitted with mechanical stokers and were experimented with on the Carlisle jobs. I had no experience of them, but this was soon to be rectified. There had been a new oil and petrol depot opened at Bromford

Bridge and I was booked for a few weeks working empty fuel tanks from there, bound for Avonmouth Docks, as far as Gloucester, then worked a return train heavily loaded with fuel. My fireman for these few weeks was Ken Griffin, a tall chap who had recently returned from army service in the Palestine police. Unfortunately, in later years, he was laid up with severe arthritis and ended his days as a driver, coming to work in an invalid car for shunting duties.

However, on the first day of these jobs we had No 92135 and worked down to Gloucester without incident. On the return journey Ken remarked, 'You're working the engine too light. Open her up a bit.'

It was unusual for a fireman to say this - they usually complained if you worked too heavy. Passing Abbotswood Junction I could see that we were 3 minutes late, so Ken had been right, having worked on these trains

By 1962 Saltley had acquired about 20 of the new Class '9F' 2-10-0 freight locomotives. My first experience of driving one was with No 92135, seen here, to Gloucester and back. *M. Payne*

before. On the following day I let Ken do the driving to Gloucester and I drove back. On the Wednesday I drove to Gloucester and told him to drive back. At first he refused, saying 'It's too hard for you.'

'I'm still fit,' I retorted. 'If I get tired I'll let you know.'

I proved my point by firing it home. This train's weight was over 1,000 tons and as well as the Class '9' locomotive we needed three bank engines up the Lickey incline.

I was still not finished with learning. In December 1962 I was surprised to see that I was rostered for another week at the DMU school at Derby. I said to the roster clerk, 'I've already attended a school for DMUs at Bescot while I was at Monument Lane.'

'We don't count that at Saltley,' he replied. 'Derby school is the proper place.'

I saw Jack Allen again as a lecturer, and as he was living at Great Barr, I enjoyed travelling with him throughout the week. It was a more intensive course than before, and on the last day we were taken to the Derby workshops to see units being made and refurbished, seeing parts that were normally invisible.

That month I also worked my first Brush/Sulzer Type 4 from New Street to Sheffield on a special from Bristol to Leeds, returning with D41. On the following day I had the same workings with Nos D135 and D142.

On Sunday 30 December I was rostered to book on at 10.30 am to work a special train from New Street to Sheffield, but there was heavy snow overnight and it was impossible to ride my motorcycle, so I travelled into New Street by bus, and as we were booked to relieve the train there, I rang the timekeeper to ask him to book me on duty. He replied, 'Your train hasn't left Bristol yet, and we're working a relief train with you. The engine has gone to Kings Norton to fetch the coaches. Stay there and I'll send fireman John Bloor to you.'

The train arrived with BR Standard Class '5' 4-6-0 No 73134 on front. This Class had a nice double cab for a snowy day. We worked to Sheffield and were booked to take the locomotive to Millhouses loco and travel home as passenger, but as all trains were running late, we were instructed to turn our engine on the turntable at Sheffield station and work a special train back with our coaches to Birmingham. However, there were so many passengers for stations beyond that we were relieved for Bristol. I gave my timesheet to John and went home from New Street station, not having been to the depot that day.

During the week of 28 January 1963 I was rostered to book on at 1.50 am to work the 2.30 am Newcastle to Bristol Mail from New Street to Bristol via Worcester. I had worked on this train as a fireman many years before, but with diesels it was an easier job for the fireman as he had only to work the oil-fuelled boiler to provide heat for the train.

On the Saturday, just before our departure with the 7.40 am from Bristol, I was given a special stop order for Berkeley Junction station. I had never stopped there before as a fireman or a driver, and was at a point where we should be doing our top speed of 75 mph, which was the line speed, although our diesel locomotive, D164, had a maximum speed restriction of 90 mph. Passing the intermediate block signal at Wick, I closed the power handle and started to apply the brake. We were running rather fast approaching the platform but I had a few inches of vacuum in reserve, which I used and made a good stop. About 100 children were there to join the train.

A new job had been allocated to the depot, which entailed booking on duty at 8.45 pm to travel to Walsall to relieve a parcels train and work it to Derby via Brownhills and Lichfield. Then another parcels train was worked home via the normal route through Tamworth. This work had been placed in the top passenger link, but most of the drivers did not sign the road from Walsall to Wichnor. I had several weeks conducting the drivers when on an afternoon shift, until they learned the route. One week I can recall I was with driver Ernie Mapp, an elderly man, on 'Black Five' locomotives in heavy frosty weather, and he was frozen standing behind me. I tried to get him to ride in the train where he would be warmer, but he refused as the rule book stated he should be on the footplate. As I write this he is still alive, aged 95.

One Saturday morning I relieved a DMU at 7.30 am coming from Redditch to work to Leicester. As I was running towards Castle Bromwich I noticed that we were not going as fast as we should have been. I checked the engines, and all were showing a light. At Water Orton I stopped at the platform to see if I could see anything wrong, and spoke to the guard who said he would ride in the last unit to check it out. At Coleshill he came up to me to say, 'There's a lot of smoke and a smell of burning oil from one of the engines on the rear coach.' I and walked back and could hardly approach the engine, it was that hot! I had heard of a similar incident when at Monument Lane where the engine had caught fire, so I suspected that the final drive had not reversed at Redditch.

I shut down the engine and tried to isolate it from the final drive, but without success. I said to the guard, 'We'll have to get all the passengers off the train, then we must go into the sidings to clear the main line so I can examine it properly.'

I informed the porter to tell the signalmen what we needed to do. When we were safe in the sidings I had to open a door in the floor of the coach to see that the tell-tale arrow above the final drive gear box was pointing in the wrong direction. I again tried to isolate it manually without success, so decided that we needed fitters with appropriate tools. After about an hour two fitters arrived; I explained to them that I thought the forks that operated the final drive must be broken. When Mick Merril removed the top of the box holding the final drive, we could see that this was so.

'How did you guess that?' asked the fitter.

'The same thing happened with a Monument Lane man,' I answered. 'The final drive light only shows that it's fully over, not which direction it's in.'

The fitter used his tools to do the isolating and on completion I went to the signal box to speak to Control. They instructed me to take the unit to Derby Works for examination. On arrival there I made out a repair card reporting the defects.

About a week later I was called into the shedmaster's office to see Mr Lowe, who used to be at Monument Lane depot. He recognised me and, after a few pleasantries, asked me for an explanation of the incident. I told him everything and how I had suspected that the selector forks had broken.

'There must be some distinction in the final drive light to indicate which direction of travel the engine is in,' I said.

He agreed with me and said that he would make recommendations for this to be altered. It was never done, however, and afterwards I used to watch the final drive light when reversing to see it go out momentarily as the change-over occurred.

Another night conducting job involved booking on at 9.00 pm, walking to Bordesley Junction, which took about 25 minutes, then conducting Western Region men on a Swindon to Longbridge freight train via New Street station, carrying car bodies for the Austin motor works. The first night we had a Class '9F' 2-10-0 on front and were stopped between the mouth of Proof House Tunnel and New Street station. When the signal cleared I had a struggle to restart the train. The next night we had No 73012, a BR Standard Class '5' and were again stopped outside New Street station, but this time I could not start the train at all, owing to the bigger driving wheels slipping and the weight of the train pulling us backwards into the tunnel. As we got into the tunnel we were covered in smoke and steam, which nearly choked us.

I stopped the train and sent the fireman to New Street No 5 signal box for the West Pilot engine to give us a pull through the station to Five Ways Junction. While we waited for our return train at Longbridge I telephoned New Street No 5 signal box and said to the signal man that if I did not have a clear distant signal at Proof House to indicate I was clear to run through the station, I would stay there until it was clear, so I could have a run with the train through the tunnel and the sharp curves of the platform roads. When I signed off duty I made out a report stating what I intended to do. The rest of the week I stopped at Proof House Junction until the distant signal cleared and had a trouble-free run.

In February we heard of the death of inspector Jack Bates, and a good crowd of us footplatemen attended his funeral. A few days later I was due to work the 12.40 express from New Street to Sheffield, booked with a 'Peak'. I inquired how it was running from the West Country and was informed that it was reported 45 minutes late. I said to my mate, 'We'll go into the mess room', and added 'I bet we have a steam locomotive on it!'

After a while a platform inspector looked in and said to me, 'Inspector Locke is on number 7 platform asking for the driver of the 12.40 pm.'

After 45 minutes we wandered over. Mr Locke spotted me and shouted, 'Where have you been?'

I replied, 'In the mess room. I don't fancy standing on a draughty platform for 45 minutes', adding, 'I expect it's got a steamer on front.'

He snorted. 'It can't have. We have a dynamometer car on the rear testing the route.'

The train arrived 55 minutes late and we relieved the Bristol men with their inspector on 'Jubilee' No 45577 *Bengal*. They said the diesel locomotive had failed and this was the only replacement available. While we stood at New Street Mr Locke put some overalls over his suit and exchanged his bowler hat for a beret. He said, 'I don't know this route. I'm covering for Mr Bates', and added, 'I'll rely on you to obey the speed restrictions correctly.'

'I'll do my best,' I replied, 'considering we have no speedometer.'

We had a good run and when we entered the short tunnel just outside Sheffield station I heard Mr Locke, who was standing behind me, give a shout.

'What did you say?' I shouted back.

We had cleared the tunnel by now and were running over the points at the south end of the station. He said, 'I've lost my hat, it's blown off in the tunnel.

'It's a good job you have a bowler to put on,' I said, jumping on to the platform when

we stopped to change over with the Leeds men. I remarked to them, as had been said to me some years before, 'The inspector's going through to Leeds with you. Don't trust him - he would report his own grandmother.'

As we were about an hour late, our return train was waiting for us with D27 on front, and it was a case of eating our sandwiches as we worked home.

On Whit Sunday, 2 June, I was rostered on another Blackpool job, with drastic results! I booked on at 7.50 am with fireman Colin Lucock and 'Black Five' No 45040. On the return trip we approached Moore water troughs where we needed water. I shouted to Colin, 'Don't put the scoop down too soon. There is a farm level crossing just before the troughs. I'll tell you when.'

At the appropriate time I shouted to him, but we did not get a drop of water. I looked at the water gauge approaching Crewe and could see we had only 500 gallons, insufficient to get us to the next water point at Whitmore troughs between Crewe and Stafford. I decided to stop at Crewe station and told my mate to telephone the signalman to inform him that we needed water.

The overhead electrification had taken place some years before and in order to get water we had to hook our engine off the train and move into number 3 bay, which had no overhead wires to endanger anyone climbing on to the top of the tender. We went forward over the North junction and reversed to run into the bay, then I heard a rumbling and a crash of metal. I immediately stopped and climbed on to the ballast, expecting to see us derailed. However, all I could see was the bottom part of the water scoop on the track. We picked it up, placed it on the footplate and carried on into the bay, where we filled the water tank.

When Colin telephoned the signalman to tell him that we were ready to rejoin our train, he informed us that we had damaged the points and he could not get us back to the train. He added that we had to change over to the South standby locomotive, 'Britannia' Class '7P' 4-6-2 No 70051 *Firth of Forth*.

The Crewe men had backed on to our

train, so we climbed on to the footplate and explained about our water scoop, departing about 30 minutes late. It was the first time either of us had been on one of these locomotives and we were amazed at the extra power we had compared with the 'Black Five'. We were able to pull back 15 minutes of our delay to New Street. When we dropped 70051 at our depot around 7.00 am on the Monday morning, Les Mitchell, the outside foreman, exclaimed, 'We don't want that Class of engine here! Why didn't you take it to Monument Lane or Aston?'

'We've been on duty since 7.50 am yesterday,' I replied. 'Get someone else to take it.'

When signing off duty I made out a report explaining the circumstances at Crewe. The sequel came a couple of weeks later. I was asked for a further report, then after another fortnight I was issued with a Form 1, charging me with damaging the water scoop and the points at Crewe station. I asked for a union representative for the hearing, and was allocated Mr Les Felton.

Mr Edwards was the superintendent who read out the charge, and asked for my explanation. I told him as accurately as I could what had transpired. He said, 'Water scoops are regularly damaged by the farm crossing at Moore through being dropped too soon. You must have done that.'

'I was most careful delaying my mate from operating the scoop as I knew of the crossing,' I replied. 'If it had been damaged there it would have been knocked off there instead of at Crewe. It must have been damaged at Blackpool and was trailing to Crewe. When we reversed it met resistance and was broken off.'

'How do you know that?' asked Mr Edwards.

'I picked it up and put it on the footplate,' I replied.

He tried another approach. 'Did you examine the engine before you left the depot at Blackpool?'

'No,' I replied. 'The engine was prepared for me and backed on to the train, and we had only 5 minutes when we got on it before we departed.'

After a long interview, with Les Felton stating that I was an experienced driver over that route, having worked trains there for over 5 years and not having experienced trouble getting water at Moore before, it was decided to adjourn the interview to inquire from Crewe whether the scoop was on the footplate when No 45040 arrived at Crewe depot.

I never heard any more on the subject so I presumed they were satisfied with my explanation.

9
NEW ROUTES
1963-65

When I reviewed my route card in June I inquired if I could have a refresher run from Rotherham to Carlisle, which I had asked for six months previously without success, otherwise I would have to cross it off my card. The roster clerk remarked, 'We have plenty of spare drivers signing that road now we have diesel locomotives, different from the steam days. But we have some new work over the old GWR route from Bordesley to Banbury and Oxford. I'll book you to learn that route from next Monday.'

I duly booked on at 8.00 am and travelled on the 9.00 am DMU from Snow Hill to Oxford via Solihull, Leamington, Banbury, Aynho Junction and Oxford Hinksey sidings.

One day, after walking around Hinksey sidings for a couple of hours looking at the elaborate GWR signals, I arrived back at Oxford station for my train back to Birmingham. As a Paddington to Worcester express with a 'Castle' Class locomotive on the front ran in behind me, I heard a lot of whistling. As the locomotive drew abreast of me it stopped, the driver jumped off and dashed towards the rear of the train, and the fireman shouted to me 'Look after the engine', and dashed to the signal box in front.

The guard came up to me saying, 'Did you see what happened?'

'No,' I replied. 'I had my back to the train.'

He said, 'A woman stood on the level crossing as we ran in.'

I got down on to the track and had a look at the front of the locomotive to see blood splattered around the buffer beam. I thought with all the rodding and connecting rods of the pistons underneath she must have been chewed up! The driver eventually came back and drew the train to the end of the platform, so I went back to the rear to see a policeman picking up shoes and human remains and putting them into a bag.

There were three other drivers learning the route to Banbury at the same period and I used to meet them en route. One was Fred Cooke, who was a committee man on the Saltley Self-Help Fund. This had been started in 1922 to provide sickness, convalescence and death benefits for the staff at Saltley depot. Fred informed me that the annual general meeting was to be held on one of the Sundays during our route learning, and asked me to come along. When the nominations for committee were called for he nominated me, and I was duly elected, so I was again involved with welfare work.

I finished my route learning after four weeks and signed my road card for this new route, but it would be a few weeks before I would work over it. During this wait I was rostered for a week's work booking on duty at 5.25 pm to work an express passenger train from New Street to Sheffield, returning with the Newcastle to Bristol Mail train and arriving at Birmingham around 1.00 am. When booking on for this turn on the Thursday I was called into the running shift foreman's office where the foreman, Harold Evans, was waiting for me. He said, 'I'm taking you off your job to go on the breakdown train.'

'Is it an emergency?' I asked. 'Where is it going?'

'Nowhere,' he replied. 'It's standing by because the Royal Train with the Queen on board is to run in our area from Kenilworth for the Royal Show.'

'What about my mileage payments for the Sheffield job?' I asked.

'You'll be paid any loss of earnings - you're the only driver available who signs the route to Kenilworth via the three routes: the Berkswell branch, Coventry and Leamington. The train with engine 44660 coupled to it is standing on No 1 road and we may need to turn it out at a moment's notice, so take your fireman and stay on the engine. Don't go into the mess room.'

We made a can of tea and joined our locomotive, which was in full steam. I spoke to the breakdown train foreman, Tommy Mackintosh, and could see that he had his crew in their mess van on the train. We all sat in our appropriate positions patiently until around 10.30 pm, when Jobie Leight, the outside foreman, came across to us and shouted, 'The Queen is tucked safely in bed and she says you can do the same', so we had an early finish without turning a wheel.

On August Bank Holiday Monday I again worked the 'City of Birmingham Holiday Express' as I had done in 1958 when at the Monument Lane depot. It had gone to Weston-super-Mare in the morning and we worked a West Country train around 4.00 pm from New Street to Bristol with D39, with Brian Heath as my mate. We then relieved a steam locomotive, 'Black Five' No 44659, as it returned from Weston to Birmingham. As we were travelling at top speed towards Coaley, a flurry of feathers scattered around us, and I remarked, 'It looks at though we've hit a pheasant.'

We stopped at Gloucester South Junction for water and while Brian filled the tank, I walked around the locomotive making a cur-

sory examination. As I looked on the framing under the smokebox door I could see a dead swallow. I picked it up and climbed back on to the footplate. I could hear Brian busy on the top of the tender, and I spotted his black jacket hanging in his corner, so I dropped the bird in his pocket. We worked into New Street around 10.30 pm and took the empty coaches to Monument Lane carriage sidings, then started tender first to our depot. Because of the chilly night air Brian put his jacket on, and I could see him in the firelight put his hand in his pocket and withdraw it quickly. Then, more cautiously, he put his hand in again, and pulled out the swallow.

'Look at this,' he said to our guard. 'I remember we hit a bird coming down to Gloucester, but how did it get into my jacket pocket?'

There followed a discussion between them on aerodynamics and the theory that the bird had been sucked into the cab by the front of the tender and into the corner of the footplate! I kept quiet and smiled in the darkness. He spoke about it many times for years afterwards and it was when he was about to take a managerial position on the Eastern Region some 10 years later that I informed him how the swallow had really got there.

In September I had my first trip over the newly learned road to Oxford. It entailed booking on duty at 11.30 am to go light engine to Washwood Heath and work a fully fitted braked freight train for Southampton as far as Oxford North Junction, where we uncoupled from the train and turned the locomotive at Oxford Loco. We then ran light engine to Hinksey sidings and worked another fully fitted train to Water Orton.

I had the regular link fireman, Fred Lloyd, and when I climbed on to No 44966 I could

On 25 June 1964 '9F' 2-10-0 No 92087 arrives at Oxford beneath the fine gantry of Western Region lower-quadrant signals, which had replaced earlier GWR signals in 1959. Oxford Station North signal box is behind the locomotive, while Oxford North Junction is indicated by the distant forest of semaphores. *K. C. H. Fairey*

see that he had cleaned up the footplate and washed the coal down for our tender-first run into Washwood Heath. We had an uneventful run both ways. I could see that he was keen on his job, so when we backed on to our train at Hinksey the next day with No 45647, I asked him, 'Do you know the road?'

'I think so, but I've not driven over it,' he replied.

'Come over this side and try your hand at driving,' I answered. 'If you're not sure of anything, shout out.'

He worked the train quite well without any trouble! On the following Wednesday I told him to work the train outwards with No 45674, but after getting water at Aynho troughs, the exhaust injector, which puts water into the boiler, started to give us trouble by not working and we had to use the live steam injector to get us to Oxford. On the loco depot I reported the failure to the foreman fitter, who sent a couple of his men to repair it.

After about half an hour, when they had dismantled the injector, they said, 'One of the cones is damaged and we haven't got a spare one here. You'll have to take another engine.'

I reported it to the shed foreman, who said, 'The only locomotive we have is 6928 (an ex-Great Western 'Grange' Class 4-6-0). Will you take it?'

'We'll have a go with it,' I answered.

We worked back without any trouble, and as the engine was right-hand drive compared to our left-hand drive ones, I could see some of the Western signals placed on the right-hand side of the track, which was much better than looking from an ex-LMS footplate.

A few weeks later we had another new train. We booked on duty at 2.15 pm to work a semi-fitted freight train from Washwood Heath to Cardiff as far as Gloucester, and work a return freight home. We were booked an ex-GWR 'Hall' Class 4-6-0 and I had fireman Brian Heath with me again. We had no trouble all week with this strange class of engine, except that the relieving fireman complained to Brian that the coal in the tender was out of reach.

I interjected, 'We've come non-stop from Bromsgrove and my mate isn't climbing into the tender while we're on the move.'

On Saturday Jack Siggs, who had passed out as a driver with me some years before, was acting shift foreman. As I booked on duty he came to me and said, 'Your Great Western engine has been failed by the fitters - will you take one of our "Crab" 2-6-0s?'

'I will,' I replied, 'but I don't know about the Cardiff men at Gloucester.'

As we had no return workings, and travelling home as passenger meant an early finish, I said to Brian, 'We'll have to persuade the Cardiff men to take to this locomotive.'

When we arrived at Gloucester the new driver was a bit apprehensive and inquired, 'What sort of locomotive is this?'

'This is one of our top express freight locomotives,' I explained, 'better than your engines we've had all week.'

I explained the working parts, and Brian said to the fireman, 'You've got plenty of coal today - our tenders have doors on for easy access.'

At last they agreed to take it and we stood on the platform and watched them depart over the river bridge with the exhaust beats disappearing in the distance.

I was working the 5.52 pm Sheffield turn again a few weeks later, and on the Thursday we had trouble with the 'Peak', D34. When I shut off power to coast through Clay Cross Tunnel the engine stopped, but I managed to restart it with the starter button while on the move! We were not booked to stop at Chesterfield so I could not look for the cause, but I sent my mate to have a look in the engine room, but he could not find anything amiss. When coasting again at Dore & Totley the engine cut out once more. I restarted it on the move, but at Queens Road cutting it stopped again. This time it would not restart, and we ground to a halt within sight of Sheffield station. I made out a Wrong Line Order for my mate to take to the signalman to allow an assisting locomotive to come and pull us into the platform. While he was away I looked into the engine room and diagnosed low lubricating oil, which I reported to the fitters who came to meet us on our arrival. Incidentally, that was the only

Wrong Line Order I ever made out in almost 30 years of driving.

In October I had a Sunday turn conducting Gloucester men via the Sutton Coldfield line to Derby, returning over the site of the disaster in which their men had been involved some years before. At the end of October more DMU training was the order. Gloucester men were working Western Region four-car sets, called 'Inter-City' units, which came from Cardiff to Sheffield all week, but on Sundays Saltley men were booked to take over from Birmingham. These units comprised two power cars on either end of the train, with two trailer cars in the centre. They could be coupled to another unit and there was a corridor throughout the train which could be connected to both units. This meant that the driving compartment was small, tucked into the left-hand side of the coach. There was no room or a seat for a mate or for anyone training or road learning.

At the end of the week I passed out with inspector Charles Weston who had replaced the late Jack Bates. He was an ex-Great Western man from Wolverhampton and I found him an extremely fair man in the years I worked with him. I was soon driving these, as on the following Sunday I booked on at 11.45 am to relieve two units, Nos 52134 and 52132, and found them far more powerful when climbing up the bank from Chesterfield to Bradway Tunnel and on the return run from Sheffield to Dore & Totley.

In the winter workings, which started in October, two drivers, who had been at the now closed Bournville loco depot, had been promoted to the top passenger link. In the November I was rostered for a week's work, booking on at 9.10 am to work the 10.10 from New Street to Bristol with fireman Jack Gregory (one of my Blackpool firemen). On the Monday these men came and asked if they could ride with us to learn the road to Bristol. I handled the controls on the first day and asked how long they had been learning the route, and explained some of the intricacies and speed restrictions on the way.

On Tuesday I invited them to drive, telling them that if they were uncertain of anything to shout out. They took it in turns

outward and returning for the rest of the week without any trouble, until returning on the 1.30 pm from Bristol on the Friday. After leaving Mangotsfield we were travelling through Westerleigh sidings at about 60 mph with all signals clear when, after going through the overbridge at Westerleigh North, Tom Porter, who was driving, shouted, 'The starting signal's at danger!'

He made an emergency stop, but we were over a train's length past the signal when we stopped. I sent Jack back to the signalman to find out what had gone wrong. In the meantime, Tom was quite upset, saying, 'I'm sure all the distant signals were clear.'

I tried to reassure him, although he was about 20 years older than me, by telling him that I had seen the clear signals as well. My fireman returned some 10 minutes later to say that the signalman at Westerleigh South box had spotted a door handle partially open when we passed him and had signalled to the North box to stop us. Jack had informed the guard, who had rectified it, so we could proceed some 15 minutes late.

On the last week of 1963 I was rostered on duty at 9.22 pm to work the 10.40 pm Royal Mail train to Sheffield and a parcels train back home, with fireman John Williams (a son of a Saltley driver, who eventually left the railway and worked alongside my son). On New Year's Eve we should have had a diesel locomotive, but on arrival at New Street we found that we had 'Jubilee' No 45612 Jamaica. I had taken a small bottle of brandy to work with me, and while standing at Derby for mail to be loaded, with Jack on the top of the tender getting water, I went to the Carriage & Wagon examiner's cabin and made a can of coffee. As we approached Ambergate I could see that it was about 2 minutes to midnight, so I poured the rest of the brandy into the remains of the coffee. As we passed Crich signal box we could see that his clock showed midnight, so I whistled a couple of 'crows'. The signalman came to the window with a cup of something in his hand and waved at us.

I shouted to John 'Happy New Year!', and offered him the tea can, saying, 'Sorry, we've only got coffee to let the New Year in with!'

I looked at his face in the firelight and saw his expression change. He laughed and remarked, 'It should be a good year if this is a taste of it.'

We had our usual diesel on the return trip.

The next night we arrived at New Street to be informed that our train was 1½ hours late from Bristol. We expected the worst, with a steamer on the front again, but were happy to see diesel D42 arriving 100 minutes late. We managed to pull a bit of time back, arriving at Sheffield only 86 minutes late, but our return train had left so we had to travel home on the first passenger train around 7.00 am, so we showed 11 hrs 23 mins on duty.

The following week I was rostered on duty at 3.12 am with fireman Gordon Hopkinson to work a freight train from Washwood Heath to Banbury and back. We had a mixture of steam locomotives from new British Railways Standard Class '9F' 2-10-0s to ex-GWR 'Hall' and 'Grange' 4-6-0s and our own Class '8F' 2-8-0s.

On the Thursday when we arrived at Banbury with Class '9F' No 92236, instead of being relieved by Didcot men for Moreton Cutting, the yard foreman instructed the shunter to unhook us from the train, and said to me, 'Go to the loco depot and turn your locomotive. One of the diesel locomotives on the Southampton to Bromford Esso oil depot has failed and left half of the train here for you to work.'

We backed on to the oil tank train and on the slight incline out of Banbury to Fenny Compton I could feel its weight. I had the Leamington distant at clear and again at Warwick, so in the slight downhill run I got up as much speed as I could for the climb up the stiffer gradient to Hatton. As we neared the summit we were hardly moving, although Gordon was providing me with a good head of steam, just under the blowing-off mark at 225 psi, and I had the regulator wide open and the reversing lever right down to its limit.

'If she slips we've had it,' I said.

We gradually breasted the summit and on the easy running through Hatton station I got the train running faster for the slight rise towards Rowington water troughs, where we had enough speed to fill the tank. We carried

Type 3 Sulzer Bo-Bo diesel-electric (later Class 33) No D6533 passes Fladbury, on the Oxford-Worcester line with an up fitted Esso oil tanker train on 18 May 1963, the same year that we had to relieve such a train with a Class '9' - and struggled up Hatton Bank! *Michael Mensing*

on to the Esso sidings and brought the locomotive back to our depot.

I remarked to Gordon and our guard, 'Those Sulzer diesels [later Class 33] must be strong, as two of them regularly work the train and we've had only half of it with the strongest steam locomotive that British Railways has, and only just managed it.'

We had snow and icy weather in the last week of January 1964, and I was rostered to sign on duty at 8.45 pm with fireman Brian Knight to travel to Walsall to work a parcels train coming from Worcester to Derby, then relieve a fully fitted York Dringhouses to Washwood Heath freight train with an ex-LNER 'B1' 4-6-0 on the front. Brian was an old hand fireman and it was his link's working, and after watching him work on the first day I worked a day about with him, with each of us driving or firing on alternative days. When our train arrived in the early hours of Saturday morning, the Derby men were quickly off the footplate and gave us our loading, but made no mention of the condition of the locomotive, No 61275.

When the signal cleared I opened the regulator and we were enveloped in steam. I thought that as we got moving it would clear, but it got worse. I could not see Brian and he in turn could not see the coal in the tender. When we passed Repton & Willington signal box I whistled to indicate that I needed to change locomotives at Burton; we were routed via the goods line from Clay Mills and stopped at Leicester Junction. I looked around the locomotive and could see that the blow-down pipe between the engine and tender was fractured. I informed Brian to go to the signal box to inform Control of our predicament.

After about 15 minutes Brian returned to say that they had no other locomotives there and we would have to take ours to Burton depot, and the train would have to be worked forward when they could get one.

When we arrived on the depot Brian went to take our overcoats off the hooks in his corner of the footplate. He shouted, 'Look at this!'

I shone my hand-lamp and could see icicles hanging around the window, caused by the condensed steam and the freezing weather.

'No wonder I get bronchitis every winter,' I remarked.

We travelled home passenger, making almost 12 hours on duty.

February brought thick smog even in daylight hours. We were booked on duty at 7.40 am to work a freight from Washwood Heath to Banbury, and on the Tuesday it took a long time owing to the denseness of the fog. We had 'Black Five' No 44944, and with our left-hand drive engine and the ex-GWR signals being on the right-hand side of the track, it was difficult to see them, so approaching each signal box and travelling with caution was the order of the day. We stood at the end of the relief line at Lapworth for ages, waiting to be turned out on to the main line for the run to Warwick; eventually we were on duty for 9 hours.

The guard walked up to us, worried about the delay, and said that he would go to the signal box, where my mate had been for a couple of hours signing Rule 55, to remind the signalman of our presence and inquire how long we would have to wait. He came back after about 15 minutes to inform me that there was no chance of a main line run now as the commuter rush-hour would soon

be started. We would have to put the train in the sidings as the relief line was needed for the local passenger trains. I then had to negotiate the signals going tender-first back to our depot, where we arrived about 6.00 pm, then had to drive my motorcycle home in the darkness and fog.

One interesting trip took me along the old North Stafford line. We booked on at 2.15 am to relieve a train of oil tanks coming from Avonmouth Docks to Longport sidings, just north of Stoke-on-Trent. We usually had a '9F' on this train, and as I did not sign the route beyond Stoke, I had a conductor driver to Longport sidings and back to Stoke loco depot. On the Thursday of that week the Stoke man said, 'They want loco No 92139 at Crewe South loco depot', so when we had put our train off at Longport we had a run along the line I had first fired over 20 years before - I took a nostalgic look as we passed my old depot at Alsager.

A few weeks later I was rostered on further main-line diesel training, this time on the smaller Type 2 Sulzer/AEI locomotives of the D5151 series, which developed 1,250 hp. There were four of us drivers on the training programme and at the end of the week we were to be passed out by the redoubtable inspector Locke. We all trooped into his office around 9.00 am and immediately he started questioning us on the different items of machinery on the locomotive. He drew a long oblong box on a piece of paper, then asked us where each item was placed in the box representing the engine room, and he wanted everything in its correct place. I made a few comments early on, then he said to me, 'You be quiet, I know you have knowledge from a few years ago.' I had only to lift my head and offer to speak and he would stop me.

When we stopped for lunch, Sid Harrison, an ex-Bournville man, remarked, 'Who's inspector Locke's favourite driver then?'

'I'm surprised,' I replied, 'as I've crossed swords with him a couple of times, but he must think I know something!'

We took D5194 on a local freight train in the afternoon, and again he watched the three others drive except me, saying, 'I've seen you drive before.'

When we returned to the depot he said that we had all passed.

A few weeks afterwards I was rostered on the 11.30 am Washwood Heath to Oxford fully freight train, and instead of the 'Jubilee' or 'Black Five' we were booked one of these diesel locomotives. I still had a fireman booked with me, George Watson, and he remarked that he was going to have an easy week. I was surprised how weak they were compared with the steam locomotives we usually had, and we had a job to keep time. I had to work the controller fully open whenever we were on a rising gradient.

As we approached Fenny Compton at around 15 mph I remarked to George, 'If I was working a steamer as heavy as this you'd be entitled to hit me with the shovel. We'd be travelling at around 30 mph with the steamers!'

Towards the end of the week we were approached Banbury North with all signals clear through the station when I shut off to coast through for the station speed restrictions and everything went quiet. The engine had shut down. I attempted to restart it with the starter button on the driving panel, but to no avail, and we came to a stand at Banbury North station signals.

I sent George to the signalman to tell him of our predicament while I had a look in the engine room. Immediately I entered I could feel the heat, and when I looked at the engine temperature gauge it was showing 195°F, far higher than the normal 165 to 175. I looked at the coolant water gauge and could see that, instead of the glass being three-quarters full, the water was just showing at the bottom. I put the coolant fan to emergency and opened all the engine room doors (an old trick of the English Electric Type 4s). After about 10 minutes an assisting engine came to rescue us, and I could see that the temperature had dropped to 175°F, so I successfully restarted the engine. We drew on to the goods line behind the station, where we hooked off the train and went on to Banbury loco depot. I informed the foreman fitter that we needed coolant water and the cooling system checking for leaks, but the fitter and his mate said that they did not

know anything about diesel locomotives as Banbury had not been allocated any. I showed them the water filling point and one of them remarked, 'I remember a connection to fit that coming to the stores a few weeks ago, and we wondered what it was for.'

Once the radiator was successfully filled I started the engine and had a look around the cooling system, where I found a Jubilee clip connection leaking; the fitter tightened it up with a screwdriver. When I was satisfied that there were no other leaks we rejoined our train and carried on to Oxford, and worked back again with our locomotive without further trouble.

As we signed off duty George remarked, 'I thought we were going to have a steamer from Banbury and my easy week would have been spoiled - it's a good job they found that connection.'

These locomotives were tried out on the Water Orton to Carlisle trains, but although they meant that the working was easier for fireman and driver, they made hard work on the 'Long Drag' from Settle to Blea Moor compared with the 'Black Fives'.

A few weeks passed and I was rostered on more main-line diesel training. This time it was the Sulzer/GEC Type 2 of the D5300 series. The Sulzer engine was the same, but with GEC electrical equipment and a more comfortable cab than the spartan AEI version. In working them I found them actually weaker than the AEI type, although they both had 1,250 hp engines and were more likely to overload, which shut off power immediately. At the end of the week four of us had to pass out, this time with inspector Weston.

He started off by saying that he would only be asking questions on the differences between the GEC locomotive and the AEI. He then added, 'There'll be no dead signalmen in here today!'

Evidently, during the previous week inspector Locke had four top link passenger drivers to pass out, and when he asked questions about a locomotive failure on the main line, one driver quite rightly answered that the signalman must be informed as soon as possible. Mr Locke replied, 'What happens if the signalman is dead?' This led to a long discussion on rules and regulations, which culminated in Mr Locke failing all the drivers for any driving at all! This put a spanner in the works of the rosters - as it was Friday afternoon, the next week's rosters had already been published, and taking these four drivers off their booked work for another week meant that their work had to be covered on a day-to-day basis.

Charlie Weston duly passed us out. This meant that I was now trained on seven main-line diesel locomotive types and five types of DMUs and shunters, and was still expected to take any type of steam locomotive, whatever Region they came from. I brought this to the notice of our trade union by asking for extra payment for every type of traction trained on, and I quoted the British Army, where soldiers were paid extra for their proficiency. However, although our branch meeting agreed and a resolution was sent to the union's head office, it was never attained.

A few weeks later I was rostered on an afternoon Washwood Heath to Banbury freight turn with fireman Ron Matthews and Standard 4-6-0 No 73139. This was an unfitted coal train with just the locomotive brake and that in the guard's van to stop it. This locomotive had Caprotti valve gear and Timken roller bearings on all axle-boxes, which made it freer running when coasting.

We had a good run from Washwood Heath, with hardly any use of the brake necessary. After passing over Rowington water troughs I shut the regulator and coasted through Hatton station and over the slight rise, then started to brake as we began to descend the steep bank. I instructed Ron to put the tender brake on to bring the train together, then I started to use the locomotive brake. Even though I told Ron to put the tender brake on harder, and had to use the power of my brake, we were still gaining speed. I gave a series of popping whistles to indicate to the guard that we needed his assistance to brake the train, and were then just holding the speed at around 20 mph.

The distant signal for Warwick was at caution, but I could do no more. As we approached the home signals we could see that the left-hand one was clear, indicating that we were being diverted into the loop line. There was a slight rise over the road bridge which reduced our speed to around 15 mph, then we were on a falling gradient. I whistled to the signalman, indicating that we would not be able to stop at his signals at the end of the loop, or at the stop blocks in front of the signal box - Ron had got the side doors open ready to jump off.

I whistled again and at the last moment the points came over and we were turned back out on to the main line. We passed the signalman waving at us to stop, but we indicated that we could not. We eventually stopped well through the station, with the guard's van at the Leamington end of the platform. The guard called us to reverse back into the loop, and when we had settled in there, I went to the signal box.

'It was touch and go whether I turned the points to let you out!' exclaimed the signalman.

'Well, we and the locomotive would have been in the box with you,' I replied.

The station master then appeared on the scene; we must have woken him with all our whistling. When I explained that we had run away, he said he would be reporting the incident as the stop block had just been replaced after being smashed when a 'Royal Scot' locomotive on a coal train had run away a few weeks before. Alf Love, one of our senior drivers who was on that train, later told me that they were only going about 5 mph when they could not stop, and when they touched the stop block it collapsed. He added, 'I reckon Bill Shakespeare built that when he was a platelayer around here.'

When we left the locomotive at Banbury I booked the brakes to be examined, and when booking off duty at Saltley I made out a report of the incident. After about a fortnight I was summoned to go and see inspector Charlie Weston. He produced a bundle of papers referring to the runaway and asked me to explain. I pointed out that we had a Caprotti valve gear locomotive.

'What difference does that make?' he asked.

I thought about saying that you could not put them in reverse for extra brake power as on a conventional steam locomotive. However, I replied, 'They run a lot freer than ordinary locomotives because of the valve gear and roller bearings.'

He looked at his papers. 'When this locomotive had its high-mileage examination at its home depot, Grimesthorpe, they found that the Duplex brake valve, which works either steam or vacuum, was seized in the vacuum position, so if you were working a vacuum-fitted train it would stop you, but you had to rely on the steam brake alone. You had only the slightest steam pressure to brake the train with.' He smiled at me and said, 'You are totally exonerated. I hope this incident hasn't affected you.'

'No fear,' I replied.

Driver Frank Marshall, one of our fellow travellers from Walsall, had a similar incident a few weeks later at Gloucester Midland station on a Sunday evening. He had worked a stopping passenger train from Birmingham with one of these locomotives, and stopped without incident at a dozen or so stations. When uncoupled from the train to go light engine to Gloucester Barnwood depot, he drew forward about 100 yards towards the level crossing to clear the points in order to reverse along the other platform. When he applied the steam brake he could not stop, and crashed through the crossing gates, hitting a bus. The side was ripped out of the bus, trapping the driver in his cab and slightly injuring him.

'It's a good job the bus was going into the town and was almost empty,' said Frank. 'If it had been coming out at that time of night it could have been full. I can't sleep thinking about it. When I shut my eyes I can see the bus and me struggling to stop to no avail.'

I told him about my incident and said that it could be a defective brake.

There was an official inquiry at Gloucester about a week later, and Frank informed me that when he entered the room the complete brake valve was on the table in front of the three officials. He was told that he was completely exonerated because the Duplex valve was partially seized, as in my incident. The responsibility lay with the servicing by the fitters and maintenance staff. However, this incident shook Frank's confidence and he did little more main-line work; he would change his turn to be on shunting duties or shed work.

During the summer of 1964 the main line from Euston to Crewe was being electrified, and on Sundays trains were being diverted from Nuneaton Trent Valley to Stafford via our route through Whitacre, Water Orton, Sutton Park, Walsall and Bushbury. One Sunday I signed on duty at 9.50 am to travel with a Saltley guard to Nuneaton to work three trips conducting men as far as Bushbury. Our first train arrived around 11.30 am; it was the 'Royal Scot' with English Electric Type 4 D318 and 12 coaches. The Camden train crew were booked through to Carlisle, where they lodged overnight. When I stepped into the cab, the driver remarked, 'I don't suppose you're trained on these locomotives?'

When I answered, 'I was trained on them at Monument Lane', he said, 'Good. You can handle her, and my mate can go into the train to Stafford.'

'I'm only booked with you to Bushbury,' I replied.

'That's no good to me,' he snorted. 'I don't sign from there to Stafford.'

'We'll see if there's another conductor there,' I answered. 'If not, I'm OK to Stafford.'

Over the heavy climb from Water Orton to Aldridge I noticed how much weaker this locomotive was compared with our Sulzer ones. When we arrived at Bushbury my guard alighted from the train, but there was no other conductor driver, so the Camden driver said, 'I don't want any more delay - this diversion has cost us an hour already.'

'I'll carry on,' I said.

At Penkridge I saw my return train from Bushbury and, after getting off the locomotive at Stafford, I went to the station inspector's office to telephone Control to tell them why I had come through. I expected them to say, 'Who authorised you to do it?', but instead they thanked me for not delaying the 'Royal Scot', as there had been a mistake at Bushbury. They instructed me to wait at Stafford for my last train to Nuneaton around 4 hours later.

English Electric Type 4 No D330 on the southbound 'Royal Scot' near Brinklow on the Trent Valley line in 1961. Later, when this and other trains were diverted because of work on the electrification of the main line, the Camden drivers were introduced to the delights of 'Sunstroke'! *Michael Mensing*

Type 2 diesel No D7531, sister locomotive to D7587 on which Bob Tudge and I ran away near Sutton Park! *J. Crook*

Two weeks later it was my rostered Sunday to work, and I was again conducting the 'Royal Scot' from Nuneaton. It was a day of heavy thunderstorms and warm sunshine, and as we traversed the speed restriction at Shustoke station, the Camden driver, seeing the station sign, remarked in his best Cockney slang, 'Cor blimey mate, we're at Sunstroke!'

A few weeks later I was rostered on local 'tripper' No 64 for a week's work between Sutton Park, Aldridge and the Walsall Wood colliery and brickworks branch line close to our old house. We were booked a Class '3F' or '2F' 0-6-0 steam locomotive, but on the Thursday we were delighted to see that we had Type 2 diesel locomotive No D7587. Our last trip was to work a coal train around 6.30 pm from Aldridge and stop at Sutton Park to pick up traffic to load to Washwood Heath sidings. I started the train out of Aldridge, then coasted down the bank towards Streetly. On the slight rise here I started to control the train by gradual use of the brake, and instructed my mate Bob Tudge to put the handbrake on, but like the Hatton runaway incident, I quickly realised that I was losing control. Approaching Sutton Park I sounded the horn to indicate

to the signalman and guard that I could not stop. The shunter was waiting by the vans we should have picked up, and looked amazed as we passed, waving him goodbye.

We slowed up a little on the rise to Penns station, but on the falling gradient to Park Lane Junction we speeded up again. I sounded the horn to the signalman as the signals were against us, and was relieved to see the signal clear, directing us towards Castle Bromwich. We took the 20 mph restricted curve at around 40 mph with wheels squealing. The signals at Castle Bromwich were against us. I again sounded the horn frantically, and said to Bob, 'Get our bags together. If we don't get the signal to turn us out main or goods line we'll go into the old British Industries Fair sidings and a dead end, so get ready to abandon ship!'

As we approached the signals they cleared for us to go out main line over the junction at around 30 mph. Signalman Armstrong came to his window to see us career by, and we eventually stopped outside Dunlop's factory about a mile along the main line. I dropped on to the ballast and inspected the brakes and wheels, which were glowing hot.

'Do you want to make some toast?' I asked Bob.

We then carried on to Washwood Heath, where we disposed of our train. The young yard inspector asked, 'Where's the Sutton Park traffic?'

'We couldn't stop there today,' I replied.

When we arrived at our depot, I booked the brake gearing to be examined and put in a runaway report to the foreman.

The following day we had a traffic inspector riding with us on another Type 2 diesel, No D5197. He inquired about the incident of the previous day.

'Do you want to try it today?' I asked. 'We've only four pairs of wheels and about 80 tons in weight compared with six pairs of wheels and 120 tons in weight of a steam engine to stop the train.'

'I've come to see if we can find some vacuum-braked wagons to put next to the locomotive to assist with the braking,' he replied.

We did this and with the extra brakes of four wagons we had a more leisurely run down the bank!

During this period drivers were expected to take over any steam engine from any Region of British Railways, whether they had seen one before or not. However, notices were issued to staff forbidding them to drive any diesel locomotive or DMU on which they had not been trained.

— o —

After a few weeks I was again rostered to learn new routes. This time it was from Walsall to Droitwich via Dudley, Stourbridge and Kidderminster. This was the busy line running through industrial areas from Walsall to Stourbridge, with signal boxes situated about every mile. From Dudley it was former GWR signalling, with a large amount of them situated on the right-hand side of the track. This took me three weeks to learn, and as there were no passenger trains to ride on from Walsall to Stourbridge I had to rely on local freight trains.

Derby men were rostered a new turn of duty that entailed taking empty coaches, after their arrival at New Street, to Kings Norton, then returning light engine to New Street and Monument Lane sidings to work a parcels train back to Derby via Walsall, Lichfield and Wichnor Junction. They did not sign the road from New Street over this route and I was booked on quite a few occasions to sign on duty at 9.15 am to travel to New Street to pick up the Derby men, usually with a Type 4 'Peak', and conduct them as far as Wichnor Junction. I would then carry on with them to Burton, where I could catch an express home, making an early finish and a nice day turn of duty.

In December 1964 Monument Lane warehouse handled extra Royal Mail traffic, and from there I worked trains to Sheffield via Walsall, and to Crewe via Wolverhampton. I had applied for leave on Christmas Day as usual, but when I booked off duty around midday on Christmas Eve the roster clerk said, 'We've got a job booking on at 10.00 am on Christmas Day from Monument Lane to Derby, and we've no one to work it.'

'I vowed many years ago not to work on Christmas Day,' I replied.

'You'll travel home as passenger from Derby,' he said.

'That's what happened before,' I remarked. 'I was stranded there until the Mail train at 8.00 pm, so I'm afraid you're still short of a driver.'

During the last week of the year I was rostered on duty at 9.18 am to work from New Street to Bristol with the 10.10 am express. One day we had D33, and when proceeding between Yate and Westerleigh sidings, the engine began to cut out. I nursed it until we were in the protection of signals at Westerleigh North, and came to a stop. I sent my mate, Doug Hazzard, to the signal box while I investigated the cause. I was rather baffled as the symptoms showed fuel starvation, but the fuel gauge showed over 300 gallons. I tried to clean the fuel oil filters in case there was a blockage, but to no avail. We eventually had to be towed by a freight locomotive into Mangotsfield and Bristol Temple Meads, and at Bath Road locomotive depot I duly reported fuel starvation. The following day the foreman fitter there informed me that the fuel gauge was not working, and there was no fuel at all on the locomotive.

On the first Sunday of 1965 I was rostered

on duty at 4.07 pm with No D98 and mate John Beck to work a special train coming from Sheffield to Cardiff as far as Gloucester. Our return working was with two 'Inter-City' DMUs. These were fitted with the ex-GWR automatic brake system whereby if the distant signal was at clear a bell rang in the cab and no action was needed by the driver, but if the distant signal was at caution a horn sounded, which the driver needed to acknowledge and cancel by lifting a plunger to make a normal stop. If this was not done the brake would automatically go on, bringing the train to a sudden halt. I had worked ex-GWR steam locomotives with this on without trouble, but on the DMU things were to be different.

We left Gloucester Central station on the Sunday night and the first distant signal for Barnwood Junction was at caution. The horn sounded, and in the dark I felt for the cancellation plunger on the driving panel, but to no avail. The automatic brake operated and we came to a sudden stop halfway between Tramway Junction and Barnwood Junction.

The horn was still sounding. I put the cab light on and John and myself searched for the elusive plunger, but could see nothing resembling one. We traced the sound of the horn to behind my driving seat, and there was the cancellation plunger. When a driver was in his normal driving position he would have to put his hand behind his back and feel for it. We had been delayed about 10 minutes; as we passed Barnwood Junction, now with clear signals, the signalman came to his window with both hands open, indicating the delay. When I signed off duty I made out a report stating the cause of the delay, criticising the positioning of the ATC equipment.

Another new job came to the depot. We booked on duty at 9.20 pm, relieved a parcels train at Landor Street Junction, some 10 minutes walk from the depot, at 9.30 pm and worked to Derby, where we were relieved for Leeds. After our food break we relieved a fish train coming from Burton Salmon near York to Curzon Street, Birmingham, via Wichnor Junction, Lichfield City, Sutton Coldfield and Aston Junction, before taking the locomotive back to our depot. When I was on a

night shift I worked this train regularly until the men in the link in which it was placed learned this route.

Another new working was booking on at 7.00 pm to work a DMU to Leicester. We were then booked to bring a Sulzer/AEI Type 2 diesel off Leicester loco depot to work a parcels train to Walsall via Nuneaton, Water Orton and Sutton Park. The first night we had D5200, and when we arrived at Walsall around 2.00 am the Ryecroft driver who should have relieved me said that he was not trained on these locomotives, and he was booked to work another parcels train into New Street and Birmingham Central sidings via Five Ways Junction, then light engine to Saltley. We telephoned Control and they asked me to stay with him as instructor. This meant an extra 5 shillings a day, and as it was around 7.00 am when I signed off duty it was a good night's work, and this happened all week. In that month we had a wage rise, bringing a senior driver's pay to £16 8s 0d.

During this period, and for the next 18 months, New Street Station was being rebuilt. The old Midland and LNWR sections were made into one, with the old Queen's Drive between platforms 6 and 7, which was the boundary between the stations, done away with. Prior to this, although the two railways had been amalgamated into the LMS in 1923, the two sections were still worked separately. Each had its own supervisors, platform inspectors, porters, and even its own passenger guards. It was said that it needed an Act of Parliament for a North Western train to be put into the Midland side, and vice versa. Drivers only signed the side of the station that was theirs, and needed a conductor if they were diverted. As I had worked at Monument Lane depot on the old LNWR lines I was fortunate to sign for both sides, so I regularly had the job of booking on duty every Monday morning and conducting Derby and Leicester men into the station; as we did not know what alterations had been done over the weekend, it was a case of creeping in and getting ready to stop quickly at any new signal! There were also jobs booking on at 6.00 am, 2.00 pm and 10.00 pm to stand by at New Street to con-

A dramatic view of the rebuilding of new Street station in 1964. The former Midland-side roof is being dismantled on the right; the North Western side was to the left of the picture. No wonder 'foreign' drivers needed conducting through the works - even we weren't sure what changes to find each day!
Michael Mensing

duct 'foreign' drivers on any diversion of trains into other platforms.

During 1939-45 Sutton Park warehouse had been extended to accommodate the American Army Postal Service, and trains had been worked into and out of there. When the war finished the Royal Mail took it over, using it as a customs clearing office. We still worked trains to and from Bristol, Liverpool and other docks there. One such job entailed booking on at 7.45 pm to work a Sulzer/AEI Type 2 diesel locomotive from Sutton Park around 8.30 pm to Walsall, then, after detaching a couple of vans, running round the train and proceeding to Derby via Lichfield City. Then we would work back to New Street via Tamworth.

One evening I was surprised to see, when looking at the locomotive allocation board, that I had a 'Black Five' steam locomotive allocated to us, No 44856; as the foreman said to me when I queried it, 'We have no other.'

We duly worked from Sutton Park to Walsall. When the shunter hooked us off after disposing of the two vans I said, 'We need to go and turn the locomotive around Pleck Curve and Bescot station as we're not going tender-first to Derby.'

There was an hour's delay while we did this manoeuvre, and when we eventually backed on to our train the Walsall station inspector came and asked the reason.

'The wrong type of locomotive for these workings,' I replied. 'Talk to the locomotive arranger in the Control office who authorised it.'

We did not have a steamer for the rest of the week.

One morning I booked on at 7.00 am spare duty with Johnny Beck, and the foreman said, 'I've got a nice little job for you. D58 is on the depot coupled to crippled locomotive D1748, which has to be towed to the Brush locomotive works at Loughborough.'

This meant that a driver or fireman had to ride on the 'dead' locomotive. I had not yet been on the 2,750 hp Brush Sulzer Type 4s since my training some 12 months previously, so before leaving the depot I had a good look both outside and in; a fireman had been chosen to ride on it, but I was responsible for both locomotives. We had an uneventful trip via Leicester, leaving D1748 at the works at Loughborough, and took our locomotive to Toton depot, which had been expanded to do major servicing and repairs on diesel locomotives.

There was a Welfare Fund at Saltley depot, which had been formed with money left over when the depot Cricket Club had been wound up in 1960. Its aim was to provide an annual reunion dinner each October and to provide Christmas parcels for staff that had been off duty ill for a long time. Money for this was raised from weekly raffles run by Mrs Connie Baker, one of our office staff, and by a weekly tote run by committee members. At Christmas, staff were asked to contribute tins of fruit, cream, cooked meats, sugar, cheese, etc, to enable us to make up the parcels for the needy. At 1965's Annual General Meeting I was elected on to the committee and served on it for 20 years until I retired.

10
FREIGHT LINKS
1965-67

When a driver's seniority took him to the top of the special link, he would be issued with a form to sign indicating whether he wanted to work passenger or freight trains, then he would be placed in the appropriate links.

In the summer workings in May 1965, myself and three other drivers, Tom Wootton, Len Biss and Bob Clarke, had received these forms. At our next union branch meeting I protested about them, as New Street station was being rebuilt and no one knew if the passenger work would be transferred there, along with Monument Lane depot. We could get no assurance as to what was happening, so I suggested that the forms be held in abeyance until such time as a decision had been made. This was rejected by our Local Departmental Committee, so Bob Clarke and I refused to sign the form and stated that we wished to make our decision when the requirements at New Street were known. This was to cause a big upheaval a few years later.

I was placed in the bottom freight link; my years doing a variety of work were over and I was now on mundane work. At least I knew what work I would be doing around the 12 weeks of the link and I had a regular mate, John Beck, who had occasionally worked with me before; he in turn had been promoted from the firemen's special link. Our boundaries would be Nuneaton, Derby and Gloucester.

We had an afternoon freight turn to Nuneaton, where we were relieved for Peterborough, and then had to go to Nuneaton loco for a locomotive to work a local freight back to Washwood Heath. Jack Siggs, who had passed out with me as a driver, had been appointed running shift foreman there, and he was always on my turn, so we would talk about Saltley. As he was also still a member of our ASLEF branch he would pay me his quarterly subscription.

In June we did have a run out. We booked on at 8.30 am to work a local freight to Gloucester, but when we signed on duty the foreman asked me to come off my booked turn to work an excursion train to Oxford. I asked for my own mate to come with me and we relieved a Mothers' Union special coming from Sheffield with D178 on the front. When we arrived at Oxford, a conductor driver was waiting for me to take our coaches to Didcot and leave the locomotive on the depot there. As we progressed along the ex-GWR line, signalmen came on to their verandahs, taking photographs of the unusual locomotive on their metals.

We had arrived at Oxford before time, but we had a lot of delay going to Didcot as this area had recently been re-signalled with the new electric multiple-aspect signals replacing the semaphore ones, and they were controlled by a new signal box at Reading, some 15 miles away. They were having 'teething troubles', as it was termed, and this caused us some 1½ hours delay before we disposed of our coaches and left the locomotive at the depot. I booked a couple of minor repairs to the locomotive, but the foreman remarked, 'There are no fitters here trained on diesels.'

'It's not serious,' I answered. 'It will work back home with our men all right.'

As we were late, we had missed our passenger train home and we were instructed to travel home via London Paddington and Euston. We went this long way round, and as we walked from Vauxhall & Duddeston station towards the bridge outside our depot at 8.30 pm, our return train was passing by above us. We could have waited at Didcot and travelled home on it, or even worked it back!

My son, Robert, had left school some 12 months previously and his boss needed him to learn to drive a car or van. He said that he did not have time to teach him to drive at work, but would pay for his driving lessons as long as he took them in his own time. I said I would make it interesting for him; I would also take driving lessons, as I had only a motor cycle and would be learning to drive something else.

After about four months we took our test on the same day, me in the morning and Robert in the afternoon. I failed because of a bad reversing movement, and when Robert came home at lunchtime he was despondent, saying, 'I've not got much chance if you failed with your motor cycle experience.'

I tried to cheer him up by saying, 'I didn't have to reverse on a motor cycle,' and added, 'I'll give you a £5 note if you pass.'

He came home later with his face wreathed in smiles.

'You owe me a fiver,' he said.

I eventually passed my test at the second attempt.

One of our link workings was to take a steam locomotive from our depot around 3.00 pm into Washwood Heath sidings and work a freight train only as far as Tyseley where we were relieved, as it was routed via the North Warwickshire line and ex-GWR metals to Stratford-upon-Avon and Cheltenham, then Gloucester and Bristol. As we had no return working our shift foreman would inform us if any diesel locomotive needed to come out of the large diesel maintenance depot after refurbishment or heavy repair. It was interesting to see the locomotive hung up on large cranes with some of the working parts taken out and placed on the floor of the workshops. I used to try and explain to John what the parts were. He was quick to learn as he was a good mechanic (he used to race a motor cycle and sidecar).

One Friday night we were taken off our rostered work to travel to Walsall to relieve as far as Gloucester a pigeon special coming from the Manchester area en route to Bath. It was running about 2 hours late when it arrived behind 'Black Five' No 45429. We were booked home as passengers on the 2.30 am Royal Mail train, which was standing in Gloucester station when we ran in. John had a motor cycle race meeting on that Saturday so he needed to catch this train home, as the next one was about 4 hours later and would not get us home until around 8.30 am. As we were handing over to the Gloucester crew we could hear the station staff blowing whistles to start the Mail train, so we jumped on to the ballast, climbed into a parcels van from the off-side just as it moved off, and sat on the mail bags.

The first stop was at Worcester, and when the doors opened we decided to move into the passenger coaches, but a police officer was standing there.

'How did you get in there?' he asked. 'It's supposed to be locked up.'

I explained about getting in on the other side, which had not been locked.

'We'll have to watch that in future,' he remarked.

In the October 1965 review of wages and conditions, the mileage payment bonus system was overhauled to give men on short mileage some payments, because it was realised that drivers working local passenger trains, stopping at most stations, worked just as hard as the top express men, although they worked shorter distances. The agreement negotiated was that men working below 65 miles had 40 minutes mileage payment on top of their normal pay. At between 65 and 84 miles they had 60 minutes extra, 85 to 104 they had 80 minutes, and so on until 133 to 139 miles equalled 2½ hours pay. Then the long mileage of over 140 miles was altered to 147 miles, which equalled 2½ hours pay, 148 to 153 miles equalled 3 hours pay, then half an hour was added for each 7 miles worked. An important concession was that any overtime incurred was also paid; the old mileage agreement disbarred this.

A 'Manning Agreement' was also drawn

up, with single manning of diesel locomotives permitted as long as a 'physical needs' break was shown on the diagrammed workings between the third and fifth hour, and no train heating was required. We had already been working DMUs on our own, but this new agreement came into force at the start of the New Year of 1966.

Early in January I was rostered to sign on duty at 2.30 pm to take D7596 and a guard, who was to act as second man for protection purposes, to Kings Norton to work a train loaded with motor cars from the Austin Longbridge works to Nuneaton. There we were unhooked and the train worked forward to London Willesden sidings with an electric locomotive. I was shunted into the sidings where I had my physical needs break, then worked a mixed freight train back to Washwood Heath.

A few weeks later I travelled with a guard to Water Orton to relieve a train loaded with sugar beet from March on the Eastern Region to Kidderminster sugar refinery, via Walsall and Dudley, with Type 2 No D5404. On arrival there, we returned home light locomotive via Droitwich and Bromsgrove, as I did not sign for the more direct route via Stourbridge and Old Hill.

In March, after a family conference, we decided to buy a car. Charlie Lindley's son, Malcolm, who worked at a garage at West Bromwich, told us of a good second-hand car for sale. It was an Austin 1100, just 12 months old, and as my son had been driving an Austin A40 van for some months without any trouble, we decided to look at it. It was more expensive than we had anticipated, but after a little haggling over the price we decided to buy 593 TEA.

Later in the month George Wilkins, the man who introduced me to committee work and ran our sick club, retired, and we arranged a presentation evening for him in Walsall, where about 50 of his fellow travellers to Saltley attended to give him a good send-off. He was later to become Mayor of Walsall!

A couple of days later I handled my first Brush Sulzer 2,750 hp Type 4, No D1843, on a train, after a wait of 18 months since my

George Wilkins's retirement party; myself and Frank Marshall in the foreground, with Sid Lloyd and Howard Warley behind. *Author's collection*

training on this type. I booked on at 3.40 am and relieved the freight train to Crewe Basford Hall in the dark at Landor Street. The signals were clear when I took over, so I had no time to look over the locomotive. I arrived at Crewe thankfully without any trouble, where the guard came up and rode with me to Crewe South depot, where I had a good look around the engine to refresh my knowledge. Two weeks later I was allocated

The first Brush Sulzer 2,750 hp Type 4 that I drove was No D1843, after an 18-month wait since training on them. Here is sister locomotive No D1834 at Saltley. No 3 shed has at last been rebuilt (see pages 49 and 124), but the chimney of the sand-drying oven still survives! *Derek Sharpe*

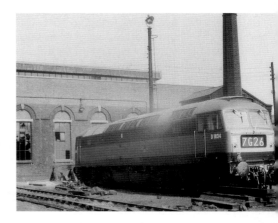

one every day of the week, working Bathgate car trains from Kings Norton as far as Derby; as I was single-manned I travelled home as passenger!

In the middle of April I had the first long run in the car. Elaine took a day off from school and we toured around Evesham and Stratford-upon-Avon to see the apple and pear trees in blossom, but we ran into a snowstorm which deprived us of the nice view. A fortnight later we travelled again by car to May's brother's home at Tilehurst near Reading for the weekend. We travelled via Warwick, Banbury, Oxford and Didcot. We crossed the main railway line about half a dozen times during the journey, and I said to the family, 'As long as I can see the railway line every 10 miles or so I'm not lost.'

On Sunday 22 May Stanier 'Pacific' No 46235 *City of Birmingham* was placed in Birmingham Science & Engineering Museum. It had been towed by diesel locomotive to Lawley Street sidings, then the engine and tender were separated and placed on a Pickfords lorry and driven through the city streets to the museum. My family and I went to see it, and it looked massive standing in the road outside. A wall had to be knocked down to get it in, which was then rebuilt. It was like putting the locomotive in a tomb, where it still is. I thought at the time, and still do, that it would have been better preserved as a working engine.

In July we were issued with our first uniforms. They were green with the letters 'BR' in yellow on both lapels of the coat. I was walking one day between Moor Street and New Street stations via the Bull Ring shopping centre when a man stopped me to inquire about a certain shop.

'I'm sorry, I don't know,' I said.

'I thought you would,' he said, pointing to the 'BR' on my lapels. He evidently thought I was a Bull Ring security man!

Later that month I had a mixed week's work! On the Sunday I worked the 2.40 am Royal Mail to Gloucester via Worcester with D44 outwards and returned with a Cardiff to Leeds express with D77 on front and Gordon Hopkinson as my mate. The rest of the week we were rostered to book on duty at 3.15 pm to work a local freight trip to Longbridge and the Austin car factory. On the Tuesday the shift foreman asked me to come off my job to work a special banana train to Rotherham with Gordon. We relieved the train at Landor Street to find in amazement that we had 'Britannia' 'Pacific' No 70045 *Lord Rowallan* on the front; as it was a banana train, steam heating was provided to the train. We worked it uneventfully and were relieved at 7.00 pm to travel home as passen-

On 27 July 1965 I worked a special banana train to Rotherham; when we relieved the train at Landor Street we were amazed to find 'Britannia' No 70045 *Lord Rowallan* on the front. While we were standing at Duddeston Road Junction, Dave Lacey, one of the clerks, took this photograph of me on the footplate. *Dave Lacey*

ger. While we were standing at Duddeston Road Junction just outside our depot offices, Dave Lacey, one of the clerks, took a photograph of us and later presented it to me. He told me he was train spotting on the Settle & Carlisle line on the following Saturday, taking more photographs, when the same locomotive came by working a passenger train, on the same film four days later and 150 miles away.

On the Wednesday we were again asked to come off our booked workings to travel to Crewe to work a special test freight train from Basford Hall sidings to Washwood Heath with Type 2 diesel D5246 on front. Behind our locomotive was a dynamometer car, which was testing the drawbar pull on the different gradients along the route. This train was tested over the weekend on the Whitacre to Nuneaton line, and they even set up a wind measurement gauge at Arley to test the wind drag on a train.

On Thursday the shift foreman was again waiting to ask us to come off our workings to take 2-6-0 No 76052 towing D5243 to Crewe Works. The passed fireman who rode on the 'dead' diesel locomotive was Alan Binder who later emigrated to Australia, and the last I heard of him he was an engine driver in Queensland. We had a lot of delay on this run and also had to wait for a conductor driver to take us into Crewe Works, and it was around 9.00 pm when we disposed of the locomotive. We had to wait until 12.45 am to travel home, so we had a drink at the railway club, and as we walked back to the station we called for some fish and chips. It was now around 11.00 pm and the lady at the shop said, 'Are you hungry? I'm just finishing.'

We naturally said 'Yes', and asked for three portions. When we opened them in the mess room on the station, Alan and myself had two fishes each and plenty of chips, and Gordon had three fishes with his chips!

On Friday we *did* work our booked train to Longbridge, and Gordon remarked, 'I thought this was going to be a boring week, but we certainly had plenty of variety.'

We had a job in our link where I booked on at 3.17 am, single-manned, to work a freight train to Redditch with a Type 2 diesel, then work a local passenger train back to New Street. We arrived at Barnt Green around 4.30 am and, as the signal box at Redditch was closed at night and did not open until 5.30 am, we had to wait there.

One summer morning, after it had just turned daylight, we stood on the embankment looking down into a field about 50 yards away, and watched a vixen playing with her cubs for about an hour until the signal cleared for us to go down the single line. On these locomotives there was a 'dead man's button' on the off-side of the cab, which enabled the driver to leave his seat and release the 'dead man's treadle' in order to lean out of the window to catch the single-line tablet, which he had to carry when working down the branch line. One morning I failed to catch the tablet and automatically moved to open the cab door, thereby letting go of the button. This operated the brake and we stopped rather suddenly. I waited for the signalman to walk to me with the tablet, then carried on to Redditch, where I had to apologise to the guard for the rough stop!

In the late summer of 1966 we had our annual holiday in Newquay, Cornwall, and this was the furthest run yet in the car. We travelled with Charlie Lindley and his family, who also had an Austin 1100. The M5 motorway then terminated at Tewkesbury, and the rest of the journey was via the A38 most of the way. We left around midnight on Friday night, stopped three times for refreshments, and arrived in Newquay at 9.30 am, clocking up a total of 262 miles. During the week it was like learning to drive a car all over again, travelling down narrow roads and having to reverse two or three hundred yards to allow buses and lorries to pass coming the other way.

I took a railway pass with me in case anything happened to the car, so we could get home, and on the second Saturday we left at 9.40 am but did not arrive home until 8.30 pm. As we stood in traffic jams I said jokingly, 'I wish I'd sold the car and come home by train.'

On Sunday 2 October I booked on duty at 4.30 am with John Beck and No D7577 to work a special freight train from Washwood Heath to Bescot. We were stopped by the signalman at Sutton Park station and informed that cattle had been seen on the line in front of us. After going through the first bridge we saw about six cows and heifers. We tried to overtake them slowly to try and send them on to the side of the track, but they kept walking in front of us. We entered a cutting through the park and had to be content to go slow until we came out in the open ground at the Streetly end. There was a cattle-crossing there and gates into either side of the park, so I stopped the train about 300 yards short of the crossing, opened one of the gates, and John and I tried to round up the cattle and drive them into the park. One Hereford would not go where we wanted it, but fortunately the guard had walked up to inquire why we had stopped. With his help we managed to round up the last one and closed the gate.

As we approached the next open signal box at Ryecroft, the signalman, Harry Hadley, stopped me with a red flag.

'I might have known it was you!' he shouted. 'Where have you been? You're more than an hour late!'

I explained about rounding up the cattle and putting them into the park. He replied, 'I suppose you've cut one up and are taking it back to your mates at Saltley.'

The following Monday we booked on at 2.50 pm for our local 'tripper' workings, but the foreman asked me to come off my job to take D177 to Doncaster Works for major repairs. I took my own mate John with me and put him in the driving seat. He knew the road as far as Derby but was unsure beyond, so I said, 'I'll keep my eye on you - a light engine is ideal for feeling the route.'

Jack Gregory disposing of 'Jubilee' 4-6-0 No 45574 *India*. Tragically, in 1966 Jack was knocked off his bike and killed while cycling home. ASLEF sought and obtained substantial compensation for his widow. *Derek Sharpe*

At Rotherham we had a conductor driver to take us the rest of the journey. We travelled home as passengers, booking off around 4.00 am.

On Monday 4 November, Jack Gregory, a Saltley driver and a near neighbour of mine, was knocked off his push-bike by an opening car door as he cycled home from work. He hit his head on the kerb-stone, which killed him. I was a bearer at his funeral a week later, and the car driver was subsequently fined heavily. Our trade union claimed compensation for Jack's widow and I took our branch secretary, Jack Coxsey, to see her to get statements and such things as their wedding certificate and birth certificates of their two children so the union could assess the damages. Mrs Gregory later received several thousand pounds.

A few weeks later I was to have further training, this time on the new air pressure braking system of the Liner freight train, which gave us a far better brake than the vacuum-controlled one. We could work these heavy trains at 75 mph and stop comfortably in the distance allowed. At the end of the week I passed out with inspector Weston.

A fortnight later I had a week's work booking on at 12.10 pm to work an air-braked train of tanks from the new gas works at Coleshill, going to Birkenhead, as far as Crewe, and I gained plenty of experience with this brake. At the end of the week I allowed my mate to work it for his experience.

Towards the end of 1966 steam locomotives were being phased out, and there were only two steam-hauled trains at Saltley. One was a late evening train from Stoke-on-Trent to Washwood Heath via Stafford and Walsall, and the other an early morning train from Water Orton to Stoke via Burton.

One week in December I was again taken off my local job to book on duty at 4.15 pm to travel to Stoke, prepare a steam locomotive at Stoke depot, then go light engine to Cockshut sidings and pick up a semi-fitted freight train for Birmingham. My mate was John Bloor, who used to change his turns to work on steam engines. On Monday we were allocated 'Black Five' No 45263, the type of locomotive I used to like, but this one was in a run-down condition with steam leaking everywhere and the exhaust injector wasting water. It was a shame to see such a good locomotive in such a bad condition. We had to make a special stop for water at Walsall and this meant a dead start for the climb to Lichfield Road Junction and Aldridge.

As we travelled to Stoke on Thursday of that week it started to snow and it was quite heavy when we trudged from the station to Stoke loco. There was no locomotive allocated to us on the engine board; the shift foreman said, 'There's No 48266 on the ashpit - I'll tell you when it arrives on the preparing pit for you.'

About an hour later it was ready. When we climbed on to the footplate the steam pressure was only around 50 psi and there was only a handful of fire in the firebox. John got to work with a will, putting a dozen or so shovelsful into the firebox to gradually build up the fire. Meanwhile I got the oil bottles and feeders and started to oil the vital parts. It was snowing well and we were out in the open getting covered in the stuff.

After a while I could hear John using the fire irons to spread the fire, and more coal was being shovelled in. When I had finished my job I clambered into the cab to see a good fire going, but still only 75 lbs of steam. John managed to get the injector working to put some hot water in the bucket for me to wash the oil and grease off my hands.

We had to wait another half an hour for

Towards the end of 1966 many steam locomotives were in a very run-down condition, including '8F' 2-8-0 No 48266 on which we struggled from Stoke to Birmingham. She is seen here in happier days in 1958 bringing a mineral train off the Whitacre line at Water Orton. The main Midland line to Kingsbury and the north swings away to the left, towards the distant chimneys of Hams Hall Power Station. *Michael Mensing*

the steam pressure to rise to 200 psi before we could move off the shed to go tender-first into the snow to Cockshut. I remarked to John, 'You must be mad to change from a nice enclosed diesel job for this. I've a good mind to cross this route off my card!'

We struggled along and had to stop again at Walsall for water. The signalman at Park Street box said that Control wanted to know what we had stopped for.

'I've already whistled at Pleck Junction that I needed water,' I replied, 'so you could have told them, but I'll do it myself.'

The controller said, 'You're not booked at Walsall for water.'

'Do you want me to burn the boiler because of a shortage of water?' I replied. 'If these locomotives were properly maintained and not allowed to get into this bad condition I wouldn't stop here, as it prevents me having a run at the Aldridge bank.'

We arrived at Washwood Heath about 3 hours late.

The week before Christmas I was rostered to sign on duty at 2.17 am with John Bloor, who had changed from an 8.00 am shift, to work a freight train from Water Orton to Burton with a steamer and return with a Type 2 diesel. On Tuesday we had No 45139 on the outward trip and we left the sidings around 4.00 am. The locomotive was again in poor condition and we had to stop at Kingsbury sidings, only some 6 miles away, as we were low on steam and boiler water. John was very downcast and kept on saying, 'I'm doing my best.'

'Don't worry,' I replied. 'If this locomotive was in proper condition it would be capable of working to Carlisle without any trouble!'

We had a variety of 'Black Fives' and Class '8s' the rest of the week, all run down. On the Saturday, which was also Christmas Eve, we were allocated No 48615, but when John tested the exhaust injector he could not get it to work. I reported it to the fitters, who also failed to repair it, so after half an hour they said, 'Tell the foreman you'll have to be

given another locomotive.' After an hour's wait we were given 45428, again low on steam and fire, and we eventually left the depot about 2 hours late, and struggled again to get to Burton. As we were so late we missed our return train and travelled home as passengers.

Although I did not realise it at the time, this was the last steam locomotive I would drive, and I am happy to say that it is now preserved on the North Yorks Moors Railway.

The last week of 1966 John changed turns with my booked mate to be on an afternoon shift with me, and we had a variety of work. The day after Boxing Day we booked on at 1.08 pm to take D1742 light engine to Walsall to change locomotives on a Manchester to Plymouth special passenger train and work it to Bristol. We returned to New Street with D152 on another special from the West Country going to Leeds. The extra running to Walsall put another 30 miles on our mileage bonus, so we were paid 13 hours for the day's work.

On the Friday we worked an air-braked train from Coleshill gas works to Crewe, and on Saturday we relieved Sheffield men in New Street to work as far as Worcester a spe-

The last steam locomotive I drove, on Christmas Eve 1966, has happily been preserved. 'Black Five' 4-6-0 No 45428, now named *Bishop Eric Treacy*, is seen here on the North Yorks Moors Railway in September 1985. *D. A. Idle*

cial passenger train going to Great Malvern, with a brand new Type 4 Brush Sulzer diesel. At Worcester Foregate Street we unhooked from the train and a Western Region locomotive hooked on at the rear. Putting our locomotive on the depot to wait the 6 hours for the train to return, we took a leisurely walk along the riverside.

'This is better than firing a steam locomotive,' I remarked to John.

'It isn't as interesting,' he replied.

John is now a driver at Inverness in Scotland, where there are still occasional steam workings.

The following day, New Year's Day 1967, I booked on at 12.40 pm to conduct Gloucester men to Derby and back via Sutton Coldfield and Lichfield. When I resigned my route card early in January I asked to be refreshed on the routes to Leicester, Nottingham and Toton, as I had not been over them for more than six months, owing to being in the local freight link, and to my surprise I was rostered for a week to refresh my knowledge at the end of January.

Early in March we had another wage increase. My rate of pay was now 351 shillings (£17 11s 0d) a week. The end of the month saw me and John Bloor signing on at 9.15 pm and standing by at the depot on the breakdown train with D1904 for the passage of the Royal Train with Prince Philip travelling to Bristol.

The new shunting yard had been opened at Tinsley, Sheffield, and I had a job there booking on at 6.26 pm with John on D143. As I did not sign beyond Treeton Junction I needed a conductor, so we picked up a Barrow Hill driver at Staveley sidings. He took us into the massive sidings, then light engine to the new depot. This new railway centre was placed miles from anywhere and we had to travel by railway bus for about 25 minutes to Sheffield station to travel home as passengers.

On Monday 10 April I was shown on the daily alteration sheet to sign on duty at 7.15 am, single-manned, to relieve a liner braked train of tanks with D1669, to work to the new gas works at Watery Lane, Tipton. We went from Landor Street via Sutton Park,

Walsall and Wednesbury, then over the single line to Prince's End and Tipton. We arrived at the signal protecting the level crossing around 9.00 am, and when it did not clear I spoke to the signalman from the signal telephone.

'We're waiting for the Mayor of West Bromwich to declare the works officially open,' he said.

The signal cleared after about half an hour and as I approached the signal box a red flag was shown. As I brought the train to a stand, a traffic inspector climbed into the cab, saying, 'Do you smoke?'

I thought he was going to offer me a cigarette, so I replied 'No, I gave them up years ago.'

'You have to hand over all matches, lighters, oil lamps, etc, to the security cabin before we enter the gas works sidings,' he explained.

We arrived at the entrance gates, which when opened revealed a yellow ribbon. I was asked for any combustible materials, then about 20 men in their best suits appeared to watch me break the ribbon and proceed into the sidings. Apart from the traffic inspector, no one spoke to me. The guard who climbed into the cab was most indignant as he had left his cigarettes and matches with the security guard.

'I've counted how many there are,' he said.

We set the tanks to the emptying pipes and pumps. The council and railway officials disappeared, no doubt to have a champagne breakfast, while we returned light engine to Bescot loco depot and left our locomotive there, travelling home as passengers. The rest of the week I worked from Landor Street with the full tanks to the new gas works and returned to Landor Street with the empties we had delivered the previous day.

In May I had a new mate allocated to me, Dave Buckingham. On his first day, he said, 'I know this is the bottom freight link but I hear you get taken off your booked turns to go over routes many drivers don't know.'

'I was fortunate to be at Monument Lane depot for five years,' I replied, 'so I sign a lot of ex-LNW routes.'

'I'm looking forward to going over them,' he said.

It wasn't long before he did. On Sunday 14 May we signed on duty at 9.30 am to travel by our depot bus to Berkswell to relieve Coventry men on D5229 on an engineering ballast train to work between there and Kenilworth, and at the end of work take the train to Coventry and go light engine back to Saltley. The rest of the week we signed on duty at 6.55 pm to work a Freightliner train from Lawley Street sidings going to Willesden in London via Nuneaton to Rugby, where an electric locomotive took over, and we waited for a return train to Lawley Street.

On the Spring Bank Holiday Monday, 29 May, we had an unusual trip. We signed on duty at 3.25 pm to travel to New Street to work a special passenger train going from Bristol to York as far as Derby, with D1111 on front. I told Dave to do the driving outwards, as he would not know the return route. We relieved another special coming from Matlock around 9.00 pm to work to Walsall via Lichfield City and Brownhills with D5186 on front. We then took the empty coaches to Tyseley carriage sidings via Bescot, Perry Barr Junction, Soho, Monument Lane and New Street, before returning light to our depot.

'I'm certainly seeing some different railways,' Dave remarked.

We had a new 'tripper', No 55, placed in our link, which entailed working to Nuneaton Trent Valley, running around the train and carrying on to Hartshill gravel and stone sidings near Atherstone. After picking up a full train of stone we would work it to Tamworth Low Level, run around the train, then proceed to Nuneaton Trent Valley, and run around the train again before returning to Washwood Heath.

I was despatched to learn the route from Nuneaton to Tamworth, and when I was ready to sign my route card for it, I remarked to the roster clerk, 'I now sign the road from Rugby to Tamworth and from Walsall via Rugeley to Stafford and Crewe. Shall I learn the little bit along the Trent Valley line between Tamworth and Rugeley?'

He thought for a while and agreed, saying, 'We never know when it will come in useful.'

We also had another new train booked to us, signing on duty on Sundays at 7.25 am, working a passenger train via Worcester to Cheltenham and returning via Spetchley and Stoke Works Junction, making it a pleasant day turn.

In August, when it was the Crewe Works annual holiday, we were rostered to book on at 4.25 pm to travel to Crewe, prepare D1966, then pick up 10 coaches from the carriage sidings and propel them into the station to work an overnight train around 9.00 pm to the West Country. A lot of Crewe workers lived along the ex-North Stafford line (a special workers' train was run for them every morning from Stoke-on-Trent right into Crewe Works). As I did not sign the route from Crewe to Stoke I had a conductor driver and we stopped at Radway Green, Alsager (my wartime depot), Harecastle, Longport, Etruria and Stoke, where the conductor left us. We then worked non-stop via Bushbury, Walsall and Sutton Park to Duddeston Road, where we were relieved around midnight.

I booked on duty one Saturday morning at 7.40 to work a local 'tripper', No 28, to Longbridge. However, the running shift foreman, Harold Evans, called me into his office and said 'I want you to come off your job to act as instructor on English Electric D334 coming from Wolverhampton with a holiday train going to Paignton. Our men are booked to work it from New Street, but are not trained on that type of locomotive. The engine is diagrammed to come off the train at Bristol and work a return train around 6.00 pm. Another set of our men are booked to work down to Bristol in the afternoon to bring this back, and I want you to stay with the locomotive at Bristol.'

We relieved the Wolverhampton men around 9.00 am and the driver was evidently expecting to go through Bristol, saying that Saltley men were not trained on those locomotives; I explained about my five years at Monument Lane. We arrived at Bristol around 11.00 am and went on to the Bath Road diesel depot, where the foreman said, 'I have no men trained on these.' I again explained that I was staying with the locomotive all day, so he said, 'Stay and marshal it into a siding after it's been fuelled and serviced, then it won't be moved until it's time for its return workings.'

I eventually shut the engine down around 12.00 noon and this gave us plenty of time to have a walk around the docks and the town and get some lunch, as I only had sandwiches to last me 8 hours; I also telephoned May to tell her I would not be home until 9.30 pm. I returned to D334 around 5.00 pm for our men to work it back home. I had it ready for them to proceed to Temple Meads station to change over with a 'Western' diesel-hydraulic locomotive coming from the West Country.

On another Saturday, a fortnight later, I was on the daily alteration sheet to sign on duty at 4.50 am instead of my booked time of 6.30 am. Dave and I prepared D1707 and took it light to Rugby, where we picked up 10 empty coaches, took them into the station and worked a Plymouth train, stopping at Coventry and New Street, as far as Bristol, where we were relieved. After half an hour's break we relieved D89 coming from Penzance going to Sheffield as far as Landor Street, bypassing New Street station via the Camp Hill line from Kings Norton. I told Dave to do the driving as it was over a route he knew. This working amounted to 245 miles, equalling 15 hours pay.

On Wednesday 20 September I was rostered on duty at 10.25 am to conduct Ryecroft men on D5223, an officers' special train, which consisted of a single observation car. We had to propel this so that the district engineer and his staff, who were stationed at Walsall, could examine the lines we would traverse. I took over at Duddeston Road, worked into New Street station, then departed via Bournville with instructions to stop at certain bridges and at Lifford Curve, where the engineer would examine the points with

instruments. After leaving Lifford we stopped at Camp Hill, then carried on to Landor Street Junction, Castle Bromwich, Water Orton and Whitacre, where we were shunted into the sidings for the engineering staff to have lunch, provided by a chef who accompanied them. After about an hour we carried on to Nuneaton Abbey Street, then returned pulling the coach. I alighted at Water Orton to travel back to our depot; the Ryecroft driver knew the route to Walsall via Sutton Park and did not require me.

In November I arrived at work early, as was my habit, to book on at 1.17 pm for a local freight train, but the timekeeper instructed me to book on at 1.00 pm to work the Bathgate car train, as the booked driver had reported sick. I looked at the locomotive board to see that D1616 was allocated to this train. As I dived into the cab, the guard, Brian Timms (who was later to become a guard's supervisor) was waiting for me. We went light to Kings Norton to pick up our train loaded with cars from the Austin factory at Longbridge. We worked it to Crewe via Sutton Park, Walsall, Bushbury and Stafford. At Crewe Basford Hall we were relieved by a Preston crew and travelled home passenger.

In December I booked on at 1.03 am to work a freight train to Derby, but again the foreman asked us to relieve a train that was standing at Duddeston Road; it was oil and petrol tanks coming from Immingham Docks to Bromsgrove, where a new oil depot had been erected. On arrival there we had to wait a couple of hours while the tanks were emptied, then we took the train as far as Derby to be relieved for Immingham Docks.

So, although I was in the bottom freight link, I was still wandering about the railway system!

11
FIRE, STORM,
AND TRANSFORMATION OF LINKS
1968-71

In January 1968 I had further diesel loco-motive training, this time with the English Electric Type 1. These were built with just one cab, and if they were worked with the engine end in front of the cab, a second man was needed for an extra look-out. It was necessary to walk along the out-side framing, like a steam locomotive, to open various doors to inspect the different machines housed inside. Very often two locomotives would work in tandem with the cabs at the outer ends, thus saving the sec-ond man, as the old fireman was now called. Two of us had the redoubtable Inspector Locke to pass us out at the end of the week and he contrived to make it last all day, although the only locomotive available was

Bob Fletcher on English Electric Type 1 Bo-Bo No D8075. *J. Crook*

under repair and could not be started up or moved.

In March I was promoted to freight link No 6 and had Norman Webb as my booked mate. One of our turns of duty was to book on around 6.30 pm, take a light engine to Birmingham Central parcels depot, where Stanier House now stands, work a parcels train to Redditch, then return with another one to Walsall, via the Camp Hill and Sutton Park line, where we were relieved. Then we waited to relieve another parcels train to work to Nuneaton Trent Valley and dispose of our train before returning light engine home.

Norman had worked with me previously as a fireman on steam locomotives, and I knew his character, so we immediately worked a day about so I could teach him the intricacies of the diesel locomotive. He became a diesel instructor a few years later, and had the doubt-ful pleasure of training me; he is now a run-ning shift foreman. A new turn of duty entailed us booking on duty at 8.07 am to work an iron ore train from Water Orton sid-ings to the huge Spring Vale steelworks at Bilston, via Walsall, Wednesbury and Tipton Curve, and return with a steel train.

One week we had Brian Phillips as our guard, who had been a fireman for me work-ing to Rhyl. He had resigned from the rail-way to find other work, but had then returned; as he would have to start at the bottom in the footplate grade, he elected to be a guard. As we went to Water Orton he remarked, 'It'll give me the greatest of plea-sure to hang on as many wagons as I can behind you, then sit in the van and watch you do all the work.'

'Don't forget,' I replied, that if we have to stop through overloading, you're the one to walk back for assistance, and it's a long way from Sutton Park to Park Lane Junction, and from Streetly to Sutton Park.' We were never overloaded!

One Easter Sunday we signed on duty at 7.25 am, went light engine with D7508 to Walsall to work an excursion train going to Great Yarmouth as far as Leicester, and returned with a DMU to New Street. Norman was driving up the bank to Arley working the engine full out to keep time.

'It's a good job we didn't have to work steam locomotives like this,' I said. 'I've looked at the timings and you'll have to go like hell on the down gradient to Nuneaton and work it full out again climbing to Hinckley.'

We booked on one Saturday at 12.25 pm to work a freight train to Derby, but the foreman had our time cards. He said, 'Book on immediately - the loco bus is waiting to run you to New Street. There's a derailment at Ashchurch and the Bristol men who should work the Leeds-Plymouth express are stuck the other side of it. Work their train via Worcester and there'll be a conductor to take you over the old Great Western line via Honeybourne and Broadway to Cheltenham, then you carry on to Bristol.'

We duly took over D35 and worked to Bristol. The Bristol men were not trained on these locomotives and it was normal for us to take the loco to Bath Road depot while the train was taken on by one of the WR's diesel-hydraulics. The Bristol station arranger was waiting at the end of the platform when we stopped.

'I'll look after this,' he said. 'You go over to platform 3 right away - there's another express waiting for men, so work it back to Birmingham.'

No D1574 was on the front (these locomotives were worked by Western men as well as us). I put Norman in the driving seat while I made a can of tea on the stove. As we approached Cheltenham we were again signalled over the diversion line and there was another Worcester driver waiting to conduct us. We carried on to New Street where we

were relieved by Derby men around 7.00 pm, booking off around 7.30 pm, with 214 miles recorded, equal to 14 hours pay.

Saturday 18 May was Cup Final day, and we booked on at 3.25 pm to work to Derby with D170. West Bromwich Albion were playing and Norman brought a portable radio so he could hear the match. Extra time was being played around 5.00 pm when we stood at Tamworth High Level station. Geoff Astle scored the winning goal for Albion, and Norman jumped right out of his seat in his excitement.

As there was heavy permanent way work on our normal line after 7.00 pm, we were diverted on our return journey via Lichfield and Sutton Coldfield to New Street with D61. As we approached Lichfield Trent Valley the boiler, which provided steam to heat the train, stopped working, and Norman went into the engine room to ascertain the reason.

'It looks like fuel starvation,' he said.

When we stopped at Lichfield City station he dropped on to the ballast to look at the fuel gauge and came back alarmed, saying 'We've only about 30 gallons registered on the gauge.'

It had been estimated that these Type 4 locomotives used about a gallon a mile, so I sent him to the signal box to tell control we would try to get to New Street, but if we stopped in a section they would have to be ready to pull us in.

I worked the engine as light as possible, coasting where I could, not bothering to keep time. We arrived safely at New Street, then we were booked to take the empty coaches to Walsall. The station arranger came to meet us and asked if we had enough fuel to get us there. I pointed to the fuel gauge, which was showing zero, and said that I did not know if we could get out of New Street.

'Will you try to get to Vauxhall Carriage Sidings?' he pleaded.

'Send our relief there and get ready to tow us in,' I replied.

'These gauges very often stick,' he said.

'When there's fuel in the tank,' I answered, 'not at zero!'

We arrived at Vauxhall and Harry Rodent

and his mate were waiting. I explained about the fuel.

'You worry too much,' he said.

We alighted and walked to Saltley Loco just down the hill, about an hour earlier than had we gone to Walsall.

About a fortnight later, Harry spotted me in the depot. He said, 'We never managed to back the coaches into the sidings. The engine stopped completely and the shunting engine had to couple up to us to move the train and haul us to the depot.'

We booked on one evening at 5.10 pm to work a local freight trip to Bescot, but once again the foreman was waiting for us saying that there was an English Electric Type 4 in front of a train of steel *en route* from Stoke-on-Trent to Severn Tunnel Junction. 'You're the only driver available trained on these locomotives, so will you come off your job?'

'If I can take my own mate.'

He agreed and we relieved D269 about an hour later at Lander Street. As it was a heavy train we had a bank engine to Camp Hill, and when approaching King's Norton I noticed a fault light showing on the driving panel. I sent Norman to look in the engine room. He came back as we approached Barnt Green, saying 'We've high coolant temperature.'

When we stopped at Blackwell to have the wagon brakes pinned down before descending the Lickey Incline, I put Norman in the driving seat and went into the engine room. I could see that there was not much water in the gauge glass. These locomotives were fitted with a pump that enabled water to be transferred from the boiler water tank into the coolant system, but it would be a long job. I returned to the cab and told Norman to carry on down the hill when the guard was ready, as I would be a while pumping the water. By the time we had stopped at Bromsgrove South to have the wagon brakes released, I had filled up the coolant system and the gauge glass looked respectable. The high water temperature had reduced, the fault light had disappeared, and no further trouble was experienced.

At Gloucester, a Cardiff driver stepped into the cab and said, 'I'm not trained on these, so I've got to conduct you to Severn Tunnel.' We arrived there around 9.00 pm, expecting to be told to take the locomotive back home as no one was trained on them, but were told to take it to the loco depot, where the shed foreman said, 'Home passenger on the 10.35 pm to Bristol, then travel on the Mail from there.'

The Cardiff men had to wait until the 10.30 pm train home, so the driver said, 'Do you fancy a pint?'

I naturally said that I did and he said, 'Come on, I'll show you the Railway Club.'

We sat there enjoying our beverage when the door opened suddenly and the foreman came in. He spotted us and came over, saying, 'I'm sorry, I've made a mistake. I thought that locomotive was an English Electric Type 3.' (This was an easy mistake to make looking at the silhouette, as I was to find out later. 'Will you work it back with a train for Gloucester,' he continued, 'then take it back to Saltley if I give you a conductor driver?'

While I hesitated, he said, 'If you want some food I'll make arrangements at the railway lodging barracks for you to have a meal. There's no need to hurry - the train's not due to leave until 11.30 pm.'

We had another pint, then the Cardiff men showed us the way to the barracks. The cook was waiting for us with lamb chops, potatoes and peas, followed by rice pudding. We enjoyed this repast and signed the chits for the cost to be deducted from our wages. We duly worked back to Gloucester and home light, booking off duty at 6.25 am.

'I'm going to enjoy being with you,' Norman remarked.

I replied, 'We worked a lot more hours than this during the war, but we couldn't get food as easy as tonight.'

In June 1968 we had an offer from the West Bromwich Council to buy our council house for £2,749 10s (my rate of pay then was £18 2s per week - what a comparison with today's prices!). There was an insurance society called The Engineers' Assurance Fund that had started at the Saltley depot, with offices at Washwood Heath Road, and was run for footplatemen. It employed a full-time secretary and office staff, and covered all footplatemen to protect them if they failed their railway medicals and were demoted to another job. It also lent money for housing purchase, so I applied for a loan. At the end of July, after a couple of interviews, I had a letter informing me that I could borrow £2,475 at 7 per cent interest for 25 years - I had to find 10 per cent myself, which amounted to £374 10s. It was November before our solicitors and the Council finalised the sale and I was instructed to pay the cheque from the Engineers' Fund plus the solicitor's bill of £378 17s 6d. On 12 November I was informed that the house was ours and I was to pay no more rent.

Some more new workings had come to the depot. One was a parcels train from Curzon Street to Derby via Aston, Sutton Coldfield, Lichfield and Wichnor Junction, and this had been placed in the No 2 passenger link. In August I booked on at 8.10 pm to work a local freight to Nuneaton and the foreman asked me to conduct our driver over this route. This train arrived at Derby around 11.30 pm, and as their workings returned on the normal route via Tamworth, I was not required, so I caught the 12.30 am mail train, arriving in New Street at 1.30 am, booking off duty around 2.30 am, which was an early finish. I was required to do this all week.

There was permanent way work being done on the Whitacre to Nuneaton line every Sunday for about eight weeks, and the New Street to Leicester and Peterborough DMU trains were diverted via Coventry and Nuneaton. I was required for conducting over these routes for quite a few Sundays, stopping at Nuneaton, then conducting another train to New Street, then the same journey once again.

This was quite efficient working, but one Sunday I booked on duty at 9.10 am to conduct the 10.10 Peterborough train only as far as Coventry, where a Coventry driver took over, and I was booked to stay there until 2.45 pm to work back home. As I was sitting in the mess room having a cup of tea, Don Robertson, an ex-Saltley and Monument Lane man now stationed at Coventry, looked in, and when he saw me asked what I was doing. When I told him I wasn't doing any-

thing until 2.45 pm, he remarked, 'You're interested in the ASLEF union - we have our branch meeting at 12.00 pm and Terry Clarke, our area secretary, is coming today. I'm the chairman, and you're welcome to attend.'

It was a good meeting, and when it finished around 2.00 pm Terry Clarke had to wait for my train at 2.45 pm to Birmingham to catch another train home to Manchester, where he lived. We shared a can of tea and had a good talk about trade union activities. We both knew Les Felton, our area secretary, who used to be our branch secretary. We became good friends and he eventually became President of the union and signed my retirement certificate.

Sunday trains were also interrupted by resignalling on the New Street to Gloucester line, and our link's booked Sunday passenger train to Cardiff, which we worked as far as Gloucester, was diverted via Tyseley, where we picked up a conductor to Stratford-upon-Avon, Honeybourne and Broadway, rejoining our line at Cheltenham.

We booked on at 7.35 am and went light to Vauxhall Carriage Sidings to take 10 coaches into New Street, then ran around the train as we were to depart on the diversion route from the opposite end of the station. On the first Sunday we had quite a lot of delay as most of the old ex-GWR signal boxes were closed, which meant long block workings, and we arrived at Cheltenham over 2½ hours late. Our return train, which we should have taken over at Gloucester, was waiting for us, so it was a case of out of one cab and into another. Eight weeks later we had the same workings with no improvement in time-keeping. One day there was a party of nurses in the front coach going to Cardiff for the day. I said, 'It'll be time for you to come back when you get there!'

One November Saturday morning we booked on at 3.10 am to work a freight train from Washwood Heath to Staveley as far as Derby with D7529. As we approached Burton at about 5.30 am, we were signalled to go up the goods line from Branston Junction. As we proceeded in the darkness, my mate remarked, 'There's one of your loco-

Myself in the cab of a Type 2 awaiting signals at Burton. *Author's collection*

motives on the down goods line - an English Electric.'

When we stopped at Leicester Junction someone popped his head out of the relief cabin and shouted, 'Driver, Control wants a word with you.'

When I picked up the telephone, the loco-motive controller said, 'I want to ask you a favour. There are Barrow Hill men on an English Electric locomotive working to Washwood Heath at Branston, but no one at Burton is trained on them. I've spoken to Saltley depot and they tell me you're OK on them, so will you change over?' I could see a chance of an early finish, so I agreed.

As the signal cleared for us to go out main line, I said to Norman, 'You've driven these before - take over while I make the tea.'

At Elford we were diverted into the loop line. As we stood there I decided to put the cab light on to catch up with the writing of my daily duty statement, and asked Norman, 'What's the locomotive number?'

'D6707,' he replied.

I almost dropped my pen. 'What?' I cried. 'This is a Type 3! I'm not trained on these, only on English Electric Types 1 and 4.'

'What are you going to do?' asked Norman.

'It's too late to do anything now,' I answered. 'We'll have to carry on.' I went and had a look in the engine room to see if there was any difference from the Type 4s.

It was getting daylight when we left Elford and we arrived at Washwood Heath without any trouble. When we arrived at our depot, we had been on duty for only 6 hours. The outside foreman shouted, 'Where have you got that one from?'

I told him of the changeover at Burton.

'I suppose you were trained on them at Monument Lane?' he said. 'No one knows them here so will you fuel and service it and put it at the back of No 3 shed out of the way?'

This suited us, and we went home with only 7 hours on duty on a Saturday.

However, there was a sequel to this. When we signed on duty on Monday at 1.50 pm for the Sutton Park tripper, the shift foreman said to me, 'Take that English Electric you brought here on Saturday back to Barrow Hill depot.'

Norman smiled at me and we had to do as we were told; we were forbidden to drive any diesel locomotive on which we were not trained, and I daren't admit that I should not have brought it in on Saturday. I could now understand how the Severn Tunnel foreman could not tell the difference.

January 1969 found me with a new mate, Ray Reynolds, who again was later to become a diesel instructor, and is now a locomotive inspector. I was still in freight link No 6, working between Bescot, Derby, Leicester, Nuneaton and Coventry, and had requested route refreshing between Gloucester and Bristol and Derby to Sheffield and Rotherham at the annual review of my route card, but this had been declined, so I had to cross these routes off my card.

Part of my booked week's work was a sin-gle-manned turn for which I signed on duty at 5.35 am to work '34 tripper' taking empty coal wagons from Washwood Heath Sidings or Hams Hall Power Station to collieries on the branch line between Nuneaton and Coventry; we would then haul loaded wagons of coal to Hams Hall. I usually had a 'Peak' locomotive on front.

One Saturday lunchtime I was working my second trip with D19 and about 30 loaded wagons down the sharp incline from Arley towards Whitacre Junction, with just the locomotive and guard's van for brakes. I had complete control of the train, trundling along at 20 mph with about half of my brake power applied, when a driver on a passing light locomotive at Daw Mill Colliery started blowing his horn erratically and his second man started waving his arm alarmingly from their side window. I dropped my side window and looked backwards but could not see anything untoward. I crossed over to the other side of the cab, and held the dead man's button while I looked out of the other window. To my amazement I could see flames covering that side of the locomotive. I resumed my seat, increased the braking and brought the train to a stand just short of the crossing points at Shustoke station. There was a signalwoman there, and as I jumped to the track with a fire bottle in my hand I shouted, 'Ada, send for the fire brigade and stop trains coming on the opposite line, as I can't see me putting this fire out with this.'

The flames were above the top of the loco-

motive and I used the hand fire bottle to no avail. The fire alarm in the cab then started to ring, which indicated a fire in the engine room. I climbed into the cab and broke the glass covering the emergency push-button, and exploded the internal fire bottles to work the engine room sprinkler system. I could do no more but wait for the fire brigade, who arrived about 10 minutes later in the station yard opposite my burning locomotive. They soon had hoses out and commenced to put out the fire.

The officer in charge asked, 'How much fuel have you got?'

'About 700 gallons.'

He ordered one of his men to spray foam on the roof of the locomotive. We then heard more sirens, and an ambulance and police car screeched to a halt in the yard, men jumping out and racing towards the railway line. They stopped in amazement when they saw that it was a freight train, as they had been told it was a passenger train on fire.

After about 20 minutes the fire was out and the officer ordered one of his men to check the engine room. I informed him that I had operated the sprinkler system, so he instructed him to put on his breathing respirator, and I opened the door to show him the way. He returned about 10 minutes later to tell us that there was no fire in there.

A fire brigade car then arrived with a supervisor from Nuneaton who examined the seat of the fire, which was judged to be the

Above left D19, the locomotive that caught fire in the dramatic incident at Shustoke station in January 1969. It is seen here some years earlier at New Street in 1964, with rebuilding of the station under way. *Michael Mensing*

Left Shustoke station in 1966, being passed by a Birmingham-bound DMU. *Michael Mensing*

cast iron brake blocks overheating on the steel wheels and setting fire to the oil and grease that had accumulated under the locomotive framing. Ada, the signalwoman, brought a tray of cups of tea for us all.

One of the policemen said, 'Do you want your picture in the paper? The local reporter is here.'

'No fear,' I replied. 'Someone might recognise me.'

The firemen had loosened their tunics and I could see that they had civilian clothes on underneath. When I remarked on this they told me that they were a part-time brigade stationed at Coleshill and had to stop what they were doing to man the fire engine. I knew about part-time firemen as my father had been one from about 1930 until after the war.

They still had one hose spraying over the rear end of the locomotive some 20 minutes after the flames were out, and I asked why.

'That 700 gallons of diesel can be very volatile when heated up, so we're cooling the final tank down.'

'That's the water tank that end,' I said. 'The fuel tank is my end of the engine room.'

An assisting locomotive had arrived by now on the other line, and when the firemen had rolled up their hoses and loaded their equipment, Ada crossed it over to couple up and tow me and the train to Hams Hall.

When we arrived at our depot with the two locomotives the outside foreman was waiting for me to tell me that the shift foreman wanted a report of the incident. I explained all the details and praised Ada for the quick way she acted in stopping trains on the opposite line and sending for the fire brigade. I had a wash and put my belongings in my locker, but then to my dismay found that my car had a flat tyre.

I arrived home around 5.00 pm instead of the usual 2.00 pm. May said, 'I thought we were going shopping and to visit my mother. You're always late when I want to go somewhere.'

'Make a cup of tea and let me cool down for a few minutes,' I replied.

I found out the next day that D19 was towed to Derby Works for refurbishment and I never heard any more of the incident.

The following day I should have been on duty around 2.00 am, but with having to have 12 hours rest I signed on at 4.15 am and was given a job to take D7536 to work a ballast train between Whitacre Junction, Shustoke and Daw Mill, and to my surprise it entailed removing the crossover points at Shustoke which had proved useful the day before - I think that must have been the last time they were used. While the platelayers were engaged in this I had time to go to the signal box and talk to Ada about the day before.

The rest of the week we booked on at 10.24 pm to work a London Willesden freightliner train from Lawley Street Sidings as far as Nuneaton Trent Valley, where we hooked off and an electric locomotive took the train for the rest of the journey, while we waited for a return train to Lawley Street. On Wednesday I worked outwards with Ray and D1647; we arrived at Nuneaton around midnight and waited in the sidings for our return train. Within an hour it arrived and we got ready to couple up, but when the electric locomotive hooked off and was negotiating the way into the sidings it became derailed, blocking our exit. By the time the breakdown train arrived from Rugby an hour had elapsed, and because of the overhead electric wires they could not use the crane, so the heavy locomotive had to be jacked up and slewed across to the rail, which took about 8 hours. Around 7.00 am I sent Ray to the station cafe to get some bacon sandwiches; I could see that we were going to be on duty a long while as we could not get out of the sidings and there was no relief crew at Nuneaton. It was around 10.00 am when we backed on to our train and departed for Lawley Street and our depot, booking off with 13½ hours on duty.

One cold frosty February morning I was rostered to sign on duty at 7.26 am to travel to Coventry to conduct an engineering department driver on a Matisia track-repairing machine to Kingsbury via Nuneaton and Whitacre Junction. There was no protection on these earlier machines, just a roof with no sides on it. There was only one seat for the man driving, and as I was not trained on them I had to sit on an oil drum and instruct the engineering man regarding the signals and so on. It was a good job the maximum speed was only 10 mph as in the frosty air I thought I would be frozen to the oil drum. When we arrived at Kingsbury sidings some 5 hours later I remarked, 'We ought to have a rum ration before we work these jobs.' An engineering department bus was waiting to take their driver back to their depot, so I scrounged a ride home with them.

On 31 March I booked on at 6.25 pm with Alan Tregenna as my mate to work a freight train to Gloucester, which was cancelled, so we were instructed to stand spare. We adjourned to the mess room and after a while noticed that men who had booked on after us were being given jobs. I asked the timekeeper, Arthur Nichols (for whom I had fired for about 12 months but who had failed his eyesight test for footplate work, so had been accommodated in this job) if he had forgotten us.

'I have a job for you with a Toton depot "Peak" and a train of coal for Westbury,' he replied. 'You're the only driver available trained on them.'

Some 30 minutes later we were called out and told to relieve D3 at Duddeston Road Junction signal box. The Toton men were surprised; 'I didn't think Saltley men were trained on these locomotives,' remarked the driver.

It was a loose-coupled train with only four continuously braked wagons. Around midnight we arrived at Bristol expecting to be unhooked, with a 'Western' locomotive to work the train forward. However, a Bristol driver climbed into the cab saying he was to conduct us via Bath to Westbury. We arrived there around 4.00 am and were instructed to take the locomotive back to Saltley. As a freight locomotive running light is not important we had a bad run and did not arrive home until 9.50 am, signing off duty at 10.10 am with 15¾ hours on duty and 240 miles completed. In 1965 the mileage payment had been altered and overtime and mileage payments were paid separately, so we also had 9 hours mileage payment as well as the overtime.

When the summer timetable came into being in May 1969 the 24-hour clock came into force. British Rail had run an advertising campaign to get the public used to the times and the staff had been made aware of the change in leaflets and notices for some months previously. At our trade union monthly meeting this had caused our members to revive the request for drivers to be provided with watches. They raised arguments that guards, signalmen, control officers and other staff had clocks or watches provided to keep the trains running to time, but the drivers who actually worked the trains were not provided with one. It was also mentioned that as half-minute timings were now in force in the working timetable, watches should show these half minutes.

'Let's get any watch first,' I said. 'We can improve on them later.'

Alas! It was to be over 20 years before we achieved our goal.

New electric colour light signalling was by now in operation from Blackwell to Gloucester, controlled by a new signal box at the latter place. British Rail had opted for the three-aspect type of signalling - one red, green and yellow light on each signal post - instead of the more efficient four-aspect - red, green and two yellows. The latter meant faster working, as I had been used to on the ex-LNWR lines from New Street to Euston and Crewe to Liverpool.

One summer evening I was working a return freight train from Gloucester South Junction with D28. There was a thunderstorm in progress and after I had passed Abbots Wood Junction with green signals I noticed that there were no lights showing at signal G63 at Spetchley. As I was working a fully fitted braked train I managed to stop, as a no signal light had to be treated as a danger signal. I climbed on to the ballast in the pouring rain and rang the Gloucester signalman to inform him of the situation. He was surprised, said that the signal should be at green, and told me to wait at the phone. I stood there in the downpour, and after a long wait he told me that lightning must have affected the electricity cables, and instructed me to carry on to the next signal. This was G62, which was also out, so I stopped again. The signalman again told me to carry on to the next signal, but it was now getting dark and I had a job to find it; the new signals had only a slim post about 12 feet high, compared to the larger, taller old semaphore signals. I eventually stopped at signal D61, at Dunhampstead level crossing. I again called the signalman, who told me that all signals were out as far as Bromsgrove. He checked that the level crossing gates were in our favour before telling me to carry on. I proceeded slowly and found another half a dozen signals before arriving at G55, which protected Stoke Works Junction. It was now pitch black, and when I phoned again he said 'You're now at Stoke Works Junction.'

'I know,' I said.

'We can't operate the junction points because of the power failure,' he continued, 'so engineers are having to travel from Gloucester by van to operate the junction manually.'

I instructed my guard to protect the rear of the train with detonators, one at a quarter of a mile, one at half a mile and three at three-quarters of a mile, in case a following train missed a signal and collided with us.

After an hour someone banged on the cab door, and when I opened it a man in civilian clothes could be seen in the rain, who introduced himself as the Station Master from Worcester. He climbed into the cab looking like a drowned rat, as had had a long walk from where he had parked his car. I informed him what the signalman had told me.

'Have you told the guard to protect the train?' he asked.

'I didn't start on the railway yesterday,' I answered. 'We've been protected over an hour.'

Another half-hour elapsed, then we could see lights moving about at the junction in front of us, and the Station Master climbed down from the cab to meet them. After another 20 minutes he said that the junction was lying right for me to proceed over it towards Bromsgrove. As I approached the Bromsgrove South signal it was nice to see it at green and working properly. We arrived at Landor Street Junction and relief around 3 hours late. The Derby train crew were surprised when I told them the reason for the late running, as no rain had fallen in Birmingham.

We had another new job in the link, which entailed booking on at 18.26 to travel to Nuneaton Abbey Street to relieve a train of cement tanks coming from Ketton with a Crompton Parkinson 2,500 hp diesel to work to Queen's Road, Handsworth, via Nuneaton, Landor Street, New Street and Oldbury, returning with empty tanks to Landor Street for relief around 2.00 am. As Queen's Road was on the ex-GWR line between Snow Hill and Wolverhampton, a route I had never traversed before, I had to have a fortnight's route learning.

In November I had another unusual conducting job. This time it was showing Bescot men the route with the Chief Engineer's observation coach from Water Orton to Nuneaton, returning to Whitacre, where they stopped for lunch. We then carried on to Tamworth and Wichnor Junction and back to Walsall via Lichfield and Brownhills.

From the sublime to the ridiculous, a fortnight later I had to conduct another Matisia track machine from Hawkesbury Lane on the Coventry to Nuneaton line via Sutton Park, Walsall, Wednesbury, up the single line at Tipton Curve to Spring Vale sidings on the New Street to Wolverhampton line. Once again I was perched on the oil barrel exposed to the cold weather. I had asked our foreman for a tot of rum when I was detailed for the job, but he had declined. On arrival at Spring Vale I was quite happy to get into the warmth of the engineering department's warm bus to journey home.

— o —

The year 1970 started rather poorly for me as I had a severe bout of bronchitis, something I had experienced for the last few winters, but this was more severe. My doctor sent me for a chest X-ray examination at Hallam Hospital at West Bromwich and they diagnosed me as having coal dust in the lungs, similar to the coal miners' disease of pneumoconiosis. They said it could not be cured, but could only be relieved with drugs. It took six weeks before I was fit to resume work.

When I restarted in mid-February I found I had a new mate, John Crook, who is now a driver at Inverness along with John Bloor, another mate of mine (I spent a week with them recently renewing old friendships). New work was still coming to the depot; one job entailed signing on duty at 20.41 to take a light locomotive, usually a Type 2 AEI to Curzon Street to work a parcels train to Leicester via Walsall and Nuneaton, then return with a train of steel coming from Corby with a Type 4 Crompton Parkinson on the front via Walsall and Tipton Curve, to the new steel-handling depot at Wolverhampton. To get into these sidings we had to travel 'wrong line' for about 200 yards from a point where the old Monmore Green signal box used to be, before coming off the up main line into the sidings. Twelve months previously this movement had resulted in an electric multiple unit crashing into a freight train, killing the driver and injuring several passengers in the EMU.

There had been a lot of disquiet among drivers at the depot regarding link positions, as a lot of them had refused to sign to select to go into either passenger or freight links. This had been fermenting for over a year, and I was one of the first to refuse this selection of links until we knew if men from our depot would have to move to the new Birmingham New Street depot with men from the closed depots at Monument Lane and Aston. It had now become clear that the Saltley men would not be involved, and drivers who had been placed in freight links because of their refusal to sign were now pressing for a review of links' positions. As I had raised this matter at branch meetings a couple of times, without success, I organised a petition of the men concerned and presented it to the Local Departmental Committee (LDC).

Bob Clarke proposed and I seconded a motion for the next branch meeting that all work at the depot be shared, and that passenger and freight work should be worked in all links in line with ASLEF policy.

On Sunday 10 May a special union meeting was called to discuss this subject. I objected to this date as I was booked to work, and

felt that it had been picked deliberately so I could not attend. The branch secretary, Jack Coxsey, said that if I gave him a letter that outlined my reason for the links to be changed, he would ensure that it was read out to second Bob's motion. I duly wrote a long letter pointing out union policy of work sharing, drawing attention to the fact that junior drivers were working passenger trains to Sheffield while senior men, who had declined to sign the declaration form, were working freight trains only as far as Derby, Nuneaton and Bescot. There was a full turn-out for the meeting and, after a long discussion, our proposal to amalgamate passenger and freight work in all links was carried, although it was six months before this came into operation with the winter workings.

A few weeks later an ex-passenger driver, Bill Cumberland, who was also running a newspaper shop, stopped me in the shed, saying, 'I've a good mind to shoot you, but it would have to be a silver bullet to kill you.'

'I work on the railway for my living, I replied, 'and I don't have a side-line as well!'

In June I was sent to learn the road from Tyseley to Cheltenham via Stratford-upon-Avon via the North Warwickshire line. I had been over this route a few times on our 7.25 am Sunday turn with a conductor driver, but new freight work was being booked over it to alleviate the traffic on our normal route via Barnt Green and Bromsgrove.

It was quite a picturesque run; within 5 miles of Tyseley we were in countryside going through Earlswood, Henley-in-Arden, Stratford, Honeybourne, Broadway, and through Winchcombe Tunnel to Bishop's Cleeve, where a good view of the Malvern Hills could be seen, along with the side of Prestbury Park and Cheltenham's racecourse station, near where we rejoined our main line.

In August I had my first week's work over this line, booking on duty at 12.58 with John Crook as my mate, working a freight train for Cardiff from Washwood Heath as far as Gloucester Central station. We then walked across to Gloucester South to relieve a return train coming from Stoke Gifford to Washwood again via the North

Myself posing beside a Crompton Parkinson Type 4 at New Street, probably on a Gloucester-line service. *John Crook*

Warwickshire line. We had a variety of locomotives from Type 4 Crompton Parkinson and Brush to AEI Type 2s. One Thursday we were allocated two Class 1 English Electrics working in tandem. When we arrived at Gloucester, the relieving driver said, 'I'm not trained on these - Control have asked me to conduct you as far as Severn Tunnel Junction.'

So away we went. This was another lovely run, following the River Severn through Chepstow. On arrival at Severn Tunnel Junction we were hooked off our train, changed into the cab of the other locomotive, and returned light to Gloucester, where we dropped off our conductor; we then returned via the North Warwickshire line to Saltley, booking off duty at 1.30 am.

When the winter timetable came into operation in October, the amalgamation of passenger and freight work came into operation. One turn entailed signing on duty at 18.55 to work a parcels train, again with John Crook, and a Class 2 AEI diesel locomotive, from New Street to Leicester, where we were relieved for the train to carry on to Peterborough. We then relieved a train of steel ingots coming from Corby to Bescot via the Sutton Park line. This was a heavy train, and we usually had a Crompton Type 4 locomotive on front. At this time of the year the leaves of the Sutton Park trees were falling on to the line and I had quite a struggle to keep the train moving with the wheels slipping, but with the Cromptons I had full control of the power application. However, one Thursday in the middle of October we had a Brush Type 4, No 1809; this class had an anti-slip device fitted which shut off power automatically when the wheels slipped, but was very slow to regain power. As we climbed from Water Orton to Sutton Park station we were working with full power on and just

kept going. On the easier running just past the station we regained a bit of speed, but when we hit the wet leaves of the park the wheels started to spin and power was automatically shut off. I tried to regain power but it came back slowly, causing the train to come almost to a halt, but we struggled on until we met some more wet leaves and the slipping started again. Once more the anti-slip device came into operation, and we slowed up, but I managed to get some speed into the train. Alas! At the third bout of slipping we came to a complete halt and I could not restart the train. We were in sight of Streetly station and I remarked to John that had we reached there we could have made it, as there was about half a mile of downhill running before climbing up to Aldridge. John walked back to our guard to tell him that we needed assistance; he in turn had to walk back to Sutton Park signal box, some 2 miles in the rear, and put detonators on the track to protect the train.

While we waited, a light locomotive came along the other line and the driver sounded the horn to indicate that he was coming behind us, having just pushed another train through. He pushed us up to Aldridge signal box and we carried on to Bescot. A couple of weeks later I had a letter from the Control office asking for the cause of the delay. I replied that it was an annual occurrence for leaves to fall off trees.

We had a new footplate inspector at the depot, whom we shall call Mr Jones (not his real name), a highly-strung man who would upset men as soon as he stepped into the cab. He would not wish you good morning, but would launch into a tirade of, 'Have you got your rule book, speed notices, hand lamp, etc?' and demand to see them. One Sunday I booked on at 11.10 to conduct one of our drivers, Bill Cumberland, from New Street to Derby via the diversion line through Sutton Coldfield, Lichfield and Wichnor. It was most unusual to see a footplate inspector on a Sunday, so we were very surprised when he climbed into the cab just before our departure from New Street. His first words were, 'Who is the driver?'

Bill Cumberland said he was.

Mr Jones then said to me, 'What are you doing here?'

I informed him that I was there to conduct Bill as he did not sign for this route. 'How do you know the route?' he asked.

'I was at Monument Lane depot from 1955 to 1960,' I replied, 'and I've worked regularly over this road for 14 years.'

The second man decided to go into the back cab and I drove the train, Bill sitting in the second man's seat, leaving the inspector to stand up. I worked over the route correctly, making sure to keep to the speed restrictions through Aston Junction, Sutton Coldfield and Lichfield City, and stopped at Lichfield Trent Valley High Level for passengers. From there to Wichnor Junction there was an overall speed restriction of 50 mph and we were cruising along at this speed with the Alrewas signal box colour light distant, which was about a mile from the stop signal, at green. As we approached the distant I noticed that it went to yellow, and as we were coasting and I had plenty of stopping distance I said nothing.

Mr Jones had seen it.

'Stop!' he shouted. I thought he had seen something untoward, so I stopped within about 500 yards.

I said 'What's wrong?'

He replied that the distant signal had gone from green to yellow.

'I know that,' I answered, 'and I was prepared to stop at the danger signal, not here half a mile away.'

I restarted the train and stopped correctly

at the home signal, which was some 200 yards from the signal box. As there was a telephone provided to communicate with the signalman, I made towards it, but Mr Jones intervened, asking, 'Where are you going?'

'To phone the signalman' I explained.

'It's the proper driver's duty to do that,' he replied.

'That's ridiculous,' Bill complained. 'If he tells me any place along this line, it will be a waste of time. I sha'n't know what he's talking about.'

But Mr Jones insisted that Bill did the phoning. After a few moments Bill returned, saying that a door had been left open on the train when we started from Lichfield Trent Valley. He instructed the second man to go back to the guard to close it.

While we waited, Mr Jones climbed down on to the ballast. Bill said 'Where's he going?'

'To catch a bus, I hope,' I answered.

We could see him on the telephone talking to the signalman, and when our second man returned to say that the door had been closed, we could see that the signal had cleared for us to proceed.

'Shall we leave him here?' I said.

I touched the horn and took the brake off, at which Mr Jones quickly put the phone down and dashed back to us. As we proceeded he said, 'I've been telling the signalman he could have given us a heart attack putting signals against us, and I shall be reporting it.'

'He didn't give me heart failure,' I said. 'I had over a mile to stop at 50 mph - it was nothing.'

'So you're not going to report him?' he asked.

'Nothing more than the normal procedure of a door open,' I replied.

We were relieved at Derby and he carried on with the Sheffield crew. I tipped them off not to trust him, as he reported everything.

He upset a lot of drivers, and on more than one occasion drivers had ordered him out of the cab because he was affecting their concentration. He started asking men questions on rules and regulations when they were travelling along, and it was brought to the notice of our union, who reminded the management of the safety aspect when working trains, and stated that if there was a need for a rules and regulations examination it must be carried out in an office, not on the road!

A few weeks later I was working an express passenger train from New Street to Gloucester when, as I was coming out of the short tunnel between Bournville and King's Norton at the regulation speed of 30 mph, I could see someone on the line with his back to me. I blew the horn sharply and the figure jumped clear. As we passed I could see that it was Inspector Jones. Evidently he was operating a radar speed trap, checking train speed along the curve. About a fortnight afterwards he approached me at the depot saying, 'I've got to thank you for blowing the horn to alert me to the dangerous position I was in.'

'I did it automatically,' I replied, 'but the men at the depot aren't speaking to me.'

'Why?' he inquired innocently.

'Because I missed you.'

'Huh!' he exclaimed, stamping away. He was not amused.

At the December union branch meetings when the officials for 1971 were elected, I was made a trustee responsible for all monies received and paid out, and to ensure any surplus was sent to head office.

With the workings of the new links we had a good variety of work. One of the busier turns entailed signing on duty at 8.36 with John Crook, travelling to New Street and working an express to Gloucester with a Crompton Type 4, getting relief for Cardiff, then relieving another express from Cardiff and working it to Derby with a 2,750 hp Brush Type 4 locomotive, getting relieved for Newcastle. We then relieved another express from Leeds going to Bristol with another Crompton on front as far as New Street. This was quite a busy job, clocking up 188 miles, equal to 13½ hours on the mileage bonus scheme. There was no physical break allowed as I was double-manned with John, and we had to eat our food while travelling along. As John had been with me a few months I had assessed his work and I allowed him to drive

One of our busier turns in 1971 involved working an express from New Street to Gloucester with a Crompton Type 4, getting relief for Cardiff, then relieving another express from Cardiff and working it to Derby with a Brush Type 4, where we relieved another express from Leeds going to Bristol. On 18 May 1971 John Crook stands beside Crompton Type 4 No D165 at Gloucester, then later in the day photographed me in the cab of Brush Type 4 No 1691 waiting to return from Derby. *J. Crook*

the train to Gloucester, then I would work it to Derby and John would work it back from Derby and reverse the procedure the next day. One day, as we approached Derby with John driving, a train was coming out with our men on front working from Sheffield, and I noticed that they had the notorious Inspector Jones with them.

The following day I drove from Gloucester to Derby, so when we relieved our return train I indicated to John to get into the driving seat. Just as we were ready to depart the cab door opened and Inspector Jones burst in to the cab shouting, 'Caught you!'

'Doing what?' I answered.

'Letting your mate drive,' he said.

'That's how they get experience,' I replied.

John stood up to get out of his seat, but I said, 'Stay there. If he doesn't like it he can get off.'

The 'right away' signal showed, so I said, 'Right, away with it John.'

Mr Jones started to protest, but I said, 'Shut up until we get to New Street. I don't want you upsetting John's handling of the train.'

He worked it perfectly as I had trained him. At New Street, when we had been relieved and were standing on the end of the platform, I confronted Mr Jones. 'Now what's this all about?' I asked.

'I saw your mate driving yesterday,' he replied, 'so I decided to catch you today.'

'I also saw you yesterday,' I replied, 'but it made no difference. This is the way to train men to be drivers.' I added, 'I've driven steam engines on expresses even on the Carlisle route as a fireman, when the driver has been occupied firing the engine and couldn't watch me all the time. On these diesels I can watch every move John makes and train him properly.'

'There's a drivers' school just been set up,' Mr Jones said. 'That's where they'll be trained.'

'Never!' I retorted. 'You can't teach drivers in a classroom. You can report me if you want to, but he'll be driving again tomorrow if you care to come along.'

I heard no more of this episode.

Another turn of duty involved booking on at 23.30 to take a Type 4 locomotive from the depot to Curzon Street parcels depot, working to Derby, being relieved for Leeds, then walking to Derby loco depot, bringing an AEI Type 2 into Derby station and picking up half a dozen parcel vans to work to Wolverhampton via Lichfield, Brownhills and Walsall.

One winter's morning we arrived just two signals from Wolverhampton on the bank from Portobello Junction around 5.00 am, and it had started snowing. John phoned the signalman, who said he was having difficulties with his points and would we ring him every 10 minutes if the signal did not clear instead of the 3 minutes designated? We were on an embankment looking down on a factory with an empty car park. After an hour's wait the signalman instructed us to ring up every half hour as the snow was drifting into the points. He said, 'We don't know when we shall be able to get you into the station.'

We watched the car park gradually fill up as the workers arrived for their day's work, and it was around 9.30 am before the signal cleared. By the time we stabled our locomotive and returned to our depot we had been on duty for 11½ hours.

When the summer workings commenced in May 1971 with more new work being put into our link, I was sent to learn the route from Derby to Sheffield and Rotherham, which I had crossed off my route card a couple of years earlier. I was also instructed to learn into the new sidings at Tinsley. When I signed my card for these routes, the roster clerk said, 'Will you learn the way from Stenson Junction to Toton and from Derby to Toton?' I agreed and added some more lines to my route card. I also had a new mate allocated to me, Tony Pountney, and when I asked him if he had done much driving, he replied, 'Not a lot, but I'm getting near to being passed out as a fireman.'

'Right,' I replied. 'I'll teach you what I know including not being afraid of Inspector Jones, who you will no doubt come into contact with.'

Colour light signalling was now in operation between Birmingham and Chesterfield Tapton Junction. The signals from Wingfield, south of Clay Cross, were operated from Trent Power Box, some 15 miles away on the Toton to Leicester line. The signalmen could not see us, except as a moving light on their panel, and we never passed anywhere near them. These modern signals did not operate beyond Chesterfield, and Tapton Junction was the first semaphore box open. One of the duties of the semaphore signalman was to observe the tail lamp of trains as they passed to ensure that the train was complete; if the lamp could not be seen, he would order the train to be stopped at the next signal box to tell the guard to check if the train was complete or if the tail lamp was out.

One of our new turns of duty was signing on at 21.03 to relieve a freightliner train coming from Cardiff at Landor Street and work it via Sheffield and Holmes Junction curve to Rotherham Masborough, where a new freightliner yard had been built. We would have about an hour's wait while the train was unloaded and reloaded, then work back home via Staveley to Chesterfield. This night's work was equivalent to 12 hours on the mileage bonus.

We were working this train on a wet and windy night when we were stopped at Unstone signal box on a steep embankment. When Tony went to the signalman he found that the signalman at Tapton Junction had sent the 'Stop and examine train' code as he had not seen our tail lamp. As this was a freightliner train without a guard's van at the rear, the guard rode in the back cab of our locomotive, so Tony informed him of the situation and he got set to walk to the rear of 20 liner vehicles. He returned after about 20 minutes wet through to say that he had re-lit the oil lamp at the rear of our train.

The next night we were stopped again at Unstone, and as Tony was driving I went to the signal box and was informed again that we had been stopped for train examination as no tail lamp had been seen at Tapton.

I remarked, 'That tail light could have gone out anywhere from Cardiff, as there is colour light signalling all the way, and no semaphore box to look at it.' The guard went back in a howling gale and returned some 20 minutes later with the lamp, saying that he

had used a box of matches to no avail and needed the shelter of the cab to re-light it. He borrowed a match from Tony, as I did not smoke, checked that there was oil in the vessel and lit it. When it was showing a bright red light he proceeded again to the back of the train, and another 20 minutes elapsed before he returned for us to carry on with our journey.

The following night, as we walked to Landor Street to relieve the Cardiff men, he said, 'I'll check that tail lamp before we leave here, and if it's out I can re-light it in the shelter of high buildings, not on that embankment at Unstone.'

Before he gave me the 'right away' signal he climbed into the cab to say that it was out again. A lot of delay occurred to these trains because the old lamps were not suitable to being exposed on a low wagon with the speed of the trains being a maximum of 75 mph. A shield was later fitted, but without much success, and later an electric battery lamp was used.

We had a Sunday turn signing on at 8.45 am, which entailed taking a locomotive from our depot to Vauxhall Carriage Sidings to take 10 empty coaches into New Street to work the 10.03 train going to Leeds and Bradford as far as Sheffield, then returning on a York to Bristol express. One Sunday, owing to work being done on the permanent way at Tamworth and Clay Cross Tunnel, we were diverted via Lichfield City to Derby, then were booked to run around the train to go via Trent to Toton where I was booked to pick up a conductor to take me as far as Chesterfield. When the guard came to tell us the loading of the train at New Street, he remarked, 'I see we're being diverted via Sutton Coldfield and Lichfield and Toton.'

'No,' I said. 'I know that's the normal Sunday diversion route, but I've looked at the special train timetable and we're booked to stop at Walsall for 2 minutes, then via Brownhills to Lichfield.'

He had a look at my timetable and agreed, saying he had missed it.

We departed at the right time but at Aston Junction we were signalled via Sutton Coldfield. I managed to stop at the signal at the end of the station as there was a 20 mph speed restriction in force. I said to Tony, 'Telephone the signalman and tell him he's got the wrong route for us.'

Tony came back saying, 'He says "Are you sure?"'

'Tell him to look at page 21 of the special notice,' I retorted. He did this and the signals were changed to the Walsall route. When we approached Great Barr station the signals changed from green to red. When I stopped the train Tony climbed down to speak to the signalman on the phone, and came back saying 'There's something wrong. The signal boxes at Rushall level crossing and Norton Junction aren't open, so we can't go beyond Walsall. I'll have to phone him again to see what they decide to do.'

After about 10 minutes he returned to say that we were to go into Bescot and another locomotive would hook on to the rear of our train to drag us back to Vauxhall, then proceed via Sutton Coldfield. This was done and we arrived at Derby about an hour late.

As we were recoupling to our train after running around, someone put their head out of the first carriage window and said, 'You will make your mind up which way to go today?'

As we were so late at Chesterfield, the platform inspector informed us that our return train was approaching and Control wanted us to change trains there, so it was a case of getting a can of water and boiling it on the cab stove, and eating our food on the run. Tony remarked, 'This is going to take our 13 hours mileage off us.'

'No fear,' I retorted. 'We're booked to do the 200 or so miles, so I'll see we get paid for it.'

When we arrived at our depot to sign off duty the timekeeper said that the foreman, Ted Brown, wanted a word.

'What have you been up to today?' he asked.

I explained to him and showed him the Special Train Notice showing the 2-minute stop at Walsall. He rang Control and told them of the page concerned, and after a pause he put the phone down saying, 'They

say there was a telegram sent out cancelling that Walsall stop.'

'I've not had one,' I said, 'and neither has our guard or the signalman concerned, or they would have queried my timings.'

I heard no more of this incident and do not know on whose shoulders the blame for the delay was placed.

On the next occasion that we worked this train we were diverted again, this time via Whitacre Junction, Nuneaton, Leicester, Trent and Derby. Tony drove to Leicester and, as I waited for my conductor driver to turn up, sine I did not sign the route between there and Trent, Tony was looking along the platform from his side window and he remarked, 'There's a smashing looking girl coming towards us.'

On arrival at the cab, she said, 'When do we stop at Tamworth?'

I replied, 'Not today! You should have caught the special bus from New Street station.'

'Mother will be upset,' she replied.

I said, 'Don't get out of the train here. Carry on to Derby and there will be a special bus running to Burton and Tamworth from there.'

By then my conductor had arrived, so I told Tony to go back into the train with the girl and explain what I had said to her mother and the guard of the train. He needed no second telling! As we were being hooked off the train at Derby to run around the train to go via Toton, Tony, the girl and her mother came to the cab. Tony said, 'This is Tom Williams's wife and daughter.' (Tom was one of our Saltley drivers.) 'They're going to Tamworth to look at a house they're thinking of buying.'

The next time I saw Tom Williams I asked him if he was trying to get rid of his wife and daughter.

'I was at work,' he replied, 'and they decided to go without telling me.' He said he had been diverted himself that day going to Bristol, and I said that I would not tell my worst enemy to travel on a Sunday with all the permanent way work being done. 'It's bad enough for us, and we're being paid for it!'

12
TYSELEY CHANGEOVER
1971-74

For a couple of years there had been rumours going around the Saltley and Tyseley depots that one of them would close and men would be transferred from one to the other. We thought that it would be our depot, as Tyseley had the adjacent carriage sidings, locomotive repair shops and fuelling facilities, but in July 1971 it was decided, surprisingly, that Tyseley would close, leaving only 16 drivers there to marshal DMUs in the carriage sidings and locomotive shops, plus two other drivers to work the Small Heath shunt engine and one other to man the Knowle & Dorridge shunter.

There had been meetings with the railway Board and the trade unions and our Local Departmental Committees (LDCs) as to how the changeover would take place. There was quite a difference of opinion between the two LDCs. The Tyseley men and railway management wanted the ex-Western Region men to keep their work separate from us and continue to work to London Paddington, Basingstoke and Bristol, via the North Warwickshire line, as before. We did not agree to this, as the Worcester depot had done this some 40 years before without success. Our opinion was that all work should be integrated, with men being placed in the links that their seniority dictated. After lengthy meetings our point of view won the day. This meant that some ex-LMS men found themselves in links going to places on the former GWR, and Tyseley men working to Sheffield, Leicester, Crewe and Bristol via the ex-LMS routes.

In August I had two ex-Tyseley men, Harry Redfern and Carey Evans (who became a footplate inspector at Derby), riding with me learning the route to Sheffield, so I got to know them personally. The same happened when we travelled with the ex-Tyseley men learning their routes, so everyone got to know one other better. There was a lot of banter in the mess room about 'God's Wonderful Railway' and 'Brunel's Boys' versus the LMS, Stephenson's *Rocket*, etc.

In October I was sent to learn the road from Didcot to Reading, and in November I had my first week's work over this route, booking on duty at 7.32 am to work the 8.12 am from New Street to Southampton as far as Reading, with Tony Pountney and a 2,750 hp Brush Type 4 locomotive. On arrival at

Following the demise of steam in 1968 Saltley's steam locomotives were replaced by a sizeable allocation of diesel locomotives. This is the view from the top of the coal hopper showing a wide selection of types. *J. Crook*

Reading we uncoupled and another locomotive came on the other end to work the train via Basingstoke. We followed the train along the platform to stable our locomotive in the sidings, and about 45 minutes later hook on to another train coming from Poole to work it back to New Street.

The following week I was working the night freightliner train to Rotherham, which was now diagrammed as a single-man turn; I did not need a second man for steam heating of the train, and was booked on a physical needs break at Rotherham. In the middle of the week I had what was by then known as a Class 47 diesel-electric, D1926, in thick fog, and after a temporary speed restriction at Castle Bromwich I attempted to pick up speed, but when I applied power I heard a loud bang in the engine room and the engine stopped. I managed to coast to the signal protecting Water Orton West Junction, where I phoned the Saltley Power Box signalman. I explained what had happened and that I would take a look in the engine room to see if I could rectify it. On investigation I could smell burning rubber and I noticed that two electric circuit breakers had tripped; these I reset and managed to get the engine running, but I still could get no power to the traction motors. I called the signalman again and told him that I could not carry on; he said, 'There's another Class 47 at Saltley loco which they will send to rescue you.'

About half an hour later D1749 arrived with two ex-Tyseley drivers on board, Ken Edgington and Alf Shaw, the latter a diesel instructor. They had been instructed to hook on to the front and we were to carry on to our destination with both locomotives. Alf said he would ride on the crippled locomotive to see what he could do, and I carried on with Ken, riding up front with me. I soon got the train running at the 75 mph maximum, and as we ploughed through the heavy fog, Ken remarked, 'I hope you know where you are - it's like looking into a blank wall to me.'

'I've been on this route for about 30 years,' I replied.

The lights of Derby station soon appeared and Ken said, 'I've never been beyond here.' However, the fog stayed so he did not see

much of the route. When we arrived at Masborough freight yard the inspector told us to stable the crippled locomotive on an adjacent siding, and Alf said, 'There's a notice in the electric control cabinet stating that there are experimental traction motors fitted, and if any failure occurs there's a phone number to call to inform the person concerned.'

It was now around 2.00 am, so I told Alf to phone Control with all the relevant information and they could have the pleasure of waking him up. They both rode back in my cab sharing a can of tea, so we were well and truly mixing with one another.

In December we were working the 7.32 am turn to Reading with another Class 47 Type 4 Brush locomotive when we lost power after passing Aynho Junction, between Banbury and Oxford. Tony phoned the signalman at Oxford while I investigated the engine room. I reset a circuit breaker and regained power, but on attaining 40 mph power was lost again. This happened on three occasions, and I told Tony to inform Oxford that we would endeavour to get there, but we would need a fresh locomotive.

When we crawled into Oxford about 30 minutes late there was no fresh locomotive available, but an electrician and fitter were waiting to look in the engine room. There was a lady Station Master at Oxford and she came to us asking what was the trouble, whereupon I explained the situation. I invited her to come into the engine room to show her what was happening, but she declined. After about 10 minutes the electrician came out to say that he had cleaned some electrical contacts, but he needed about half an hour to do it properly.

'We have that time at Reading,' I said. 'Come with us in case we break down again and you could do the job there.'

He agreed, so we departed and got up to our top speed of 75 mph towards Didcot. I looked across to see that he was standing holding the back of Tony's seat, and his knuckles were white. I shouted to Tony, 'Give him your seat before he keels over when we reach 95 mph on the Didcot to Reading line.'

When our return train arrived we rejoined our locomotive and the electrician said that he had fixed the electric circuits but if I didn't mind he would ride in the train back to Oxford, and that he would be in the front coach if I needed him.

Tony drove back home without any more trouble and at Oxford the electrician came up to us to ask if everything was OK. We said it was. 'I don't know how you can stand the bouncing about at that high speed,' he said.

'It's a case of everyone to their own trade,' I replied.

One Saturday morning towards the end of December I booked on at 5.35 am and my freight train was cancelled, so I waited spare in the mess room. Around 7.30 am the foreman came rushing in with the special train workings book and job card, which he gave to me saying, 'The driver for the West Bromwich Albion excursion to Leeds hasn't turned up and we haven't missed him until now. The locomotive was due off the depot 10 minutes ago. Do your best to recover this delay.'

I looked at the train board to see D1956 allocated to the job, but the engine was not even running, so I had to start it up and wait for air pressure to rise while I did the cursory examination. We left the depot about 30 minutes late and had a bad run to Oxley carriage sidings, where we arrived about 45 minutes down. While we were being hooked on to the train I took a quick look at the workings and could see that I had to work it to Rotherham, and we were booked to stop at Wolverhampton, Tipton, Dudley Port, Oldbury, Smethwick and New Street. Then we were non-stop to Rotherham. The guard came up to inform me that we had 10 coaches for 355 tons behind us.

We arrived at Rotherham only about 15 minutes late and got relieved by a Leeds driver. I thought we had done well, pulling back 30 minutes of our late start, but when I went to sign off duty Ted Brown, the foreman, asked, 'Why did you miss Spon Lane station this morning?'

'Because we weren't booked to stop there,' I replied.

'Have you got the Special Train Notice?'

'Yes.'

'Have a good look at it.'

I looked and could not see Spon Lane mentioned. When I showed him the page concerned, he smiled and said, 'Turn the page sidewards.' Having done this I could see that Spon Lane had been placed in as an afterthought, and we had been booked to stop there for 1 minute. Ted remarked, 'Control tell me there were five passengers waiting to go on that excursion, so it will be reported, and no doubt you will hear more of this.'

It was the middle of January 1972 when I received a Form 1 charged with failure to stop at Spon Lane. I requested an interview with my trade union representative present, as was my right. It was another week before the interview took place in front of Mr Edwards, the superintendent of the depot, who read the charge out and asked for my reason for not stopping. I explained that it was not my booked turn and I had rushed off the depot without studying the timetable, and pointed out that the Spon Lane timings had been added as an afterthought, and showed it to him, as I had retained the special notice.

Mr Edwards said, 'It's your duty to study all notices, and just because other people make mistakes it doesn't mean that you can do likewise.' He added, 'You deprived five football supporters of an enjoyable day at Leeds.'

I smiled and remarked, 'Albion lost 3-0.'

'You don't seem to be taking this seriously,' he retorted. 'I'm thinking of suspending you from duty for two days.'

Les Kirk, my union representative, intervened, saying, 'You can't do that, he has no misdemeanour on his record card.'

They both argued while I stood there, and eventually it was agreed that a reprimand would be recorded on my record card. This would be my punishment for doing my best in exceptional circumstances.

In February I was sent to learn the route from Moor Street station to Tyseley and from Hatton to Stratford-upon-Avon. The new job in the link consisted of signing on duty at 14.15, travelling by the depot bus to Tyseley carriage sidings to work an empty DMU into Moor Street, working the 17.40 to Stratford-upon-Avon via Solihull, then working the 20.10 to Leamington and stabling the unit in the sidings. To complete the day's work I would relieve a one-coach diesel parcels train coming from Reading and work non-stop into New Street, where I was relieved, then travel back to the depot to sign off duty after just 8 hours. One evening we left Moor Street at 17.40 for Stratford with a double DMU comprising of six non-corridor suburban coaches. When we arrived at Hatton North the signals were at caution, and I was brought to a stand at Hatton curve at the signal protecting the single line to Bearley Junction. I climbed down to telephone the Saltley Power Box, which controlled these signals, and was informed that there was an electrical failure and that they could not clear the signals to Bearley. Had the line been controlled by Saltley all the way to Stratford they could have authorised me to proceed at caution, but as Bearley Junction was still a semaphore box I would have to wait for a pilot man to ride with me. This was around 18.20 and I asked the guard to tell the passengers the cause of the delay. After an hour or so some passengers asked if there was a toilet anywhere.

'Only behind the hedge,' I replied.

Some desperate travellers did do this, although I didn't have a lady ask!

Around 20.00 the pilot man arrived. He was the Station Master from Leamington, and he informed me that he had been at a

When this view is compared with that on page 77 it can be seen how much rationalisation has taken place around Saltley, now that many of the sidings have been lifted and the semaphore signalling replaced with colour lights controlled from the new Saltley Power Box. Class 37 No 37087 (formerly D6787) heads towards Water Orton in 1975. *Michael Mensing*

restaurant with his wife and had just ordered a meal when he was contacted about our predicament. After he had spoken by phone to the Bearley Junction and Saltley signalmen, he instructed me to pass the signal at danger and proceed at caution. We arrived at Stratford at 20.30, where I was relieved and told that my 20.10 train was waiting on the other platform. The pilot man rejoined me in the cab, saying that the fault had cleared. 'It must have been us running over the track, but my car is at Hatton station so I'll ride with you.' When he left me at 21.00 I remarked, 'I hope your meal is still warm!'

We also used to book on duty at 1.07 am to work a freight from Washwood Heath to Derby, but when I booked on duty one Thursday I was instructed to work a special train of Austin motor cars from King's Norton to Wakefield as far as Rotherham, with English Electric Type 4 (now Class 40) locomotive number D285. When we arrived at Rotherham around 6.00 am the Leeds driver who was to have relieved us said that he was not trained on the locomotive, so Control wanted me to work through to Wakefield and he would show me the route. We arrived at Wakefield around 7.30 am and had to take the locomotive to Healey Mills depot, arriving about 8.30 am. I asked the foreman for a service home as it seemed as if we were in the middle of nowhere, and I had to wait about an hour for the depot bus to run me to Wakefield where I caught a train to Sheffield and another to Birmingham, resulting in my being on duty 11 hrs 53 mins.

In late March I was seconded on to the LDC as one of the members was off duty through sickness. Work was needed to be done on the new links for the summer workings coming into operation in May 1972. This entailed a fortnight's work.

At the annual meeting of the Self-help Sick Club in May, it was decided to form a sub-committee to review the rule book and look at subscriptions and benefits. I was elected to this along with the secretary, Jack Randle, the treasurer, Vic Pattison, and another committee man, Jack Evans. We had to apply for a day's leave from work and were paid for loss of earnings by the Sick Club. It

took a full day to do this and we recommended that a new rule book be published to bring
the rules we had altered up to date.

In June I was sent to learn the route into
Oxley carriage sidings from Wolverhampton
High Level. This line had previously only
been accessible from the ex-Western Region
Low Level station, but a new stretch of line
had been put in at the North Junction to
enable all coaches to be cleaned and maintained there.

As a child, when on holiday, I used to go
with my father on his brewery lorry, and he
had made deliveries at Jones Road Club in
Wolverhampton, which was about 100 yards
from the two viaducts carrying the railway
and the canal. I used to sit on the barrels of
beer on the lorry and watch the movements
of the gaily coloured boats and the green and
brass of the Great Western steam locomotives, the drivers, firemen and guards with
their red and green folded flags protruding
from their bags - it was quite a kaleidoscope
of colour and movement for a child of 12 or
13 to enjoy.

For over 30 years I had travelled around
the ex-LMS railways of Wolverhampton and
had never found this place of my childhood,
and I sometimes wondered whether I had
dreamed of it, or it was a figment of my imag-
ination. On that Monday morning, however,
as I rode on the locomotive towards Oxley,
there it was, the place I had tried to find.
The access to the street was by way of about
60 steps, which I negotiated and stood view-
ing that childhood scene, soaking it all up
again. Unfortunately, there were no green
and brass locomotives, only the diesels.

On a sadder note, in 1946 my father had
collapsed and died while delivering to the
Jones Road Club, so on my lunch break I
went to the club and inquired if anyone
remembered him. The elderly doorman did,
and he introduced me to a couple of the
committee who I thanked for their floral trib-
utes of 26 years previously.

We had one evening turn where we
booked on duty at 18.30 to travel to New
Street to work a York express coming from
Bristol as far as Sheffield, where we were
relieved and travelled to Rotherham to catch

a depot bus to Tinsley locomotive depot.
After our physical needs break we would
relieve a Leeds crew on a Bristol air-braked
freight train and work it via Treeton,
Staveley and Chesterfield to Landor Street.
One night as we worked back with D1649 the
engine stopped as we approached Belper station. As we were coasting, Tony went into
the engine room and was back in a couple of
minutes to say that we were out of fuel. Had
this been a vacuum-braked train and the
exhausts stopped working, the vacuum would
have leaked away, applying the brakes and
stopping the train. However, as we were an
air-braked train, although the compressors
were not working the air pressure remained
constant, so we cruised along in silence. I had
to apply the brakes gradually for the 15 mph
speed restriction in Derby station, knowing
that I could not regain the pressure I had
used, and managed to run to the Birmingham
end of the platform where I stopped the train.
We had coasted some 8 or 9 miles.

I asked Tony to tell the signalman that we
were out of fuel.

'This is an ideal place to stop with the
diesel depot just across the sidings,' he said.

'It was no use stopping at Belper,' I
answered. 'It would have taken an hour or
more to rescue us. Besides, they give Green
Shield stamps here.'

The guard, Jack Lane, came along the platform with his hand lamp and detonators and
said, 'I've been waiting to use these when the
engine stopped out in the country.'

'There's no need now as we are protected
by the Derby signals,' I replied.

Eventually a fresh locomotive arrived and
towed us into the sidings, then rejoined the
train for us to carry on with about 30 minutes
delay.

My 50th birthday was in June and again I
had to go to Derby for my medical examination. The doctor passed me, but said that I
had put on a stone in weight since the last
examination five years earlier.

'It's the change-over from steam to diesel
traction,' I remarked.

'I hope you've taken some of it off when I
see you in another five years,' he replied.

One day in July we booked on duty at

17.55 to work a freight train to Gloucester, but the foreman instructed me to work the breakdown crane and vans to Littleton Colliery sidings near Penkridge on the Wolverhampton to Stafford line, where the down line was blocked with derailed coal wagons. We had D7527 and Bill Hicken was the foreman fitter in charge. We arrived at the site of the incident around 19.15 pm to find a dozen 'merry-go-round' coal wagons piled up. Evidently the train was being propelled from the main line into the colliery sidings when one wagon became derailed and the rest of them piled up on top of it. It took the breakdown crew until about 2.00 am to clear the main line. I thought we had finished then, but Bill came to us and said, 'I want our train put in the sidings and the crane marshalled alongside an electric overhead gantry upright post that has been damaged. The concrete base has got to be taken out of the ground.'

This base was about 3 feet in circumference and was inserted about 7 feet into the ground. When we got into position I remarked to Tony, 'This looks like being a long job', and told him to go and get some sandwiches from a road transport cafe on the nearby A449. The gantry was taken down, then the crane fastened to the bolts that were in the concrete base. Bill gave instructions for the crew to keep a watch on the crane when he gave the order to lift, as one had tipped over doing the same job a few months previously.

It took about ten or a dozen pulls with only about a couple of feet pulled out before the watching men shouted to stop. When the crane eased off, the base sank back into the ground with the suction underneath it. It was like pulling a huge tooth! It was around 6.00 before it eventually came out completely. As we re-marshalled the crane on to the train ready to go back to the depot, the signalman told Bill that we were needed at Nuneaton for another derailment.

'We've been on duty over 12 hours now,' I said, 'so instead of going via Walsall we'll go via Wolverhampton and Birmingham New Street, then we can get relieved outside Saltley loco.'

I thought the breakdown crew would also be relieved, as they were the 14.00 to 22.00 fitting staff, but when we arrived at Saltley there was a driver, second man and guard, but the original breakdown crew carried on. By the time we signed off duty we had 13½ hours to our credit. I don't know what time the others booked off.

Later in the month I booked on at 17.00 for a freight train to Toton, and again the foreman was waiting for me. He said, 'I need you to work a special DMU to York. The Plymouth to York express is delayed considerably.'

I was sent on a bus to Tyseley to pick up two three-car DMUs and take them into New Street to work to York stopping at Burton, Derby, Sheffield and Rotherham, where I picked up a conductor driver. We arrived at York around 22.00, and were placed in a bay platform. The Station Inspector said, 'Have your physical needs break and tell me when you are ready to leave to go back empty coaches.' This we did, but we had a bad run back because of the large amount of express freight trains that ran through the night, compared with which empty coaches were not important. I was on duty 11½ hours and the mileage was 254.

The mileage bonus scheme had been altered during a recent wage increase, with 200 miles being equivalent to 8 hours pay, instead of the old 140 miles, but all overtime was to be paid for instead of losing it to mileage, as in the old scheme, so I had 4 hours mileage plus 3½ hours overtime, and night rate. It was a profitable night's work! This was the first time I had worked into York, and I did not think that in a few years time Saltley men, myself included, would be working there on a regular basis.

At the beginning of August I heard the bad news that George Wilkins, who had introduced me to trade unions and committee work, had died. He had been a Town Councillor at Walsall for many years and in the spring of that year had become the Mayor. I and five other ex-Walsall drivers acted as pall-bearers, wearing our best uniforms. The cortege had police motor cycles in front of the hearse and also as outriders, and it stopped at the Town Hall for the staff to pay their last respects. He was cremated at Ryecroft cemetery and we returned to his terraced house in Palfrey to mix with Council officials, trade union representatives and railway bosses. George's wife, whom I had known for many years, told me that his doctor knew he had cancer before he took the Mayor's office, but had said that 'George had worked for that position for many years, so let's hope he can finish his year in office.' Unfortunately he only lasted about five months.

In October five other drivers and myself were sent to learn the route into London Paddington from Banbury on the 'new road', via Bicester, High Wycombe and Old Oak (it had been built as late as 1906, thereby the 'new road'), and from Reading via Slough, Southall and Ealing. We signed on duty at 06.40 to travel on the 07.20 to Banbury, changing trains for Reading and arriving around 09.00. For the first two weeks we attended the route-learning school run by Inspector Stan French. This was necessary because of the four-aspect colour light system of signalling, which called for fast running of trains on the two main lines and two relief lines, plus several loop lines and sidings. The old semaphore system had various signals on gantries to show visibly any diversion of route, but the colour light diversionary signal was normally not visible unless set for the diversion; thus when drivers were route learning it was impossible to see the diversions that could be used, yet at some signals up to six different routes could be indicated. We were accompanied in the school by drivers and guards from Bristol, Cardiff and Swansea, and a series of colour slides were shown on all the important signals, giving us each diversionary route and the speed restrictions involved.

The approach to Paddington station from Old Oak Common was highlighted as trains could be switched between the six lines on four occasions before arriving at the platform indicator signals. The various goods yards at Reading, West Drayton, Slough, Southall and Acton were also shown, with all the internal signals, the locomotive and DMU depots at Old Oak Common and Southall, and all carriage sidings. We were also shown

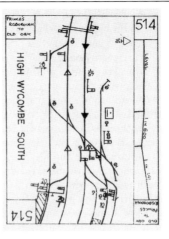

This portion of the BR route map for the 'new road' from Banbury to Paddington shows that semaphore signals were still in wide use at High Wycombe, and remained so well into the 1980s. After about four weeks schooling we rode two at a time in locomotive cabs to get a feel for the gradients, etc.

the signalling of the single line from Aynho Junction through Bicester, Princes Risborough, High Wycombe and Greenford (where we could be diverted over the branch line to the Reading line or to Old Oak Common). The signals between Aynho and Princes Risborough were 8 miles apart and line-side phones were provided 3 miles apart in case of emergency. From Princes Risborough to Park Royal, which was only a few miles from the centre of London, and across the branch line between Greenford East Junction and West Ealing, the old semaphore signalling was still in operation.

After a fortnight in school we were taken on a single-coach DMU along these routes into Paddington, returning along the main and relief lines into the different freight and carriage sidings; questions were invited and explanations given by Stan French. After about four weeks schooling we rode two at a time (the maximum allowed in the cabs of expresses, local passengers and freight trains) to get the feel of the gradients and the braking capabilities. As one instructor remarked, 'It's easy to go at speeds of 95 to 100 mph with the power we have, but it's stopping them that causes the problems!'

We would be working express passenger trains into Paddington, car trains with over 100 Rover cars from Knowle & Dorridge for Dover or Harwich as far as West Ealing, Acton or Old Oak Common, and coal trains for the coal concentration depot at West Drayton. After a fortnight of this we returned to the route-learning school to be polished up, with Stan French asking questions on the tricky part of the route, before returning to Saltley to sign our route cards.

It was 29 December when I had my maiden trip to Paddington, working the 7.20 am from New Street with my regular mate Tony Pountney. We had a good run to Banbury, stopping at Solihull and Leamington *en route*. We then ran into heavy fog over the new line towards Bicester and this persisted all the way into Paddington station. As we were travelling at 95 to 100 mph on the falling gradient from High Wycombe to Old Oak Common, looking for the semaphore distant and stop signals through a wall of fog, Tony remarked, 'I hope you learned the route properly.'

'I'll tell you when we arrive at Paddington safely,' I replied.

The return journey was via Reading and Didcot and we ran out of the fog at Oxford. The following day was clear and frosty and I told Tony to do the driving to Banbury, where I would take over, and he could do it again from Oxford, until he became conversant with the route.

As we approached Greenford East Junction the signals were against us. I brought the train to a stand at the junction signal, and Tony went to the signal box to discover that the points were frozen towards the branch line and the signalman was waiting for permission from Control to send us that way. This we did, and we travelled along at 20 mph, the maximum speed allowed, until we joined the main line at West Ealing and ran into Paddington about 20 minutes late.

On Sunday, the last day of the 1972, we signed on duty at 3.55 am to work the 4.20 am from New Street, the Royal Mail train from Penzance to Newcastle, as far as Derby, with a diversion via Aston, Lichfield and Wichnor Junction. We returned with a six-car DMU to New Street and took the emp-

ties to Tyseley, and were bussed back to Saltley around midday. Tony and I adjourned to the railway club to celebrate the end of an eventful year together.

At the December ASLEF branch meeting I had been elected as Vice Chairman and was made a delegate to Birmingham Trade Council where all trade unions in the area met once a month.

In February 1973 I was rostered to learn the route from Gloucester to Bristol, of all places, which I had been travelling since 1942 as a fireman, and since 1956 as driver, but as I had not been over the route for over 12 months I had crossed it from my card. However, I found out that it had been altered. I knew that the old LMS station, Gloucester Eastgate, had been closed and all trains had to go into the old GWR Central station. There trains for Bristol and the West Country had to reverse, with another locomotive coming on the other end, or the train engine had to run around it to work forward. This diversion into Central station and the return to our original route at Gloucester South Junction added over 10 minutes to our running time. At union and management meetings I often advocated that passengers for Gloucester and South Wales should change at Cheltenham and be taken into Gloucester on a DMU. This would limit the delay to a few passengers, rather than cause a lot of delay to a train full.

Another big alteration on the Bristol route was from Yate Junction. Originally the old LMS route took us via Westerleigh, Mangotsfield and Fishponds and entered Temple Meads station at Barrow Road Junction. Now we joined the ex-GWR line at Yate Junction, then carried on to Stoke Gifford where a new station, Bristol Parkway, had been built at the junction of the Severn Tunnel and South Wales line with that into Bristol Temple Meads via Filton Junction. The old LMS locomotive depot at Barrow Road had been closed and a new diesel depot built on the old steam depot at Bath Road, and a DMU depot at St Philips Marsh had opened on the triangle around the station.

At this time the railway trade unions were in dispute with management regarding wages and conditions of service, and at the end of February, as our branch chairman was in hospital, I chaired a noisy open meeting at the Olive Branch public house about 2 minutes walk from our depot, with about 200 men in attendance. Les Kirk, the Midlands area ASLEF secretary, was in attendance, bringing the meeting up to date with the negotiations. I managed to control the meeting, and after 2 hours and numerous proposals and amendments being put forward and voted upon, it was decided we embark on a series of one-day strikes.

On 10 May it was the annual assembly of delegates meeting of ASLEF, which met at the union headquarters in Hampstead, London. The weekend prior to this a meeting of all the local branches took place to make certain suggestions. I was elected as chairman from the floor, and it was a lot quieter and more orderly than the last meeting, which had lasted about 3 hours. On 30 May, after many one-day strikes and a ban on overtime and Sunday work, the dispute was resolved, and we had a wage rise from £30.75 to £33.00 per week.

With the summer workings starting in May I had a new mate allocated to me, Ray Reynolds, who had fired for me in steam days. He is now a footplate inspector in Birmingham.

We had a single-manned Sunday turn allocated to us called the 'Paddington stand-by'. This entailed signing on duty at 13.30 to be bussed to Tyseley to prepare a DMU and be prepared to work anywhere on the ex-GWR route to London, taking passengers who had missed their connections because of late running of trains through permanent way work. One day in June we had waited all afternoon without being called on and had resigned ourselves to having to go back to Saltley around 21.00 when suddenly there came a phone call from Control to say that passengers needed to be taken to Banbury and Bicester. Although our day's work was almost over and we were not keen to go, with passengers stranded we could not refuse. By the time we had got to Bicester and dropped army personnel coming back off leave, and returned empty coaches home, we had been on duty 13 hrs 50 mins. I should have been on duty at 12.59 on the Monday to work the

13.40 to Paddington, but as I had not signed off duty until 3.20 am I could not sign on until 15.20, so I missed my train and had to do spare duties. However, as it was not my fault I was still paid my mileage bonus payment of 3 hours.

On the Tuesday I was on my own job with my booked mate and D1707, and as we approached Fosse Road signal box between Leamington and Banbury, in heavy thunder and rain, we had a power failure and I coasted uphill until we were inside the signals protecting both ends of the loop line, so that if needed another locomotive could get to us from either direction. I sent Ray to the signalman to explain our difficulties, and as he got on to the track in the heavy rain, he shouted that there was smoke coming from one of the traction motors. That gave me a clue, so when I entered the engine room I isolated a pair of traction motors (this could only be done in pairs). I then went back to the cab and tested for power, but to no avail, so I returned to the engine room, reconnected that pair and isolated another. This time I was successful and power was regained. Ray had returned by then, wet through, and I told him to inform the signalman that we would endeavour to get to Banbury, but would need a fresh locomotive there, as we would not be able to keep time with two out of our six traction motors isolated.

When we arrived at Banbury the locomotive foreman was at the end of the platform and asked if we were trained on English Electric locomotives. Ray put his head in his hands, saying 'Not a Type 3!'

The foreman said, 'No, a Type 4.'

'Yes,' I replied, 'I'm all right on those.'

After our crippled locomotive had been removed we therefore carried on with D248 via Oxford and Reading, arriving at Paddington about an hour late. The station locomotive arranger was waiting for us and said, 'Where have you dug that up from?' Nobody here is trained on them. Shut it down when the shunter hooks it off and another locomotive is coming on the other end for you to leave about the right time.' He added, 'We shall have to get some men from Willesden to move it.'

It was therefore a case of picking up a can of water as we walked along the platform, which I boiled and made the tea to have with our sandwiches while Ray drove back via High Wycombe and the 'new road'.

During the journey he complained that he was still wet through, and that it was his birthday. I laughed and said, 'Never mind - I'll buy you a drink when we sign off duty.'

We also had night freight trains to Harwich Docks from Knowle & Dorridge, going as far as West Ealing, or to Dover as far as Old Oak Common. For the West Ealing train we booked on at 23.00, went light to Knowle and picked up a train of 20 long, flat vehicles carrying about 100 cars, then worked via Reading. At West Ealing our guard hooked us off and we came back to Southall to pick up a train comprising another 20 car flats, either empty or carrying Italian or French cars. For the Old Oak Common train we signed on at 21.35 and went via the New Road to Old Oak up sidings and, after hooking off, crossed over to

Class 37 No 37117 (formerly D6817) on a mineral train near St Andrews, Birmingham, in 1975. I was trained on these locomotives in 1973, although they were not very different from the English Electric Type 4 with which I was already familiar. *Michael Mensing*

the down sidings under the Power Box to pick up our return train.

In July we were on the Old Oak Common turn and found that we had been allocated English Electric Type 3 locomotive (Class 37) D6778. I informed the foreman that I was not trained on it, but he said, 'That's the only locomotive we have. I'll arrange for a traction conductor driver to accompany you.'

I could see that it was going to be an uncomfortable night with three of us in a cab with only two seats, so I sent Ray to get a chair out of the mess room. I drove on the outward journey, as the accompanying driver did not sign for the route, and Ray did the honours on our return journey.

The following night our train was cancelled and we were instructed to work a special iron ore train to Corby steelworks as far as Leicester. But again we were allocated another Class 37, D6997, and I had to have another traction conductor, so Ray borrowed another chair. However, on arrival at Leicester, another route conductor driver stepped on to show us the route to Corby. I remarked to Ray that we should have got two chairs, as there were now four of us in the cab. On arrival at the massive steelworks (now closed down) we returned light locomotive back home.

It was September before I was trained on these locomotives, and I had to go in front of the indomitable Inspector 'Jones', who had Charlie Lindley and myself for 7 hours of questioning, although there was not much difference from the English Electric Type 4, with which we were already conversant. After 4½ hours I said, 'I'm entitled to a physical needs break between the third and fifth hour, so I'm going to the mess room and will be back in half an hour.'

When we returned he carried on grilling us until the last minutes before he made out our certificates to drive that type of locomotive.

At this time there were important LDC meetings regarding Bank Holiday workings, and as our branch chairman was still off duty ill, I was again co-opted on to the LDC. We had several meetings with the local management and got the conditions we wanted.

On Sunday 14 October I was again on the

13.30 'Paddington stand-by'. Around 20.00 we were called upon to go into New Street with three-car DMU set No 534 and take passengers to Banbury, Oxford, Reading and Bicester. At Reading I sent the guard to make a can of tea while I went to the toilet, and when I returned I noticed that we had only one passenger, a WAAF girl sitting in the rear of the train. I introduced myself and inquired where she was going. She told me she was going to Bicester, so I invited her to ride in the 1st Class compartment behind my cab, as it would take another hour before we got to her destination. The guard produced the tea and we invited her to share it as we proceeded via West Ealing, Greenford and High Wycombe, arriving at Bicester around 00.30.

When I asked her how she would get to her barracks, she replied, 'I'll phone them and they'll send a car to pick me up.' The guard explained where the public telephone box was situated, as there was no staff on duty. It was 02.15 before we signed off duty and again I missed my Monday turn on the 12.59 Paddington. It was Tuesday when I resumed my own turn of duty with a new mate, Brian Hammond, who had been allocated to me with the winter workings starting on 8 October. He was a passed fireman eligible for driving duties and signed the route as far as Reading. I told him to do the driving there, and I would take over and explain the route from Reading and also work the 17.40 from Paddington via the new road as far as Banbury.

This return train carried a lot of Paddington officials and we had D1714 as our steed. After we had passed through the 25 mph speed restriction at Old Oak Common Junction towards Park Royal, I opened the power handle fully, but when we reached 60 mph no further acceleration was possible; we passed Ruislip at that speed, where we should have been travelling at 75 mph, and lost 8 minutes to High Wycombe. From my driving seat I diagnosed that the last stage of weak fielding was not operating (this was similar to not being able to engage top gear in a car). Brian went into the engine room a couple of times and confirmed this. I instructed him to tell the High Wycombe platform inspector to inform Control that we needed a fresh locomotive at Banbury, the first available place. When he returned he said, 'Some of the railway officials are grumbling about us losing time.'

'If they can do any better let them try,' I answered.

I managed to get up to 75 mph on the falling gradient between Bicester and Aynho Junction and arrived at Banbury some 20 minutes late. The locomotive foreman came to us with the bad news that he did not have another locomotive and we must carry on with our crippled one. Brian took over from there and we lost more time, arriving at Birmingham about an hour late.

On arrival at our depot I booked the defects in the repairs book and showed it to the foreman fitter, Derrick Lynk. About a month later I received a letter from Paddington Control inquiring why we had lost 8 minutes to High Wycombe. I answered by saying that I had informed them of the problem at High Wycombe and had asked for a fresh locomotive at Banbury. I also asked why they were not concerned at the other 52 minutes we lost on the rest of the journey.

On Saturday 27 October 1973 I was in the biggest trouble of my railway career. Brian and I had signed on at 3.37 am to work a parcels train from Exchange sidings to Didcot with D5243, a Type 2 locomotive. We returned light via Leamington and Coventry to Nuneaton, where we were booked to leave the locomotive for other workings. When we arrived around 9.30 am we were told that the loco was not needed and to take it to Saltley, so we proceeded via Arley Tunnel. The signalling on this line had been recently modernised with three-aspect colour lights, and as we approached the old Arley Colliery Sidings signal box the signal was at danger. When I stopped, Brian climbed down to speak to Saltley Power Box and discovered that a Birmingham to Peterborough DMU had failed near Daw Mill colliery. We were needed to pull it to Nuneaton, so we would have to cross over to the other line. The redundant signal box was still being used to work the crossover points, although there was no signalman there. Our guard went to the box but after about 5 minutes came back to say that he did not know how to do change the points. I went back with him and spoke to Graham King in the Saltley box, who told me what levers to pull in the correct order according to the interlocking. I managed to do this correctly and the ground signal cleared. I went on to the verandah and signalled to Brian to take the locomotive on to the other line, then I replaced the points. As there was no ground signal to clear in order to run in the wrong direction, I again called Brian, who was standing some 100 yards away, to come towards the signal box. I could see him start to move, then to my amazement the locomotive started to sway and bounce and I thought it would turn over on its side, but it stopped at a crazy angle, above a road bridge, blocking both main lines. I immediately phoned Saltley box to tell them we were derailed and we were now blocking both lines.

I went to our stranded locomotive to assess the position. Brian was very white. He said, 'I thought we were going over the bridge into the road below.' I calmed him down and could see that all wheels were off the line and the points were damaged. After about 15 minutes the guard told us that Saltley had ordered the breakdown train, but it was out on another job and would get to us as soon as possible. In the meantime the failed

D5200, class leader of the Sulzer Type 2 Bo-Bos; No D5243 landed me in trouble at Arley Colliery Sidings in October 1973! *Michael Mensing*

Peterborough train would have to be pulled back clear from Whitacre Junction.

Brian was still shaky so I suggested that we had a can of strong tea with plenty of sugar (the railwayman's pick-you-up!). We waited until around noon when a couple of cars arrived with railway officials who assessed the situation, but it was another hour before the breakdown train arrived with Derrick Lynk in charge; he was a friend of mine, as I had known his father at Monument Lane depot. Brian was starting to get worried by this time as he had tickets for a West Bromwich Albion match. I suggested that he rang them to tell them he would be late and they might delay the match for him. His reply is unprintable!

The breakdown crew had moved into position and had taken a pull on the locomotive, but to no avail. The crew looked all around it, then Mr Hall, the area manager from Stanier House, approached me saying, 'Driver, I know you are in charge of this locomotive, but I'm asking you a favour. Will you go to Nuneaton Trent Valley by car where we have another locomotive but no men, as we need it to pull yours clear of the bridge before we can lift it.' I agreed and the area inspector, Trevor Williams, took us in his car. As we approached Stockingford village I asked him if there was anywhere we could get some sandwiches, as we had been on duty for over 10 hours already, and heaven knew how much longer we would be.

'There's a pub nearby which should be serving food,' he replied.

The landlady said she could do us some cheese and ham rolls, but would have to make them, so I ordered three pints of beer while we waited. I hardly tasted it, I was that dry, and Trevor ordered another one before the food arrived. He said there was no great rush, as they would have to place packing around my locomotive to keep it away from the bridge wall.

We carried on to Nuneaton Trent Valley where D1701 was waiting for us. I said to Brian, 'You book to drive this as I can't be in charge of two locomotives. It'll be a driving turn and rate of pay for you. It's an ill wind that blows nobody any good.'

At Nuneaton Abbey Street we again had

to cross over to the other line, which had been the cause of our derailment earlier. We then travelled in the wrong direction to Arley. It took three pulls to drag our locomotive clear of the bridge, and there was a delay of 10 minutes between each pull while blocks of wooden packing were placed around it and pneumatic jacks were placed to guide it towards the rails. During one of these waits I spoke to Harry Hughes, who used to be one of our bus drivers but had recently transferred to be a fitter's mate.

'I hope this doesn't take long as I've got tickets for Birmingham Hippodrome tonight,' he said.

Eventually we dragged the loco clear so the crane could get a straight pull. While this was going on I heard one of the Stanier House officials say, 'There was a derailment at Coventry and the Rugby breakdown train was on its way, but they needed ours as the stanchions carrying the power lines were damaged.' I spoke to Harry, pulling his leg. 'You'd better give me your theatre tickets. I'll take your wife as you'll be too late to go.' However, he declined the offer, saying 'We sha'n't be long.'

Our locomotive was eventually re-railed around 16.00 and Mr Hall asked me if I would tow it to Nuneaton Trent Valley with the area inspector Trevor Williams riding with me, and my mate Brian riding on the dead locomotive. We arrived at Nuneaton and as we were stabling the locomotives we saw the breakdown train, which had followed us, progress to Coventry over the branch line. We caught the 17.21 to New Street, where we found hundreds of passengers hanging about because both the Nuneaton and Coventry lines had been blocked, and each one was a relief line for the other. We signed off duty at 19.15, showing 15 hrs 38 mins on duty, and we should have been on duty at 03.15 on the Sunday following, but having to take 12 hours rest, we were told to sign on at 07.15 am. As I drove into our car park on the Sunday morning, I could see the breakdown train just arriving on the depot, and saw Harry Hughes alighting from the mess van.

'I told you to give me the theatre tickets,' I said.

'There'll be a divorce when I get home!' he exclaimed.

He had been on duty from 06.00 on Saturday. I have a newspaper cutting of the incident to this day.

It was the beginning of December when I had the Form 1 accusing me of not ensuring that the points were correct to travel over, causing the derailment of D5243. I once again asked for an interview with the superintendent of the depot, with my trade union representative in attendance. I had spoken to Graham King, the signalman who was on duty that day, and he had informed me that when single-line working had been operated on the Sunday previous to our mishap, the points were loose and had to be clamped.

At the interview with our new superintendent, Mr Stan Vaughan, I explained what had happened, and he asked 'What were you doing operating the points in the defunct signal box?'

I told him that our young guard did not know how to operate the points and I had tried to help him. Mr Vaughan then asked me if I had looked at the points. I explained that I was too far from them to see them, and as they were in the normal position they should have been correct. I went on to say that they had to be clamped on the previous Sunday and we were not provided with clamps to do this. I also mentioned that a few hours later I had to do the same movement at Nuneaton Abbey Street when I fetched the second locomotive.

He gave me a fair hearing, but said, 'If you had remained on your locomotive and the guard had operated the points and called you, it would have been him answering the Form 1.' He added, 'I'm afraid you were doing your best under difficult conditions, so I will give you a verbal caution and you must observe that all points are correct in future.' I gave a sigh of relief, as I had expected one or two days suspension at least.

In November, when working a train of chemical tanks with two Class 37s, Nos D6671 and D6760, single-manned to Gloucester, approaching Abbots Wood Junction I was signalled into the loop line. Half-way into it I lost all air-brake pressure

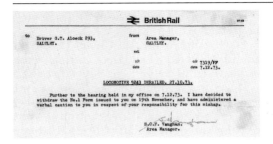

When I received this letter I breathed a sigh of relief, as I had expected one or two days suspension at least for my part in the derailment, the only one of my career.

and came to a sudden stop. I climbed on to the track to speak to my guard, who was riding in the rear cab of the second locomotive; he was a young chap sitting quite unconcerned with his feet up. I shouted to him to go back to the end of the loop to see if we were clear of the main line, and if not to telephone the signalman at Gloucester Power Box and tell him, in case he reverses the points and clears the road for a passenger train. In the meantime I said I would investigate the cause of the loss of air-brake pressure. I stood on the ballast watching him go, thinking, 'This is going to be a long job testing two locomotives and 30 vehicles on the train.'

However, in the quiet countryside I could hear a hissing sound. I walked a couple of tanks back and found the culprit! One of the air pipes between the second and third tank had burst and the air was escaping from it. The British Rail air-brake system worked on two pipes, unlike the continental system of one pipe, so it was possible to isolate the pipe in front of the burst one and close the valves on the first two. I now had control over the brakes throughout the train, although the brake would be slower to operate. When the guard returned I instructed him how to isolate the tanks concerned and I climbed into my cab to see the brake pressure return.

We then drew the train clear into the loop and about 2 minutes afterwards an express train came by, picking up speed, with the driver blowing his horn indicating that we had stopped him. I explained to the signalman what had occurred and told him that we would be travelling a bit slower and would

need the carriage and wagon repair men to put on a fresh pipe when we were relieved at Gloucester South Junction.

— o —

In January 1974 our trade unions and BR were again in conflict, and I attended another open meeting. As our chairman was now back at work, I was one of the audience. After a hectic couple of hours it was agreed that we stage a series of national one-day strikes and a work to rule! For the second week I was rostered to book on duty at 6.35 to work the 7.20 to Paddington, but the one-day's strike fell on the Tuesday, so I did not work that day. Instead, I was the senior man on our picket line from 6.00 to 10.00 am. It was a bitterly cold morning with snow on the ground and a heavy frost. which was reported as -10°C. We had a steel barrel filled with firewood scrounged from the local factories to keep us warm; we were frozen on one side and warm on the other, as we stood close to it.

At about 9.45 am we noticed our assistant area manager walking down the road. He normally came from Four Oaks by train but had travelled by Corporation bus; he would not risk coming to work by car owing to the bad road conditions. As he approached us, one of the lads shouted, 'Put a report in for being late on duty,' which was our normal instruction from the timekeeper when late.

He stopped to talk to us, warming himself in front of our fire. 'It's warmer here than in my office,' he said.

Charlie Lindley retorted, 'It will be this morning - the gas workers are in sympathy with us and have cut the heat off to your office!'

These one-day strikes were organised on a regional basis, with each region having a strike on different days. On the first Tuesday in February we were rostered to sign on at 12.59 to work the 13.35 to Paddington, but it was the day when the Western Region were on strike. I inquired from our regional secretary what we should do and was instructed to do our own work only.

The next Monday, Brian and I discussed how they would get another locomotive on to our train at Paddington to work the 17.40 back. When we booked on duty on Tuesday we found out how the management had solved that problem. Instead of our normal 10-coach train and a diesel locomotive, the foreman told us to travel into New Street, where there were two three-car DMUs for us. Brian drove outwards with the train packed with standing passengers. Our top speed was 75 mph instead of the normal 95 mph, and we arrived at Paddington at 17.45, 1¼ hours late.

Platform 4 was crowded with passengers for the 17.40, but it was eerie with all other platform lights out, as we were the only train there. I said to Brian, 'Shut the engines down and put the hand brakes on, as we are taking our physical needs break.'

As we climbed out of the cab our guard asked us where we were going.

'For our physical needs break,' I replied.

'You can't do that,' he said. 'You have a second man.'

'Many times I've taken a can of water and boiled it on our locomotive,' I retorted, 'but there's no stove on a DMU, so I'm having my food in a civilised way.'

We entered the mess room, which would normally be crowded with train crews from Bristol, Gloucester, Cardiff and local men, but it was empty. The train crew supervisor looked out of his office window, but said nothing.

After half an hour we returned to our train; we could see that it was full, and platform staff were standing by our cab, one with gold braid on his cap, but they walked away from us as we neared. I started the engines and sent Brian to take the rear hand brakes off.

When the air pressure was sufficient, I sounded the horn to say we were ready. The platform inspector came to the cab to ask if I was OK. He was the only person to speak to me at Paddington. He blew his whistle to attract the guard, the platform signal cleared and we left about 45 minutes late.

When I stopped at High Wycombe there came a tap on my side window. Three passengers stood there, and one said rather grudgingly, 'I suppose we'd better thank you.

It doesn't seem that our Western Region crews are bothered about us.'

'Don't put yourself out thanking me,' I replied. 'I'll not only be on strike on our region tomorrow, I'll be on the picket line, so don't expect this train to run!'

In April I had another run to Westbury, but this time via Didcot. I booked on duty at 14.40 with Graham Mills to be told that a parcels train was waiting at Landor Street with Class 46 No 46017 on front (these locomotives had been re-numbered, this one having previously been D154). We had a good run via Banbury and Oxford to Didcot, where a Didcot driver stepped on to conduct me via Swindon to Westbury, where we were instructed to return light engine. We were on duty 10 hrs 20 mins, and the mileage was a lot more than the 240 miles that we clocked up in 1969, via Bristol. This time it was 272 miles, which entitled us to 3½ hours mileage bonus.

We had an eventful day in April. We were rostered on the afternoon turn to Paddington and travelled to New Street to relieve the locomotive that had worked the return morning train from Paddington. When I climbed into the cab, Joe Carlton, our morning driver, said, 'I've informed Control at Banbury that you need a fresh locomotive - the boiler room is flooded.'

He took me to the opposite end to show me water about a foot deep. It was a good job there was a step between the cab and the engine room, or water would have penetrated into both of them. I informed the platform inspector, Mr Lovell, who, after telephoning Control, instructed us to take the locomotive to Saltley and bring a fresh one back.

When we arrived at the loco depot and booked the locomotive in, the outside foreman, Colin Porter, remarked, 'That's the failed one. I've sent another one to New Street.'

'We should have taken it!' I protested. 'We're the men to work that Paddington train!'

He telephoned Control to ascertain what was happening. Brian, my mate, whispered to me, 'The train is due out now - what if the men who took the locomotive work our train?'

'I hope they do,' I answered. 'We'll still be paid our mileage as the mistake is theirs.'

After some deliberation we were told to wait for the railway bus to return to the depot to take us to New Street to work our train. We eventually arrived at New Street and left about an hour late. Consequently, when we arrived at Paddington, we were already due out again, and had to go straight back to our locomotive, which was backing on to our train. Brian picked up a can of water along the platform which he boiled to make tea to help our sandwiches down.

At Bicester, after the passengers had alighted, the guard gave me the green 'right away' signal and we had only drawn out of the station about a couple of coaches length when the brakes of the train were applied. I looked at the air pressure gauge to see that we had lost about 20 lbs. I said to Brian, 'It looks at though the communication cord has been pulled.'

He walked back along the platform to confer with our guard, but after a few minutes the air pressure returned. Brian returned to explain that it was an American serviceman and his family of four travelling 1st Class with a lot of luggage who were slow in getting out of the train (Bicester was near the Upper Heyford American airfield).

Brian went on to say, 'We've caused an accident on the car parks. The leading car departing must have stopped suddenly to see what was happening as we stopped quickly, and two other cars have crashed into the rear of one another.'

'I wonder if we'll be asked to witness it for an insurance claim,' I said.

A few years earlier the Welfare Fund had decided to generate more money, and suggested fruit machines, 'one-armed bandits', in the mess room. Mr Reg Lowe, our area manager (and no relation to Jack Lowe, our previous shedmaster), gave his permission, but insisted that we keep a close watch on men overplaying them, who could lose their wages, and we undertook to put it in the rules that we would reimburse any wife or mother who complained of loss of wages. Fortunately, it never happened.

The machines were highly successful and resulted over the years in a surplus of funds in the bank. At the annual general meeting of April 1974 it was decided that three trustees be appointed to supervise the investment of the cash and to be responsible for it. I was elected as one of these, and after a meeting shortly afterwards we recommended that £1,000 be invested in City of Birmingham bonds, at 13.5 per cent for a minimum of five years.

At the end of May it was the annual general meeting of the Self-help Sick Fund, which had been founded in 1922 and operated separately from the Welfare Club, which provided sickness, death, retirement and convalescent grants. The present secretary, Jack Randle, was retiring from the railway to take a job in outside industry, so a new secretary was needed. I was nominated for this position, as was our trade union branch chairman, Fred Orton Jones. At the ensuing ballot I was elected, and so took over the job of administering this old fund for the benefit of Saltley employees.

In the summer workings starting in May I lost my mate Brian, who was replaced by Ray Reynolds. This was the third time we had been booked together.

13
UNION MATTERS,
AND THE NORTH LINK
1974-80

In July 1974 I was still learning about my railway career, and was rostered to train on the Mirrlees Class 31 locomotive. Another driver should also have been with me, but he was off duty ill, so it was just me with instructor Cyril Rist, who is now a footplate inspector. He gave me a good grounding and at the end of the week I had to pass out with the inscrutable Inspector 'Jones' at 8.00 am. He said that he had a meeting at Stanier House (the regional head office) at lunchtime, so Cyril and I thought we would be having an early day. How wrong we were! He had me in his office asking questions pertaining to this locomotive until around midday. He then said, 'As there isn't one of these Class 31s on the depot today, I'll see you at Vauxhall Carriage Sidings at 14.00, when one is booked to be there.'

We duly met him and climbed into the cab, where he asked me questions regarding the driving panel and gauges. We then entered the engine room where I had to identify the equipment and explain the working parts, and after 1½ hours we emerged in the other cab.

'I can't think of anything else to ask you,' said Mr Jones, and I gave a silent sigh of relief. 'We'll go into the other cab where I've left my briefcase.'

I thought he was getting out the Ministry of Transport Certificate to fill in, passing me out. Instead, he got the Mirrlees handbook out and started to leaf through it.

'If you're going to ask me any questions from that book,' I said, 'I'll get my book out for the answers.'

Cyril then entered the cab and exclaimed

to Mr Jones, 'Do you know what time it is? It's after 16.00 and we shall be showing overtime when we walk back to the depot.'

'He can't think of anything else to ask me,' I said, 'so he's trying to find something in his book.'

Cyril said, 'Baloney! If he's not up to standard he'd better have another week's training.'

Mr Jones's attitude suddenly changed, and he said, 'You've answered every question. I was trying to find something you didn't know. You should apply to be an instructor,' he added.

'No thanks,' I replied. 'I've been told that before, and I've been told to apply for a foreman's position, but I'm more interested in trade union affairs.'

Mr Jones duly filled in the MOT form, while Cyril looked at his watch. 'It's now 16.30, and we need 15 minutes walk to the depot, so we'll be showing 55 minutes overtime.' With that parting shot we left Mr Jones. As we walked down the hill, Cyril remarked, 'I don't think he's got a home to go to.'

On the Friday morning before the August Bank Holiday weekend, ASLEF headquarters asked me to arrange entertainment for three Russians (two footplatemen and an interpreter) who were visiting Birmingham. I made various enquiries about arranging visits for them, and placed notices at the depot inviting our members to come and meet our celebrities.

We met the party on Sunday at the Midland Hotel. Mr Parvel Popov was the general secretary of the locomotive engineers'

Our Russian visitors, Parvel Popov and Nikolai Bikov, being shown round the Birmingham Post & Mail premises on 26 August 1974. I am looking over their shoulders. *Birmingham Post & Mail*

steam locomotives in different stages of repair, culminating in a ride on a pannier tank that Mr Bikov was allowed to drive. He afterwards said through the interpreter that it had been over 20 years since he had been on a steam locomotive. We had afternoon cream tea in the old GWR Directors' coach, and before they left Pat Whitehouse offered them a toast in vodka, but somewhat surprisingly they said they preferred whisky. Altogether it was an enjoyable and interesting interlude.

In the winter workings I was again allocated a new mate, Alan Tregenna, who was passed out to drive, and one day in October we booked on duty at 06.15 to go light locomotive to Oxley carriage sidings, to work empty coaches to New Street to work the 08.10 express to Cardiff as far as Gloucester. We had No 45001, which had just had extensive repairs.

As we were about to depart, the door opened and our Inspector Jones appeared. Alan was in the driving seat, but I motioned to him to stay there. Jones said nothing, the 'right away' signal light appeared at the end of the platform, and away we went. The locomotive had not been worked heavy from Oxley, but heavy work was needed on the climb through the tunnels towards Five Ways station.

As we approached Bournville, Mr Jones, who was standing by the engine room door in the centre of the cab shouted, 'Stop! We're on fire!', and dashed into the engine room. As he opened the door, smoke entered the cab. Alan stopped the train at the signal outside Kings Norton station, and Mr Jones, who had reappeared coughing, shouted to Alan, 'Tell the signalman we need a fresh locomotive.'

I grabbed the portable fire extinguisher and entered the engine room, but the smoke had eased off with the engine idling. I could then see that it was coming from the new lagging on the manifold pipe on top of the engine. I looked for signs of burning but found none, so returned to the driving cab and said to Mr Jones that we did not need another locomotive, as it was only the new grease on the lagging that had got hot. I told Alan to tell the signalman that we were OK. Mr Jones intervened and told Alan to tell Gloucester to have one standing by in case it was needed.

union, Nikolai Bikov was an electric locomotive driver from Leningrad, and Mr Alexander Burgushersky was the interpreter. It was the first time I had spoken through an interpreter and had to pause after each sentence for my words to be translated. On Sunday evening, following a tour of the depot, we arranged a welcoming meeting with our branch members at a local club, where I presented them with some Terence Cuneo railway paintings and a series of pen-and-ink drawings of BR steam locomotives by Dick Potts, one of our talented drivers. Other presentations were made, then we had a good social evening where I introduced them to our committee and to Birmingham beer!

On the Monday we showed them the city and the Council House, where they were entertained to a tour; I remarked to Jack that we were taking them to places we had not been to ourselves!

After lunch we caught the train to Tyseley Railway Museum where Mr Pat Whitehouse and Mr Michael Satow OBE welcomed the visitors and took them on a tour, showing

'On your head be it,' I said. 'I've said we sha'n't need one.'

We re-started the train, and when coasting down the Lickey Incline Mr Jones entered the engine room, and before we stopped at Cheltenham was in and out a couple of times. As we stood there I looked at the new lagging and there was no smoke. When we arrived at Gloucester we could see a fresh locomotive in the bay platform, and the shunter came to hook us off. I shouted to him, 'We don't need another locomotive', and the platform inspector queried, 'You asked for one!'

'Not me,' I answered, and pointed to Mr Jones. 'He's the one who's panicked.'

During the year Inspector Jones continued his harassment of train crews, and two or three drivers stopped their trains *en route* to order him off the footplate. One, on leaving New Street, was surprised to hear the engine room door opening as he approached Proof House Junction, and Mr Jones appeared.

'What are you doing?' the driver shouted.

'Riding with you,' said our inspector.

'You're not - you've frightened me to death coming in unannounced like that', and he stopped the train at Landor Street Junction and ordered him off.

I once saw him walking between Northfield station and Longbridge Junction after such an incident, but it reached a climax when he presented himself to driver George Harrison at New Street just before he was departing with an express to Sheffield. They had clashed before, and George told him to get out of the cab as he did not want any interference while driving the train. Mr Jones refused to get off, and when the signal cleared George refused to move the train. The station inspector came to the cab to see what was amiss, and George explained that he was not moving with Inspector Jones on board. After 10 minutes of arguing, Jones climbed down in more ways than one and the train worked forward.

He reported driver Harrison, who came to our union for support, claiming that he could not work the train safely with an interfering man on board. We supported him at the formal enquiry and the driver was cleared.

A few weeks later Mr Jones was transferred to a distant railway school (no doubt lecturing on personality and how to handle men). A couple of months went by and George Harrison was promoted to the Stoke-on-Trent Control Office.

At the beginning of 1975 we had a new footplate inspector allocated to us, Jack Boulton, who was an old cleaner friend of mine at Ryecroft Loco in 1937, and had spent his last few years as a driver and instructor at Bescot. One winter's morning we were standing at platform 1 with No 47054 waiting to work the 7.18 am to Paddington when I saw Jack about to get into the train. I shouted, 'Come in here, it's warmer. The train's still cold, as we've only just put the steam heat on.'

'You're not inviting a footplate inspector to ride with us?' said Alan.

'You'll find this one a bit different from old Jones,' I replied.

Jack told us that he was meeting Inspector Stan Barratt at Leamington and that they would be coming to Paddington with us to acquaint him with the new routes. As we had

Class 47 No 47054 which I drove in 1975 with a new inspector, Jack Boulton, in the cab to acquaint him with the Paddington route. It was a very pleasant journey, very different from the days of old 'Jones'! *Michael Mensing*

just made a can of tea we offered him a cup, and as we ran into Leamington station Stan Barratt was standing at the end of the platform waiting to join us in the cab. He had travelled with me on a few occasions and his first words were, 'Hello Bill, have you made the tea?'

'Yes, and drank it,' I replied.

We received the 'right away' signal so I got away smartly. Alan offered his seat to one of the inspectors and stood behind me. When we stopped at Banbury we got a can of water and shared another can of tea on the journey to Princes Risborough. I pointed out the line-side telephones every 3 miles along the track, places of interest and the best places to observe the signals controlling the running into Princes Risborough and High Wycombe, as there were still semaphore signals right down to Old Oak Common.

We arrived at Paddington at 9.40 am right time, where the shunter was waiting to unhook us, and we shut the engine down and secured the locomotive. All four of us went to the mess room for our food. Stan said, 'Give us your can and I'll buy some tea as I've not brought any tea and sugar.' We chatted about the weather, football, politics - in fact, everything except railway work.

On relieving the Old Oak men to work our return train with No 47066 via Reading, I asked Stan if he would like to handle it, but he declined, saying that he was not sure of the road at the high speed we would have to attain. He added, 'I'll have a go from Didcot.' So I said to Alan, 'Go on, show them what you can do.' We had a good run, and as we coasted over the Didcot curve at 50 mph, they changed places.

At Leamington Stan and Jack alighted, Alan got back into the driving seat and said, 'It's been a good trip. If we'd had the other clown with us I'd've been a bag of nerves!'

At the January union meeting I was nominated as delegate to the West Midlands Trade Union Congress to represent branches from Wolverhampton, Stoke-on-Trent, Bescot, Rugby, Coventry, Leamington and Stratford-upon-Avon. At the first ballot I received the most votes, but as I did not have a two-thirds poll majority, a second ballot had to be made

between the Stoke nominee, Bob Jones, and myself. I polled 745 votes and Bob 313, so I was elected to this important body.

There was a monthly full day's meeting, and if I had to take leave of duty to attend ASLEF paid loss of earnings. At the AGM in June I was elected to the committee and this meant more meetings with different politicians, managing directors of industry, social services representatives, as well as our monthly meetings.

One important meeting was with Michael Foot MP, who was then Minister of Employment in Harold Wilson's government. We visited factories in the West Midlands, discussing the running down of industries in the area and workers with great skills being made redundant, and no apprentices being appointed to learn these skills. As I write this in the 1990s, how things have carried on to the detriment of the workers!

One night, having worked the car train from Knowle & Dorridge to West Ealing, the guard inquired about our return train from Southall but was told that there was no car train for us, but an empty coal wagon train at West Drayton coal concentration depot. We duly backed on to 50 wagons, with only the first half a dozen fitted with the continuous brake. This meant that we would not be able to run at 75 mph as we did normally, but only 45 mph maximum. As we were facing towards West Ealing, we would have to travel via the Greenford branch and High Wycombe. We were on duty for over 13 hours and thought we had missed our next night's work, but when we booked on an hour later than usual we were told our normal train was waiting for us as no other staff were available.

Another night turn involved booking on at 17.00, working a DMU to Worcester, then working a freightliner via Dudley and Walsall to Derby. As we had no return workings from there, we were shown 'as required', which meant that Control could use us to work a spare train home, or we would travel as passenger on the midnight Mail train.

One night at Derby Control had said that they did not require us and to travel home. As we had 45 minutes to wait we decided to go to the fish and chip shop for sustenance. When we returned some 30 minutes later, we learned that Control wanted to speak to us.

'Where have you been?' exclaimed the voice on the phone.

'To get some fish and chips, which I'm eating now' I replied.

'We've a train standing at Wigston [just south of Leicester] without a locomotive or train crew, going to Rowley Regis oil depot. Will you take a locomotive from Derby depot and go light to Wigston to work this train forward?'

'I don't sign the route between Derby and Leicester,' I replied. Then I had a thought. 'Hang on,' I said, and asked Alan if he signed for it, which he did. I therefore said that we could do it, but what about the guard?

'Take your own,' he answered.

'Tell him we need relief at Saltley,' said our guard, 'as I don't sign the route from New Street to Rowley Regis.'

We were not long preparing No 46015 and ran non-stop to Wigston. Our guard hooked us on to the dead train and we were soon on our way, via Nuneaton.

We were on duty around 10½ hours, and when I telephoned Control at Derby the next night, the train man inquired, 'Were you the crew from last night? Thank you very much. You were pretty fast getting to Wigston and got my colleague on the Leicester panel out of a mess. We don't need you tonight, so you can get your fish and chips!'

'There's no driving turn for you tonight,' I said to Alan, who I had told to make out a driver's sheet for the run to Wigston.

One night in January 1976 we booked on at 22.37 to work our normal car train to West Ealing, but the foreman said that he had another car train coming from Halewood for Southampton Docks, and needed us to work it as far as Basingstoke.

'I only sign the route as far as Reading,' I replied, but again Alan came to the rescue, saying that he signed the route.

We relieved Crewe men on No 40107, an English Electric Type 4. When we arrived at Basingstoke, a Southern Region driver stepped on, saying, 'I'm not trained on these locomotives, so I've got to conduct you for-ward.' We arrived at Eastleigh around 04.00 am, where the trains terminated, and we were instructed to take our locomotive back home. We were on duty 10¾ hours and the mileage was 280, equal to 4 hrs 20 mins extra.

One weekend in March the main line from Birmingham to London Euston was closed for important bridge renewal between Coventry and Rugby, and Euston express trains were diverted into Paddington via Leamington. On the Saturday we were rostered to sign on duty at 06.15 am to travel on the 6.37 from Vauxhall & Duddeston into New Street and relieve New Street men on No 47544 to work the 06.48 Euston train into Paddington.

The New Street crew were most truculent, accusing us of taking their work. I said, 'Do you sign the route to Paddington? If not, you can't work the train, can you?'

On the way into New Street I had looked at the Special Train Notice and spotted that we were booked to stop at Hampton-in-Arden and not at Birmingham International, as I had expected. We arrived at Paddington right on time.

We had No 47488 on the return train and were booked to work through to Wolver-hampton. I told Alan to drive back, and as we ran into the platform at New Street I noticed a New Street crew, Jack Beenham and his mate, boarding our train. On arrival at Wolverhampton they came up to relieve us. I knew Jack very well; in fact, he had been my fireman on my first driving turn, some 20 years previously. They did not look very happy. I said, 'Why didn't you relieve us at New Street? We have to travel back now.'

'You've pinched our work,' said Jack. 'I wouldn't help you in any way.'

'You're being childish,' I replied. 'You know as well as I do we have to do the work diagrammed to us by management. I'm not the only Saltley man working Euston trains into Paddington today. There's about a dozen!'

It took us about an hour and a half to travel home, and as travelling time after mileage was extra, we were paid that as well as the 3 hours for the 281 mileage payment.

On Whit Sunday bridge work blocked the route from Saltley depot into New Street. We signed on duty at 15.25 and were booked light locomotive via Sutton Park, Walsall and Perry Barr into New Street, to work our train to Bristol, and traversed the same journey when we arrived back at New Street. This put over 40 miles on our mileage, so we were paid an extra 3 hours plus 1 hr 10 mins overtime.

When the summer workings commenced in May new workings were put in our link. One of them entailed signing on duty at 17.03 to take a light locomotive into New Street to work to Bristol. Our return train was a car sleeper coming from Plymouth to Stirling in Scotland, and we took it as far as New Street before taking our locomotive to the depot while an electric one took it forward. This train varied from 14 to 18 vehicles, half of them sleeping coaches, and the rest conveyed the cars of the passengers. The loading limit up the Lickey Incline for Class 45 locomotives was 515 tons, Class 46 525 tons and Class 47 545 tons. We had become used to travelling through Bromsgrove non-stop, but 14 vehicles equalled 503 tons, and when extra vehicles were added at Bristol, this took us over the limit (18 vehicles equalled 740 tons). When the guard at Bristol gave us the loading we had to tell the platform inspector to inform Control that we needed a bank locomotive at Bromsgrove. The old locomotive depot there had closed, and English Electric Type 3 locomotives were used, provided by Worcester depot.

For years I had advocated that the ASLEF AGM should be held in towns and cities where it was more accessible to our members to watch the proceedings, rather than the seaside towns they normally went to. We were fortunate in 1976 as it was to be held in the Midland Hotel, just outside Birmingham New Street station. As I was on a late afternoon turn on the first week, I was able to attend the opening ceremony performed by the Lord Mayor of Birmingham, and listen to the debates throughout the week.

Our branch and Bescot branch put on social evenings, so that our members could meet the 50 delegates from all over the country in a more relaxed atmosphere, and talk about resolutions that were down for debate.

I changed turns of duty to an 01.00 am shift for the second week of the meetings so that I could attend.

During this fortnight there was a court case being held at Birmingham Crown Court, where a Euston driver was being charged with manslaughter after an accident at Nuneaton Trent Valley some 12 months before. Our union had engaged legal representatives to support our driver and at the end of one of the debates one afternoon, Ray Buckton, the General Secretary, got to his feet and said that he was pleased to announce that the Euston man had been found not guilty. There was a huge cheer and a lot of applause, as most members knew that ASLEF had spent thousands of pounds defending him!

Extra freight work was coming to the depot, which entailed working coal 'merry-go-round' (MGR) trains coming from the Nottinghamshire coalfields to Didcot Power Station. There were 25 trains rostered to run over every 24 hours, and our men worked from Landor Street to Didcot. On arriving there the driver set the locomotive to run at half a mile per hour, and the hopper wagons unloaded their coal into the huge troughs under the rails, whence endless belts conveyed it to the stock piles. We were booked to return the empty wagons non-stop and arrive back at Landor Street to be relieved by Toton crews in about 7 hours.

That was how it was supposed to happen, but quite often the unloading machinery was not working properly, and the trains were stopped by the driver when emergency signals operated. Sometimes wagons became damaged or even derailed, so instead of unloading a train in 20 minutes it would take over an hour. Meanwhile, other trains were arriving and queues of them awaited their turn to be unloaded. My mate Alan nicknamed the power station Colditz, saying that once in there, you never knew when you were going to get out!

One Saturday morning we booked on at 2.10 am to work a freight train to Gloucester, but were informed it was cancelled and instructed to work an MGR train to Didcot. I

One of the new freight turns at Saltley was 'merry-go-round' coal trains coming from the Nottinghamshire coalfields to Didcot Power Station. There were 25 trains every day and we worked them from Landor Street to Didcot. On 15 August 1978 No 47276 runs through Banbury station with an up MGR. *K. C. H. Fairey*

particularly wanted to finish duty on time and informed the timekeeper.

'You should have a good run today,' he replied.

We did, as far as Oxford, but were placed along the goods line to Hinksey sidings around 5.00 am. Alan phoned the signalman and came back with a long face.

'The signalman doesn't know how long we'll be delayed as the power station is having trouble with the unloading machinery.'

We stood there until around 8.00 am, then had a run into the power station sidings to find three other trains waiting. I climbed down and telephoned the power station train controller to inquire how long would we have to wait.

'The way the plant is working, about 4 hours,' he replied.

I asked him to pass a message to the Didcot train crew foreman, asking for a relief as I needed to finish work on time. I rang again after 15 minutes, but his reply was 'No chance', as they had no relief available.

We had raised questions regarding the long hours being worked on these trains at LDC meetings and with railway management, and had been assured that relief would be available when late running could be seen to be taking place. I explained this to the power station controller, as we could not

speak direct to the Didcot foreman, but he replied 'It's no concern of mine - it's between you and the railway foreman.'

I had a discussion with Alan and the guard, and we decided that we would hook off the train and return home light. I again telephoned the controller, and when I told him of our intentions he became concerned, saying, 'Don't do it yet - I don't want a dead train there. Hang on the phone while I contact the train crew foreman.'

Within a few minutes he came back to tell us that as we were about 2 miles from Didcot station, and relief would be coming to us by taxi, which would take us back to catch a train home. We still made about an hour's overtime, and I dread to think how long we would have been on duty. Some men used to like these trains because of the opportunity of overtime, but if I was rostered on a week's work on them, I would find an overtime man to exchange turns of duty.

One Sunday we were booked at 7.15 am to bring empty coaches from Oxley carriage sidings to work the 09.10 to Cardiff as far as Gloucester. We had No 46037, and as I approached Ashchurch at 90 mph I suddenly lost power. I closed the power handle, then opened it slowly and regained power, but at Cleeve I lost power again and could not regain it. I managed to coast to Alston Road level crossing, just outside Cheltenham station and controlled by the Gloucester Power Box, where the signal and barriers were against us. As I brought the train to a stop the barriers rose and the signal cleared, but it was too late, as I could get no power. If the signalman had been quicker clearing the crossing we could have run into the station. I instructed Alan to telephone Gloucester to tell him we were a dead train, while I entered the engine room to see if I could rectify the fault. However, when I saw sparks coming from the main generator I realised that nothing could be done.

We therefore told the signalman that we needed another locomotive to pull the train. This took 90 minutes; meanwhile some of the passengers climbed out of the train and, despite our warnings, walked along the line to the station, some 200 yards or so away.

I remarked to Alan, 'It's a good job we're not miles away in the countryside.'

There was an annual ASLEF school based at Dorking where branch officials received training on all aspects of office - chairman, secretary, treasurer, and accountancy - the correct way of debating and overseeing a branch meeting, and the everyday running of the union. I had been selected to attend this school at the December meeting and in February 1977 I and two dozen other locomen from all over the country attended the fortnight's course at Beatrice Webb House (named after the wife of Stanley Webb, a Labour MP in 1922, and a Minister in the 1929-31 Labour Government; she had left the house and grounds to the Labour and Trade Union movement for adult education).

We had to apply for a fortnight's leave of absence and were paid ASLEF officials' rate of pay. I gained a lot of knowledge and made friends with fellow locomotive men from as far afield as St Blazey, Glasgow, Darlington and Tonbridge. One of my outstanding memories is of a stained-glass window, placed in the house in 1910, showing the elite of the Labour movement of that time including George Bernard Shaw, George Lansbury, H. G. Wells, Sidney Webb, and others who were leading members of the Fabian Society.

One Saturday evening we were working the 17.40 from Paddington and were stopped at Ruislip semaphore signals. Alan contacted the signalman and was told that owing to a shortage of staff there were no boxes open between there and High Wycombe, and a local DMU had just departed. As we knew that this could take 10 minutes to clear, we did not phone him every 3 minutes, as specified in the rule book. After 10 minutes I sent Alan to phone again, and to our amazement the signalman told him off for not phoning him earlier; he then said that there was a block telegraph failure and instructed us to pass the signal at danger. When working in these conditions we had to proceed at caution, so we arrived at High Wycombe some 20 minutes late.

About a month later I had a letter telling me to go and see the footplate inspector, Jack Boulton, who wanted to know about the delay at Ruislip. I explained what had happened, and he pointed out the 3 minutes rule, which I accepted, but pointed out that I knew the distance between there and High Wycombe, and we would not deliberately delay a train on a Saturday evening as we wanted to go out socialising. He warned me not to do it again and told me to phone the signalman every 3 minutes even if it upset him.

In June 1977 I was 55 years of age, so once again I had to go for a medical examination, but instead of travelling to Derby we now went to New Street station where the railway doctor was based. He passed me as fit to carry on with my railway career, and had only been on duty for a couple of hours when I returned to the depot, but was paid the full day's pay!

The Depot Welfare Fund, of which I was a trustee, had been in negotiation with the railway management to hire a train to take our retired staff, their wives and widows, to Weston-super-Mare for a day's excursion. This was the first of many such trips we would arrange. (Now I myself am retired I enjoy going on these excursions. Recently we went to Lake

A group photograph taken at the ASLEF National School at Beatrice Webb House, Dorking, in February/March 1977. I am second from the right on the front row. *Author's collection*

Windermere, but unfortunately by motor coach, as the railway management had priced themselves out of the business.)

We always paid for the train, although we could travel free at other times. It was due to depart from New Street around 9.30 am, and we organised three double-decker buses to collect our members from different parts of the city. We arranged for a packed breakfast and coffee on the train, and a four-course lunch was waiting for them at a hotel in Weston. We left there again around 19.00 and arrived in Birmingham about 21.30, with the buses waiting to take us home.

— o —

When the new winter workings were announced in October 1977 our depot was allocated new express passenger and freight trains to York. The routes from Rotherham via Normanton and Castleford, and from Wath Road Junction and Pontefract to Burton Salmon Junction, were completely new to our depot, and most of the senior dri-

Route learning involved travelling in locomotive cabs and making notes of all the signals, signal boxes, stations and other landmarks along the line. These notes could then be drawn out more neatly at a later date. Here are my notes of the line in the Pontefract area between Burton Salmon and Wath, showing a mixture of semaphore and colour light signalling.

vers, who were entitled to this work, were over 60 years of age and too old to learn new routes.

An open meeting was called to discuss the problem of where to place the work in the link structure. After a 2-hour discussion it was decided to form a new link called the North link, which would cater for all work beyond Derby, and volunteers would be called for.

Within two weeks the LDC produced the 12 weeks' work with the earliest booking-on time of 5.35 am, no night work, and the latest booking-off time of 02.10, after working the Mail train from Sheffield. My present work in the Paddington link consisted of 48 weeks' work, with a lot of night work and weeks booking on at 2 and 3 in the morning for day shifts, so I volunteered for the North link.

My near neighbour, Charlie Lindley, and the only ex-Tyseley man, Trevor Floyd, were sent to learn the road from Sheffield and Rotherham. Most of this route was still signalled by the old-fashioned semaphore signals, and I remember one driver saying to Trevor, who was used to the former Great Western Automatic Train Control audible cab-signalling system, 'There's no hearing aids along here'.

York station was different altogether. It was one of first major stations to be colour-light signalled in the late 1930s, and was a complicated system with ground signals at each pair of points, which meant that as many as six or eight signals could be negotiated between the 'platform number' signals outside the station junction and the platform itself.

After a few weeks learning the semaphore signals and gradients by riding in the cabs of trains, we had a fortnight in the road-learning school in York station, where we were shown slides of the signals showing the different routes available, and were taken on walking tours, with the instructor pointing out different anomalies. We were joined by men from Darlington and Newcastle, who were amused by our accents, and we pulled their legs about their 'When The Boat Comes In' accents! It took us eight weeks to learn this and sign our route cards, but it would be a long wait before I drove over the route.

The south end of York station on 24 May 1981, with No 45117 on a southbound evening passenger train. The complex system of points and ground signals can clearly be seen. To us it seemed even more complicated than Crewe or Bristol! *Roger Siviter*

During this period I had to take a day's leave to audit the Welfare Fund books, and on 2 December we decided to issue £10 food vouchers to the active staff at the depot, as well as the Christmas parcels we regularly gave to our retired staff. Charlie and I thus had to take another day's leave on pay day to supervise their issue.

In February 1978 I signed on at 6.20 am to work a return empty MGR train coming from Didcot to Staveley sidings, just beyond Chesterfield, and work a loaded one back. Our train had been delayed at Didcot and it was around 10.00 am when we relieved it, arriving at Staveley around 13.00. The yard inspector informed us that there was no return train, and instructed us to take the locomotive to Barrow Hill loco depot, just along a branch line. This depot had an ancient building preservation order placed on it and it was like travelling back 50 years or so as we went into the old roundhouses with the turntables in the centre and locomotives stabled all around. There were the old frost fires blazing and a furnace burning under the sand for the sanders, to dry it out.

When we reported to the shed foreman, he said, 'Where have you been? We're waiting to go home. You're the last locomotive to arrive before we close down for the weekend.'

'We were 3½ hours late relieving it,' I replied.

'Our bus driver is waiting to take you to Chesterfield to catch a train home.'

This he did - on two wheels most of the way to get us there in time.

Saturday 6 May was Cup Final day, and it was my maiden trip to York. We booked on at 7.05 am to relieve a train at Landor Street coming from Oxford and going to Harrogate with No 47108 on front. We had a good run, diverting from Sheffield via Staveley and Rotherham, and travelling via Wath Road and Pontefract, arriving at York around 11.00 am. We were met by the shunter, who said, 'The limit is ten coaches on the Harrogate line, so I want you to take the first coach of the train and dispose of it in the Scarborough Bay line.'

'We're booked to travel home on the 11.38 am,' I replied, 'and it's my first trip since learning the road, so get moving and keep your eyes on me in case I make a wrong move.'

He spoke on his walkie-talkie phone to the Power Box, and uncoupled the first coach. The signal cleared for the Scarborough branch line and the shunter rode on the coach. We then reversed into the bay, he uncoupled us and spoke again to the Power Box. The ground signal cleared for us to go again on to the branch line, then we had to do a 'double W' movement to cross from one side of the north end of the station to the local depot right on the other side. The shunter rode with us in the cab, barking instructions to the signalmen, and we made the movements without delay and left the locomotive with about 15 minutes to spare to catch our train. It met with some delay approaching Birmingham and was stopped at Landor Street, opposite our Loco, so doors opened and drivers, second men and guards jumped out to save time going into New

The north end of York station in March 1978. The Scarborough line curves away to the right behind 'Deltic' No 55006, and the depot is over to the left, so the complex back and forth manoeuvre necessary to get from one side to the other can be appreciated.
T. J. Edgington

Street in order to get home in time to watch the Cup Final.

On Saturday 14 June there was another one-way trip. I signed on at 8.04 with my new mate Anthony Brewer to relieve No 45109 at 8.30 am at Landor Street, coming from Bristol to York. We arrived at York at 11.15 am and were booked to take the coaches into the sidings. When the shunting locomotive had taken them off us, we made the 'W' movement across the junction to take our locomotive to the depot. It was good experience to do it in daylight, as I would have to do it many times in darkness. We then travelled home on the 12.50 pm.

The following Friday I signed on for my first two-way job to York, a single-manned turn on the 13.30 train from New Street via Normanton, which terminated at York. There the shunter hooked me off the train and rode with me while we ran around it to back on the other end. I then had 45 minutes for my food before working back at 17.45, stopping at Pontefract, Sheffield and Derby. The mileage was 240, equal to 4 hours pay.

One of our jobs was working the Bristol to Leeds express from New Street to Sheffield at 8.20 after travelling in from Saltley. One morning I was surprised to see it arrive with an English Electric Type 3, No 37026, on front. As I had not worked on this type for

over six months, I had requested a refresher course on them, and explained this to the Saltley man who had worked it from Bristol; he said he would come with me as far as Landor Street, if another man would take over from there.

This was arranged with the platform inspector and caused about 5 minutes delay while we stopped to change drivers. When I signed off duty in the afternoon the assistant shedmaster, Mr John Wardle, inquired about the delay. I explained that the train was diagrammed for a Class 4 locomotive and I was surprised to see a Class 3 on it, and that I had requested a refresher some three months previously, and produced my diary to show the date. I then went on to show him that I had also applied for refreshers on Class 40s, 20s, 25s and 26s.

'Right,' he said. 'You'll have your refreshers next week.'

This suited me fine, as I should have been on a DMU turn, booking on at 15.40, which included working Saturday afternoons, whereas I would be signing on at 8.00 am with Saturday off duty. I was duly rostered with instructor Harry Willets.

'What's brought this on?' he inquired.

When I explained, he said, 'There must be dozens like you.'

I agreed, but said, 'Unless they make a stand they won't have a refresher, but if anything goes wrong and they've not been on that locomotive for over six months, management will blame them.'

Harry got his books out and said, 'We'll be able to go on to all of the locomotives, one each day. However, all the Class 26s have been allocated to depots in Scotland.'

During the course of the week we met Cliff Fletcher, one of our drivers who had recently been promoted to footplate inspector. He inquired, 'When are you going to refresh the Class 26s?', and smiled.

'We've already got our travel passes to travel to Inverness, but it means stopping there for the weekend,' I joked.

'Like hell you will!' he retorted.

In fact, we spent the Friday perusing the Class 26 traction instruction books in the classroom.

The sequel to this came later in the year when we had a fortnight's holiday touring Scotland by car. The middle weekend we stayed overnight at Kyle of Lochalsh, and on the Sunday I got up early and had a walk towards the station before breakfast to find a Type 26 shut down in the platform. The cab door was open, so I went in and looked around, and put the engine room lights on and examined the equipment and components in there. The town itself was completely silent. I wondered what would be said if I started it up!

When I returned to work and was signing on for a Sheffield job, I mischievously knocked on the door of Mr Wardle's office and told him of not being able to get on a Type 26 when on my refresher course. 'However,' I said, 'I've just been on holiday in Scotland and had a look at one at Kyle of Lochalsh on a Sunday and wondered if I could be paid for that day.'

His reply was as expected. 'You must think I'm barmy!' he exclaimed.

One day we were working the 8.20 am to Sheffield and my mate, Anthony, was driving when the engine shut down approaching Wichnor Junction while we were coasting. I told him to attempt to restart it with the button on the driving panel. It started twice, but shut down again. However, we managed to run into Burton station.

I looked into the engine room to find that the lubricating oil pressure gauge was showing low, and on testing the dipstick in the oil sump I could see that it was very low. I informed the platform inspector that we needed another locomotive, and they produced two English Electric Type 1s for us to work forward, after leaving our crippled one in the sidings. I expected a passenger locomotive would be provided at Derby, but they did not have one, so we carried on to Sheffield where the Leeds men were surprised to see these locomotives on front, but had to carry on with them.

As already mentioned, Saltley depot had two funds to provide benefits for staff illness, or death of members or members' wives. I was secretary of the Self-help Fund, which paid sickness, convalescence and death benefits, and was trustee of the Welfare Fund, which gave retirement grants, Christmas vouchers or parcels, annual dinners, excursions and grants for long-time sickness. At the AGMs of these funds it had been decided to have a joint meeting to find out whether it would be beneficial to amalgamate them, but at a special meeting held in September it was decided after a long debate not to do so.

At the AGM of the Welfare Fund it was decided that instead of issuing grocery vouchers for the active staff, we would give free tickets up to the value of £12 for theatres or night clubs, etc. This was to prove a headache to administer. Instead of members getting their own tickets and the fund reimbursing them, the committee decided that members should inform the secretary, Norman Beckett, of their venue, and he would book the tickets.

I was off duty ill with bronchitis for a fortnight and when I came to the depot on the Friday with my doctor's certificate to report fit for work the following week, Norman, was also the roster clerk, said, 'I've covered your Crewe job for next week, but the theatre tickets idea has proved a nightmare for me. Could you do it for me?'

'If management will allow it,' I replied.

'Come on, we'll go and see the shedmaster,' he said.

After Norman explained the size of the problem, Mr Lowe agreed that I would be given a week's unpaid leave if the Welfare Fund would pay me loss of earnings, and he would allocate an office and telephone for me to use. I had to contact theatres as far away as London, Stoke-on-Trent, Kidderminster and Worcester, as well as the Birmingham area. It was a full week's work for me before the tickets were issued on the Friday, and everyone was satisfied except the railway telephone switchboard manageress, who complained of the number of outside calls from Saltley depot.

In November I had a quite unusual job. This entailed signing on duty at 7.30 am and travelling to Tyseley to pick up a single-coach DMU, which had been transformed into a travelling route-learning schoolroom. On arrival at New Street station, drivers and guards from Old Oak Common, Reading,

Liverpool Edge Hill and Bristol, boarded, together with a route-learning instructor, Ken Beesley, and we proceeded to Coventry, Wolverhampton, Bushbury and Bescot, showing these 'foreign' men the intricacies of signals, stations and freight yards in the area.

Sunday 31 December saw me rostered on duty at 11.00 am for a stand-by North turn at Tyseley, and it started to snow around midday. I and my guard were called out about 14.00 to take two three-car DMUs into New Street to work a special train to Derby, with special stop orders for Tamworth and Burton. When I stopped at Burton the guard came to me from the rear unit to tell me that we had a lot of passengers for Sheffield and York.

'Tell the platform inspector to inform Control and that I sign the route to York.' I replied.

'I'm OK as far as Sheffield,' he said.

At Derby it was decided that we carry on to York, stopping at Chesterfield and Sheffield. It was snowing heavily when we arrived at Sheffield, and it was decided that we terminate there and work a special train to Bristol, stopping at principal stations *en route*.

'I'll take it as far as Birmingham,' I said. 'Tell the Midland Control to have another driver and guard to take over.'

We arrived at New Street at about 20.30, signing off duty around 21.30, just in time to dash home for a quick wash and change to go and celebrate the New Year at our local social club.

— o —

On the first day of the new year, 1979, I was rostered to sign on at 12.50 to work the 13.25 to York. As it was diagrammed a steam-heating locomotive, I was booked a second man, Michael McLeland. We relieved our men who had brought the empty coaches in from Oxley with No 45059 on front, and as we approached Derby we ran into heavy snow. This caused us a lot of delay and we arrived at York some 90 minutes late. We were relieved, the locomotive was taken to the depot and No 46010 was shunted on to the other end of our train.

We should have departed with the return train at 17.35 but it was now 19.15, and the platform inspector came to us and explained that the local DMU was cancelled and we were given special stop orders for all the small stations to Sheffield via Pontefract, such as Ulleskelf, Church Fenton and Bolton-on-Dearne. It was still snowing heavily when we set out and I had difficulty finding the tiny platforms holding three or four coaches with our train of ten, and I was concerned about losing time. I need not have worried, because when we arrived at Wath Junction we were directed along the slow line to Aldwarke Junction; this was operated by electric colour lights and power-controlled points.

It was around 20.30 when we came to a stand at a signal about half a mile from the signal box, and Michael telephoned the signalman, who informed us that he could not operate the points to turn us out to the fast line because of the snow drifting into them.

I phoned again at around 22.00 and the signalman informed me that platelayers were on their way to attempt to clear the snow. I inquired whether he had a national phone in the box to telephone my wife to tell her that I was going to be home late, as I was supposed to have been home at about 21.30. He said he would ask Control to contact my wife, so I gave him our telephone number. We stood there for another 3 hours and melted snow in the tea can to make some tea.

The platelayers were eventually successful and we got the green signal to go out fast line at around 1.30 am. We eventually arrived at New Street at 3.55 am, instead of our booked time of 20.25. We had been on duty for 15 hrs 55 mins, and as it was a Bank Holiday we were entitled to a day off in lieu. I remarked to Michael that I thought we should be entitled to two days. When I arrived home at about 5.00 am there was a note from my wife to say that she had received the telephone call from Sheffield Control to say that I was snowed in, and she could go to bed without too much worry.

The trade unions were again in conflict with the railway Board regarding wages and conditions and at the January meeting of our branch a series of national one-day strikes each week was announced. After a fortnight of this, discussions resumed and the trade unions were given certain assurances and concessions, and the industrial action was called off.

One of my turns was single-manned mixed passenger and freight workings, signing on duty at 13.40, taking an express passenger train to Derby and, after relief, travelling on it to Chesterfield and working a train of cement tanks coming from Buxton, going to Cardiff, as far as Landor Street. The Buxton men went home as passenger and, on Saturdays especially, liked to be early to catch an earlier train home. Normally they would be waiting on the goods line as we got off the express. Therefore instead of the guard and I having our 30-minute physical needs break, we would depart early, which enabled us to arrive home about an hour early. This also suited the Gloucester men, who also wanted to get back home on a Saturday night.

We arrived at Chesterfield one Saturday in March and it was raining heavily. To our surprise there was no train waiting for us. My guard remarked, 'It's a sign I wanted to get home early tonight - I've got a party to go to.'

We adjourned to the relief cabin behind the station buildings and telephoned Control to inform them that we had arrived. They told us that the train had left Buxton early, but did not know where it was at present. We made a can of tea and ate our sandwiches (which we usually did on the move), and after an hour's wait my guard rang Sheffield Power Box to ascertain the whereabouts of our train, as he was getting anxious because of his party. The signalman could only say that it had not arrived on his part of the signalling system at Dore & Totley Junction, but would inform us when it did.

The guard said to me, 'My wife will kill me if I'm late. I've told her to be ready when I get home.'

Another hour had gone by when the telephone rang and the signalman told us that our train had passed Dore & Totley and should be with us in about 25 minutes. We got our bags and tea can together, but after

30 minutes the phone rang again and we were informed that the train had stopped in Bradway Tunnel, and they were now sending a passenger train that had stopped behind it to push it through. Another half-hour elapsed before another call, when the signalman said that our train had coasted down the bank from Dronfield and was now standing at Tapton Junction awaiting the express to push it on to the goods line again.

'Will you go to that signal,' he continued (it was about half a mile away), 'to see if you can assist in finding out the cause of the trouble?'

We buttoned up our macintoshes as the rain had turned to sleet, and trudged towards our crippled locomotive, No 45033. The Buxton driver was also single-manned and, on entering the cab, he said, 'The engine's running all right and when I apply power it starts to move for about 30 seconds, then I lose power again.'

'I'll go into the engine room,' I said, 'then after about a minute put power on, and I'll try to diagnose the fault.'

This he did and immediately I could smell burning rubber from the main generator. I came back into the cab to tell the driver, and then telephoned the signalman that we needed a fresh locomotive as the generator was burning out. After he had consulted Control, he phoned me back at the signal, standing in the driving sleet, to ask if we could unhook the locomotive from the train and shunt it into the bay platform so that the fresh locomotive could come right on to the train. I had a discussion with the Buxton man and we discussed the risk of getting stranded with the failed loco, as it meant reversing twice to get from the goods line into the down bay. We decided to risk it and managed to stable it safely, then he and his guard caught a train into Sheffield, and we sat on our crippled locomotive with the engine running to work the cab heaters, which worked off the auxiliary generator, to dry out our wet clothing. I suggested to my guard that he telephoned his wife from the national telephone on the station to inform her of our delay.

Eventually No 47023 arrived from Tinsley depot and we departed about 3 hours late, instead of 45 minutes early, which we had hoped for. When we approached Saltley we were signalled to go along the goods line into Washwood Heath Sidings. It was around 23.00 when we stopped at the West End signal and the guard quickly dropped on to the ballast and got in touch with Saltley Power Box. When he came back he shouted up to me, 'Our relief has gone home. We're too late and there's permanent way work in the Bromsgrove area around midnight, so Gloucester Control don't want the train tonight. We have to leave the train here and take the locomotive light to our depot.' It was around 23.45 when we signed off duty, and the guard was very dejected as his night out had been spoiled.

In April I was single-manned again working the 14.15 freightliner from Lawley Street sidings to Holyhead as far as Crewe. I had Brian Timms, who is now a guard's supervisor, as my guard, and we negotiated the Sutton Park branch inclines with No 47474 and ran all right through Stafford. However, on approaching Norton Bridge Junction I lost power and managed to coast to the signal protecting the junction. I told Brian to inform Stafford Power Box that we were in trouble, and I was going into the engine room to see if I could rectify the fault. However, I could see nothing wrong. All circuit breakers and fuses were all right and each time I tried to get power, nothing happened.

Eventually, another locomotive came behind us from Stafford and hooked on to the rear of the train to propel us to Crewe Basford Hall Sidings. Our relief men climbed into the cab along with a fitter and an electrician, who asked for the symptoms of the failure.

'Is this an electric train heating locomotive?' he asked.

'Yes,' I replied, 'but I've no cause to use it.'

He disappeared into the engine room and within 30 seconds shouted, 'Try the power', and when the Crewe driver opened the controller we regained power. When the electrician returned I asked him what was wrong; I had looked at everything I could think of.

He replied, 'Come with me', and took me and the Crewe man into the electric train heating compartment to show us the circuit breaker, which had tripped.

I said, 'But we never had any train heat on.'

'We've had this happen a few times,' he replied, 'and when I knew it was this type of locomotive I guessed what it was.'

A few weeks later I had a note to see Cliff Fletcher, the footplate inspector, who asked me about the failure. I told him about the circuit breaker, which I did not know existed, and that I had spoken to other drivers who had no knowledge of it either. I told him that we only knew of an 'on and off' switch in the cab, and that the second men had been trained on train heating but we had not. He agreed with me and said, 'There's been a lot of trouble with this and all drivers will be given a day's training on train heating.'

With the numerous one-day strikes that we had undertaken in the previous couple of years our union branch funds had become depleted, and it was decided to hold a grand raffle. On 12 July I was allocated £150 to purchase prizes. The first prize was a black and white portable television and there were about a dozen small prizes. When the draw was made at the August branch meeting, the first prize was won by a driver working on the London Underground. It had been sold by Les Felton, our representative in ASLEF headquarters at Hampstead in London, so we informed him that he could have the honour of taking it to the Underground man's depot at Ruislip.

At the end of July I and three other drivers were rostered to train on the new Class 56 freight locomotive. I was pleasantly surprised to find that our two instructors were ex-firemen of mine from steam days, Norman Webb and Ray Reynolds, who is now a footplate inspector.

'You're told you're getting old when policemen look young,' I said, 'but when traction instructors are old steam mates you must be old!'

We had a pleasant week and Bob Clarke and myself passed out with a New Street inspector, Arthur Bullock.

At the June branch meeting I had been nominated to sit on industrial and social

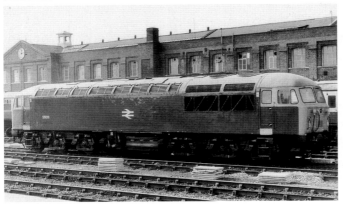

In 1979 I had my first experience of the new Class 56 locomotives. This is No 56011 brand new in the yard of Doncaster Works on 26 February 1977. *K. C. H. Fairey*

trained on them. The platform inspector stood nearby, so I said to him, 'If you want to blame someone for the noise, he's the one who's booked it to work the train.'

On a Sunday in December I was rostered on duty at 11.00 am for the stand-by at Tyseley, prepared to work south. At around 15.00 we were told to work DMU No 412 into New Street to take stranded passengers to Reading. We stopped at various stations *en route* and at Reading the guard came up to say that he had found a passenger for High Wycombe. He informed the platform inspector that we signed for the route, so again we had to negotiate the Greenford branch to High Wycombe and returned via Bicester to Tyseley. This gave us 4½ hours mileage bonus and 1 hr 50 mins overtime.

The depot Welfare Fund had installed cigarette machines and catering machines providing hot and cold drinks for men working throughout the 24 hours, and we had a spate of forged 50p coins being used. One week, early in 1980, when I was rostered on duty at 18.50 to work to Sheffield, I received a phone message at home on the Thursday afternoon from the shedmaster, requesting me to come to work at 18.00 and stay in the mess room for 8 hours to watch activities around the machines. I relieved one of the other trustees who had been watching since 10.00 am, and I was to be relieved at 2.00 am. We did this for two days, but no forged money was used. We were later informed by the City of Birmingham police that these 50p coins were prevalent in the clubs and pubs in the area. After a few months they found the culprits, who had been stamping metal blanks in the shape of a 50p in one of the local factories.

The year 1980 was the centenary of ASLEF, and different functions to celebrate

security appeal tribunals. I went for an interview at the Social Security offices at Five Ways House, Birmingham, and after about a fortnight I received a letter from the Lord Chancellor stating that I had been appointed to sit on these boards. I also received a letter from the area office inviting me to sit on an appeal tribunal to see how they worked. I was supplied with a huge book on social security law and other small booklets explaining the workings of the tribunals, and in August I sat on my first tribunal.

One Friday in October I signed on duty at 14.35 to work the 15.35 to York, and was informed that I had a Class 40, No 40120, which I had to take to New Street and change over with the Type 2 locomotive that was bringing the train in. At New Street we were placed in the middle sidings near the platform inspector's office to await our train. After a while he came out to remonstrate with us as he could not hear his telephones because of the noise of the locomotive. I replied, 'Think yourself lucky you've only a few minutes of it - I've got eight hours.' (They were indeed a noisy locomotive and our union is now negotiating with the railway Board for compensation for loss of hearing. I have been examined by an audio specialist and it has been confirmed I suffer from it.)

When we backed on to our train, a man came to the cab whom I recognised as one of our controllers. He said he was the traction controller and had authorised the locomotive to work the train, after finding out that I was this were held throughout the country. On Good Friday a dinner was arranged by the Wolverhampton branch at the Bushbury Railway Club, and my wife and I and other Saltley branch committee men and wives were invited to attend. After-dinner speeches were made by the union's assistant secretary, Don Pullen, our own Les Felton and others from the Midlands trade unions, and I spoke as the West Midlands TUC committee man. This was followed by a dance.

Our branch had discussions as to how we ourselves would celebrate the centenary, and Jack Evans, the assistant secretary, and myself, as vice-chairman, were delegated to arrange a function. The Lord Mayor of Birmingham at the time was George Canning, who had been a fireman at our depot before being called up into the Navy during the war years. Jack and I arranged a meeting with him and his Chief Clerk and they agreed that we could use Birmingham Council House. We were told that we could not bring in our caterers as we wanted to, but they introduced us to their chef who promised to supply any food we needed.

When the New Street branch heard what we were arranging they asked if they could join us. As the dining room at the Town Hall could accommodate 500 people, we were glad to have them with us. We arranged a five-course meal with different table wines, and a dance band, singer and comedian were booked for after dinner. George Canning gave us a speech of welcome about his years on the footplate at Saltley, and the ASLEF

General Secretary, Ray Buckton, replied on behalf of the union. We then went into the ballroom where entertainment was arranged until midnight. At the next branch meeting Jack and I were thanked by the members for the efficient and enjoyable evening that had been arranged.

In June we were both involved again as trustees of the Welfare Fund when we took our retired staff, wives and widows on a train trip to Butlin's Barry Island holiday camp, being the only place at this resort that could cater for 400 people. On the way down we counted how many actual travellers we had and found that we were about 30 short of our total, so as soon as we arrived Jack and I went hot-foot to Butlin's camp and informed the manager how many short we were and requested a refund for the lunches and high teas that had been arranged for us. The manager said he was glad we had informed him early as he could now allow 30 other visitors into the camp.

On Friday 18 July I booked on at 12.54 single-manned to travel into New Street to relieve our driver who had fetched the empty coaches from Oxley carriage sidings with No 47511 on front, to work the 13.40 to York and return with the same train. Things went well until I was descending from Dore & Totley towards Sheffield, with all colour light signals at green. These had been in operation for about six months, controlled by a signal box at Sheffield station. At Beauchief I received a green signal, which meant that I should have received a double yellow near Heeley carriage sidings; I was travelling around 90 mph and was surprised to see only a single yellow light, indicating that the next signal, not the next but one, was at danger. I applied the brake in the emergency position, and the next signal at Queen's Road was indeed at danger, but I had no chance of stopping and passed it at about 25 mph. I was again surprised to see the points set for the loop line, and stopped with the locomotive and about four coaches past the signal, with the loco and two coaches in the loop. I jumped down on to the ballast and dashed back to the telephone on the signal. The guard put his head out of the train to inquire

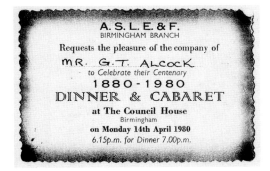

My ticket for the ASLEF centenary celebrations at Birmingham Council House in April 1980.

why we had stopped so suddenly. I told him and inquired if he had observed the signals coming down the bank. He replied that he had not, so as I was single-manned it would be my word against that of the signalman if an argument arose.

I was pleasantly surprised when the signalman answered my call and said, 'What have you stopped there for? You've the line clear into platform 1.'

I informed him of the signal's malfunction, and that part of the train was in the loop. It was now his turn to be surprised, and he told me to hang on at the phone. After a few minutes he came back and said, 'Come at caution through the loop - the signal at the end will be at clear right into the platform.'

When I arrived, the platform inspector was waiting near the end of the platform and asked me to speak to the signal box controller on the telephone. He inquired which signals I had seen coming from Dore & Totley, and I told him I had all greens to Beauchief, then one yellow instead of two at Heeley, then a red signal at Queen's Road, which I could not stop at because of the short distance from the yellow signal. He thanked me and said, 'Carry on to York.' I had been expecting to be taken off, which was the normal procedure after having passed a signal at danger.

I ran around the train at York as normal and worked back home. On arriving at Sheffield the train crew supervisor was at the end of the platform and climbed into the cab. He recognised me from earlier.

'All right, Brummie,' he said, 'what happened early on this afternoon?'

I explained about the sequence of the signals, and he said, 'Be sure to report it when you get back to your depot. A Manchester driver and one of our men have had similar difficulties with these signals, but the signal and telegraph department won't acknowledge any faults with them.'

As I climbed the bank out of Sheffield, I could see men at all the signals on the opposite line. I duly reported the incident, and on the following Monday Jack Boulton asked me about the incident.

'How long have you been working into Sheffield?'

'About 35 years.'

'You should know what you're talking about,' he said.

'Yes,' I replied, 'but these new signals have been in operation about six months and they should make things much simpler than the old semaphores.'

About three weeks later I received a letter from management admitting a wrong-side failure of these signals. This took me by surprise, as they never usually admitted any signal malfunction. I took this letter to our branch secretary and asked him to take copies of it for his use and to send a copy to ASLEF headquarters, and I also asked for a copy for myself to take to the Sheffield branch the following week when I was working there. After their secretary read it he thanked me most profusely, saying, 'This is what I need to get some of our men out of trouble.'

A few weeks later I was involved with signal irregularities again, but this time I had a surprise witness. I was working a return express from York and, on arrival at Sheffield at around 13.35, I got a can of water from the shunter's cabin and put it on the stove in front of the second man's seat; it would be just about boiling when I stopped at Chesterfield, and the 2-minute stop enabled me to put the tea in the can. On this occasion, when I came to a stand there was a well-dressed man standing nearby. He opened the cab door, showed me his footplate pass and said, 'I'm Mr Taylor, the Nottingham Divisional Manager, and I'd like to ride with you to Derby.'

I welcomed him aboard by saying, 'The can has just boiled. Here's the tea and sugar - make yourself useful as I haven't a second man.'

By the time we emerged from Clay Cross Tunnel the tea had mashed, so I said, 'The milk and cups are in my bag - pour the tea out.'

As we were travelling down the bank, he explained that this was a piece of his railway that he did not see very often, even though it was in his area. It was controlled by Trent signal box, some 15 miles away.

At Crich Tunnel we were going about 90 mph, and I had closed the power handle to prepare to brake for the 30 mph speed restriction around the curve at Ambergate Junction, and as we emerged from the tunnel the next signal, which should have been at least a double yellow, was at red.

Mr Taylor shouted, 'It's red - stop!'

'I'm already doing it!' I replied.

We managed to stop right alongside it. He exclaimed, 'What the hell is going on? You've had green signals all the way.'

'I'll go and find out,' I said. 'This isn't one of your signals - it's the first one of Derby's.'

'Never mind,' he said. 'Don't mention that I'm here with you.'

When I contacted the signalman he said, 'What have you stopped there for? You've got green signals as far as Belper.'

'Not here,' I replied. 'I've got a red one.'

He must have looked at his panel, then exclaimed, 'The points at the junction must have moved over! I'll reset them and you'll have to wait 2 minutes while they operate.' (This was the built-in safety margin.)

Mr Taylor looked quite upset and white-faced. I explained what the signalman had said and remarked, 'We'd better have another cup of tea from what's left in the can.'

'You're very calm,' he said. 'My heart is still racing.'

'You get used to it,' I explained. Then I took my cap off and said jokingly, 'I used to have a lovely head of black hair before I became a driver. Look at it now, grey and very sparse.'

When we arrived at Derby he asked me for my name and depot and said, 'Be sure to report this incident when signing off duty. I'm going to the signal box to sort them out!'

About a fortnight later I received a letter from Mr Taylor, thanking me for the calm and efficient manner with which I had handled the situation, and going on to say that the signalman responsible had been suitably disciplined.

In November I was sitting on a social security appeal tribunal when one of the cases concerned a man of Pakistani extraction; as was allowed, he had an interpreter with him, who turned out to be Mr Ray Darr, one of our depot timekeepers. When he entered the room and I recognised him, I explained to the chair-woman, Mrs Earle, that I knew him. After a discussion, she ruled that as he was not the appellant and acting only as an interpreter, I could sit on the case. Mr Darr spoke with an Asian accent and I had to interpret what he had to say. After they left the room, Mrs Earle said, 'It's a good job you were here - we would not have understood either of them!'

The Pakistani chap did not have good grounds on which to appeal, and it was turned down. For about three months afterwards, whenever Ray Darr was on duty when I signed on or off, he would buttonhole me to try to explain aspects of the case.

One cold Saturday, towards the end of the year, I was rostered on duty at 07.37 with another driver, Malcolm Smith, to work a train-spotters' special coming from London Marylebone and going to Manchester via Burton-on-Trent and Toton, and booked to stop at Mansfield Parkway for a photographic session, then carrying on via Clay Cross Junction and Staveley to Rotherwood sidings, near Darnall, on the old LNER. As I did not sign the route from Toton to Clay Cross and from Staveley to Rotherwood, Malcolm drove over this part of the route.

When we relieved the train at Landor Street we were surprised to see two English Electric Type 1 locomotives on front, apparently requested by the enthusiasts. It was a bitterly cold day with flecks of snow drifting down and we were both frozen with cold, as these locomotives did not have much heat when travelling at their maximum 75 mph. At the photo stop, where hundreds of rolls of film must have been used, people came to us to ask if they could look into the cab.

'Why have you picked these ice-boxes to work the train?' I asked. Then I realised that the coaches of the train would be as cold, as these locomotives had no facilities to generate train heat.

At Rotherwood we were uncoupled and an old 'EM1' electric locomotive backed on to the train to work it to Chinley and Manchester. We went light locomotive via Sheffield and I took over the driving. Surprisingly, we did not stop between Rotherwood until we arrived at our depot, a distance of nearly 90 miles.

14
HSTs AND SHUNTING
1981-85

The first Sunday in January 1981 I signed on duty at 15.25 with second man Bob Dunn to take No 47476 off the depot to New Street station to work the Bristol to York express at 16.15 and return with the same locomotive and coaches. This train had worked into New Street via Camp Hill and Grand Junction because of track work at Selly Oak, and we hooked on to the rear to work it in the proper direction. We arrived at York around 20.00, and as we ran in I spotted a Class 40 waiting in the middle bay.

'It's unusual to see one of these up here,' I remarked to Bob.

When we stopped, a set of men climbed into the cab and said that there was another locomotive going onto the other end, and they were taking ours to the depot.

'I bet it's that English Electric Type 4,' I said to Bob, and so it was! As I had driven to York, Bob, who was an old hand passed fireman and who signed the route, drove back, so we had a noisy return trip home.

In early March my ex-fireman, Ken Griffin, died in his early fifties. He had suffered for a number of years with acute rheumatoid arthritis, which culminated in him being off duty for over 12 months, and having gold treatment on his wrist, elbows, knees, ankles, etc. He had been bedridden for a long period and had to go to Droitwich brine baths for treatment to get his limbs working again. As secretary of the Self-help Sick Fund, I used to visit him in hospital. He was determined to come back to work; a shunting driver's position was found for him on regular nights at Washwood Heath so that his daughter could bring him to work by car at 21.30, and the shunting engine was

placed at the end of the sidings, so he had only a few steps to walk. He was eventually provided with an invalid car, which gave him greater freedom. About 100 train crew men filled the crematorium at Perry Barr for his funeral.

Our latest turn of duty involved signing on at 18.57 to work the Cardiff to Sheffield train from New Street at 19.35. One Monday we had No 47558 on front of our normal 10 coaches. Our first station stop was Burton and I shut off power when travelling at 90 mph, as usual, approaching Branston Junction. I started to apply the brake when running under the bridge at Branston Sidings (this was a good guide in foggy weather), but my first application did not seem to have much effect, so I put more pressure into the braking system and as we passed Burton Loco at about 60 mph, I remarked to Bob, 'We're not going to stop here tonight.'

We ran through the station at around 25 mph, and eventually stopped with only five coaches in the platform; the other five and the locomotive were opposite Ind Coope's brewery. After a while the guard called us to set back into the platform, where the mail bags could be unloaded from the first guard's van. This caused about 10 minutes delay.

As there was a 30 mph speed restriction approaching Derby, I stopped there without a problem. When we approached Chesterfield at 90 mph, I shut off power earlier than normal and started to brake as we passed the old Hasland loco depot. Even then I had a job to stop, with the locomotive ending up beyond the end of the platform. There were some black looks from the Post Office staff who had to wheel their barrows some four coach lengths from our normal stop. I approached Sheffield station very cautiously and stopped safely. The Sheffield men relieved us to take the coaches to the carriage sidings and I told them about the poor brakes.

The following night Bob drove outwards with No 47050 without any trouble. On Wednesday night we had No 47341, and again at Burton and Chesterfield I had trouble stopping despite running up to them cautiously. When I arrived at Sheffield I asked the platform inspector to send for the carriage and wagon examiner as I wanted the brakes examined at Nunnery Carriage Sidings.

The following night Bob had no trouble stopping and when we arrived at Sheffield the carriage and wagon examiner was waiting for me. He said, 'Half the brake blocks on last night's train weren't touching the wheels because of bad adjustment. I could tell when I went round the train before it left for Nunnery because the ones not working were cold and the others quite warm. These coaches were serviced at Cardiff,' he continued, 'and they were allocated to this train on alternate nights, so that's the reason for the difference between the brakes on Monday and Wednesday.' Needless to say we had no further trouble that week.

Our return train was the Post Office Mail train with no passengers on board, stopping at Derby and New Street only. We arrived there at 00.55, making an early finish on our late turn.

A few weeks later I received a letter from management, asking for the reason for not stopping properly at Burton, thus causing delay to occur. I replied that the brakes of the coaches were defective for at least three days and gave them the name of the Sheffield carriage examiner.

In August we went on holiday to Sorrento and Rome with the Railway Touring Club. The weather was very hot, and one evening as I emerged from the shower in our room I slipped on the wet marble floor and fell with my side on the bidet! I was in terrible pain and May helped me to my feet and on to my bed. Being a nurse, she tried to ease my pain, and advised me to go to hospital as she thought I had broken some ribs. I decided

against this as we only had one more day remaining before we travelled home, and I did not want to stay in hospital. Another lady in our party gave me some ointment, which helped to ease the pain.

We travelled home on the 15.25 from Rome and at nightfall I tried in vain to sleep in the couchette, but could feel every sleeper we ran over, so I stood in the corridor most of the night.

I was booked on duty at 07.50 am on the following Monday, and as the pain had eased I went to work to Sheffield and return. When I built up speed on No 45069 around Castle Bromwich, I could feel the arm of my chair hitting my rib cage with every bounce of the locomotive. Eventually I arrived at Sheffield feeling very sore. During my physical needs break I purchased some aspirins from the bookstall. I worked back home on No 47545 and I was not too bad on the slow climb up to Dore & Totley, but on the fast running down to Chesterfield the bouncing, which normally I never noticed, caused the pain to return.

I was stopped at signals at Proof House Junction just outside New Street station, and after waiting the customary minute I had to climb down to telephone the signalman.

'We're a bit congested in the station,' he explained, 'but we should have a platform for you shortly.'

The ballast there was about a foot deep below the rail level and I had to reach for the hand rail to pull myself into the cab. This caused me immense pain and I hardly made it. What wouldn't I give for a second man now, I thought. I managed to drive the train into the station and when the Cardiff men came into the cab I was in a state of collapse. They called for the platform inspector, Gordon West, who helped me from the cab and wanted to call for an ambulance, but I declined.

'Help me over the footbridge to the Vauxhall & Duddeston train - there should be some of our chaps travelling to the depot who'll help me.'

On signing off duty I managed to drive my car home and made an appointment to see my doctor the next day, so I rang the depot to book off duty sick. When I saw the doctor he examined my ribs and made an X-ray appointment with Sandwell Hospital for the next day. They diagnosed I had cracked three ribs, and this caused me to have six weeks off duty.

At the September union branch meeting change was in the air, and although I was still off duty I attended, and found that the LDC was proposing to alter the structure of the links again, with men placed in strict seniority within them. Paddington and Bristol work would be in Link 1, York work in Link 2, and so forth. This would comprise 48 weeks' work in each link to contain rest days, with the long-distance jobs being rostered three days one week and three days later on in the link to keep drivers conversant with the routes.

I and most of the men who had volunteered for the York link objected to this plan, but although we were large in voice, we were small in number (there were only 12 of us in that link). We were out-voted when the vote was taken, so I was back in the Paddington link again.

Before the new workings came into operation with the winter timetables in October, I had an unusual job to York. My second man was Bill Jones, who was the son of a signalman friend of mine, Maurice Jones. We signed on duty at 06.58 to relieve No 45074 at Landor Street, coming from Ealing Broadway with a party of schoolchildren. It was a cold, wet morning and we were surprised to see there was no heat going into the coaches. When we spoke to the Banbury men they said that the boiler was not working as it was isolated and out of service.

When we arrived at York, we waited to be unhooked to take the locomotive to the depot and a couple of teachers who were in charge of their pupils complained to me about the cold coaches. I said that I sympathised with them entirely, explaining about the boiler. I went on to say that if they wanted heat on the return train, they should complain to the Station Master, or they would have the same locomotive again.

They must have done this because when Bill phoned the shed foreman on arrival at the depot to inquire where to leave the locomotive, he was told to put it on the cripple road, as it would not be working the return

train to Ealing Broadway. We had our break, then walked across to the station to relieve a football supporters' excursion coming from Newcastle to watch their team play West Bromwich Albion. We relieved Gateshead men on No 46001, whose boiler was working, and we were routed via Wichnor Junction through Lichfield, Walsall, Perry Barr Junction to Smethwick. After the supporters had unloaded, we took the coaches to Oxley carriage sidings, and were then instructed to take the locomotive to Bescot depot. This meant us travelling home from there as passenger, so we had 45 minutes travelling time on top of our 5 hours mileage bonus, and we were on duty for 9 hrs 57 mins.

The new links started in late October, and as I had not been over the Bristol and Paddington routes for almost three years, Charlie Lindley and I were rostered again to learn them. There was also fresh work to Leicester and Lichfield via Sutton Coldfield. One day, when reviewing around London, we decided to have a run from Ealing Broadway over the branch line to Greenford, which was essential for diversions. We joined the Southall driver on a single-coach DMU, and I asked if much had changed in the three years.

'Nothing has changed,' he said, then thought for a moment and added, 'There's a new pub been built outside Barr Park station.'

When we stopped there Charlie exclaimed, 'They've have named it after you!'

The sign outside showed a London policeman and it was called 'Old Bill'!

That evening at home I said to my wife, 'They've named a pub after me.'

'You have been in enough of them,' she retorted, 'so it's about time.'

It was the middle of January 1982 before we completed our route learning, and once again the trade unions were in conflict with the railway Board, and we were involved with another series of two-day strikes that lasted about four weeks before an agreement was reached on wages and conditions of service.

My first trip to Paddington was at the beginning of February on the 14.35 from New Street. Class 50 English Electric locomotives

At the age of 60 I was still learning, with the introduction of Class 50s on the Paddington run. In March 1982 I had a Class 50 on the 18.40 from Paddington via Reading and Oxford, but was provided with a traction instructor. This photograph taken on 21 January 1984 shows No 50016 on the 10.09 New Street-Banbury-Paddington service framed in the signals at Aynho Junction, cleared for the Oxford line. *Roger Siviter*

had been allocated to the depot, but as they had been working on the Paddington and Bristol trains, I had not been trained on them. One was allocated to me now, so I had to have a traction instructor with me for the three days of the week that I was rostered on for this week's work. This way of working carried on when I was allocated these locomotives until the end of April, when I was trained on them, so at the age of 60 I was still learning!

In March I had a Class 50 on the 18.40 from Paddington via Reading and Oxford, and I was provided with a traction instructor who was stationed at Reading. As he knew the route and the locomotive, he did the driving. As we approached Kennington Junction, just outside Oxford, we had yellow signals, but unfortunately we approached the red too fast and ran the locomotive and first coach past it. The Reading driver shot out of

his seat and shouted, 'I'll phone the signalman.'

When he returned he said, 'They've got points trouble at Oxford station and the area manager is in the signal box, so it looks as though I'll get reported.'

When I signed off duty at 22.15, I was asked for a report of the incident, and when I signed on the next day the senior footplate inspector from Stanier House, Eddie Alcock (no relation to me), was waiting to interview me. I explained to him that I was not handling the locomotive as the traction instructor was acquainted with both the locomotive and route, as per the rule book. He replied, 'It looks as though you're in the clear and the Reading man will be held responsible.' I heard no more about it.

On the Spring Bank Holiday I was rostered to sign on duty at 16.18 to travel to Paddington, then catch a local train to Ealing Broadway to relieve an excursion train coming from Brighton, going to Wolverhampton. My second man did not turn up for duty, so a spare driver was instructed to come with me. He was Ken Mitchell, one of our LDC representatives. When we arrived at Ealing Broadway we had to use the porter's room to make our can of tea and await our train. There was a set of Bristol men also there awaiting a train from Eastbourne. When I telephoned the Old Oak Common signalman at the station inspector's office inquiring about the running of our train, he told me that the locomotive was having trouble and a fresh one was being provided, so it looked as though there would be some delay. After about an hour the station inspector came to tell the Bristol men that their train was coming along the down relief line, so off they went.

About 10 minutes later the inspector burst into the room shouting, 'There's been a mistake! They've taken your train. Come and have a word with the signalman.'

When I spoke to him he admitted it was his mistake, giving the wrong train to the station inspector. 'Your train is standing at Hanwell station,' he said. The guard had spotted the mistake when he looked at the train papers and had applied the brake.

'Where's the Bristol train?' I asked.

'It's standing here at Old Oak changing locomotives,' he replied.

I suggested sending the Bristol men on to Reading, and we would take their train there and change over with them. However, this was over-ruled by the signal box controller, who authorised our train to propel back about 3 miles and over a dozen or more points; this would not have been allowed under the old semaphore manual signalling. It eventually returned to us, and when I stepped into the cab, I smiled and said, 'I've heard of Bristol men stealing Saltley men's work, but this is a bit blatant - and I've got one of our LDC men with me as a witness!'

This mistake caused over an hour's delay and we had been on duty for 9 hrs 45 mins by the time we returned from Wolverhampton.

In May of every year ASLEF held its annual conference, where 46 delegates from England, Scotland and Wales met to put forward branches' suggestions for improving the footplate staff's way of life and air their experience of the way the union was run by the appointed officials. I was fortunate to be elected to represent the Birmingham No 2 area, which comprised the Saltley, Bescot, Coventry, Leamington and Stratford-upon-Avon branches. Birmingham No 1 area consisted of New Street, Wolverhampton, Stourbridge and Kidderminster, and Ernie Bennet, of the New Street branch, who had served with me on the Monument Lane LDC, was their delegate. For the fortnight of the conference we were granted unpaid leave by the railway management and were paid the trade union rate of pay. The conference was held at the union headquarters in Arkwright Road, Hampstead, London, from Tuesday 18 May.

My branch had sent two resolutions, which I had to propose. One was on health and safety, which proposed that heart complaints and hearing difficulties be classed as industrial diseases, because of the increasing number of drivers suffering from them due to the increase of speed and the high intensity of the modern workings. Both were carried, which meant that our union had to negotiate with the railway Board to achieve this. They also had to improve cab insulation to keep out noise and draughts, which I explained could affect the ears under circumstances of extreme pressure when working at high speeds through tunnels, etc. They also had to get the Ministry of Health involved in these negotiations.

(Early in 1992, after retirement, I had to attend an audio specialist provided by ASLEF for a series of tests, so that a claim for loss of hearing through my work could be lodged against British Rail. I was eventually granted over £1,000 compensation, and I know of other men who received over £3,000.)

Another important discussion, which was to become the principal debate of the conference, was the railway Board's insistence on train crews' variable rostering of 6 to 10 hours for a day's work. We opposed this, as we were of the opinion that the simplest way of working throughout the 24 hours was three shifts of 8 hours. Train crews already had the most unsociable hours of work throughout the country. For example, my rosters show that I was to sign on duty at 00.21, 02.17 and 03.42, booking on and off at odd minutes through the 24 hours, seven days a week. I still have a copy of my roster, which comprises 48 weeks work. It shows that on some weeks I was to book on for three days at the same time and two

A meeting in progress during the 1982 annual delegates' conference at the ASLEF headquarters in Hampstead. I am second from the left on the front row. *Author's collection* other days at different times. On early morning shifts the alarm clock was continually being altered, and a proper sleep pattern could not be attained!

In a debate that lasted all day I spoke against the Board's proposals, and the delegates instructed our union officials to oppose them, even as far as to going on all-out strike. It was a hard day and we were glad that a coach trip had been arranged by General Secretary Ray Buckton's wife, Barbara, to Grim's Dyke House, former home of W. S. Gilbert of Gilbert & Sullivan fame, where we had a relaxing evening.

On some of the evenings we were invited to ASLEF branches in London, such as Kentish Town, Southall, Old Oak Common, and the London Underground branch at Acton and Northfields. Incidentally, the London Underground had three delegates at our conference.

One evening Leslie Huckfield MP, who was our union's representative in Parliament, invited a party of us to the House of Commons, where a debate was in progress on a section of the Transport Bill. It was quite surprising; we watched and listened to a Labour Party amendment when there were only about two dozen MPs in the chamber, but when the division bell sounded around 23.00, hundreds of MPs walked through to record their votes, and the amendment was lost, with over 600 MPs voting.

It was back to earth on the Sunday, signing on duty at 16.56 to travel to New Street and relieve a train coming from Peterborough and take the coaches to Duddeston carriage sidings, then bring the locomotives to our depot. I was then booked to travel back into New Street to relieve a train coming from Paddington with No 50032 on front, and run around the train to work the 20.40 to Paddington as far as Banbury. This was the day that the Pope was visiting Coventry, and extra trains and staff were provided to carry the extra passengers expected.

Leamington Spa's up platform has a sharp curve on the London end, and I had to take the locomotive off the platform to get all the coaches on. This meant that I could not see

An April 1971 view of the London end of the up platform at Leamington Spa, showing the sharp curve to the right that restricts a driver's view back along the train. W. Adams

my guard, and I had to rely on one of the station staff to relay the 'right away' signal. When I received this I opened the power handle and started to move away, but after going about three coaches length I was brought to a stand by a severe brake application. I looked at the brake air pressure gauge and could see it was too much for a communication cord operation, so I decided it must have been done by the guard. As I had no second man, I could not send him to ascertain what had gone wrong, and as I was still on the sharp curve I could not see what was happening on the platform.

I waited for 3 or 4 minutes, then two railway officials with gold braid on their hats approached the cab. One of them asked, 'Who gave you the signal to move?'

'One of the station staff,' I replied.

'Not the guard?'

'Come and see for yourself,' I replied. 'I can't even see the platform - but what's the matter?'

'A woman has fallen between the coach and the platform,' he answered. They walked back to the platform and after a long delay I again received the 'right away' signal and carried on to Banbury. When I was relieved I dashed along the platform to speak to the guard, who was carrying on to Paddington. I asked him about the incident and he told me that a woman had got into the train to see a passenger off, the door had been closed, and he had signalled the 'right away' to the station staff, and as the train started to move she tried to get out of the train by opening the door and fell between the coach and platform.

'She was unconscious and had to be taken to hospital by ambulance,' he said. 'It's not your fault.'

He gave me his name and depot for verification in case I had to report about it. I asked who the people in gold braid hats were.

'Staff,' he sniffed. 'They've been brought in for the Papal visit - we manage without them normally.'

I expected Control at Banbury to have words with me, but worked my normal train home without trouble. When I signed off duty around 1.00 am the foreman wanted a report of the incident for Control. I fully expected that further reports or an inquiry would be required, but I never heard any more of it.

Since the abolition of the York link I did not relish working early morning shifts and, when possible, used to exchange with a driver on a late day turn. One week I should have been on duty at 03.17 for a Didcot coal train, and I changed for a local DMU turn, booking on at 10.15 am, working to and from Lichfield and Longbridge. The Saturday working entailed signing on at 9.32 to travel to New Street and relieve a six-car DMU coming from Leicester and going forward to Barry Island in South Wales. I was booked to work this to Gloucester, then wait there for 4½ hours to work the same units home with the return Barry Island to Leicester train.

I had spoken to a driver in that link and he said that rather than wait at Gloucester he would travel on the train, and he had about half an hour for his food at Barry Island. I decided to do this too, and when the Gloucester driver came to relieve me I asked if he minded my coming with him. He was glad of the company, worked the train to Cardiff and was relieved by a Cardiff Canton driver for the short run to Barry Island. We made a can of tea and had our food while the train was being cleaned in the platform for the return journey. When we walked along the platform about 10 minutes before the departure time, I was surprised to see one of our drivers, Ron Jackson, who had recently had a heart attack, and his wife.

'What are you doing here?' he said. 'Saltley men don't sign the route.'

I explained that I had come for the ride, and said, 'But more important, what are you doing here? The last I heard of you, you were in hospital.'

'I came out about ten days ago and this holiday at Butlin's camp had been booked previously, so within three days I was taking it easy down here to help my recovery.'

On the return trip I had a good run until Barnt Green, where we were stopped by signals. When I spoke to the Saltley signalman he said, 'We're having trouble with the track circuits between King's Norton and New Street. You're in the queue.'

It took us about 2 hours to travel the 3 miles to Northfield. Mrs Jackson gave me a cup of tea from her flask and a piece of cake. When I spoke to the signalman at King's Norton he said, 'There are six trains in front of you waiting their turn into New Street.'

'Do you know we're a six-car DMU?' I said.

'What difference does that make?' he asked.

'We could come into New Street via the Camp Hill line,' I replied, 'and enter New Street from the other end, and the Leicester driver could drive out from the rear cab.'

'That's a good idea,' he said. 'I'll have a word with the box controller.'

Within a few minutes the signal cleared for the branch line and we ran non-stop into New Street, arriving at about 20.00 instead of 16.55.

I was on holiday touring Scotland when it was my 60th birthday, and when I returned I was due to see the railway medical officer on 27 June, but the NUR were on strike and it was postponed. Meanwhile ASLEF had been negotiating with the railway Board regarding the variable rosters, but without success, and on 5 July we were called out on strike. As vice-chairman I was appointed as strike committee chairman, as Fred Orton Jones was selected to join the executive committee, and instead of standing on the picket line for about 4 hours at a time, I had the doubtful pleasure of sitting in a back room of the Orange Tree pub near to the depot from 10.00 am until closing time around 23.00.

On the following Sunday I attended the Bescot board meeting as their delegate, and after a stormy meeting it was agreed to support the union and stay on strike. When we came to pick up our delayed wages on Friday 16 July, we were handed letters from the railway Board indicating that if we did not return to work on the following Monday we would be deemed to have resigned from the railway service!

An open meeting was called for the following Sunday, where all branches I represented attended. I chaired the meeting, which lasted over 2 hours, and it was agreed that we continue to support the strike. That afternoon I had to take an aunt of mine, who had been staying with us, back to her home in Mid Wales, and I did not know until Monday that our executive had called the strike off on Sunday afternoon.

ASLEF head office called us delegates back to a meeting at Arkwright Road on 27 July, and the week before I attended the branches I represented to get to know their opinions. I was instructed to try to get a compromise on the 6 to 10 hour day, although my personal feeling was to oppose any variable rostering, even if it meant striking again. When I spoke at the re-scheduled conference, I had to eat humble pie and the statements I had made at the first conference had to be withdrawn in line with the feelings of my branches. After a full day debate, the officers of our union were instructed by the delegates to negotiate for a 7 to 9 hours daily agreement. After about a week the railway Board agreed to this, so as well as the unsocial shift workings, we also had unsocial daily hours.

This produced a lot of problems for the LDC and railway management, and eventually the solution was for each man to work 312 hours in an eight-week cycle, some weeks working as little as 35 hours, and other weeks up to 45 hours. It was also a problem

for the running shift foreman and timekeeper to remember if a man was booking on for a 7-hour or up to a 9-hour shift. Extra clerical staff had to be employed to monitor and transfer the hours over a 40-hour week to a week where fewer than 40 hours were worked for our wages. I do not know who gained from this agreement, but it certainly was not the locoman or guard!

One of our major grievances regarding rest days was that periodically we would be booked on duty late on Friday night, and work 6 or 7 hours into our Saturday rest day. On one occasion second man John Clamp and myself signed on duty at 22.41 to work the car train from Knowle & Dorridge to West Ealing with No 40060. We had a good run and arrived right time, to be informed that our return train was at Southall. As we waited to go into the sidings, we could see a train of empty car-flats departing with one of our train crew, who had signed on at 21.35 to work to Old Oak Common. The driver was Andy Harrison, a noted overtime man.

We duly departed some 30 minutes later with a train of Italian cars, and had a good run to Banbury, where we were placed along the goods line. When my mate phoned the signalman to inquire the reason for this, he was told that the other train was having difficulties ahead of us. We were delayed for some 3 hours, and I asked for relief when we had been on duty for 8 hours, but was informed that no Banbury driver was trained on the Class 40.

We had a spasmodic run to Leamington, where we had more delay, and we arrived outside Knowle & Dorridge around 10.00 am to be told that the other train was in the sidings, and there was no room for us. After about half an hour it was decided that the other train would be sent to Bordesley, as our train of cars was needed to be unloaded at Knowle & Dorridge.

We eventually disposed of our train around 11.00 am, and prepared to travel light engine to our depot. When our guard told the signalman that we were ready, he was told that the other train had become derailed near Widney Manor station. I suggested that we go via Leamington and Coventry, but this was turned down, as we would be needed to take the rear vehicles off the train in front.

While we waited I managed to phone my wife to tell her that I would be very late, as we had arranged to go shopping.

'You're already very late,' she replied. 'You should have been home around 7.00 am.'

We were eventually instructed to go forward at caution towards Widney Manor and couple up to the rear of the empty car-flats. We could see that the Saltley breakdown train and crew were in attendance. We towed the rear vehicles back to Knowle & Dorridge and stabled them in the up sidings, but still had to wait while the other vehicles were put back on the rails and taken on to Bordesley sidings. We passed Andy Harrison marshalling his train at Bordesley, and gave him a rude whistle!

We arrived at our depot at 13.10 pm, signing off duty at 13.35 pm, showing 14 hrs 44 mins. One consolation was that as we had worked over 12 hours into our rest day, we would be paid 8 hours compensation for spoiling our day off.

On Wednesday 4 August I had my delayed medical, with rather surprising results. I passed my eyesight, electro-cardiograph and blood pressure tests, but when the sample of my urine was tested, the assistant called the doctor into the outer office. After a few minutes he came back to me and gave me another blood pressure test, shone a light into my eyes, looked at my hands and feet, then after a while told me to get dressed, but not to go until he had spoken to me. When I returned to his office he said, 'You are showing signs of diabetes. I cannot allow you to work on the main line until you have seen a specialist. Make an appointment with your own doctor who will arrange for you to attend a clinic.'

When I returned to the depot the foreman already knew and told me to sign on duty the next day at 8.00 am for shed marshalling, instead of my rostered turn of the 5.35 am Bristol. I saw my own doctor on Friday and he examined me and took urine tests, then arranged for me to go to Mr B. Smith's clinic at Sandwell Hospital the following Monday. Mr Smith gave me a strict medical and informed me that I had diabetes, but I was

not showing any signs of blood pressure, poor eyesight, etc; he said he thought that it could be controlled by diet. I explained about my job and that I had been taken off the main line. He replied, 'We'll see what dieting will do. Come back and see me in four weeks time. In the meantime, go and see the dietician next door.'

This was a comical interview, albeit meant to be serious. She had papers in front of her, no doubt from Mr Smith, and remarked 'You are overweight at 13 stone 10 pounds. You need to lose 4 stone.'

I protested, 'That means I will be under 10 stone. When I was at my fittest, I was cycling over 20 miles a day back and forth to work, and firing on the top expresses. I was always over 12 stone.'

She looked very stern and said, 'These are my instructions from Mr Smith. Now what do you have for breakfast?'

'It all depends what time I go to work, I replied. 'On early mornings a piece of toast will suffice, but on later shifts I have bacon and eggs or sausages and tomatoes.'

She cringed. 'They're both out,' she said. 'Now, what do you have around 11.00 am?'

'What do you mean?' I queried.

'Do you have coffee and biscuits?'

'No,' I said, and tried to explain the shifts I worked over the 24 hours, the different hours and minutes signing on duty every day in every week, and more recently being on duty anything from 7 to 9 hours.

'That's no good for a diabetic,' she said. 'You should have regular meals. The best I can do is to give you a list of prohibited foods and ones that will keep your sugar content down.'

I returned to work on Tuesday and was rostered to travel to Knowle & Dorridge to cover for the out-station driver, who was on holiday, on the shunting engine, marshalling car trains, which were being loaded with Rover cars for the night train that started from there and which I had worked. The following week I booked on at 12.18 to travel to Bordesley to work on the shunting engine there. I then had a week booking on at 7.15 am, travelling to Tyseley carriage sidings to marshal DMUs.

After a month of this and a strict diet, I visited the specialist again. After another examination he said, 'You've lost 16 pounds and your sugar level has dropped dramatically. I'll give you a letter for your railway doctor stating that you're fit to take up your proper duties, but I will need to see you in three months time.'

I took this to our chief clerk when I booked on at 15.15 the next day for a Tyseley job, but it was another week before an appointment could be made to see the railway doctor. After his examination he said, 'You've made good progress - I will see you in six months time.' (The normal period at 60 years of age was 12 months.) 'I'll recommend that you can go back on the main line again.'

— o —

Earlier in 1982, when I had been chairing one of our monthly union meetings, I had announced that the new 125 mph trains would be worked by Saltley men to Bristol, Cardiff, Leeds and York. There was cheering in the room by some of the younger men because it had been rumoured that Saltley

I warned my colleagues early in 1982 that the new 125 mph trains would mean that they would cover 'more miles in a shorter time, and your mental alertness will have to be higher, and this causes heart trouble and high blood pressure, and more work will be diagrammed to you in a day.' Here an HST climbs the Lickey Incline northbound on 17 February 1983 - certainly less stressful for the fireman! *Roger Siviter*

would be left out of the programmes for these South West to North East trains. I calmed them down and remarked, 'Don't forget - with these higher speeds, you will be covering more miles in a shorter time, and your mental alertness will have to be higher, and this causes heart trouble and high blood pressure, and more work will be diagrammed to you in a day.'

In the October winter workings the 125 rosters came into being and I was booked on one of these new trains. This entailed signing on at 9.55 am and taking Class 50 No 50023 to New Street to work the Manchester to Plymouth as far as Bristol. I was then booked to relieve an HST (High Speed Train) 125 coming from Plymouth to work it through to Derby, then relieve an ordinary express with No 47362 on front to work back to Birmingham. The mileage clocked up was 265, so my words were coming true! As I had not been trained on the 125s, I had Charlie Morgan as a traction instructor to accompany me on the Bristol to Derby run.

Later in the month I exchanged my early morning shift to sign on at 9.10 am to work a DMU turn to Lichfield and Redditch. When signing on duty on the Wednesday, the foreman asked me to come off my job as there was a locomotive at Old Oak Common depot that was needed at Saltley. He found me a second man, Nigel Sloper, and we travelled to London Euston, caught the local train to Willesden and walked to Old Oak Common. It was about 14.30 when I reported to the foreman. He told me that the locomotive was No 31300, and if we did not leave the depot before 15.30 the signalman would not allow a light locomotive to run because of the high intensity of the rush-hour trains.

We left the depot around 15.00 and were routed via the High Wycombe line. At Ruislip we were stopped by signals and my mate telephoned the signalman to be told that a local train had just left, and there are no signal boxes open until High Wycombe. He did not know if he would be able to let us go until the rush-hour was over, around 18.00. I climbed down and spoke to him, saying that we were in a hurry and did not want to stay there for 2½ hours.

'Let us go,' I said, 'and I'll travel at the highest speed this locomotive will do, which is 90 mph. The local DMUs only do 75 mph.'

He said he would see what he could do, and shortly afterwards he cleared the signal. We went like a bat out of hell over the 'new line' through High Wycombe, Princes Risborough, Bicester and Aynho Junction, and ran non-stop to our depot.

In November I was in trouble. I was rostered on a single-manned turn at 15.03 to work the 15.45 to Paddington with No 47481. It was a day of heavy fog and I worked the train all right, stopping at Coventry, Leamington, Banbury, Oxford and Reading. The fog had cleared from Didcot and when I received the 'right away' at Reading I was signalled along the relief line. This was not unusual, as an HST 125 was due along the main line. We ran towards Ruscombe Junction and I received a double yellow signal followed by a single yellow. The 125 had not passed me, so I expected to be stopped before following him along the main line. I had reduced my speed, had the train under control and was looking at the red colour light signal, when I heard the automatic train control warning horn blow. This meant that I was only about 20 yards from the signal. I was astounded - I had been looking at another red signal some 300 yards away! I braked immediately, but as we were travelling at 25 mph I stopped beyond the signal with the locomotive and two coaches on the wrong side.

I walked back and phoned the signalman at Reading Power Box.

'Get back behind it,' he said. 'You'll be following the 125.'

This passed by when I was climbing into my cab. Normally when a driver passes a red signal he is relieved and sent back to his depot, but as we were about 8 miles from Reading and 10 miles from Slough, so there was no way I could get relieved. After I reversed the train behind the signal, I looked at it and the one I had mistaken it for, and could see that it was showing a higher intensity of red light. The signal then cleared for me to go out main line.

I was still thinking of the incident and my mind was not concentrating on my driving as

we were running through Slough at 95 mph. I realised I was not doing my job properly, so I shut it out of my mind until I arrived at Paddington. The train crew inspector was waiting at the buffer stops at the end of the platform. When I shut the engine down after the shunter uncoupled me, he climbed into the cab.

'Are you all right, driver?' he said. 'You've had a bit of trouble at Ruscombe, I hear.'

'I'm all right now,' I replied. 'It was when I was speeding along afterwards that I was vulnerable by not concentrating properly. I could have caused another mishap.'

'Are you all right to carry on,' he asked, 'or do you want relieving?'

'I'll be OK when I've had my cup of tea.'

He tapped me on the shoulder. 'Good,' he said, 'and if it's any comfort to you, you're not the first driver to run past red signals there.'

When I signed off duty around midnight, our foreman was waiting for me and asked for a report of the incident. On 10 December I had to report to Stanier House on a Form 1 charge of passing Reading 179 signal at danger. Mr Mitchell, who I had never seen before, held the inquiry and I had with me Les Kirk as my trade union representative. Mr Mitchell read the charge out, and as I had already admitted passing the signal at danger, he asked for my reason for doing so. I explained that I had slowed down on receiving the yellow signals, but the intensity of the red light at signal R181, 300 yards beyond signal R179, was so strong that I was looking at that one to stop at. I had been in touch with Les Kirk a couple of weeks previously and had mentioned that the Paddington train crew inspector had said that other drivers had made mistakes there, so Les had spoken to the ASLEF area secretary at Reading.

He told Mr Mitchell, 'Other drivers have run by there, so there must be something wrong with the sighting of the signals at Ruscombe.'

After a lengthy discussion Mr Mitchell said he would adjourn the inquiry for tests to be made on the sight of the signals.

'It's no use doing it in daylight,' I said. 'It's

in the dark it needs to be done.' I had worked past those signals the week before in daylight and could see nothing wrong.

It was two days before Christmas when I was recalled to Stanier House for the resumed Form 1 inquiry. It lasted only half an hour. Mr Mitchell had a pile of papers in front of him, and he started off by reading out the tests that had been carried out on the signals' sighting. No fault had been found on the lighting, but better alignment of R181 should be made to prevent it from being confused with R179. Then he read out another paper stating that Cardiff, Bristol and Gloucester drivers had run past R179 in the last six months, but went on to state that the local drivers at Reading, Southall, Paddington, etc, did not have any trouble. He read out another report from the train crew inspector from Paddington, who stated that he had spoken to me and was satisfied with the calm way I had answered his questions, and he felt I was quite capable of carrying on with my return workings.

Mr Mitchell summarised by saying, 'I think a verbal warning to you to be more careful in future will suffice. So carry on with your work.'

This was a good Christmas present to me as it had been hanging over me for almost two months. A couple of weeks later I worked the same turn of duty, and again ran along the relief line from Reading to Ruscombe without any trouble. I wondered if R181 had been realigned!

At the beginning of December I had been sent to learn the route from Reading to Basingstoke, as we had trains in the link going from Birmingham to Bournemouth and Southampton as far as there. Little did I know that it was to be the last route learning I would do!

— o —

The DMU depot at Tyseley was staffed by 18 drivers who signed on duty there, working over the 24 hours shunting DMUs in the carriage sidings and the huge maintenance depot commonly called the 'factory'. Twelve worked over the 24 hours on 8-hour shifts in the carriage sidings, three in the factory, two on the Bordesley shunting engine and one on the Knowle & Dorridge shunter. These jobs were reserved for drivers with eyesight or medical failures, but any vacancies not thus filled could be filled with volunteer drivers.

In January 1983 three vacancies were offered to men with over 20 years main-line driving with slight medical difficulties, although not failed by the railway doctor. Since I had been diagnosed with slight diabetes some five months before, I had to keep to a strict diet, but the 24 weeks work in my link of variable shifts of 7 to 9 hours meant that proper dieting could not be achieved. I therefore applied to be considered for one of these vacancies, and about a week later I had a letter stating that my application had been granted on the condition that if the railway doctor seriously failed a main-line driver, I would return to my original place in the links.

On 24 January I transferred to Tyseley. It was administered by Saltley with drivers signing on duty at Tyseley, but daily duty statements were sent to Saltley, and wages and discipline was administered from the parent depot. At the January union branch meeting it was discussed whether I was entitled to retain my position of vice-chairman, but it was decided that as I was still Saltley employed I could keep this position. This also made a precedent for me keeping my positions of trustee of the Welfare Fund and committee member of the Self-help Sick Fund.

After I had settled in at Tyseley I was surprised to find out that eight drivers who had remained there when its closure had occurred were not in our Welfare Fund, although they had made applications to join. The reason for non-acceptance had been given as per the rule book, that membership of the fund was open to men signing on duty at Saltley, but men who had joined and then moved away to other depots could remain in it. I found out that there were ten Tyseley men who had worked previously at Saltley in the fund, and the other eight out of it. This seemed wrong to me, and at the next meeting I raised this point and proposed that the eight should be allowed to join. Members of the committee quoted the rule regarding booking-on at

Saltley; I countered by saying that they technically signed on there, but my proposition was defeated.

At the AGM some months later I proposed that the rule be altered to 'men whose wages or salaries are paid by the Saltley depot'. I received a seconder, and this caused a long debate. Some members claimed that they should not be in the fund as they were not in a position to play the one-armed bandit (our main source of income). I countered this by saying that the clerical staff at the depot did not use our mess room and did not play the bandit, yet they were allowed to be members. At the end of the debate the voting indicated that the majority of members present agreed to accept them. I was told afterwards that I would be responsible for all the Tyseley men, collecting subscriptions, issuing Christmas vouchers and keeping them informed of rule alterations and activities of the Fund. I was also designated their unofficial ASLEF representative at Tyseley, bringing complaints and ideas to our branch meetings, and posting copies of correspondence from ASLEF HQ and other notices in the official notice case.

In the first few weeks working there I found that I was not used to a lot of walking about, and at the end of the shifts my legs were quite tired. The reason for this was that the carriage sidings comprised 16 stabling roads, each holding around 18 coaches. There were three fuelling roads, two of them with pits beneath for fitters to examine the DMUs and do running repairs. (If a more serious defect was found the DMU had to be shunted out and taken to the factory.)

After fuelling and examinations we would drive the units towards the dead-end stop blocks near Tyseley station, change ends and drive them into the road designated by the traction foreman. After shutting the engines down a long walk back to the fuelling line was necessary for the next unit. This happened about a couple of dozen times a shift, and with the climbing up and down to the driving cabs and the walking, it certainly tested my legs. However, after a few weeks my muscles got used to it.

During 1983 the famous preserved steam locomotive No 4472 *Flying Scotsman* hauled the 'Orient Express' train of Pullman coaches to Stratford-upon-Avon, and brought the empty coaches to Tyseley for cleaning and watering. I helped to marshal them into position with a diesel shunter, and managed to have a good look at the locomotive and the coaches inside and out; I also took a few photographs before No 4472 went to Saltley for coal and servicing for its return journey.

In between the carriage sidings and the factory was the Tyseley Railway Museum run by Mr Pat Whitehouse, and occasionally we assisted them in moving locomotives and giving technical advice. An ex-Tyseley driver, now at Saltley, Mr Bernard Rainbow, was their main voluntary driver, giving many hours of his own time to keep the museum going, especially on Saturdays, Sundays and Bank Holidays, when a lot of visitors came to look at the exhibits.

Around 6.00 am one busy Sunday morning of a Bank Holiday weekend he was engaged moving locomotives out of the shed where he had been raising steam on them since midnight, to marshal them into position for the spectators to see later in the day. I was on duty at 6.00 am and after moving a DMU from the fuelling line into the sidings, I was walking back along the embankment above the museum sidings. I could see that he had brought one of our ex-LMS engines, 'Jubilee' 4-6-0 No 5593 *Kholapur* outside the shed, so I dashed to the fuelling line but there was no other unit to be moved, so I took my camera from my locker and went back on to the embankment. Unfortunately he had brought an ex-LNER locomotive and an ex-GWR tank engine out of the sheds, blocking my view of 5593, which I was interested to photograph.

'Can you bring the "Jubilee" further out,' I shouted to him, 'so I can get a clear view?'

'Come and move it yourself,' he retorted. 'You're capable!'

I scrambled down the bank and climbed on to 5593. Bernard had a good fire going and a good head of steam.

'Bring it forwards over the points,' he said.

'Where are we going?' I asked.

'On to the turntable at the other end of

'I then reversed 5593 on to the pit, put the hand brake on, worked the water injector to fill the boiler, shovelled about two dozen shovelsful of coal into the firebox and shut the dampers. . .' Quite like old times at Tyseley Railway Museum in 1983! On the extreme left a diesel locomotive can be glimpsed entering the BR maintenance depot. *Author*

the yard. It'll make it easier for me if you drive out and I'll set the points.'

I took off the hand brake, opened the regulator and moved forward over the points where Bernard was standing. When he changed them I reversed the locomotive down to the turntable. I stopped on it and Bernard put the vacuum pipe from the locomotive on to the turning machinery and turned us to one of the pits surrounding it. I then reversed 5593 on to the pit, put the hand brake on, worked the water injector to fill the boiler, shovelled about two dozen shovelsful of coal into the firebox and shut the dampers so that it could stand about an hour or so without attention.

Bernard thanked me. 'That saved me a lot of climbing up and down as I'm working on my own.'

I managed to get some nice photographs of 5593 and other locomotives on which I had worked some 20 years or so before.

As I was now looking forward to retirement, I decided I needed a pastime, especially now that I was on regular shifts, so I joined our local Crown Green Bowls Club and had a season learning the intricacies of the game. In the spring of 1984 the treasurer, George Watson, died, and at the AGM I was elected to that post.

In June I had my usual 12-monthly medical and, after dressing and going to the doctor's office, I could see him studying my electro-cardiograph. He told me to sit down and said, 'I have some bad news for you. According to this graph you have the left bundle branch blocked in your heart. This has happened before with other people, and on taking a re-test nothing has been found wrong, so I want

to see you in a month's time. You'll be restricted to shunting duties.'

'I'm doing that voluntarily now,' I replied, and asked whether I could have a copy of the graph as my wife was an electro-cardiograph technician, but he declined.

When I got home I told May of the doctor's examination and diagnosis, and she said that she would get me a private test. A fortnight later I attended the ECG clinic where some of May's colleagues were in attendance, and after all tests they announced that they could not find anything amiss with my heart. One remarked, 'It's nice to get some good readings for a change, as most of our patients are already suffering from heart trouble when they get here.'

I went to see the railway medical officer a fortnight later, and after his cardiograph test he told me, 'I can't find anything wrong with you now.'

'I know that,' I replied, and produced the graph I had obtained.

He compared it with his and remarked, 'You shouldn't have gone to this trouble.'

'I told you my wife was a heart disease technician and she insisted on my having these tests.'

'You're now all right for main-line working,' he said, 'and I'll see you in six months time because of your diabetes, which you seem to have controlled.'

In August we had a holiday at Pickering in North Yorkshire with a friend, Bill Smith, and his wife Chris. He was a keen railway enthusiast and we rode on the line from

Pickering to Grosmont on the preserved North Yorkshire Moors line. We explored the loco depot, where one of my favourite 'Black Fives', No 45428, was stabled, and I explained to Bill the working parts. It was during this period when the closing of the Settle to Carlisle line was being mooted, so we travelled in Bill's car to Settle and caught the train to Carlisle where I again showed Bill, Chris and my wife the outstanding parts of this scenic route. After about 4 hours in Carlisle we returned to Settle and Pickering.

At our next branch meeting I raised the subject of the Settle to Carlisle line and proposed that we oppose this closure of one of the most beautiful routes in the country, as it was part of our heritage. The proposal was carried. I then suggested that we ran a special train over this route to Carlisle for the benefit of the staff and retired people at Saltley who used to work over it (we had many a hard day's graft on the steamers, but after we had switched to diesel and the work became easier, BR had diverted the traffic that would normally have gone via this route to Bescot, Crewe and Preston). The day fixed was 10 November and we made a charge of £5 for our members.

A travel agent in Birmingham was arranging a similar trip a fortnight later and protested to the railway Board that we were undercutting their fare by half. We said that it was for ASLEF members only, but the Board refused our trip.

It was 20 April before we could rearrange it without any objections, and we put our price up by a pound to make it £6, but we put on free coffee and biscuits for our members. We left New Street on a lovely Saturday morning at around 8.15 am. A path could not be found for us over our normal route via Derby, Rotherham and Leeds, so we had to go via Crewe, Preston, then across country, to join our old route at Hellifield. We had a special stop at Dent, the highest point on the line, where a lot of photographs were taken.

Jack Coxsey, our branch secretary, said, 'That's the first time I've come up the "Long Drag" without getting into a sweat!'

We then carried on along the beautiful Eden Valley through Appleby into Carlisle. After about 3 hours there, we returned via

Jack Coxsey, our Branch Secretary, poses in front of the ASLEF special at Dent station on 20 April 1985. *Author*

Hellifield, Leeds, Wakefield, Huddersfield, Stockport and Crewe, over a lot of railway that we had not seen ourselves. We arrived in Birmingham around 22.00 vowing to do all we could to keep this lovely scenic line open.

In the winter workings in October 1985 there was a loss of work at the depot and 13 redundancies were declared. I received a voluntary redundancy form on 19 October and, after considering it, I sent a letter of acceptance on 22 October, and on 25 October I received my official redundancy notice giving me 12 weeks notice, which meant that I would retire on 21 January.

On 31 October the 13 drivers who had accepted the redundancies attended a meeting in the shedmaster's office with the Area Manager from Bescot, Harold Hook, his Chief Clerk, a Social Security representative and Fred Orton Jones, our ASLEF area secretary. He surprised us by speaking first and informed us that he had been negotiating with the railway officials and any of us with less than two years until our 65th birthday could waive the 12 weeks notice, and could retire as soon as it could be arranged.

This suited me as I did not fancy the winter months tramping about in the open, so I and five other men decided to take this offer.

The Chief Clerk informed us what our redundancy pay would be and that our British Rail concessionary travel would be maintained. The Social Security man informed us we could sign on for unemployment benefit for 12 months, but he emphasised that we could be offered work. I thought, 'I don't suppose there will be many railway locomotive driver's vacancies going.' The meeting finished around midday and as we adjourned to the Olive Branch pub to celebrate, Fred Orton Jones said he was sorry he could not join us as he had to go to Bescot on a similar errand.

'You'll have to go near our home in Great Barr,' I said, 'so pop in and warn May that I'm finishing in about a week's time. She's only just getting used to me retiring in January!'

Two days later I received a letter stating that my official date of retirement would be 23 November, and as I had some holiday and Bank Holiday lieu days owing to me, I would finish on the 11th.

Friday 8 November was my last day actually driving. I was on the 15.00 to 23.00 shift and around 20.00 the foreman, Arnold Sears, sent me to bring DMU set No 502 from the factory into our sidings. I thought nothing of it until I brought the unit towards the mess rooms and about two dozen detonators exploded under it! He and my work mates came out and cheered me when I clambered down from the cab for the last time! They all shook hands with me and I adjourned to the Railway Club nearby to have a drink with some of them.

On Monday 11th I signed on at 9.00 am to empty my locker of my timetables, notices, general appendices, rule books, satchel, handlamp and wrist-watch, to take to Saltley. I arrived there around 11.00 am and

Terry Kenna, the shedmaster (who had fired for me at Monument Lane on the steamers), and the running shift foreman, Ray Power, shook hands with me and took my satchel, books, etc, off me. They did not ask for the railway watch and I did not remind them.

On 22 November my wife, myself and the other five drivers and their spouses were invited to attend at the shedmaster's office at 12.30 pm to receive our retirement certificates from Mr Harold Hook, the Area Manager. He gave us all a run-down of our railway career from the records and thanked us for our 48 years' railway service. He then presented our wives with bouquets of flowers and remarked that they deserved more than that for putting up with our shifts and the loss of social life.

He then told us to load up in cars and took us to the Bradford Arms at Castle Bromwich where he provided lunch and drinks for us all. At the end of the lunch he shook hands with us, and I left the railway service after 48 years with a lump in my throat.

A few weeks later I attended the Welfare Fund's annual retired staff's dinner and reunion and received a certificate showing 45 years' union membership of ASLEF, and May received another bouquet.

On 25 November 1985 I attended the unemployment office to sign on as unemployed, the only occasion I had done this since having left school in July 1936.

On 22 November 1985 I received my retirement certificate from Mr Harold Hook, the Area Manager, in the Saltley shedmaster's office, thus ending 48 years of railway work. *Author's collection*

INDEX

Alcock, Eddie 211
Alcock, May 63, 85, 221
Allen, Inspector Jack 107, 125, 129
Alsager MPD 14ff
Ambulance trains 49
Andrews, Frank 13
Arley Colliery 53-54, 183-5
Arley Tunnel 53, 72, 73, 74, 84
Ashchurch 56
ASLEF 22-23, 89, 101, 108, 112, 114, 115, 118, 123, 124, 147-8, 151, 160, 166, 169, 173, 181, 192, 194, 196, 204-5, 212, 220; disputes 87, 180-1, 186, 201-2, 203, 214-5
Attenborough, Arthur 114
Austin, Bill 111
Austin, George 75

Baker, Mrs Connie 145
Barnett, Frank 30
Barratt, Stan 191
Bates, Jack 74-75, 80ff, 84, 124, 125, 131
Beaman, Jack 84
Beasley, Ken 121-122
Beck, John 144, 145, 146, 150
Beckett, Norman 127, 200
Beech, Walter 105-106, 112
Bennet, Ernie 123
Bennett, Gordon 89
Bescot MPD 7
Binder, Alan 150
Birks, Harry 67
Biss, Len 88, 146
Blackesley, Mr 28
Bloor, John 58, 59, 129, 152, 153, 154
Bosson, Harry 97, 99
Boughton, Sid 12
Boulton, Jack 191, 196, 206
Bounds, Sid 97
Breakdown trains 51, 61, 86, 104, 125, 134, 178
Brewer, Anthony 199
Briers, Les 69, 118, 119
Broadhurst, Ron 14, 31, 53, 63, 105
Brown, Ted 175
Buckingham, Dave 154
Bullock, Arthur 203
Burke, John 126
Bushbury MPD 13, 113
Butler, Jack 64, 71

Cadman, Inspector 18, 21
Call-boys, duties of 8ff
Canning, George 205
Carter, 'Tat' 70
Challinor, William 14, 17, 18, 22, 31, 68
'City of Birmingham Holiday Express' 111, 134
Clark, Alf 17
Clarke, Bob 104, 146, 166, 203
Clarke, Terry 160
Cooke, Archie 36, 50
Cooke, Fred 133
Cookson, Tom 30
Coughton 55-6
Coxsey, Jack 166, 222
Crook, John 166, 167, 169
Cumberland, Bill 168

Dale, Peggy 31
Diesel multiple units (DMUs) 96, 98, 99, 105, 111, 113, 115, 117-8, 130, 144
Diesel shunters 73, 118, 119
Diesel-electric locos, ex-LMS 121; TOPS Class 20 157, 207; Class 24 121, 122; Class 25 138, 142, 184; Class 26 138; Class 31 189; Class 33 137; Class 37 161, 182; Class 40 121, 122, 141, 204; Class 44/5/6 124, 125, 135, 158, 161-3; Class 47 125, 174; Class 56 203; HSTs 217
Dunn, Bob 208
Dutton, Sid 55

Eanson, Mr 117-118, 120
Edgington, Ken 174
Edmunds, Horace 49
Edwards, Mr 132, 175
Evans, Bill 22, 28
Evans, Carey 173
Evans, Harold 124, 155
Evans, Jack 176, 205

Felton, Les 132, 160, 203, 205
Fletcher, Cliff 199
Floyd, Trevor 197
Footplate training, steam firemen 18-19; steam drivers 80ff; diesel shunters 118; diesel-electrics

121, 124, 125, 138, 139, 189, 199, 203, 210-11, 217; DMUs 105ff, 113, 129, 136
Freightliner trains 151, 155, 163

Garn, Jack 12
Gibson, Bob 43, 60-61
Gilbey, George 5
Godfrey, Harold 90
Gregory, Jack 127-8, 136, 151
Griffin, Ken 128, 208
Guy, Ernie 75ff, 91

Hammond, Brian 183, 186
Harrison, George 191
Hart, 'Tiny' 78
Hazeldine, Arthur 37
Hazzard, Doug 143
Heath, Brian 134, 135
Heron, Jack 124
Hicken, Bill 178
Higgins, Bill 25, 83
Hood, George 20
Hook, Harold 222-3
Hopkinson, Gordon 137
Hughes, Mr 7, 9
Hughes, Harry 102, 185
Hughes, Taffy 101, 116

Ingram, Bernard 63, 72

Jenvey, Ken 8
'Jones', Inspector 167ff, 182, 189, 190
Jones, Bill 210
Jones, Bob 115
Jones, Ernie 113
Judge, Ron 109

Kendrick, Arthur 49
Kett, Charlie 76-77
Kirk, Les 115, 218
Knight, Brian 137-8

Lane, Jack 177
Leight, Jobie 134
Lichfield accident 1946 61
Lickey Incline 41ff, 59, 62, 159, 194
Lindley, Charles 93, 182, 186, 197, 210
'Links' 9, 20, 34, 41, 58, 67, 98, 105, 210
Littlewood, Joe 91, 93-94
Lloyd, Dick 100
Lloyd, Fred 134
Lloyd, Sid 148
Local Departmental Committees (LDCs) 105, 114, 115, 116, 118, 119,

120, 123, 146, 173, 176, 182, 195, 197, 210
Locke, Mr 118, 121-122, 131, 139, 157
Lodging barracks, Blackpool 127; Carlisle 46; Leeds 48; Mold 24; Peterborough 53; 'lodging basket' 25
Lowe, Jack 97, 107, 109, 130
Lowe, Reg 188
Lucock, Colin 131
Lynk, Derrick 183, 184

Mackintosh, Tommy 125, 134
McLeland, Michael 201
Mapp, Ernie 129
Marshall, Frank 141, 148
Massey, Fred 118
Matthews, Bert 65
Matthews, Ron 140
Mayo, Tom 11
Medical examinations 17, 32, 115, 125, 177, 216, 221
Merril, Mick 130
'Merry-go-round' trains 194ff
Mileage bonus schemes 38, 147
Mitchell, Ken 211
Monument Lane MPD 96, 97ff, 166
Morgan, Charlie 207
Morris, Steenie 113
Mutual Improvement Classes 79, 80

New Street rebuilding, 1965-6 144-5
Nichols, Arthur 164
Nichols, Ron 116, 118
Nutt, George 32

Orton Jones, Fred 188, 215, 222-3

Pattison, Vic 176
Pettifer, Joe 12
Phillips, Brian 125, 157
'Pines Express' 38, 115
Porter, Tom 136
Potts, Dick 112, 190
Pountney, Tony 170, 173, 180
Preston, Bert 105, 109, 117
Prestridge, Jack 91-92
Pulley, Tom 58

Rainbow, Bernard 220
Randle, Albert 53
Randle, Jack 176, 188

Reading, Alf 45
Redfern, Harry 173
Reynolds, Ray 161, 181, 188, 203
Riddle, Les 103
Rigby, Frank 120
Rist, Cyril 189
Roberts, 'Rhubarb' 48-49
Roberts, Bob 84, 90, 93
Roberts, Reg 52
Robertson, Don 160
Rodent, Harry 158
Route-learning, to Oxford 133-4; N Warks 166; to Sheffield 170; to Stratford 175-6; to Paddington 179
Rushden, Sid 109
Ryecroft MPD 7ff, 31, 113

S&MJR line 57, 72
Salt, Miss Maggie 119
Saltley MPD 31ff, 123ff, 173
Searle, Victor 87, 88
Self-Help Sick Fund, Saltley 50, 133, 176, 188, 200, 208
Settle & Carlisle line 46ff, 67ff, 75ff, 94, 222
Sharret, George 118, 123
Shaw, Alf 174
Sherrat, Mrs 15, 24, 31
Shorto, Mr 66
Shustoke, fire on D19 at 161-3
Siggs, Jack 80ff, 135, 146
Signalling, new, Crewe 29-30, 100; Blackwell-Gloucester 164; B'ham-Chesterfield 170-1
Simkins, George 50
Smith, Albert 27
Smith, Frank 63
Soho Pool yard 103, 119
Stacksy, Bill 102
Steam locomotives, BR '9F' 2-10-0 128, 137; 'Britannia' 4-6-2 131, 149; Class '5' 4-6-0 129, 130, 140; ex-GWR 71, 135; ex-LMS '8F' 2-8-0 47, 57; 'Black Five' 4-6-0 27, 71, 77, 82; 'Jubilee' 4-6-0 32, 59, 88, 89, 125, 220; 'Patriot' 4-6-0 86-87; Class '4' 2-6-0 84; ex-LNER 'B1' 4-6-0 71; ex-LNWR 0-8-0 'Super D' 11, 16, 21, 23, 24, 27; ex-MR

'Compound' 4-4-0 58; Class '4' 0-6-0 26, 62
Stokes, Len 124
Sturmy, George 74
Sutton Coldfield accident 1955 85-86
Sweeney, Bernard 14

Tabener, Arthur 43
Talbot, Mr 83, 118, 123
Taylor, Bill 59
Thomas, Arthur 75, 124, 125
Thorley, Bill 51, 52, 79
Timms, Brian 156, 203
Tregenna, Alan 164, 190, 193
Trueman, Arthur 102
Tudge, Mr 121, 123
Tudge, Bob 142
Tyseley MPD 173, 219; Railway Museum 220

Vaughan, Stan 185

Wakelin, Jim 61, 63, 86, 104
Wall, Cliff 117
Warley, Howard, 148
Wartime bombing 27, 29, 30, 39, 49, 50
Watson, George 139
Watts, Harry 85
Webb, Norman 157, 161, 203
Webster, Stan 51
Welfare Fund, Saltley 145, 196, 200, 204, 219
Weston, Charles 136, 140
Wheeler, Fred 12
Whitaker, George 98, 111
White, Mr 10, 31
Whitehouse, Ginger 114
Whittal, Bill 62
Wigginton water troughs 41, 45, 65, 81, 82
Wilding, Owen 23, 24
Wilkes, Harry 115
Wilkins, George 50, 51, 80, 87, 148, 178
Willets, Harry 199
Williams, John 136
Williams, Tom 172
Williams, Trevor 184, 185
Wilson, Albert 15, 17
Wilson, Tug 42, 61, 104
Wood, Tom 85
Wootton, Tom 146